818181

Communication and
Democratic Reform in
South Africa

The book examines the reform of the communications sector in South Africa as a detailed and extended case study in political transformation – the transition from apartheid to democracy. The reform of broadcasting, telecommunications, the state information agency, and the print media from apartheid-aligned apparatuses to accountable democratic institutions took place via a complex political process in which civil society activism, embodying a post–social democratic ideal, largely won out over the powerful forces of formal market capitalism and older models of state control. In the cautious acceptance of the market, civil society organizations sought to use the dynamism of the market while thwarting its inevitable inequities. Forged in the crucible of a difficult transition to democracy, communication reform in South Africa was steered between the National Party's new embrace of the market and the African National Congress leadership's default statist orientation.

Robert B. Horwitz is Professor of Communication at the University of California, San Diego. He is the author of *The Irony of Regulatory Reform: The Deregulation of American Telecommunications* (1989), which received the 1990 Ethics and Policy Award for Communications Research, awarded by the Donald McGannon Communications Research Center at Fordham University. His articles on communications media and free speech law in the United States have appeared in journals such as *Theory and Society*, *Political Science Quarterly*, and *Critical Studies in Mass Communication*, and his articles on South African communications reform have been published in *African Affairs*, *Telecommunications Policy*, and *Media, Culture, and Society*. Professor Horwitz spent 1995–96 as a Fulbright Research Fellow at the University of Cape Town and served as a member of the Technical Task Team of the South African National Telecommunications Policy Project. He is the 1998 recipient of an individual research project fellowship from the Open Society Institute and was the founding editor of the academic journal *The Communication Review*.

Politics and relations among individuals in societies across the world are being transformed by new technologies for targeting individuals and sophisticated methods for shaping personalized messages. The new technologies challenge boundaries of many kinds – between news, information, entertainment, and advertising; between media, with the arrival of the World Wide Web; and even between nations. *Communication, Society and Politics* probes the political and social impacts of these new communication systems in national, comparative, and global perspective.

Communication and Democratic Reform in South Africa

Robert B. Horwitz
University of California, San Diego

PUBLISHED BY THE PRESS SYNDICATE OF THE UNIVERSITY OF CAMBRIDGE
The Pitt Building, Trumpington Street, Cambridge, United Kingdom

CAMBRIDGE UNIVERSITY PRESS
The Edinburgh Building, Cambridge CB2 2RU, UK
40 West 20th Street, New York, NY 10011-4211, USA
10 Stamford Road, Oakleigh, VIC 3166, Australia
Ruiz de Alarcón 13, 28014 Madrid, Spain
Dock House, The Waterfront, Cape Town 8001, South Africa

http://www.cambridge.org

First published 2001

Printed in the United States of America

Typeface Minion 11/13 pt.   *System* QuarkXPress [BTS]

A catalog record for this book is available from the British Library.

Library of Congress Cataloging in Publication Data
Horwitz, Robert Britt.
Communication and Democratic reform in South Africa / Robert B. Horwitz.
p.   cm. – (Communication, society and politics)
ISBN 0-521-79166-9
1. Communication policy – South Africa.   2. Democracy – South Africa.
I. Title.   II. Series.
P95.82.S6 H67 2001
302.2'0968 – dc21   00-063041

ISBN   0 521 79166 9   hardback

To Libby, Rachel, and Marco

Contents

Tables

Preface and Acknowledgments

In early 1991, I received what can only be described as a fan letter. Most academicians, myself included, do not get fan mail. Indeed, most of us feel fortunate to have our work merit a review in some arcane scholarly journal. At any rate, this fan letter was doubly unusual in that it was postmarked South Africa. The letter's author was W. J. "Jimmy" Taylor, Deputy Postmaster General of the Republic of South Africa and head of the country's telecommunications monopoly. Mr. Taylor indicated that he had obtained a copy of my book, *The Irony of Regulatory Reform: The Deregulation of American Telecommunications,* through Oxford University Press's Johannesburg office, and was writing to commend my analysis of the communications revolution and the transformation in communications policy and regulation. Needless to say I was thrown for a loop. What did it mean that a high official of a state apparatus in one of the most repressive regimes in modern times thought highly of my scholarly work? Was there something in my ambivalent, if not skeptical, assessment of American deregulation that gave succor to authoritarian bureaucrats? Realizing I didn't know enough to address these worries adequately, I merely dashed off a thank you to the Deputy PMG, and not wanting to jeopardize any future contacts, said I would love to visit South Africa if and when democracy was put in place.

That caveat reflected the times. Taylor's letter had come less than a year following President F. W. de Klerk's famous February 1990 speech in which he announced that the South African government would "unban" political organizations that had been illegal for decades, including the African National Congress, the Pan-Africanist Congress, and the South African Communist Party. Like many, I followed news about South Africa, and knew about the February speech and the movement toward some kind of new political dispensation. I had been involved in the campaign in the mid-1980s to divest the University of California's stock portfolio of companies with investments in South Africa. But in early 1991 it remained unclear whether a political settlement could or would be reached.

A few months later I received a telephone call from a Peter Davies, head of the Computer Society of South Africa and responsible for organizing a large telecommunications conference there. This national conference, the fifth, was of particular importance because it would mark the recent creation of Telkom, the new, commercialized telecommunications company formed out of and separated from the old government-run South African Post Office. Davies, in a robust British-accented voice, was delighted to inform me that the conference program committee had selected me as the keynote speaker. Dumbfounded, indeed querying Davies whether he had the right guy, I demurred that while honored, I was at the moment unable to accept the invitation and I would have to get back to him. I thereupon spent several unsuccessful weeks trying to determine whether such a conference fell under the cultural boycott, which had remained in place at the urging of the African National Congress. When Davies called back another time and indicated that the ANC had been invited to the conference and its representative, Andile Ngcaba, had accepted, I too accepted the invitation. I then scrambled to the library to see what I could find out about South Africa. What I found was shelf upon shelf of books about apartheid, the liberation struggle, and South Africa's colonial history, but very little on how the state actually worked, much less on how state-owned enterprises – or "parastatals," as the South Africans called them – were constituted, funded, and operated. I found but one book on South African parastatals. Luckily for me, it was about the telecommunications industry: *The Crossed Line: South African Telecommunications Industry in Transition*, by David Kaplan, a professor of economics at the University of Cape Town. With the help of Kaplan's book, I cobbled together a paper discussing the history and consequences of telecommunications deregulation in the United States and Britain, and which strove to apply some of the lessons to South Africa.

My actual introduction to the country in November of 1991 was head-spinning. Peter Davies and his wife Linda drove my wife and me to the conference venue – the "Superbowl" in Sun City, Bophuthatswana – a replica in miniature of a Las Vegas resort, set in the middle of a poor black "homeland." On the way we passed through Pretoria's Church

Street to behold the jacarandas in full bloom, only to encounter a rally on horseback of the Afrikaner Weerstand Beweging (the Afrikaner Resistance Movement or AWB), the armed neo-Nazi Afrikaner separatist organization. (A newspaper story reported that the AWB leader, Eugene Terreblanche, had embarrassingly fallen off his horse during the rally, an incident of great mirth to my hosts.) Sun City presented itself as a gleaming, lush jewel amidst barren and bone-dry terrain broken by the occasional dusty, ramshackle village. A gala opening conference dinner featured as entertainment, of all things, but in keeping with the Las Vegas parallel, an Elvis impersonator.

My keynote, unbeknownst to myself, articulated an argument that approximated the position of the ANC alliance on state-owned enterprises – that deregulation, liberalization, and privatization were policy strategies that with great care could possibly be used to beneficial effect in South Africa (note all the equivocations), but could not be deployed prior to free elections and the establishment of a truly democratic government. Furthermore, I suggested that the early privatization of parastatals appeared to be a strategy designed to maintain white dominance, a way of denying the coming black majority the means to effect the redistribution of public services, wealth, and life-chances to the benefit of the disenfranchised and disadvantaged. When I delivered this speech to a conference of more than a thousand delegates I was met with barely restrained hostility. Telkom management, finally free of the Post Office bureaucracy and eager to display its new company as a forward-looking commercial venture, saw this conference as Telkom's coming-out party. Minister of Transport and Posts and Telecommunications Piet Welgemoed and Telkom Managing Director Danie du Toit opened the conference with upbeat pronouncements about the new, commercial era in South African telecommunications. In addition to the usual attendees of Telkom management, state bureaucrats, and equipment supply company directors (almost all white, of course), conference invitees included foreign telecommunications operators and neighboring African state observers. Telkom management did not want to hear about the historic benefits of regulated telecommunications monopolies and the political dangers of privatization. The speaker following me, Ben Bets, a Telkom Senior General Manager, announced pointedly at the beginning of his speech that he was not going to talk about politics, a declaration that drew loud and sustained applause. (Some of the hostile reaction to my remarks turned out to be a rather bizarre linguistic misunderstanding. Several times in my address I had used the word "regime," in the political science usage of that term, to describe the set of agreed upon rules and structures that govern a multilateral international institution. I spoke neutrally of the "old telecommunications regime," that is, of the post, telegraph, telephone state monopoly model. Most conference delegates, being communications professionals, businessmen, and politicians, not political scientists, understood the word "regime" in its more commonplace meaning, as connoting illegitimate dictatorship, and assumed that I, a guest of the country, had the gall to be referring to the South African government as a regime.) I learned later that Minister Welgemoed had angrily called the conference program committee on the carpet, he had been so offended by my remarks. I was looking forward to a very uncomfortable few days at the conference, but I was in effect rescued by the next speaker, Mike Morris of the University of Natal. Prior to presenting interesting empirical work he and his colleague, Aki Stavrou, had conducted on the sociology of telephone usage in a black shanty around the port city of Durban, Morris declared that the applause following Bets' remark about politics greatly upset him. If people didn't think there were politics to the questions about the structure of telecommunications and the possible privatization of Telkom, Morris argued, they didn't understand anything about what was happening in South Africa.

Mike Morris was a member of the Economic Trends Research Group, a cadre of left-wing academicians spread across several of the South African universities, and who had close relations with the Congress of South African Trade Unions (COSATU), the powerful, primarily black union federation. Indeed, Economic Trends researchers produced analyses of policy issues that were used by COSATU in staking out the labor federation's positions on various matters. Morris arranged for me to meet two stalwarts of Economic Trends in Cape Town, David Lewis and, to my delight, David Kaplan, author of the book that had helped me prepare my conference address. On behalf of Economic Trends, "the Daves" invited me to spend a few months in South Africa looking further into the issue of the parastatals. I returned to South Africa, with family in tow, from April through June 1992, based at the University of Cape Town under the auspices of the Development Policy Research Unit and another research unit, the Energy for Development Research Centre, which had informal ties to the ANC. My "brief" was to examine the telecommunications and electricity parastatals in the light of international trends and to suggest how they might be reorganized from apartheid to democratic institutions. It was during this stay that I experienced the excitement of the new South Africa – the rush of political activity and the sense of possibility, the self-empowerment of people so long disenfranchised, in a place in a particular time where ideas mattered, where the opportunities to do good were there to be seized and where the dangers of bad decisions were humbling. This was a time and place where the momentous negotiations between long-warring political movements were being conducted in public, broadcast live on radio and television. Here was a country whose people had the will and opportunity to rethink and reconstitute most of their institutions. I got the South Africa bug.

In the spring of 1995, I learned that I had been awarded a Fulbright to spend the 1995–96 academic year in South Africa. Preparing to go in September, I received a call in May asking if I could participate in a process convened by Posts, Telecommunications and Broadcasting Minister Z. Pallo Jordan to write a Green Paper on telecommunications policy. Though it followed the nomenclature of the British policy process, this was no ordinary Green Paper. Instead it was conceived as a consultative exercise in policy determination, encompassing all players and constituents, and designed to conclude in a White Paper in which the sectoral players, in conjunction with the minister and Parliament, would establish government policy for the telecommunications sector. It was the remarkably consultative, participatory democratic process of the Green and White Papers that focused my research project. I was fortunate to have participated in the reform process in the telecommunications sector during my Fulbright year. I was the only permanent non–South African member of the National Telecommunications Policy Project (NTPP) Task Team, the body appointed by Minister Jordan to facilitate stakeholder negotiations and to guide policy discussions from the Green Paper phase through to legislation. Being part of the NTPP Task Team allowed me to operate as a participant observer inside an intricate and complex reform process intended to transform a vital economic sector from an apartheid to a democratic orientation. My role in the NTPP also opened doors for the evaluation of other reform processes, notably broadcasting, energy, and the government information service. With a long-time interest in both political reform and participatory democracy, I found myself deeply attracted to the way these were playing themselves out in South Africa and fascinated by the emerging tensions between participatory and electoral politics as the ANC began to consolidate its political mandate. This book is the result of that fascination.

Many people and institutions helped in the years it took to bring this research to book form. The Fulbright Association set up the crucial 1995–96 year in South Africa. The Open Society Institute awarded me a generous grant in 1998 to finish the writing, and an additional grant in 1999 to help get the book published. Gail Goodman of OSI helped immeasurably. The UCSD Committee on Research provided funds to get me back to South Africa for a research follow-up.

I want to thank the many South Africans who made the research possible, including the scores of patient people who generously made time for me and endured my questions in innumerable interviews, conversations, and e-mails. Special thanks to David Kaplan, David Lewis, and the researchers and administrative staff of the Development Policy Research Unit at the University of Cape Town. David Kaplan not only served as my Fulbright sponsor, he and his family took care of us during our Cape Town sojourn. Though a focus on the energy sector dropped by the wayside, I pay parallel gratitude to Anton Eberhard and the researchers and administrative staff of the Energy for Development Research Centre, also at the University of Cape Town. Former Minister of Posts, Telecommunications and Broadcasting, Dr. Z. Pallo Jordan, indirectly got me started on the project, and I wish to thank him for naming me to the National Telecommunications Policy Project. Working with the members of the NTPP was a terrific and rewarding experience, particularly with my collaborator on Green and White Paper chapters, Gabriele Celli. Gabriele and his wife and daughters were the most gracious of hosts on several occasions. Peter and Linda Davies introduced me to the country. They helped and hosted me many times over the years, and I thank them profusely. Melody Emmett seemed to be connected into nearly every communications-oriented reform project in South Africa. She helped identify and corral many of the people whom I was to interview.

Several of my friends and colleagues read parts of the manuscript and offered much-needed critique and suggestions. For this and their encouragement, I thank them. Chandra Mukerji, Dan Hallin, Vince Rafael, Val Hartouni, and Michael Schudson participated in that collegial interchange. Robert Price offered encouragement and wrote letters on my behalf. Elliot Kanter, Larry Cruse, and especially Ronnie Coates of the UCSD Central Library, provided bibliographic assistance. My lifelong friends, Lew Friedland and Joel Greifinger, read and commented on more drafts of parts of the manuscript than they probably wished. John Keane, visiting UCSD from London one summer, made very useful suggestions for the overview chapter. In a series of e-mail exchanges, Barbara Praetorius provided comments and bibliographic recommendations from Berlin. Nicholas Garnham, Michael MacDonald, and Patricia Aufderheide read the entire manuscript and offered crucial comments and suggestions. Alex Holzman shepherded the book through the Cambridge University Press bureaucracy. My wife, Libby Brydolf, offered love, encouragement, and expert editing skills.

Rachel Brydolf-Horwitz and Marco Brydolf-Horwitz made all kinds of suggestions for a book title, all of which in the end were discarded either by me or by the publisher. We shared a fabulous, life-changing experience with our year in South Africa. I appreciate and am gratified by their willingness to experiment and experience the new and unfamiliar.

Finally, I wish to thank Willie Currie. I watched him run a delicate political process as head of the NTPP and grew to appreciate his political intuitions and value his judgment. He and his wife, Barbara Klugman, were enormously encouraging of my efforts. Without Willie's generosity, intellect, and guidance, this book could not have been written. Indeed, this could have been Willie's book, but he was generous enough to permit me to write it instead.

Acronyms and Abbreviations

ADJ   Association of Democratic Journalists
ANC   African National Congress
AT&T   American Telephone and Telegraph Co.
BC   Black Consciousness
CCV   Contemporary Community Values Television
CDITP   Centre for the Development of Information and Telecommu-
                nications Policy
CIB   Campaign for Independent Broadcasting
CODESA   Convention for a Democratic South Africa
COM   Campaign for Open Media
COSATU   Congress of South African Trade Unions
CP   Conservative Party
DIP   Department of Information and Publicity of the ANC
DP   Democratic Party
EIF   Electronics Industries Federation
EPG   Eminent Persons Group
ESCOM/
    ESKOM   Electricity Supply Commission
FAWO   Film and Allied Workers Organisation
FOSATU   Federation of South African Trade Unions
GATT   General Agreement on Tariffs and Trade
GCIS   Government Communication and Information System
GEAR   Growth, Employment and Redistribution
GNU   Government of National Unity
IBA   Independent Broadcasting Authority
IFP   Inkatha Freedom Party
ISCOR   Iron and Steel Corporation
ITA   Information Technology Association
ITU   International Telecommunications Union
JCI   Johannesburg Consolidated Investments

JSE	Johannesburg Stock Exchange
M-Net	Electronic Media Network
MDM	Mass Democratic Movement
MERG	Macro-Economic Research Group
MLO	Media Liaison Officers
MMP	Media Monitoring Project
MP	Member of Parliament
MTN	Mobile Telephone Network
MWASA	Media Workers Association of South Africa
NAFCOC	National African Federated Chambers of Commerce
NAIL	New Africa Investments, Ltd.
NALEDI	National Labour & Economic Development Institute
NEC	National Empowerment Consortium
NEDLAC	National Economic Development and Labour Council
NEF	National Economic Forum
NGO	non-governmental organization
NNTV	National Network Television
NP	National Party
NTF	National Telecommunications Forum
NTPP	National Telecommunications Policy Project
NTUG	National Telematics User Group
NUSAS	National Union of South African Students
OECD	Organization for Economic Cooperation and Development
NUMSA	National Union of Metalworkers South Africa
PABX	Private Area Branch Exchange
PAC	Pan-Africanist Congress
PEBCO	Port Elizabeth Black Civic Organisation
PMG	Postmaster General
POTWA	Post & Telecommunications Workers Association
PSB	Public Service Broadcaster
PTT	post, telegraph, and telephone
PWV	Pretoria–Witwatersrand–Vereeniging (Province)
RASCOM	Regional Africa Satellite Commission
RDM	Rand Daily Mail Ltd.
RDP	Reconstruction and Development Programme
SAAN	South African Associated Newspapers
SABC	South African Broadcasting Corporation
SACC	South African Council of Churches
SACP	South African Communist Party
SACS	South African Communication Service
SACTU	South African Congress of Trade Unions
SACTWU	South African Clothing and Textile Workers Union
SAITA	South African Independent Telecommunications Authority

SANCO	South African National Civic Organisation
SAPA	South African Press Agency
SAPT	South African Posts and Telecommunications
SAR&H	South African Railways and Harbours
SASJ	South African Society of Journalists
SATRA	South African Telecommunications Regulatory Authority
SATS	South African Transport Services
SEP	strategic equity partner
SSC	State Security Council
TBVC	Transkei, Bophuthatswana, Venda, Ciskei (homelands)
TML	Times Media Ltd.
TMSA	Telephone Manufacturers of South Africa
TSS	TopSport Surplus
UDF	United Democratic Front
VANS	value-added network services
VAT	value-added tax
WTO	World Trade Organization

CHAPTER 1

Introduction and Overview

The Mount Grace Country Hotel in Magaliesburg isn't really far enough from Johannesburg to qualify as a "bush" resort, but it has the kind of rural, almost colonial, elegance to be familiar as a posh, quiet getaway spot for the white South African elite. Perhaps this is why the Minister of Posts, Telecommunications and Broadcasting Dr. Z. Pallo Jordan craftily chose it as the venue for the National Colloquium on Telecommunications Policy in November 1995. Where once they could set foot at the Mount Grace only as busboys and chambermaids, black delegates to the colloquium would mix with their white counterparts on equal footing. Jordan had been on the job as Cabinet minister for a little over a year, since the African National Congress alliance received the lion's share of the vote in South Africa's first free election in April 1994 and took the reins of government as the dominant bloc in a multiparty government of national unity. A respected ANC intellectual, Jordan was rumored to be bored with this second-rank ministry and disengaged from its operations. Yet he had initiated an unusual policy-making process in which the public, and sectoral "stakeholders" in particular, were *directly* engaged in policy formulation. Called the National Telecommunications Policy Project (NTPP), the process was moving on schedule toward its next crucial phase, this so-called colloquium.

The colloquium was designed to bring together representative stakeholders in the telecommunications sector to discuss the future of the industry in the new, post-apartheid South Africa. A Green Paper, which described the nature of the South African telecommunications sector and its problems and posed a series of questions on various policy options, had been published some months previously. Reactions, comments, and answers to the Green Paper questions coming from all quarters of the country had been submitted to a coordinating group, the NTPP Task Team, which then "played back" to the parties a document summarizing the submissions and shaping their interpretation. The Colloquium was the next phase of the process, and holding it at the Mount Grace, away from offices, workplaces, and union halls, was intended to foster a kind of working relationship, if not camaraderie, among the delegates.

Camaraderie is not what one would have expected. After all, delegates included the old Afrikaner bureaucrats in the old Post Office, white businessmen (many of whom had for years prospered happily under apartheid structures and regulations), leaders of some of the most militant black labor unions (whose youth stood in marked contrast to the aging white delegates), officials from newly formed black entrepreneur associations (dressed more smartly than the white businessmen, and like them, armed with the latest cell phones), and representatives from telecommunications user groups ranging from large corporate clients to the disabled. Many of these people, and certainly the groups they represented, had but recently been at the literal barricades. And, given the powerful, racially structured template that governed personal interactions during the decades of apartheid, this new, relatively unstructured, ostensibly equal forum made many participants both expectant and nervous. Here were heads of major corporations sitting with township residents, black union leaders with the Afrikaner old guard. Camaraderie did not really blossom. Indeed, there were several strained moments over the three days, as there would be in subsequent interactions and negotiations. Nonetheless, the approximately one hundred delegates met in workshops and plenaries and hammered out a series of compromises that, in the main, established a set of guidelines that would become the law transforming telecommunications from a retrograde, apartheid-aligned sector to one whose central orientation is to provide service to the disadvantaged black majority. This process of sectoral reform in telecommunications, replicated also in many other economic sectors and governmental functions, was an instance where democracy – in John Keane's (1991: 190) shorthand definition, rule by publics who make judgments in public – came alive literally before one's eyes.

South Africa has been a tremendously exciting place since February 1990, the date of the unbanning of political organizations and hence the birth of the transition to a post-apartheid dispensation. Virtually all social institutions have been placed under examination, their structures and operations critically assessed to see if they comport with democratic values and whether they deliver the material goods. The examination itself is an exercise in the self-constitution of a free people, a moment of democratiz*ation* – that special phase in the forging of democracy.[1] Democracy is a project of establishing a system of rules specifying who is authorized to make collective decisions and through which procedures such decisions are to be made, so as to secure the fullest possible and qualitatively best participation of affected parties. Again, following Keane (1991: 168–169), this proceduralist definition of democracy has clear normative implications. Democracy requires, at minimum, equal and universal adult suffrage, majority rule and guarantees of minority rights, the rule of law, constitutional guarantees of freedom of assembly and expression. In this, reforming communications policy in post-apartheid South Africa was and continues to be an inspiring and sometimes maddening demonstration of how to democratize politics and policy making. The process has both invoked and helped shape voluntary associations of autonomous agents outside the direct control of the state – in current parlance, civil society – and has created viable, if still fragile, public spaces that facilitate debate among citizens and dialogue between civil society and the state. The kind of participatory, civil society–based deliberative democracy that has become the reverie of so many Western social and political theorists in recent years has been occurring on the ground in complex and grubby fashion in the new South Africa. Communications policy was both the subject and object of democratic reform: Subject, in the sense that the process of policy determination occurred through a deliberative, participatory politics; object, in the sense that the goal was the establishment of the infrastructure of a democratic public sphere and the expansion of the social basis of communication generally.

---

1 An analytic distinction can be made between the processes of transition to, consolidation of, and institutionalization of democracy. In the transition to democracy, or democratization, as Víctor Pérez-Díaz (1993: 3–4) explains, the basic rules of the game are established (both within the political class and between the political class and society at large). They chiefly concern the limits of state power, the means of access of both politicians and society to that power, and the modalities for the exercise of such power. With consolidation comes the widespread expectation that the new regime is going to stay, and its basic rules will be respected. Institutionalization describes the point at which the regime is recognized as legitimate in the eyes of most of the population most of the time, and the basic rules of the political game not only prevail de facto but have been internalized by both politicians and society. The three processes are interrelated. They are not consecutive phases of a temporal order; rather, they overlap one another.

This experience of participatory, deliberative democracy may be a phenomenon unique to the South African context due to its complicated history. Indeed, one of the arguments of this book is that it was the particular kinds of civil society activism of the 1980s that established the structures and mechanisms of the participatory, consultative politics typified in the communications reform process. The South African reform experience is an important demonstration of the need to consider the formation of civil society itself as a powerful element in democratic process. This book chronicles the process of reform and the exercise of participatory democracy through the concrete examination of reform in the South African communications sector: in telecommunications, broadcasting, print media, and the government information service.

The communications sector has a special status in modern societies. Its technologies constitute the infrastructure of an increasingly information-based, trade-oriented economy and society. Uncritical and exaggerated claims about the "information age" and the "network society" notwithstanding, it is clear that communications and information have become centrally important to modern economies. Accordingly, this is a period of dramatic upheaval in communications policy design. Old models are challenged by new technologies, the convergence of technologies and modes of delivery, impetus toward liberalization and privatization, and pressures for fully open markets. Perhaps more than in the past, communications are key to economic development (see, for instance, Saunders, Warford, and Wellenius, 1994; Castells, 1996). Their reform, then, has significant impact on the task of alleviating the poverty and inequality left over from apartheid. Indeed, if, following Amartya Sen (1999), poverty is not simply a matter of inadequate income, but rather a state of unfreedom, then reconstruction and development is an inherent component of the process of liberation and democratization. Communications also have a special status in a democracy. In large complex societies, it is in the public arena of the mass media (and now, increasingly, due to the convergence of technologies and the emergence of the Internet, includes telecommunications as well as the traditional mass media of print and broadcast) where democracy is most concretely manifest because that arena both represents and constitutes the independent political institution wherein citizens can engage in the discussion of matters of the commonweal (see, among others, Garnham, 1986; Habermas, 1996; Bohman, 1996). The mass media constitute the means by which groups represent themselves to themselves and to others. To the extent that communications reform facilitates access to the public sphere, it has effects on poverty and economic development as well. As Sen (1999) has shown, in countries that are destitute but have a free press, famines do not occur. Finally, in a country like South Africa, which is confronting a brutal past, the project of truth-seeking and reconciliation – arguably necessary for successful democratization – can only take place on a national stage through the mass media. The reform of communications is not just an aspect of political reform, the transformation of one particular industrial sector; rather it is part and parcel of the transition to democracy. Indeed, communications policy is paradigmatic of the many reform processes going on in South Africa. It gives people voice, symbolically and materially.

A great deal of the scholarly literature on South Africa since February 1990 has been concerned with plotting the process of the political transition and with analyzing the design of institutions coming out of it. Could the bitter historical antagonists arrive at a workable set of compromises, or would continual outbursts of violence throw the country into ruinous civil war? What kind of electoral system (plurality, majority, or proportional representation) would come out of negotiations? What executive type (parliamentary or presidential)? What manner of constitutional arrangement (majoritarian or power-sharing)? For scholars, whether and how the South African political elites resolved these design options implicate particular paths of a transition to democracy, reveal underlying constraints on bargaining elucidated by game theory, and, perhaps most important, serve as harbingers for the future of democracy and stability. Indeed, South Africa has become just one more case to examine in an emergent literature on the "transition to democracy."

To be sure, this literature is not really new per se. It is a part of, though somewhat at odds with, an older literature on democratization that accompanied modernization theory and emphasized structural factors, such as levels of income, education, and media consumption as the key elements – even necessary preconditions – for determining the prospects for democratization (see Lerner, 1958; Lipset, 1960; Dahl, 1971). What sparked a revival in the study of democracy was the explosion of countries that moved from authoritarian to democratic politics in the 1980s, particularly in Latin America and Southern Europe. The remarkable collapse of the Soviet system in 1989 and the emergence of tentative democratic regimes in Central and Eastern Europe likewise stimulated the resurgence of research on democratization. In contrast to the older structural theories, the new scholarly literature concentrates on process, on the perception of alternatives among significant portions of the population or major institutional actors, and, especially, on elite negotiations. The correlation between higher levels of socioeconomic development and democratization, while well-documented, does not tell us much about when, how, and if a transition to democracy will take place and be successfully completed (see Linz and Stepan, 1996). The new transition literature concentrates on a process-driven explanation of change, which highlights the political choices of actors within specific sets of opportunities and constraints. Democratization is seen as primarily the product of political leaders who have the will and the skill to bring it about. Indeed, it is the reconstruction of actors' changing cognitive frames that permits the transition to proceed (see O'Donnell and Schmitter, 1986; Di Palma, 1990).

Transition theory, as it is loosely referred to, is the product of reflection upon, and abstraction from, the historically disparate paths to democracy followed in Central and Southern Europe and Latin America. Samuel Huntington (1991), whose *The Third Wave: Democratization in the Late Twentieth Century* has become something of a standard-bearer in the subfield, characterizes four types of transition: *transformations*, when the elites in power take the lead in bringing about democracy (as in Spain, India, Hungary, and Brazil); *replacements*, when opposition groups take the lead in bringing about democracy (as in Portugal, Romania, and Argentina); *interventions*, when democratic institutions are imposed by an outside power, usually following a military defeat (as in Japan, West Germany, and Panama); and *transplacements*, characterized by negotiations between key powerful groups. South Africa is usually taken as an example of the transplacement type.

Transplacements are expected to occur when two conditions are present. First, there is a mutually perceived sense of stalemate, the continuation of which becomes untenable. A transplacement's preconditions arise when the old regime registers a split between hard-liners, who insist on continuing repressive rule, and moderates or reformers, who conclude that the regime has failed in fundamental ways.[2] Transi-

---

2 Of course, the perception of "failure" by elements of the authoritarian regime harks back to the political-economic bases of the older transition to democracy model usually associated with Seymour Martin Lipset. Empirical evidence indicates that a large majority of the coun-

tion commences when dominant groups in both government and opposition begin to bargain with one another, recognizing that neither party is capable of determining the future unilaterally. Indeed, pacts are said to work only when the prior regime type is authoritarian or "post-totalitarian" (those few Soviet bloc countries that retained elements of civil society), because only in these regimes do civil society and moderate bargaining players exist (Linz and Stepan, 1996: 38–65). Second, at critical junctures, reformers must appear to be stronger than "stand-patters" in the government while moderates must seem stronger than extremists in the opposition. A successful transition to democracy under these conditions is the result of negotiations between reformers in a ruling regime and moderates in the opposition. Reformers and moderates can use their more extreme erstwhile allies as threats but in the end must isolate them and engage in a suboptimal pact of the middle ground. But, because of the control the government reformers exercise over the machinery of state, particularly the military, the pro-democratic forces in the opposition most often must offer concessions in exchange for democracy. Fear of a coup limits pro-democracy options. Hence most successful transitions produce a dispensation that is economically and socially conservative, thus maintaining the central pillars of capitalist society (see O'Donnell and Schmitter, 1986; Przeworski, 1991).

This schematic outline does capture something of the nature of South Africa's transition. "Reform apartheid," initiated under P. W. Botha's *verligte*, or moderate, wing of the ruling National Party in the early 1980s, embodied among other things a dire need to address the contradictions between apartheid institutions and an economy that had moved from a mining and farming predominance to one increasingly defined by manufacturing. Labor shortages and skills deficits had begun to plague the South African economy, and the increasing dependence of business on skilled and semiskilled African labor meant that the old form of industrial relations – characterized by Jeffrey Herbst (1994: 39) as one "whereby managers issued diktats to a floating group of

tries that experienced a transition from authoritarianism to democracy in the 1970s and 1980s had substantial economic problems (either declining economic growth or rampant inflation, or both) prior to the transition. Stephan Haggard and Robert R. Kaufman (1995: 32–36, 366), critics of the choice-based transition literature, argue that economic crisis accelerated, if it didn't directly cause the collapse of authoritarian regimes. At the very least, economic constraints figured much more centrally in determining the political agenda, the interests, and capabilities of the central protagonists in the democratization drama than the choice-based theorists acknowledge.

nonskilled workers who often responded with wildcat strikes" – no longer worked. Reform apartheid relaxed repressive labor laws, legalized black trade unions, and embarked upon the immense task of upgrading the conditions of South Africa's black population, particularly in education.[3] The political side of reform entailed an attempt by the government to foster a nonwhite middle class whose stake in the system would stabilize a social order still largely distinguished by white domination. The culmination of the strategy rested in the creation of a tricameral Parliament in 1983 to augment the whites-only Parliament. The aim was to draw in the Coloured and Indian communities and segregate them from the still disenfranchised African majority.

But reform apartheid was a liberalization, not a democratization strategy. The difference is of some importance. As Linz and Stepan (1996: 1) argue, in a nondemocratic setting liberalization may entail a mix of policy and social changes, such as less censorship of the media, somewhat greater space for the organization of autonomous working-class activities, the introduction of some legal safeguards for individuals, perhaps some measures for improving the distribution of income, and the toleration of opposition. Democratization encompasses liberalization but is a wider and more specifically political concept. Democratization requires open contestation over the right to win control of the government, and this in turn requires free competitive elections, the results of which determine who governs. In South Africa, democratization also necessarily demanded policies that deracialize politics and society, in short, the abolition of the system of racial separation and oppression known as apartheid. The effort to maintain white supremacy while jettisoning grand apartheid served rather to reignite widespread grassroots rebellion under the newly constituted anti-apartheid umbrella group, the United Democratic Front (UDF). The 1980s were marked by widespread popular struggle and violent repression, political stalemate, and economic crisis. This was the backdrop to F. W. de Klerk's move to "unban" the African National Congress (ANC), South African Communist Party (SACP), and Pan-Africanist Congress (PAC) in February 1990, very soon after he succeeded P. W. Botha as National Party leader and State President. De Klerk's faction of the

---

3 In the context of South African liberation politics since the 1970s, the term "black" was used to encompass all three "nonwhite" groups. Indians, Coloureds, and indigenous Africans were to be considered "black" so long as they identified with the struggle against racial oppression. Blackness became a matter less of ancestry than of a raised consciousness. The term "African" refers to the Bantu-speaking indigenous majority (see Biko, 1978: 49–53).

National Party saw that it had more to gain by negotiating with the liberation groups than by maintaining the conflict-ridden and stalemated status quo. In parallel, Nelson Mandela (still, for all intents and purposes the leader of the liberation movement) had come to understand that the government could not be overthrown and that the attempt to mobilize the population for armed struggle would lead to disaster. Mandela's view was communicated in a letter to P. W. Botha in July 1989, wherein he indicated his desire to open negotiations with the government but would not agree to the government's preconditions (that the ANC first renounce violence, break with the South African Communist Party, and abandon its demand for majority rule).

[M]y intervention is influenced by purely domestic issues, by the civil strife and ruin into which the country is now sliding. I am disturbed, as many other South Africans no doubt are, by the spectre of a South Africa split into two hostile camps; blacks (the term 'blacks' is used in a broad sense to include all those who are not whites) on one side and whites on the other, slaughtering one another; by acute tensions which are building up dangerously in practically every sphere of our lives, a situation which, in turn, preshadows more violent clashes in the days ahead. This is the crisis that has forced me to act. (Mandela, 1991: 218)

It has become something of a commonplace that the fall of the Soviet Union was the final catalyst enabling the National Party to move past its hard-line opposition against the black liberation struggle and toward some kind of negotiated accommodation with it (see Adam and Moodley, 1993). With the end of the cold war, each side – the ANC and the National Party/South African government – lost its value as a proxy in a larger geopolitical and ideological conflict. After the fall of the Soviet Union, communism could no longer play the ideological bogey for the white stalwarts of apartheid; materially, the white minority government could no longer expect to receive the support it had tacitly obtained from the West (particularly from the Thatcher and Reagan governments). On the other side, the loss of Soviet material and ideological support could no longer bolster the ANC's dreams for the total destruction of apartheid and the creation of a socialist order. And within the ANC, the fall of Soviet communism would have to spark some rethinking of political positions that had gone unassessed for years. Indeed, as more than one commentator has argued, de Klerk understood before almost anyone else that communism's failure would have a profound effect on the ANC's project, and hence presented whites with the opportunity to negotiate a reasonable settlement (Herbst, 1997–98; also see Slovo, 1990).

In keeping with the transition theory model, dominant fractions of the two antagonistic parties recognized they could not dictate the future according to their respective designs. All-party talks, called the Convention for a Democratic South Africa (CODESA), commenced in December 1991, but moved slowly during the first couple of years, in large part because the ANC was trying to transform itself from a liberation movement into a political party and at the same time trying not to distance itself from its grassroots supporters. The National Party, intent on taking advantage of its position as the initiator of change and in far better command of the import of governance and policy options, pressed for substantive agreement on post-apartheid political institutions in advance of elections. These included entrenching power-sharing within the executive (with minority veto-power), securing the right to private property, establishing strong regional governments, and creating a Bill of Rights enforced by a special constitutional court (see Friedman, 1993). The ANC focused rather on reaching agreement on a procedure by which a democratic government could be formed and a constitution written. The ANC demanded an interim government and an elected constituent assembly to write the first constitution. It also challenged the National Party's dual role as government and primary political negotiator. The congress, or tripartite alliance, consisting of the ANC, the Congress of South African Trade Unions (COSATU), and the South African Communist Party (SACP), flexed its muscles, organizing mass actions to demonstrate its popular support. At the same time, de Klerk called the bluff of his hard-line internal opposition by calling and winning handily a referendum in March 1992, in which white voters were asked whether they supported continued negotiations with the black liberation groups (see Giliomee and Rantete, 1992; Jung and Shapiro, 1995).

As political negotiations dragged on, widespread civil unrest and violence threatened the transition. In the aftermath of two violent incidents that prompted both ANC and NP leaders to wonder whether the lack of progress portended social disaster (the Boipatong and Bisho massacres, in which scores of ANC supporters were killed),

10

negotiations resumed in September 1992.[4] In a classic instance of "elite-pacting," this time negotiations took place behind closed doors and between the government and the ANC alliance only, in an effort to fix the main terms of an agreement before multilateral talks began again. That agreement (called the "Record of Understanding" [1992] and the baseline for the much-used pragmatic concept of "sufficient consensus," a stratagem deployed by ANC and NP negotiators when other parties threatened continued progress in the subsequent negotiations) was signed by ANC President Mandela and State President de Klerk on September 26, 1992. It set the basic terms of an interim constitution that was adopted by the last white Parliament in its final act in December of 1993. Largely adhering to the power-sharing position of the National Party, the Record of Understanding called for a legally mandated, five-year government of national unity regardless of the election outcome, with Cabinet representation for all parties winning at least 5 percent of the vote, and a share of executive power (an executive deputy presidency) to any party winning 20 percent. Elections would be by proportional representation in closed party lists. In the end, the ANC agreed to guarantee both property rights and the security of tenure (including the payment of pensions) in posts for civil servants (see Republic of South Africa, 1993a: sects. 28, 236, 245). In what would have important consequences for future economic policy, the ANC also agreed to the nearly complete independence of the central bank, the South African Reserve Bank.

The NP gave up its insistence on racially defined "group rights" and on a Cabinet veto clothed in the formalism of mandatory special majorities for key decisions. Throughout the negotiations the NP insisted that it would settle for nothing less than a Cabinet veto. In the final hours, the NP dropped this demand and settled for a vague constitutional clause suggesting that Cabinet members ought to work together. Whereas the Interim Constitution required the majority party,

4 Boipatong was a black township in the Vaal Triangle in which 39 unarmed ANC supporters were massacred on June 17, 1992, by apparent Inkatha Freedom Party (IFP) members with the connivance of the South African police. There is some evidence of an effort orchestrated by the Afrikaner right-wing and elements of the security forces in the first two years of the transition period to foment civil unrest and disrupt the transition (see A. Sparks, 1995: 153–178). Several weeks after Boipatong, the ANC tried to mobilize some of its followers against the government of the homeland of Ciskei. Protesters were met with armed resistance from the homeland's army, resulting in the shooting deaths of 28 people. Only after Boipatong and Bisho did the dynamic of negotiations become self-supporting despite all further attempts to disturb them (including the assassination of South African Communist Party and ANC leader Chris Hani in April 1993).

in the person of the state president, to "consult" both deputy presidents – which would include the NP's F. W. de Klerk – it did not offer the latter a veto. As Michael MacDonald (1996) argues, the lack of a Cabinet veto and limiting the Government of National Unity to a period of five years meant that the agreement was not really power sharing, after all. However, the property rights, civil service, and pension guarantees indirectly secured a parallel outcome inasmuch as they thwart radical transformation. The property rights guarantee meant that by and large the interests of capital were constitutionally beyond challenge. The civil service guarantee meant that the ANC must act through bureaucracies that in many respects could function independently of the government of the day. And the pension guarantee meant that the budget had very large precommitments. These features would check the transformative impulses of the ANC alliance.

A Multi-Party Negotiating Council commenced in March 1993, by most accounts a thinly veiled process for consolidating the bargain between the ANC and NP. In October 1993 an act was passed creating a Transitional Executive Council, a multiparty executive body designed to oversee the government in the run-up to the election of April 1994. The election saw the ANC receive 62.65 percent of the vote, NP 20.39 percent, and Inkatha Freedom Party (IFP) 10.54 percent. The smaller parties who were to receive seats in the National Assembly included the Freedom Front, with 2.17 percent of the vote, Democratic Party 1.73 percent, and Pan-Africanist Congress 1.25 percent. Although many doubted the reported election results from the IFP stronghold of Kwazulu-Natal, bringing the IFP into government was seen as indispensable to establishing political reconciliation and outweighed the significance of election fraud (see Reynolds, 1994).

The South African transition thus seems to have followed much of the model sketched out by the choice-based analysis of democratic transitions. Some South African scholars and commentators use the model to argue on behalf of certain kinds of moderate politics (see, e.g., Giliomee and Schlemmer, 1994; Adam, Slabbert, and Moodley, 1997). But there are features that make the South African experience somewhat different from most other transitions from authoritarian rule. These features underscore some of the drawbacks of the "modeling" of the South African transition. Transition theory tends to concentrate on elite actors. To be sure, the skilled leaderships of the ANC alliance and the National Party were crucial in negotiating the terms of the transition. (And pointedly, the personal example, the statesmanship, and the extraordinary lack of bitterness on the part of Nelson Mandela facilitated negotiation and reconciliation.) But the democratic transition in South Africa was fundamentally the product of a general mass movement, a phenomenon downplayed or even neglected by most transition theory, and a historical fact disregarded by many South African commentators. Transition theory factors in the fifteen-year mass resistance movement only as a "left extreme" that the moderate ANC leaders had to coopt. In fact, as Glenn Adler and Eddie Webster (1995) among others have argued, the trade unions and civil society organizations in South Africa set the preconditions for the transition; the participatory political processes they engendered set the transition's political agenda and provided the kinds of alternative structures and mechanisms that continue to affect the public debate and the process of consolidating democracy.

The strength and vibrancy of South African civil society, along with the fact that the dominant political movement – the ANC alliance – is ideologically committed to the liberal Enlightenment project (where political right resides in the individual, not the group, race, or tribe), marks South Africa as a special case of transition to democracy.[5] The years of political struggle engendered multiple forms of autonomous associations in the form of community political organizations (called "civics"), students' and women's groups and the United Democratic Front itself, the vast majority of which were organizationally independent of the ANC and, of course, from the state. Campaigning for improved living conditions in black townships and opposing municipal authorities foisted on townships by the apartheid state, the civics in theory represented a cross-class coalition of collective consumers (Glaser, 1997: 6). The black labor movement, which grew enormously

---

5 The other key features about South Africa that better situate it than new democracies, for example, in the old Soviet bloc, is that it has a functioning (though highly concentrated and conglomerated) market economy, with the relevant institutions associated with a functioning market: a vibrant stock exchange, a bond market, a working banking system, a well-developed law of contracts, and a functioning, if politically suspect and bloated, civil service. Moreover, the matter of "stateness," that is, questions regarding the legitimacy of the territorial boundaries of South Africa and who should constitute the polity, were essentially settled during the transition. During most of the transition period the small Afrikaner right-wing had been agitating for a separate Afrikaner state. But after the disastrous battle of Mmbatho in March 1994, in which the Afrikaner right-wing was humiliated in its effort to assert military might in a politically crumbling Bophuthatswana homeland, Constand Viljoen, leader of the Freedom Front (the political party of the Afrikaner right-wing), turned from separatism to parliamentary opposition (see A. Sparks, 1995: 197–225). On the importance of stateness to democratic transitions, see Linz and Stepan (1996: 17–37).

after 1979, was the other key civil society actor. The twin grievances of capitalist exploitation and apartheid compelled the labor movement to seek both economic and political solutions to workers' problems and, hence, to forge alliances with community and political groups, characteristic of what has been described as "social movement unionism" (Webster, 1988; Waterman, 1991; Seidman, 1994). Indeed, after the UDF was banned by the government in 1988, the labor movement essentially took on the leadership role of the anti-apartheid movement (what came to be called in the late 1980s the "Mass Democratic Movement," or MDM). After 1990, civil society groups were engaged in their own negotiations at all levels in the political transition, including the reorganization of local government. The Congress of South African Trade Unions, the black union umbrella federation, entered into negotiations with business and government over codetermination of labor and macroeconomic policies. COSATU consistently called for the participation of the working class in the political process and in the formulation and development of national economic policies.

Central to the South African democratic transition were civil society activism and the emergence of "stakeholder forums," new arenas for the discussion and formulation of policy regarding virtually every government function. Constituted outside of government, in effect *forced* upon government by anti-apartheid civil society organizations oriented around particular issues, the forums functioned as broadly consultative bodies where "stakeholders," from business leaders to township dwellers to nongovernmental organization (NGO) representatives to old apartheid government bureaucrats, met to discuss how to transform a particular government function or industrial sector and bring services to the people in keeping with emerging democratic principles. The forums appeared in the nether world of the period between the disintegration of the ancien régime and the emergence of a new political dispensation, in which the National Party still held the reins of power after 1990 and continued to function as government, but was now a lameduck, if still powerful and dangerous, administration. The liberation movement championed the forums largely as a means to prevent the apartheid government from taking decisions unilaterally, particularly as constitutional negotiations were in motion and elections would presumably establish a new, ANC-led government. The forums represented the effort by excluded, largely black, groups to gain entry to policymaking arenas during the 1990–94 transition period. The legitimacy of the forums rested precisely in the fact that they took place *outside* the

14

regular channels of the old government. At the same time, the government felt compelled to participate in the forums because any policy government might undertake risked being vetted by the ANC alliance through strikes and street action if it proceeded without agreement from the forums. This formulation is a bit overdrawn, though the basic dynamic described is accurate. The ambiguity rests in the fact that "the government" was hardly unitary at this point in time. Some government departments and parastatals participated in the forums with intense reluctance and hostility. Other government actors, such as ESKOM, the electricity parastatal, played the key role in initiating their forums (see Shubane and Shaw, 1993).

The pedigree for the grassroots, consultative orientation of the forums lay in several sources, but two stand out: the township civic associations that grew during the 1980s and the internal democratic practices of the black trade unions. The civics had functioned as loci for intense opposition to white rule and for local self-help in the context of organizing township resistance during the internal insurrection. As part of their opposition to apartheid authoritarianism, many civics inaugurated participatory, consultative mechanisms for deciding upon political strategies. Mechanisms of accountability and reporting back to the membership were brought over from the rigorous internal democratic practices of the trade unions. Local forums had been operating in some communities since the mid-1980s (Lodge, Nasson, Mufson, et al., 1991; Shubane and Madiba, 1992; Ginsburg, Webster, et al., 1995).[6] The impetus for the formation of *national* forums came from labor. As political negotiations ensued after 1990, COSATU believed that the National Party government was unilaterally placing crucial areas of the economy

6 The degree to which the civics were simply local "shock troops" of the liberation struggle or whether they were independent manifestations of grassroots interests with strong connections to the liberation organizations, that is, more classically civil society organizations, is a subject of debate. Their founding in the crucible of the liberation struggle marks the civics and youth and student groups as different from classical civil society organizations. They were engaged in both resistance and survival. Hence, notwithstanding the consultative features of many civics, they were not always "civil." Some organizations demanded and enforced a uniformity that contradicts the notion of a civil society. And in some townships, some anti-apartheid organizations devolved into groups, little short of gangs, with quasi-political affiliations (see Seekings, 1993; Friedman and Reitzes, 1995). The "social capital" literature, whose best-known proponent is Robert Putnam (1993), argues that association breeds trust. In South Africa, because the context of association was anti-authority amidst violent state repression, the development of trust was more limited and more contradictory. The civic and youth movements' call to make the townships "ungovernable" during the 1980s, so successful in mobilizing people against the apartheid state, created an enduring strain of political culture whose unruly, sometimes violent, populism would have negative repercussions even after the ANC came to power.

outside the reach of political decision making in an attempt to limit the power of a future majority government. Following a general strike in November 1991 over the government's initiation of a value-added tax (VAT), COSATU demanded a macroeconomic negotiation on social and economic issues, parallel to the political negotiations. The Business Roundtable, an embryonic business association anxious to rationalize macroeconomic policies and labor relations, was quick to support this move, as was Finance Minister Derek Keys. The National Economic Forum (NEF) was launched. Thereafter, an explosion of forums brought various constituencies together on all manner of issues at national, regional, and local levels to discuss matters such as housing, the VAT system, drought relief, and electricity distribution. An estimated 230 forums grew in the period after February 1990 (Patel, 1993; Shubane and Shaw, 1993).

The change in political culture was plainly evident with the advent of the forums. The forums were broadly democratic in terms of representativeness, with specific participation from previously marginalized groups of civil society, in particular the civic organizations. The operative slogan of the forums – and in South African politics generally in this period – was "a culture of consultation and transparency." This was in distinct contrast to the racially exclusive, closed, and often secretive way of conducting politics in the old South Africa. The importance of the forums, of civil society and associative democratic organizations generally to the ANC alliance was reflected in its 1994 Reconstruction and Development Programme (RDP) – the alliance's broadly Keynesian macroeconomic vision for a post-apartheid South Africa. Though the original RDP document was published under the ANC's imprimatur, it was the product of a broad-based consultative process run jointly by the ANC, COSATU, the South African Communist Party, the South African Council of Churches (SACC), and the South African National Civic Organisation (SANCO). It was essentially an expression of the aspirations of the previously disenfranchised, and, although vague on many points of economic policy, was clearly located within a broadly Keynesian developmental framework. Given that it was the election platform of the leading party in the Government of National Unity, its ideals became a large part of the new government's policies. The document explicitly stated that the RDP "must work with existing forums, such as the NEF, the National Electricity Forum and the National Housing Forum, and must develop a more coherent and representative system on a regional and sectoral basis" (African National Congress,

1994b: 91). The idea was that democratization of the state was not restricted to universalizing the franchise; democracy was held to be incomplete unless civil society was assured a share in decisions.

> Democracy for ordinary citizens must not end with formal rights and periodic one-person, one-vote elections. Without undermining the authority and responsibilities of elected representative bodies . . . the democratic order we envisage must foster a wide range of institutions of participatory democracy in partnership with civil society on the basis of informed and empowered citizens (e.g. the various sectoral forums like the National Economic Forum) and facilitate direct democracy (people's forums, referenda where appropriate, and other consultation processes). (African National Congress, 1994b: 120–121)

Notwithstanding this language, the forums were not manifestations of civil society per se. The product of civil society initiatives to be sure, the forums were corporatist-type structures, institutional mechanisms for mediating state and civil society in the democratic transition period. However, in contrast to typical corporatism, which creates a restricted bargaining arena for the central institutional powers of a society (government, industry, and labor, as a rule), the South African stakeholder forums were broadly inclusive of many, if not most, groups in society. The forums represented an effort at a democratic and socially transformative version of corporatism.

The establishment of the Government of National Unity under ANC leadership following the 1994 election did not undermine the forums, though it did introduce a new tension between electoral and participatory democratic processes. The work of the forums metamorphosed into consultative processes for the formulation of Green and White (policy) Papers for various sectors, often under the cooperative aegis of the relevant government minister and the sectoral stakeholder forum. Many commentators have criticized corporatism in post-apartheid South Africa. On one hand, the corporatist mechanisms such as forums and stakeholder-driven Green Paper/White Paper processes are condemned as undemocratic, inasmuch as they insulate policy making from the electoral process and permit private parties to make public policy (see, e.g., Friedman and Reitzes, 1995). On the other hand, corporatist bodies are said to be designed to "tame" radical civil society elements, making them "play politics" in accordance with the rules laid down by the state and hence demobilizing them (see, e.g., Ginsburg, 1996). Both criticisms are well-taken and may well apply to aspects of the South African political scene. I will argue, however, that in the politics of reform of the South African communications sector, the quasi-corporatist mechanisms constituted a structured participatory democratic politics that displayed neither of these criticized features.

Why communications? Several factors point to that sector's particular importance as a window to understanding the South African transition to democracy and the political struggles of its consolidation. The fact that civil society activism was so crucial to the South African transition to democracy meant that South Africa's was an unusually communication-saturated transition. The new political culture registered a heightened sensitivity to the importance of free and open media, for only through these could consultation and transparency be realized. Broadcasting, because of its centrality to the democratic transition, was the first apartheid institution to undergo a fundamental transformation – prior, even, to the 1994 election. The government-owned and -operated South African Broadcasting Corporation (SABC), long a National Party instrument, had to be transformed into a neutral institution in order for free and fair elections to take place. No challenger to the National Party could contemplate running an election campaign if broadcasting (particularly radio, which has wide distribution and is especially important to nonliterate and semiliterate audiences) remained in the NP's pocket. The power of the state broadcaster to set the agenda, to deride and undermine the opposition, to discourage voting, and especially to foment confusion and violence, was considerable. More than that, broadcasting is voice, the ability to communicate and state grievances, to share ideas and experiences, to challenge reigning orthodoxy on a national scale – precisely those forms of interaction and representation from which the black majority had been shut out for so many decades. Freedom to communicate is clearly one of the crucial underpinnings of the quest for political freedom. Under great pressure from the civil society media groups constituted within the ideological aegis of the Mass Democratic Movement (such as the Save the Press Campaign, the Campaign for Open Media, the Film and Allied Workers Organisation, and Campaign for Independent Broadcasting), the SABC and South African broadcast practice generally were reorganized through the CODESA negotiations. Telecommunications was the first sector to take its consultative Green and White Papers to legislation and hence became a model for the reform of other sectors. The principle of universal service, enshrined in the telecommunications reform process, embodied a commitment to equalizing social access to information and communication as a democratic norm – thus placing equitable access to communication resources at the heart of the democratization process. Telecommunications reform also assumed the leading edge in the contentious public debate over the proposed privatization of state assets, charting a viable position between private and state ownership. Finally, the reform of the South African Communication Service (SACS), the apartheid government's public relations and information arm, sparked a fundamental debate over the role of the press and the proper relation between the mass media and government in the post-apartheid era. The eventual abolition of SACS and its replacement by a new agency represented, in principle, the replacement of the ministry of information, top-down government-knows-best model of communication by a model that conceptualized the relations between the government and the governed as interactive, in principle dialogic, and participatory.

The importance of and early concentration on communications reform in the broad transformation of South African political institutions was no accident, for the reform of communication institutions lies at the heart of any transition to democracy. The very idea of a society communicating freely is perhaps the core of democratic struggle. In conjunction with voting, an open and accessible public sphere protected by constitutional guarantees of freedom of association, assembly, and expression is among the fundamental features of modern democracy. Access to communication and participation in public life constitute the condition of citizenship in contemporary democracies. Citizenship here must be understood as not simply a legal status but as a form of political identity in which social beings work out their versions of the good through participation in public life (see, e.g., Mouffe, 1992). And in a society undergoing vast transformation, those social changes must be represented through the media. Societies in transition from authoritarianism need to come to grips with the past, and this can only be accomplished on a large scale through the mass media, where knowledge and acknowledgment of the past are manifested in the glare of publicity.[7] The media therefore are also of central importance in reworking

---

7 The "knowledge and acknowledgment" couplet is borrowed from Ash (1997: 33–38), who has used it in the Eastern European context.

memories and in validating a heretofore unacknowledged history and, in this respect, operating in conjunction with mechanisms of remembrance such as South Africa's Truth and Reconciliation Commission (see Boraine, Levy, and Scheffer, 1994).

The three parts of the South African communications sector underwent successful reform. The SABC, the putative public broadcaster but long the mouthpiece of the apartheid government, was remade into a nonpartisan public broadcaster with responsibility to program for all the people of South Africa in all eleven official languages. An independent regulatory body (the Independent Broadcasting Authority, or IBA) now oversees the broadcast sector as a whole and has inaugurated a mixed system of commercial, community, and public service broadcasting. Telkom, the state-owned enterprise that effectively monopolized telecommunications, is now a corporation separated from ministerial control and overseen by a newly established regulatory body (the South African Telecommunications Regulatory Authority, or SATRA). Legislation plots a phased liberalization of the sector, opening its various service markets over a gradual period of time. Resisting both big-bang privatization and retention of full state control, the new policy permitted a foreign telecommunications consortium to take a minority stake in Telkom to bring an infusion of capital and expertise. Telkom now has extensive universal service obligations as a condition of its license and so far it has been meeting these commitments. Finally, the South African Communication Service, the propaganda arm of the apartheid state, has been dismantled, replaced by a smaller central agency (the Government Communication and Information System, GCIS) whose mandate is to deliver, access, and outsource essential communication services and serve as a government–media–community liaison. After a sometimes caustic public debate over the past sins of the white print press groups and a call for their breakup, the government largely let the press alone and pledged to expand communication opportunities via policies that assist community and noncommercial media.

Each of these reforms took place via a complex political process in which civil society activism, embodying what I call a post–social democratic ideal, largely won out over the powerful forces of formal market capitalism and older models of state control. "Post"–social democratic, because, while South African civil society activism embodied an affinity with classic social democracy's concern for the underprivileged and its willingness to intervene in markets, it rejected both the statism of European-type social democracy and the cultural homogeneity historically inherent in it. In rejecting traditional social democracy's statism, the South African civil society organizations displayed a classic Deweyan pragmatism, where democracy is both a goal and a means, in which the best thoughts and actions of the entire community are necessary to reconstruct social life (Dewey, 1954; Ryan, 1995). In the cautious acceptance of the market, the civil society organizations sought to use the dynamism of the market while thwarting its inevitable inequities. In all three reform processes, the dynamics of participatory democracy constrained both capitalists and statists, and created mixed systems, embedding civic principles throughout the media institutions and thus making them more conducive to accessibility and participation. These mixed systems should be viewed, I argue, not as a less than satisfactory compromise, but as a positive good. These mixed systems embody the most viable and democratic of institutional forms in democracies at the turn of the millennium. Philosophically, the mixed systems embody a form of democratic experimentalism that acknowledges the facts of complexity, diversity, and difference and doubts whether any one person, group, party, or organization can ever be trusted to make superior choices on matters of concern to citizens. They are institutional arrangements that encourage the experimental and fallibilistic attitudes and procedures best suited to democracy. Politically, they harness the power of the newly democratized state to shape the communication sector so as to build into its overall structure media that are nonstate and noncommodified, as well as to build in conditions of contestability to the dominant service provider in both telecommunications and broadcasting.

And this process, I would argue in parallel, should not be viewed as "compromised," but rather as a vibrant, sometimes messy and conflictual, but productive interplay between participatory and electoral democratic forms. Communications reform is paradigmatic of the reform processes going on in South Africa. As I wrote earlier, it gives people voice, symbolically and materially. The process of reform in South Africa itself was constitutive of democracy. It is not often thus. In many, if not most countries, the transformation of state-owned enterprises has been pushed by political and economic elites, whose ability to bring about policy transformation derives largely from the insulation of "reform" from normal public decision-making channels and distributive claims (see Waterbury, 1992; Petrazzini, 1995). In marked contrast, communications policy reform in South Africa was conducted within a democratizing context and was itself a democratic process of a unique, participatory, deliberative kind. The South African communications policy reform processes constructed a genuine public sphere in which nearly all relevant parties had access and the ability to participate in ongoing discussions and negotiations in substantive, rather than merely symbolic ways. These were instances of negotiations among civil society stakeholders and between civil society and the state over the shape of new political institutions and a new political economy, where consensus building would have normative force for the participants. The South African communication reform process was a model of deliberative, participatory democracy in the transition to democracy phase.

An important caveat. Lest this account of reform appear as a kind of triumphalism of participatory democracy, a giddy celebration of post–social democratic institution building, it must be understood that communications, for all its importance, is but one sector in a universe of institutions, sectors, and functions in post-apartheid South Africa in dire need of transformation. Many of these have not transformed. Many may transform but not along the lines of the reform of the communications sector. Furthermore, the post–social democratic vision that largely triumphed over market and statist forces in the reform of the communications sector is always threatened by those forces. In broadcasting, for example, the absence of funding from government forces the SABC to behave in ways that mimic a commercial broadcaster. At the same time, the government's demand for guaranteed access to the SABC, hitherto resisted, may yet prevail. In telecommunications, government's desire to protect its asset Telkom may undermine the conditions that would establish fruitful competition with it. The government's promise to support nonstate, noncommodified community media through grants and trusts may fall to other budget priorities. Thus it must be understood that sectoral reform, including communications, takes place within a broader political context.

The strong moderating tendencies identified by the theorists of democratic transitions *do* exist. In the case of South Africa, now, the moderating tendencies derive not from the fear of a coup or counterrevolution, but from the constraints built into the government's prerogatives as a result of the transition agreements and from the intense constraints on the country deriving from economic globalization and the corresponding imperative to maintain the confidence of capital, of managers and investors. How to deal with these pressures has provoked a sharp policy struggle within the ANC alliance. There is evidence that in the face of these pressures and constraints the ANC-led government has elected to consolidate democracy along a conservative path of economic policies that largely perpetuate existing inequalities and power relations while partially deracializing them (and hence creating a black middle class as a new power base), and it encourages the demobilization of civil society activism in the national interest. The Keynesian-inspired Reconstruction and Development Programme has been replaced by an orthodox macroeconomic package, the Growth, Employment and Redistribution (GEAR) strategy (Republic of South Africa, 1996d). Contrary to the spirit of consultation and transparency, the government announced GEAR in June 1996 as set and nonnegotiable. The policy reduces government spending and aims to reduce the deficit dramatically, expecting that these will produce the right climate for private sector expansion and foreign direct investment. Between the time of the 1994 election and 1996, the economy grew at approximately 3 percent per annum. Gross domestic product dropped to 1.7 percent in 1997 and virtually to zero in 1998, although it was expected to recover to 3.2 percent by 2000 (Economist Intelligence Unit, 1999). While respectable, this economic performance is no way near what is required to reduce unemployment (believed to be between 30% and 40% and far higher in some townships and African rural areas) and alleviate poverty. In fact, despite GEAR's emphasis on job creation, unemployment has become worse, with the economy losing 126,000 jobs in 1996 and another 212,000 in the first half of 1998 (Economist Intelligence Unit, 1999). (Is it any wonder crime is a serious problem?) While there has been some increase in portfolio investment (stock purchases of existing companies), the hoped-for large inflows of direct foreign investment have been slow to materialize. What *has* occurred is the growth of a new black entrepreneurial and bureaucratic elite loyal to the ANC through "black economic empowerment" (see, among others, Adelzadeh, 1996; African National Congress, 1996c; Adam, Slabbert, and Moodley, 1997; Freund and Padayachee, 1998).

The moderating tendencies paradoxically favor both statism and market capitalism. And these have significant bearing on the *consolidation* of democracy. The real danger to democracy in South Africa is that the government is unable to rectify the abject poverty and extreme inequality that are the legacies of apartheid. That is, in consolidating democracy in the political sphere the government is unable to bring about the democratization of *society*. Over 40 percent of all households in South Africa were in poverty according to 1993/94 statistics, with poverty defined as incomes below the household subsistence level. This poverty is linked to deep inequality. A 1999 World Bank estimate put the Gini coefficient (the standard social science measure of economic inequality) for South Africa at 58.4, one of the highest in the world (World Bank, 1999). According to the South African Central Statistical Service, income disparities between households in the twelve major urban centers decreased between 1990 and 1995, but the poorest 20 percent of households still earned only 2 percent of total income (cited in *Business Day*, 1997d). Thus this introduction ends on a note typical of left assessments of post-apartheid South Africa. A transformation of great significance has been achieved. South Africa has a government that rejects racism, that respects democratic forms and has tried to tap the energy of civil society, that aspires to reduce poverty and promote social equity. It not only has maintained the level of social services and infrastructure inherited from the past, but has even managed to expand some of them on a deracialized basis. The country has engaged in some innovative participatory policy-making processes and in so doing has constructed very attractive democratic structures in, among others, the communications sector. But the failure thus far to find a way to attack the country's terrible inequality and poverty portends a troubled and incomplete democratic consolidation.

The structure of the book is as follows. Chapter 2 provides the historical context. It briefly describes the nature of apartheid and the South African state, and proceeds to the main focus, the history of the ancien régime in broadcasting, telecommunications, and the press within the structural context of apartheid. Chapter 3 examines the historical shift in political strategy of the National Party with the "reform apartheid" ushered in by P. W. Botha in the 1980s, the opposition to this strategy by the civics, labor, and the United Democratic Front, and the economic crisis exacerbated by civil insurrection. Here the participatory and consultative culture of South Africa's vibrant civil society is briefly explored, as are the government's moves to roll back state intervention in the economy. This chapter provides the crucial backdrop to Chapters 4, 5, and 6, each of which traces the intricate political process of reform in broadcasting, telecommunications, and the South African Communication Service, respectively. The concluding Chapter 7 addresses the meaning of black economic empowerment and the nature of the South African transformation. Footnotes are designed to extend or deepen a particular argument in the text, particularly for those readers who may be unfamiliar with South African history and politics or, conversely, for those who may be unfamiliar with issues and terms germane to communications. In this way I have tried to accommodate the different audiences that are likely to read the book. Finally, while theoretical debates on the nature of civil society and citizenship, privatization and liberalization, democracy, markets, and socialism structure and pepper the book, the focus is rather on the empirical/historical dimension. For all the importance of contemporary theoretical writing on the public sphere, civil society and the state, deliberative democracy and the like, these works often feel arid and largely disconnected from concrete, on-the-ground politics. The reason is that politics is an ongoing set of struggles within the state and between state and various levels of civil society – struggles that are situated historically and concretely. To understand politics one must understand the historical specificity of its practice, of the maneuverability of agents within structural constraints. Without often directly articulating its theoretical premises, the study is animated by a nondeterministic, materialist theory of politics (see O'Meara, 1996: 419–489). This book represents an effort not just to tell the compelling story of South African political reform, but to bridge the theoretical and the empirical in a study, in Robert K. Merton's phrase, of the "middle range" (Merton, 1967).

CHAPTER 2

The Ancien Régime in the South African Communications Sector

The structures, functions, institutions, and political forces that constituted the ancien régime in the South African communications sector prior to 1990 only make sense within the political history of modern South Africa. The institutions of communication – the press, broadcasting, and telecommunications – were central to the evolution of the South African state and the apartheid system. The press gave voice and to some degree mediated the conflict between English- and Afrikaans-speaking communities; broadcasting, a product of tense compromises between the white groups, embodied the terms of their hegemonic alliance and expressed the ideological content of racial domination; state-owned and -operated telecommunications contributed importantly to the mechanisms that coordinated the apartheid economy.

White domination of the majority black population has pretty much been the rule since Dutch settlers arrived in the Cape peninsula in the latter half of the seventeenth century. Though serious hostility has always existed between Afrikaners, the descendants of the Dutch settlers, and the English (who began settling the territory after Britain seized the Cape in 1806 in order to protect its sea route to India), they essentially made common cause when it came to the domination of blacks and the use of black labor. This was particularly the case after diamonds and gold were discovered in the latter part of the nineteenth century. Mining changed the nature of the largely agriculture-oriented South African economy and society. Massive inflows of capital and people who flocked to the new sources of wealth led to rapid growth. Mining attracted major investment in railways, as European and American investors scrambled for the minerals and the new markets inland. The great Witwatersrand gold fields were very large but of low grade and scattered very deep underground. To make money, mining entrepreneurs had to bring in large amounts of machinery and employ vast numbers of workers very cheaply. These conditions favored both the rapid centralization and concentration of capital in the mining industry and the creation of a subjugated black working class. Economic power quickly became concentrated in primarily British-connected mining houses. Afrikaner capital tended to be small, scattered, and in agriculture (see S. Frankel, 1938; Davies, O'Meara, and Dlamini, 1984). To give a sense how important mining was to South Africa, by the end of World War I minerals accounted for nearly three-quarters of the country's exports, which in turn provided nearly half of South Africa's national income (S. Frankel, 1938: 107–108). The menial labor pool consisted of indigenous South African blacks and blacks from southern Africa in general. The more skilled group of workers was drawn essentially from overseas and consisted, in the main, of experienced (white) miners who demanded relatively high wages (Innes, 1984: 50).

The clash between British colonial interests and Afrikaner nationalism – at both ideological and material levels throughout the nineteenth century – resulted in the Anglo-Boer War at the turn of the twentieth, a war won by the British at great cost to both sides. The war completed the absorption of both the formerly independent African chiefdoms and the old white settler republics into the system of British colonial administration. The emergence of an independent, British Commonwealth–linked Union of South Africa in 1910 rested on a fragile set of compromises explicitly designed to ensure that whites retained political power and control over the state, and that the state – led by Afrikaners – would come to the aid of the English-speaking mine owners against white or black mineworkers (Innes, 1984: 57–96). As Dan O'Meara (1996: 470–471) explains, British colonial hegemony fashioned economic, social, and cultural relations in such ways as effectively to exclude Afrikaans-speaking whites from ownership in all sectors but agriculture, and left them with a deep sense of economic deprivation and cultural oppression. At the same time, the Union entailed the supremacy of the white coalition against blacks.

The act that established the Union of South Africa denied blacks voting rights in three of the four provinces (the Cape was the exception) and restricted membership in Parliament to "Europeans." As the South African political system evolved, power, except for some marginal delegated capacities, was explicitly the monopoly of the white minority. South Africa would come to function as a democracy for whites, with a Westminster parliamentary system characterized by regular, free elections, an independent judiciary, and a free press. But between 1910 and 1924 the state rested upon tenuous compromises between competing elites rather than on a broad consensus of the white electorate. The absence of a consensual order led elements of the white population to engage in two serious armed rebellions and a number of violently contested strikes, all of which were suppressed militarily. Only after the election of the so-called Pact government of the National and Labour Parties in 1924 was a fragile consensual order forged around the notion of an interventionist state securing institutionalized minimum privileges for all whites regardless of their class position (O'Meara, 1996: 471).

The South African state long played a central role in the economy. In the early days, the state served two key functions. Like many states, it created the underlying industrial infrastructure, supplying and/or rationalizing services through public provision. State-owned monopoly enterprises, called "parastatals," were established in transportation (the South African Railways and Harbours, SAR&H) and posts and telecommunications (the South African Posts and Telecommunications, SAPT) prior to or at the same general time as Union in 1910. The South African state also established major public corporations in banking (the South African Reserve Bank, 1920), electricity (Electricity Supply Commission, ESCOM, 1923), and broadcasting (South African Broadcasting Corporation, SABC, 1936), among others (see E. Kahn, 1959; N. Clark, 1994).[1] The other central focus of state intervention was a massive presence in the labor market to secure an adequate supply of cheap and controlled black labor, at first for the mines, later for farms and factories as well. This is the crucial early connection between state intervention,

1 "State business enterprises" (in official government reports sometimes also referred to as "public authorities" or "central government enterprises") can be considered the South African version of the more generic state-owned enterprise or SOE. In South Africa, state business enterprises are distinct from "public corporations." While both are "parastatals," public corporations are established by special legislation (not chartered under the South African Companies Act) and are granted more autonomy than are state business enterprises. State business enterprises are run directly by government ministries whereas public corporations are not. Public corporations are enterprises with share capital in which government holds a controlling share or appoints the directors. So, the SAPT was a state business enterprise, while ESCOM, in contrast, was a public corporation. Though in practice the differences between state business enterprises and public corporations were relatively minor, the lesser degree of direct government operation and parliamentary oversight over public corporations grew to be of some significance.

racial capitalism, and the system that came to be known as apartheid. Since the early days of the exploitation of minerals the state virtually assumed the responsibility for providing an adequate supply of cheap labor for the newly founded mining industry (Greenberg, 1980; Innes, 1984; Nattrass, 1988). State intervention inexorably mixed policies designed to address labor market needs with gross coercion of the indigenous people. The Land Acts of 1913 and 1936 pushed blacks off productive land not only to safeguard such land for whites but to compel blacks to seek menial jobs in mines, farms, and factories. The 1913 Native Land Act set aside 13 percent of the land area of the country as "Native Reserves" and excluded Africans from land ownership (except by special license) in the remaining 87 percent of the country, thus destroying a whole class of peasant producers and forcing them into new social relationships as menial laborers. Not only did land dispossession force Africans into the industrial labor pool, a strict color bar kept them from skilled occupations in most economic sectors, and other labor policies kept their wages low. The color bar was part of the Pact government's deal with the white working class. These policies, along with the earlier military conquest, transformed large numbers of the indigenous people into wage laborers.

The melding of these two state roles – infrastructure creator and labor market regulator – into the racially hierarchic quasi-command capitalist political economy that we recognize as apartheid was inaugurated by the Pact government of 1924 and then consolidated in a spectacular way with the electoral victory of the National Party in 1948. The Pact government brought together the National Party, which had been founded in 1914 by the former Boer General, J. B. M. Hertzog, and represented smaller white landowners and an incipient industrial bourgeoisie, with the South African Labour Party, the party of white labor. The coalition represented an alliance of white labor interests, those of the infant Afrikaanse business sector, and white rural areas. Over the nine years of its rule, the Pact government shifted state economic policies from a general economic liberalism to those based upon economic (white) nationalism and entailed increasing state intervention into both agriculture and manufacturing (Nattrass, 1988: 26, 232). The shift toward strong state intervention became the pattern. From 1924 to the early 1980s there was continuous growth in the extent of economic activity undertaken by the South African state to encourage industrialization and to upgrade conditions in the white farming sector. The creation of ESCOM in 1923 was to provide for the massive power needs of the mining industry (Horwitz, 1994a). State intervention did not stop at typically infrastructural services. Public corporations were created across the industrial landscape. The early important public corporations were in iron and steel production (Iron and Steel Corporation, ISCOR, 1928) and the Industrial Development Corporation (IDC, 1939). The IDC was originally intended to lure overseas investment capital into local private ventures, but after the 1948 National Party victory, the IDC itself became the architect of large new parastatal ventures, notably the distillation of oil from coal (Sasol, 1951) and the production of phosphates (Foskor, 1951). Among many other parastatal ventures were oil exploration (Soekor, 1966), production of aluminum (Alusaf), weapons production (Armscor, 1964), the development of atomic energy and weapons (Atomic Energy Board, 1948), and the production of natural gas (Mossgas, 1987). The government also set up a large number of "control boards" for various agricultural and manufactured commodities over the years, which, among other things, determined the conditions of entry for firms and fixed the prices of commodities. The extensive establishment of parastatals reflected the state's commitment to an import substitution macroeconomic orientation and, later, as the apartheid government encountered difficulties in the international arena, to self-sufficiency in "strategic" sectors, such as energy and weaponry. The objective of import-substitution industrialization was to develop domestic manufacturing capability for goods otherwise imported. The model, followed by most developing countries in the post–World War II era, was characterized by import controls, overvalued exchange rates, binding ceilings on interest rates, a heavy dose of public ownership, and widespread price regulation (see Krueger, 1993).

Thus, though the South African economy was capitalist, it was clearly a mixed system in which the state played an enormous role as the dominant participant in many key sectors and as a kind of regulator in most others – all within the context of racial domination. By 1965, half of the country's fixed assets were state-owned (expressed as the percentage of the total capital stock). In the peak year of 1986, public corporations and public authorities held 59.2 percent of capital stock (South African Reserve Bank, 1998). At the center of this combination of economic and ideological state intervention was a system that controlled black labor and boosted white labor. The 1924 Industrial Conciliation Act, which effectively excluded blacks, permitted the white labor unions to set the apprenticeship rules for training and to establish staffing ratios by race, thus ceding to white unions the top of the labor hierarchy and giving them the power to shut out blacks. The so-called civilized labor policy involved paying whites at a higher rate than blacks for doing the same unskilled or semiskilled jobs. The civilized labor policy was adopted in the civil service and complemented the already existing color bar in the mines. The growth of parastatals was designed to serve another important racially based function: They provided jobs to the hundreds of thousands of landless, poor Afrikaners who had left farming (see Abedian and Standish, 1985). "Job reservation" described the system that set aside types of work for whites and specified numbers of jobs to be reserved for them (see Hutt, 1964).

The policy of racial separation known as apartheid, implicit for much of South Africa's modern history, became dramatically explicit with the success of Afrikaner nationalism and the electoral victory of the National Party in 1948. An uneasy and often hostile alliance between the two white language groups had characterized the cobbling together of the Union of South Africa at the end of the Anglo-Boer War. With most of the economy dominated by English-speakers, Afrikaners fought to gain various footholds in both the economy and the state bureaucracy, as well as to use the law as a means of protection from black labor from below. Indeed, the rise of Afrikaner nationalism had as much to do with the struggles with English colonialism as it did with the more commonly recognized fear of absorption by the *swaart gevaar*, the Afrikaans term for the "black peril." The purpose of the Broederbond, that secret society of Afrikaner elite established in Johannesburg in 1918, which served as the ideological center of Afrikaner nationalism, was to unify the Afrikaner people, provide uplift, and, in effect, seize power from the English (O'Meara, 1983). In this regard the roots of Afrikaner nationalism are to be found in perceived fears and needs around group security and identity; these factors were strongly manifested in the arena of language, culture, and religion. This was an ethnonationalism. The traditional self-conception of the Afrikaner was of a people united by a common historical, racial, language, and spiritual bond, oppressed by British colonialism from above and threatened by Africans from below (see Adam and Giliomee, 1979; Giliomee and Schlemmer, 1989).

Upon coming to power in 1948, the National Party began the process of realizing Afrikaner nationalism and constructing the institutions of apartheid. Afrikaner nationalism conceived itself as anticolonial and anticapitalist. The NP had campaigned in 1948 on a platform that promised war on the twin menaces of communism and the *swaart gevaar*, and an economic program that pledged to take hold of the key centers of economic power, nationalize the banks, the land companies, and the mines in order to create an economic democracy for Afrikaners. In power, the National Party vigorously pursued policies that favored Afrikaners, including greatly expanding and "Afrikanerizing" the state bureaucracy, and subsidizing and assisting Afrikaner capital. Indeed, while the public sector had functioned as the primary vehicle for solving the "poor white" problem from the time of the 1920s, it was in the period after the National Party came to power that the public sector grew most rapidly. Much of the growth can be attributed to the expansion of the "semi-state" of public corporations, state departments, control boards, and the like, which were among other things vehicles for Afrikaner advancement.[2] The South African state under apartheid can perhaps best be understood in terms put forward by Joseph LaPalombara (1963, 1974) to describe Italian politics. "Parentela" relations signify a kind of political consanguinity, a tight family-type relationship where a sharp distinction is made between insiders and outsiders. Afrikaner organizations' access to and influence in the state was a benefit accorded to the members of a closely knit political family, with the National Party as the electoral and parliamentary head of a remarkably coherent network of economic, cultural, religious, business, and political organizations (L. Pretorius, 1996). But, notwithstanding the triumph of Afrikaner nationalism, National Party leaders did not hazard a fundamental modification of the English-based economy, and the white pact held. Although the nationalist government mobilized the state to favor Afrikaner initiatives, it did *not* fulfill the campaign promise to nationalize the banks, land companies, and mines. Doing so would likely have precipitated a capital strike and flight of English-speakers, and very likely dire economic consequences.

2 The proportion of the economically active population employed by the state increased from 8.84% in 1946 to 14.15% in 1980. As a proportion of the economically active white population, white employment by the public sector grew from 12.36% in 1921 to 22.84% in 1946 to 30.69% by 1980 (Seegers, 1994: 40–41). Of course the other force behind the expansion (and fragmentation) of the public sector was apartheid itself, inasmuch as the policy of "separate development" mandated that each nonwhite ethnic group be required to govern itself. Hence each ethnic group was to develop a set of public institutions and bureaucracies with money allocated from the central fiscus. Black "homeland" or "Bantustan" bureaucracies constituted a factor in increasing black public sector employment, though these workers for the most part were not covered by the Public Service Act.

The apartheid system manifested itself in many nefarious features, but two central and essentially contradictory characteristics are prominent. First, as has been described, white domination aimed to control black labor. Second, apartheid was constructed ostensibly on the recognition of inherent and immutable differences between races and nations, and the desirability of their separation. At the core was a claim for the racial superiority of whites in a hierarchical continuum graded on the basis of skin color. South Africans were therefore formally classified according to race (white or European; mixed race or Coloured; Indian or Asian; black or native or Bantu or African – depending on the idiom of the time) and tribe (usually demarcated by black language grouping). The racial hierarchy resulted in a high degree of differentiation in terms of job opportunities, access to certain types of training and education, the exercise of property rights, and residential choice. As the policy evolved, apartheid required racial groups by law to live in the particular geographic areas set aside for them. Indeed, after the National Party's ascent to power, the stated goal of the total segregationists was to secure a South Africa with no black citizens. This was the logic behind the Group Areas Acts and passbook identification system, and the basis of the Bantustan system championed by the architect of grand apartheid, Prime Minister Hendrik Verwoerd. Africans were to reside in their homelands, supposedly under their own "tribal" political structures and responsible for their own separate institutions and economic development. Four of the ten homelands over the years were granted nominal independence from South Africa (Transkei, Bophuthatswana, Venda, and Ciskei – often referred to collectively as the TBVC states), though everyone other than the South African government considered these statelets dominated by militarized bureaucracies to be complete fictions.[3] Together, these two aims of apartheid succeeded in securing a low-wage industrial reserve army, but also

3 This is not to claim that apartheid was the direct result of a grand plan. As Deborah Posel (1991) has argued convincingly, although guided by broad National Party principles, the making of apartheid often took a reactive course, buffeted by a series of conflicts, negotiations, and compromises among political actors. The apartheid state, she argues, was divided between pragmatists and "visionaries" linked to particular ministries (the Native Affairs Department) and bodies (the South African Bureau of Racial Affairs). Pragmatists wanted to compromise with the demands of industrialists and accept the permanency of urban blacks while visionaries wanted to implement rigid urban segregation excluding all blacks from urban areas except as units of labor. In the 1950s, the attempts by visionary state planners to control the urban black population ("influx control") frequently came into conflict with employers seeking cheap labor. In the 1960s, state bureaucrats and capitalists more often reached uneasy compromises on influx control.

created vast inefficiencies and irrationalities at the same time. This fundamental contradiction could be seen in many ways. Because black "guest workers" were needed in cities but were forced to live far outside of them, for example, the transport system had to accommodate massive long-range daily population movements – at considerable state-provided subsidy. Blacks could be rounded up and virtually enslaved as farmworkers, but the dismal state of Bantu education meant that manufacturers were often short of skilled and trainable workers. Other inefficiencies could be seen in the outlays for police and security, which, always high, reached immense proportions in the years following the 1976 Soweto uprising.

The question as to the nature of the relationship between capitalism and apartheid has been much debated. One view is that they were mutually reinforcing: Apartheid served the interest of the capitalist class by keeping wages down and thus ensuring high profit levels. For that reason capitalists supported the government and its institutions. English liberal opposition to apartheid was more of an appearance – a stick with which enlightened English speakers who were otherwise happy to benefit from apartheid could self-righteously bash the crude Afrikaners – than a fundamental opposition. A contrary view accepts the fact that capitalists benefited from a cheap labor policy in the early years of the mining industry. But, because the institutions of apartheid prohibited the free movement of labor, prevented the education and training of workers (thus causing serious skill shortages), and imposed unnecessary political, administrative, and social burdens, at some point apartheid became a burden on the capitalist economy. Thus many large-scale capitalists came to oppose the main features of apartheid. And, indeed, a version of this critique of apartheid came to be adopted by the reform faction of the National Party in the late 1970s.

In sum, South Africa was characterized by a racially organized quasi-command but capitalist economy that gave the white minority undisguised monopoly over economic power and systematically exploited black labor and property. It was a settler, as opposed to an exploitative, colonialism, inasmuch as most of the white minority was there to stay and the economic surplus was sunk back into the country rather than exported to a colonial mother country. Unlike other instances of colonialism in Africa, the white minority in South Africa was relatively large (about a 15%–20% range of the population) and had assumed a permanent status. At the same time, South Africa was an ethnic state. The system was rationalized on the basis of the racial superiority of whites and the inferiority and "tribalism" of Africans. The double project of apartheid, in Mahmood Mamdani's (1996) rendering, was to unify its beneficiaries around a racialized identity and to fragment its victims through ethnicized identities. Apartheid was a system of white minority rule in which the black majority were statutorily excluded from the political process; but the system contained strong democratic features for whites. This delimited democratic polity functioned to mediate the tensions between and to advance the interests of the two antagonistic white groups. This is why, notwithstanding the level of exploitation and state coercion, some commentators (see Adam and Moodley, 1993: 1–38) say that South Africa more approximated a racial authoritarianism rather than a political totalitarianism – a regime-typing that comports with the transition to democracy literature. For all their violence and repression, authoritarian regimes tolerate the existence of some features of civil society. This permits the possibility for an opposition with which the government can bargain (see Linz and Stepan, 1996). In Gramscian terms, the real, but delimited democratic institutions served to facilitate the functioning of a hegemonic white bloc that was united strategically but deeply divided tactically and culturally (Gramsci, 1971). African National Congress and South African Communist Party intellectuals have called the system a "colonialism of a special type" (see *South African Communists Speak*, 1981: 284–320; African National Congress, 1987; Jordan, 1997).[4]

Communications and language issues were deeply ensconced within the apartheid political-economic agenda and apartheid institutional structures. Indeed, one of the major aims of the National Party when it came to power in 1948 was to push the ascendance of the Afrikaans language over English. The first target in this policy, and the pawns in it, were Africans. The Bantu Education Act of 1953 replaced a missionary system of education, which had taught

---

4 Apartheid policies, of course, controlled black labor to the benefit of all whites. While many English institutions registered public opposition to apartheid and deplored the treatment of blacks, NP leaders could, with some justification, counter that nothing prevented, for example, English mining interests from raising the wages of their black mine workers (O'Meara, 1996: 34, 60, 78). Thus, one common understanding was that English-speaking South Africans could be self-righteously liberal about the condition of blacks and critical of apartheid because they knew their views would not be implemented in actual policy. Afrikaners sometimes referred to English(men) as "salt dicks," meaning they had a foot in Africa and a foot in Europe, with their penises dipping into the ocean. In the Afrikaner view, English speakers were always ready to abandon South Africa for England if the going got tough. Afrikaners, in contrast, considered themselves indigenous – the white tribe of Africa.

largely in English, and put the education of Africans under state control. According to the new education act, instruction was to be in native languages, with Afrikaans required as well. The communications sector, with broad importance for cultural, ideological, and economic reasons, reflected the structure of political power. The South African Broadcast Corporation established a national broadcaster to mediate between English and Afrikaner cultural and linguistic identities, and to function as a mechanism of social control over blacks. A combination of government repression and market forces systematically undermined the struggling black press. The South African Posts and Telecommunications constructed and operated a sophisticated telephone network that served whites and business, acted as an inducement for local electronics manufacturing and as a repository for white labor, and left most of the areas of black settlement unwired and unconnected. The South African Communication Service in its various incarnations functioned as a state information agency in the service of apartheid policy.

THE PRESS AND ETHNIC POWER STRUGGLES

The press, like almost all South African institutions, was organized largely according to language and race. Because of the nature of South African politics, the press was a pivotal institution in the racially and ethnically based struggles for economic and political power. The history of the press also provides a window on the structure of the economy. The English language newspapers were profit-oriented enterprises that reflected, in the mediated fashion typical of the modern Western press, the general political-economic stance of the large English mining capital that owned them. In some contrast, the Afrikaans language newspapers tended to be much more the agents of the main factions of Afrikaner nationalist politics. Indeed, like many other language-based nationalist movements, the Afrikaans newspapers functioned as institutions for the articulation of ideology and thus constituted key sites for the development of nationalist leaders (see Anderson, 1991). The black press, when it was not repressed by the government, tended to reflect either the modernist, petitionary protest stance of the small African middle-class intelligentsia, or the revolutionary visions of left-wing political organizations.

Over the decades, the English language press gradually became concentrated under two powerful groups, Argus Holdings Limited (to become Independent Newspapers Limited in 1994) and the South African Associated Newspapers (SAAN, to become Times Media Limited in 1987). Both groups had origins in English mining capital. The original Argus paper, the *Cape Argus*, commenced publication in 1856 with a pro-native, anti-British slant, but ran into financial difficulties several years later. It subsequently received the financial backing of a syndicate of mining capitalists, including Cecil Rhodes, and reversed editorial orientation – particularly on racial matters. The *Argus* merged with a new Johannesburg afternoon daily, *The Star*, in 1888, to become the Argus Printing and Publishing Co., Ltd. The company added several newspapers to its stable over the subsequent decades, primarily by acquisition, including the *Natal Daily News*, Transvaal Newspapers Ltd., *Diamond Fields Advertiser*, *The Pretoria News*, and the Friend Newspapers Ltd. The *Cape Argus* was the group's standard-bearer and English mining interests were the major shareholders.[5] Until 1931 all directors of the Argus Group were drawn from two mining houses, Central Mining and the Rand Mines Group (known as the Corner House Group and now part of Barlow Rand) and Johannesburg Consolidated Investments (JCI, originally a Barnato company, to be brought fully into the Anglo-American corporate stable in the 1960s). Strongly pro-British, even associated with the anglicizing Lord Milner, Argus papers often recruited editors and senior journalists directly from England.[6] Criticism that the Argus papers were simply mouthpieces of foreign mining capital in part led to the setting up of a more seemingly independent structure, the Argus Voting Trust, in 1931. But the financial power behind the Argus Group has always been understood to be English mining capital in general, and by the 1950s, Anglo-American Corporation in particular through its own holdings (Anglo ultimately took

5 For example, in 1926, the major shareholders were Central Mining & Investment Corporation, with a 34.27% stake, and Johannesburg Consolidated Investments, with a 20% stake. Some of the original mining magnates owned personal stakes: Otto Beit held 9.45%, the Joel family 9.09%, and J. B. Robinson 5.46%. In 1953 JCI increased its stake to 25.43%, Central Mining had decreased its direct share to 16.59%, but Rand Mines, a subsidiary of Central Mining, held a 10.23% stake. Barnato Brothers Ltd. held 7.92% (McGregor, 1996b: 5–6).

6 Lord Alfred Milner was British High Commissioner to South Africa at the time of the Anglo-Boer War. As part of the effort to anglicize South Africa in the postwar reconstruction period, Milner oversaw official policies to downgrade the Afrikaans language. This, of course, was just an intensification of earlier policies that elevated English over all other languages. During the first half of the nineteenth century English became the language of the public service and judiciary in the Cape. In 1853 it was made the exclusive language of Parliament (see Marlowe, 1976: 132–133, 140–141; Alexander, 1989).

control of Central Mining and Investment Corporation) and later its ownership of JCI.[7]

The South African Associated Newspapers (SAAN) formed in 1955 through the merger of Rand Daily Mail Ltd. and the Sunday Times Syndicate. The Rand Daily Mail, founded in 1902, was quickly taken over by the mining magnate Sir Abe Bailey. The Sunday Times, founded in 1906, was a venture of the editors of the Rand Daily Mail and was printed by the RDM. Bailey also held a stake in the Sunday paper. The two papers, both published in Johannesburg, worked in close association with each other, although a single company was not formed until the 1955 establishment of the South African Associated Newspapers. SAAN became a public corporation listed on the Johannesburg Stock Exchange in 1962. Both the Argus and SAAN groups expanded their operations into other South African cities under a 1920 agreement not to compete directly and, together with the nominally independent, but SAAN-linked Cape Times, formed a partnership with the British news agency, Reuters, to establish the Reuter South African Press Agency (to become simply the South African Press Agency, SAPA, in 1932). By the 1960s the Argus and SAAN groups controlled most of the large English language dailies and nearly all of the English Sunday newspapers, accounting for 77 percent of the total circulation of all English dailies in 1968 (Potter, 1975: 50).[8] A good deal of interpenetration of ownership long characterized all the major English language newspapers. For example, the major shareholders in SAAN, the Union & Rhodesian Mining & Finance Co. (with a 50% stake at the time of SAAN's incorporation in 1955) had investments in Anglo-American, Corner House, and JCI – the major shareholders in Argus Holdings Limited. Union &

7 Thus, even though 1981 shareholding data show that Standard Bank Nominees held the largest share of Argus at 21%, in fact the identity of the "nominee" company was Anglo-American, which controlled almost 40% of the Argus (McGregor, 1996b: 8). South African corporate reporting requirements are fairly lax. Nominee companies are a front, and they are not required to divulge who the real owners are. McGregor, who has been studying ownership patterns for twenty years, has devised ways to pierce through the veils of many of the nominee companies (McGregor, 1997).

8 For example, the Rand Daily Mail, the Johannesburg SAAN daily, did not directly compete with the Star, the Argus daily, because the RDM was the morning paper and the Star was the afternoon paper. Arrangements such as these were struck in every major city. By 1960, the Argus Group controlled the Star (Johannesburg), the Cape Argus, the Weekend Argus (Cape Town), the Natal Daily News (Durban), the Sunday Tribune (Durban), the Pretoria News, the Diamond Fields Advertiser (Kimberley), and The Friend (Bloemfontein), for a total circulation of 613,000. SAAN controlled the RDM, the Sunday Times (Johannesburg), the Sunday Express (Johannesburg), the Evening Post (Port Elizabeth), the weekend Evening Post, and the Eastern Province Herald (Port Elizabeth), for a total circulation of 674,000 (cited in Hepple, 1960: 71–72).

Rhodesian also were connected to Syfrets, the real estate and financial firm with the key shareholding position in the otherwise independent *Cape Times*. The long-standing links between the *Cape Times* and SAAN were formalized in 1973 when the Cape morning newspaper was purchased in toto by the SAAN group.

By the mid-1970s SAAN was spread over several owners, losing money, and vulnerable to a takeover. Acting as a front for the National Party, Afrikaner businessman Louis Luyt tried to buy control of SAAN in 1975. Oppenheimer interests, the key controlling family of Anglo-American, intervened by setting up the Advowson Trust, a financial arrangement that bought the shares of the Bailey Trust on which Luyt had tendered a very high offer. The Advowson purchase was part of a financial restructuring that left the Argus Group as the largest single shareholder of SAAN. But SAAN's financial losses continued. The press group restructured radically and changed its name in 1987 to Times Media Ltd. as part of a downsizing that two years earlier closed the *Rand Daily Mail* and *Sunday Express*. It established a joint operating agreement with the Argus Group, created the nationwide business daily, *Business Day*, and took a 23 percent stake in the subscription television company, M-Net.[9]

The *Natal Mercury*, an independent paper owned for decades by the family of Sir John Robinson, required substantial capital to replace its printing press in 1982; SAAN bought a 49 percent stake. By 1989 the Argus Group held a controlling share in Natal Newspapers Ltd. (the holding company), and in 1994 Natal Newspapers became part of the Argus Group (McGregor, 1996b: 14, 20–21). The *Natal Witness*, a Durban newspaper begun in 1846, is one of the few English language newspapers not to be absorbed into either the Argus or SAAN groups. It continues to be owned by several individuals.

The consolidation of the English language press into two large conglomerates, themselves controlled financially by English mining houses, is in keeping with the larger historic patterns of the South African economy. A small cluster of families and institutions controls a large

9 The *Rand Daily Mail*'s financial woes stemmed in part from the fact that its readership was increasingly black, and the paper could not lure sufficient advertisers. According to a former *RDM* editor and SAAN general manager, SAAN's bid to set up its own distribution alternative to the prevailing monopoly distribution system also contributed to the *RDM*'s demise (Emdon, 1996). The *RDM*'s oppositional stance also had bearing on its financial situation. Its exposé in the mid-1960s on prison conditions led to a protracted and very expensive legal battle under the Prisons Act, a battle the newspaper eventually lost. The paper lost money for a decade, recording a shortfall of R15.6 million in 1984 (Jackson, 1993: 70–80).

proportion of South Africa's core mining, manufacturing, and financial assets. Because South African corporations finance expansion via internal resources or through the sale of shares in the company (as opposed to bank debt), control is accomplished largely through widespread use of listed pyramided holding companies, in which the company at the apex of the pyramid is able to control the companies layered beneath it with a minor equity share. The executive board, which includes heirs of the original families, has the power to appoint the boards of its subsidiaries, and, in effect, the subsequent layers of the corporate hierarchy. This device allows the original owners to expand their operations yet retain control. For example, despite directly owning only 8 percent of the shares, the Oppenheimer family controls the De Beers diamond-mining company and its sister conglomerate, the Anglo-American Corporation, which once accounted for a quarter of South Africa's gross domestic product (*McGregor's Who Owns Whom in South Africa,* 1997). Directorates are heavily interlocked, even across conglomerates. These corporate centers, in turn, control groups (themselves extremely large and diversified) that represent the conglomerate's interest in broadly defined economic activities. The consequence is that large, concentrated, highly diversified corporate groups loom over South Africa's economic landscape. The top five conglomerates have for decades controlled companies that account for the lion's share of market capitalization of the Johannesburg Stock Exchange. As late as 1995, for example, these five, Anglo-American, Sanlam, the Rembrandt Group, SA Mutual, and the Liberty Group accounted for 82.3 percent of the market capitalization of the Johannesburg Stock Exchange.[10] In the view of many analysts, this form of control does not result in entrepreneurial dynamism. In effect, shareholding is so concentrated that shareholders cannot easily exercise their right of "exit" without impacting

10 Anglo-American (40.5%), Sanlam (12.8%), the Rembrandt Group (10.3%), SA Mutual (8.9%), Liberty Group (6.0%) (*McGregor's Who Owns Whom in South Africa,* 1997). Anglo-American was the largest and most powerful South African conglomerate, with a majority of the total capital invested in the mining industry and with vast holdings throughout the economy. Anglo-American and its leading family, the Oppenheimers, were long regarded as the leading liberal capitalist force in South African politics. Sanlam is the leading Afrikaner insurance and financial conglomerate, with close links to key factions of the National Party, but historically with the Cape moderate wing. The Rembrandt Group began as mainly a tobacco- and liquor-based conglomerate, but has diversified into substantial industrial and mining interests. Its founder, Anton Rupert, was a leading proponent of reformist Afrikaner nationalism. SA Mutual is an investment company with holdings in many sectors. Its political role was not as open as that of other conglomerates, but according to the account of Davies, O'Meara, and Dlamini (1984: 65–85), was close to P. W. Botha and his initiatives.

significantly on their financial returns and asset values. This results in risk aversion in the investment behavior of the conglomerates. Conglomerates tend to act as portfolio managers rather than as entrepreneurs (see D. Lewis, 1995).

The English language press was essentially a part of the Anglo-American corporate stable. It is, of course, arguing too much to claim that the English language press directly reflected its owners' politics and economic policy proclivities. The English language newspapers for the most part were run as businesses and were expected to make profits; their editorial staffs hewed to standard Western theories of a free and independent press. The relative autonomy of a complex organization such as a newspaper, with its system of professional routines, standards, and conventions, complicates and dilutes the direct power of ownership.[11] Moreover, the South African English language press was never characterized by press barony. Ownership tended to be institutional, with both the Argus and SAAN groups tied to mining capital and its manufacturing-based conglomerates. Still, some generalizations can be hazarded. Both Argus and SAAN newspapers generally supported a South Africa tied to London, dominated by English speakers and in which whites held dominion over blacks. They tended to espouse a procapitalist, liberal reformist politics, backing the Unionist and United parties, and, after the United Party split, the Progressive and Progressive Federal and the Democratic parties.[12] They generally opposed apartheid and the

11 The classic analysis is Herbert Gans, *Deciding What's News* (1979). Still, the South African mining owners had indirect ways of indicating their displeasure. Former *Rand Daily Mail* editor Raymond Louw would be called in to visit the SAAN board of directors every couple of months, and the directors would ask questions about stories. They tended not to provide particular input, but in asking pointed questions they conveyed their more than implicit displeasure (R. Louw, 1997).

12 A brief account of the complicated history of the major South African political parties is in order. The Unionist Party was the party of foreign mining capital. In opposition at the time of Union in 1910, it merged with the South African Party of Louis Botha and Jan Smuts in 1920. Recall that the Pact government was a coalition of Hertzog's National Party and the Labour Party. General Hertzog's NP split in 1934. The majority followed their leader into "fusion" with Smuts' South Africa Party to form the United Party. The United Party, as befits its name, reconciled English and Afrikaans speakers in a white political party representing a coming together of major bourgeois interests to cope with the Depression and abandonment of the gold standard. At fusion the NP rump, representing certain groupings of agriculture and sections of the Afrikaner petty bourgeoisie, reconstituted itself under Cape NP leader Dr. D. F. Malan as the Gesuiwerde Nasionale Party. The United Party represented all major capitalist interests until the outbreak of World War II. Hertzog resigned as prime minister and leader of the United Party in September 1939 when the South African Parliament voted narrowly to reject his plea for neutrality in World War II. Instead, Parliament declared war on Germany. Hertzog and his following of former fusionists formed themselves into the Volksparty, which

National Party's efforts to redistribute wealth to its Afrikaner constituency. In P. Eric Louw's (1993: 163, 168) judgment, the Argus Group was critical of apartheid largely because of the negative economic implications for capital, whereas SAAN's criticism (particularly in the *Rand Daily Mail* and *Sunday Express*) was due more to the racism of apartheid. Because English big business was not directly represented in the state after the 1948 nationalist victory, the English language press, along with the Chamber of Mines and Chamber of Industry, became key forums for political expression of capitalist interests.

However liberal some English language newspapers might have been, even anti-apartheid in some cases, they did not openly support the liberation movements (and could not if they wished to continue publishing). Anthony Heard, longtime editor of the *Cape Times*, has written that, because the established English language papers were part of business life, "they placed a high premium on making profits for shareholders, and their owners were the cautious mining magnates who had to remain on reasonably good terms with government. . . . Hence, liberal editors were on more than one occasion ousted, and over-adventurous journalism was discouraged" (Heard, 1992: 173). Allister Sparks (1996b), one of four editors of major daily SAAN newspapers who were fired by their owners in the twenty years between the mid-1960s and -1980s, has argued that their dismissals were not, as claimed, for simple economic reasons. Nor were they fired for their politics per se; rather, they were fired because their politics came to be seen as a threat to profitability. In Sparks' words, their editorial stances were felt to be "discomforting" and "bad for business." The image of a muckraking, watchdog English language "opposition" press defending the rights of the oppressed is characterized by some scholars and journalists as largely a myth serendipitously reinforced by the reality of government intimidation. In Heard's retrospective judgment, the English

merged with Dr. Malan's Gesuiwerde NP in early 1940 as the Herenigde Nasionale Party (Reunited National Party). This, in coalition with the small Afrikaner Party, was the NP that captured the 1948 election from the United Party, instituted apartheid, and ruled South Africa until the 1994 democratic election. The party reverted to calling itself the National Party in 1951. The United Party became the main opposition party in the whites-only Parliament until 1977, though it registered splits. The Progressive Party formed in 1959 when a group of more liberal United Party members of Parliament broke away, accusing the United Party of betraying principles. Supported by leading capitalist interests (including Anglo-American's Oppenheimer), it called for reforms in order to create a black middle class. The Progressive Federal and Democratic parties essentially took over those positions (Davies, O'Meara, and Dlamini, 1984: 159–164; O'Meara, 1996: xxii, 40).

language press was more like a "lightweight boxer" who managed a couple of blows but nothing heavyweight (Golding-Duffy, 1997). The white press concerned itself with the issues and goings-on of the white community and did very little to bring blacks into the newsroom or onto the newspaper pages until the 1980s. Like most, if not all, South African employers, the newspaper companies applied apartheid in the workplace despite (in some cases) their public criticism of these practices. Separate toilets and canteens were the order of the day, and black workers were treated as second-class employees. And the English language papers tended to mind their owners' business. It took them a long time before they began to expose South African mining interests to journalistic scrutiny. Lawrence Gandar, editor of the *Rand Daily Mail* from 1957 until 1969, when he was fired for publishing an exposé of the appalling conditions in South African prisons, character- ized the paper as "very Rand Clubbish and Chamber of Mineish" (Pogrund, 1998). Still, because of the relative autonomy of the English language newspapers, some editors and some reporters ran critical, politically risky stories over the years, such as Gandar's prison exposé (Tomaselli and Tomaselli, 1987; African National Congress, 1997; Switzer, 1997b).

Afrikaner initiatives in the print media mirrored those in other areas of business life, namely *volkskapitalisme*, the creation of parallel Afrikaans institutions alongside and in challenge to English ones. This underlay the establishment of Volkskas in banking, the South African National Life Assurance Mutual (Sanlam) in insurance and finance, the Saambou Building Society, among many others – institutions tightly integrated into the politics, ideology, and culture of Afrikaner nation- alism. Sanlam, the large insurance and financial investment company, for example, began as a way to pool funds of small-holding Afrikaners for capital formation. The Afrikaans language press in particular was central to the project of invention and consolidation of Afrikaner nationalism against English dominance. Indeed, the Afrikaans press even today speaks of its history in the rhetoric of ethnic salvation. In a submission to the Comtask inquiry, Nasionale Koerante Beperk (the newspaper division of Nasionale Pers) Chief Executive J. H. van Deventer (1996: 167) writes, "From the earliest years Afrikaans news- papers were the press allies of the National Party, as the political instru- ment of the Afrikaner's nationalism – a nationalism born out of its struggle against British imperialism which brought him just short of cultural and economic extermination." But Afrikaner nationalism was rooted differently in different provinces. Always an ideologically contentious movement, Afrikaner nationalism was long characterized by a split between moderates and hard-line traditionalists, a split registered under the Afrikaans labels *verligte* and *verkrampte*. The National Party itself was in some ways an umbrella political party for the different versions of Afrikaner nationalism generally based in different provinces (though there was virtually no Natal NP and the Orange Free State party organization clearly took back seat to the dominant Cape and Transvaal organizations). The Cape NP was always far more openly capitalist in orientation and sympathies than was the Transvaal wing. As Dan O'Meara (1996: 54–55, 85–89) argues, the Cape NP essentially rested on an economic and political alliance between the wealthier capitalist farmers, particularly of the Western Cape, on the one hand, and a small group of financial capitalists in Sanlam and later the Rembrandt Group, on the other. The Transvaal NP was far more a creature of the Afrikaner petty bourgeoisie, whose rigid Christian-national vision of the Afrikaner *volk* stressed an ideological anti-imperialism and championed the interests of the Afrikaner "small man" against what were seen as the "imperialist-oriented" monopolies (i.e., the English mining houses) that dominated the economy. The Afrikaner Broederbond was a force in the Transvaal NP far more than it was in the Cape. Historically, while the Cape NP largely supported South Africa's decision to enter World War II on the side of the Allies, the Transvaal NP tended to support initiatives such as founding a South African republic, withdrawing from the Commonwealth, and removing Coloureds from the common voters' roll.

The regional Afrikaans press groups reflected these regional and class-based ideological positions, even as they gave collective voice to the broader project of ethnic nationalism. Like the English language press, the Afrikaanse press also evolved toward concentration under two major groups, Nasionale Pers (Naspers) and Perskor. Nasionale Pers was a pioneering example of early *volkskapitalisme* in the Cape, an outgrowth of J. B. M. Hertzog's departure from Louis Botha's government and from the ruling South African Party to form the opposition National Party in 1914. Nasionale Pers, publisher of *Die Burger* (originally *De Burger*, reflecting the Dutch influence in the Cape), the most influential Afrikaans daily, has been generally identified with the more moderate, *verligte*, Cape wing of the National Party and has been financially dominated by Sanlam. The history of Naspers and Sanlam are interlinked. Some of the original directors of Naspers were involved in the formation of Sanlam. Like Sanlam, Naspers began in the mold of small-holding Afrikaner collective investment. In 1915 two individuals held 9,300 of the 20,000 issued shares, while the balance was held by hundreds of shareholders, all of whom held under 100 shares. With time, the number of private shareholders declined and Afrikaans institutions took on a fully corporate character. Sanlam held the largest single share in Naspers in 1953 at 17.5 percent (McGregor, 1996b: 11). Future Prime Minister D. F. Malan was *Die Burger's* first editor, and Naspers became part of the Cape NP establishment. The northern nationalists sometimes pejoratively referred to this coalition as *Keeromstraat* (U-turn street), the name of the street on which the offices of Nasionale Pers were long located (O'Meara, 1996: 55). Naspers started *Die Volksblad* in the Orange Free State in the early 1920s and launched the Sunday paper *Beeld* in the mid-1960s as its wedge for a southern, moderate voice in the Transvaal.

The Transvaal Afrikaans language press took longer to consolidate. Three separate nationalist press groups each produced its own newspaper. Afrikaanse Pers published the afternoon daily *Die Vaderland,* which had been founded in Pretoria in 1915 (as *Ons Vaderland*) and was an organ of the Hertzog faction of the National Party. Voortrekker Pers published the Transvaal NP paper, *Die Transvaler,* begun in Johannesburg as a morning daily in 1937. Though *Die Transvaler's* largest financial backing came from Cape nationalists and Nasionale Pers itself, the paper reflected Transvaal Afrikaner nationalism under the editorship of future premier and architect of grand apartheid, H. F. Verwoerd. Dagbreekpers, an amalgam of English and Afrikaner capital in the mold of the old Hertzog-type nationalism, published the Sunday paper, *Dagbreek.* Although *Dagbreek's* editorial policy was supposed to be politically independent, the paper moved closer ideologically to the NP in the early 1950s and openly supported the party in the 1953 general election. This action prompted the English majority shareholder to sever his connections. The prime mover behind *Dagbreek,* Marius Jooste, succeeded in amalgamating the interests of Afrikaanse Pers and the Dagbreek Trust in 1962 to form Afrikaanse Pers Ltd. In cooperation with Voortrekker Pers, Afrikaanse Pers launched the Pretoria daily *Hoofstad* in 1968, edited by Andries Treurnicht (who led the *verkrampte* breakaway in 1982 to form the Conservative Party, discussed later). In 1971 Voortrekker Pers was absorbed by Afrikaanse Pers and the amalgamation culminated in Die Afrikaanse Pers Beperk becoming the holding company of the group and Perskor Beperk the operating company. The main institutional influences within Perskor have been the Transvaal NP, the Broederbond, the Dutch Reformed Church, and Volkskas Bank, which controlled a sizeable block of shares. The Afrikaans language press thus tended to represent and act as institutions of the main factions of Afrikaner nationalist politics.[13] National Party leaders often came from editorships of the Afrikaans press. Indeed, the close links between the NP leadership and *Die Burger* especially meant that *Die Burger* often had information about the Cabinet's decisions and discussions before these officially became public knowledge (Olivier, 1994: 93. Also Potter, 1975; Giliomee, 1982: 88–97; J. Muller, 1987: 118–140; P. Louw, 1993; O'Meara, 1996: 55, 129).

Because of the historic conflict between English and Afrikaans speakers, and the greater editorial independence of the English language press, Afrikaner nationalists viewed the English language press with much hostility. The English language press was historically seen by Afrikaner nationalists as the agent of British imperialism, the mouthpiece of the "Hoggenheimers," the contrived, anti-Semitic tag for English mine owners. Later, the press was feared as an anglicizing influence and for its potential links to critical overseas opinion. "You hate me and I hate you," Prime Minister John Vorster told English-speaking journalists at a press conference (cited in Crwys-Williams, 1994: 346). There was much bluster in nationalist circles about press "irresponsibility" and, after the nationalist rise to power in 1948, threat of formal censorship. Yet, while the nationalists denounced the English language press and menaced it with vague threats of censorship or elimination, the National Party in power did not in fact engage in nationalization or wholesale suppression. In the final analysis, the mainstream English language print press was substantially off limits given the essential terms of the social compact between the English and the Afrikaners. In the end, the primary design of the NP government was to intimidate the press into exercising *self*-censorship, and though many newspapers buckled under, some did not (Potter, 1975; Pollak, 1981; Uys, 1985; Tomaselli and Louw, 1991b; Merrett, 1994).

13 This should not be overstated, however. *Die Landstem* was a nonnationalist, nonpolitical weekly with a large circulation of 148,000 in 1960 (absorbed by Perskor in 1962), and the small *Weekblad* supported the United Party (Hepple, 1960: 73). By the 1980s *Rapport* and especially *Beeld* began departing from the role of nationalist mouthpiece, and ran stories questioning and prodding the NP establishment. *Vrye Weekblad* figured as the main Afrikaans language entrant in the "alternative" press of the 1980s (Jackson, 1993).

For most of the period of nationalist rule, censorship was conducted in powerful, yet indirect fashion. The government passed laws that removed entire areas of public life, such as defense, prisons, atomic energy, and information about strategic resources (such as petroleum) from the realm of unrestricted press reporting. The government banned undesirable people and groups, and passed legislation prohibiting the dissemination of their ideas. In the words of Dr. Cornelius Mulder, minister of information in the 1970s, the government had a responsibility to prevent items or information "which incite racial friction in South Africa or destroy the image of South Africa abroad or which endanger state security" (quoted in Hepple, 1974: 5). The coercive mechanism of choice was an extensive body of laws empowering the government to ban any publication aimed at furthering "abhorrent" ideas, particularly those of communism, race-mixing, and pornography. A series of laws prohibited newspapers from publishing any statements by a banned person without the express permission of the minister of justice, or from publishing reports or viewpoints that might support a campaign which flouted the law or might cause "racial incitement." Perhaps the most wide-ranging of these laws were the Suppression of Communism Act of 1950 and Riotous Assemblies Act of 1956. The press was required to submit to police any information concerning a crime or state security that reporters had obtained independent of the police. Selective invocation of these laws and prosecution of editors and journalists were designed to intimidate the English language press into exercising self-censorship (see Potter, 1975: 101–129; Jordan, 1985; Merrett, 1994).

Other moves to curb the press included the establishment of a Press Commission of Inquiry in the 1950s, a government-appointed commission to investigate the concentration of control and monopoly tendencies, the activities of foreign correspondents and stringers, and the accuracy, responsibility, and patriotism of South African journalists. The commission took oral testimony from reporters and compiled dossiers on journalists after *in camera* interrogations. And though the final report, thirteen years and R355,000 later, fiercely reproved the English language press for its distorted coverage (the South African Press Association came in for particular abuse), in the end less came of it than one might expect (Republic of South Africa, 1961). The government instituted a Board of Reference (to become known as the South African Press Council) with the power to reprimand journalists and editors. Under threat of direct censorship under a Publications and

Entertainments Bill in the early 1960s, the Newspaper Press Union, the association of major dailies and weeklies, drew up their own code of conduct and established a control board to administer it. This was essentially a form of self-regulation designed to forestall government censorship. As former editor of the *Sunday Express*, Ken Owen (1997), has written, "The [Newspaper Press] union devoted its efforts not to the defence of the principles of a free press, but to the defence of its cartel, negotiating with John Vorster's government to exclude their newspapers from government restrictions in return for good behaviour." The Press Code of Conduct and Press Council exempted the members of the Newspaper Press Union from the Publications and Entertainments Act of 1963.

In sum, whereas the mainstream press was frequently intimidated and as a consequence practiced self-censorship, it was not often formally suppressed and sometimes resisted government pressure. The English language press in particular operated as an adversarial press mostly within, but sometimes beyond, the confines of the English–Afrikaner nationalist accommodation. In the judgment of Anton Harber (1997), longtime editor of the alternative *Weekly Mail*, the establishment press had "adapted to censorship rules in order to survive, and that adaptation became an ingrained habit." Thus the English language mainstream newspapers normally stayed away from stories about the police, prisons, the defense forces, the ANC, and practiced a distinct brand of conservative liberalism, much like that of the Progressive Federal Party.[14]

If the hegemonic pact between Afrikaners and English put obstacles on the repression of the English language press, no such forces constrained the state's repression of the black media. African publication ventures suffered under many difficulties, including the low literacy levels and the poverty of their targeted readers (hence a shortage of advertising), racial segregation, and then apartheid. An early African mission press gave way to an independent protest press between the 1880s and 1930s that tended to articulate the modernist views and nationalist aspirations of the small professional black middle class

---

14 Even the charge that the establishment press didn't report police activities has become somewhat more equivocal in light of the work of the Truth and Reconciliation Commission (TRC). According to John Battersby (1997), editor of the *Sunday Independent*, in trying to verify accounts of police beatings, arrests, the disappearance of activists, etc., TRC researchers combed through back issues of relevant newspapers. The researchers found that there *were* often newspaper accounts of these events, but the items tended to be trivialized, placed in a small box on page 6 and treated like the weather, without depth either of facts or of analysis.

intelligentsia: African, as opposed to ethnic loyalty, modernism and the "upliftment of the race," and general support of the African National Congress in peaceful protest of the government's segregationist policies (see Lodge, 1983: 1–32).[15] The influence of Christian humanism on early South African liberation ideology was quite strong and was a key factor in the nonracialist cosmopolitanism of the African National Congress (Fredrickson, 1995).[16] Most of the publications, such as *Abantu-Batho* (in English, Zulu, Sotho, Xhosa, and Tswana), *Imvo Zabantsundu* (in Xhosa and English), *Ilanga Lase Natal* (in Zulu), and *Koranta ea Becoana* in (Tswana and English), did not survive the economic depression and political repression of the decade of the 1930s. The depression undermined an already weak advertising base. And their "petitionary" protest stance could not survive the oppressive politics of the Representation of Natives Act and the Native Trust and Land Act of 1936, which took away the franchise from Cape Africans and forbade them to buy land outside the native reserves. Many of these publications were bought out, closed down, or merged with a new black commercial press controlled by white entrepreneurs. Such mergers resulted in the depoliticization of the protest press. According to Les Switzer (1997b: 2), the number of African newspapers registered with the government had reached a high of 19 in 1930, but there were only 7 by 1954 – all of the latter owned and controlled solely by whites.

With the decline of the traditional black protest press, an early resistance press developed, which gradually embraced a popular, mostly nonracial, nonsectarian and more militant alliance of left-wing

15 In view of the writing that to some degree assumes an African "tribalism" (see among others, Lijphart, 1985; Horowitz, 1991; even Adam, Slabbert, and Moodley, 1997), it is remarkable to note how early black South Africans of different ethnicities began mixing, going to the same churches and schools, and forging new identities in cities. This mixing was in part the paradoxical consequence of their dispossession from the land and the decline of kinship-based relations attached to traditional land ownership. It was also in part the consequence of the extraordinary ideological sway exercised by the modernist African intelligentsia over African communities, an influence carried out through the African press (see Jordan, 1997).

16 In discussing liberation ideology, Fredrickson (1997: 136, 150) establishes a useful dual dichotomy between cosmopolitanism and ethnocentrism on the one hand, and between revolution and reformism on the other. The cosmopolitan stance posits that liberation will come through equal citizenship in a multiracial polity. It draws on universalist standards of justice and human rights to reject a racially circumscribed political destiny. The ethnocentric stance posits that the proper aim of the liberation struggle is the achievement of some form of independent nationhood. Emphasizing a racial or ethnic particularism, the ethnocentric position asserts that blacks cannot achieve self-realization by joining with whites in a unitary state. The second dichotomy, which is not automatically resolved by adopting a cosmopolitan or an ethnocentric orientation, concerns the nature of the struggle: Will it be carried on by reformist

working and middle class interests. These included *Inkululeko* (the newspaper of the Communist Party of South Africa), *Inkundla ya Bantu* (set up by the African National Congress), *Workers' Herald* (the mouthpiece of the Industrial and Commercial Workers' Union, the largest and most influential black trade union before World War II), *Torch* (the publication of the Cape Non-European Unity Movement), *New Age* (under the editorial control of the South African Congress of Democrats, a small white left group allied to the ANC), *Contact* (closely allied to the Liberal Party, white anti-Communist supporters of the ANC), and the *Guardian* (linked to the Communist Party). According to one source, the *Guardian* and *Inkululeko* had a weekly circulation in 1945 of 67,000 (cited in Lodge, 1983: 28). The ownership structure of the black papers varied. Some were owned by individual entrepreneurs, some by political and worker organizations, some by community trusts. Most of these resistance publications were banned following the Suppression of Communism Act of 1950 or following the Sharpeville massacre in 1960.[17] The relative political tranquility of the 1960s was a result of the effective repression of the liberation organizations and the suppression of the black resistance press.

A brief note on South African black liberation politics will help tie this history of the black press to the broader contours of the liberation struggle. Led originally by middle class African conservatives interested in fair treatment and social mobility, the ANC, created in 1912, evolved from a petitionary politics in the 1930s, to a nonviolent mass protest movement in the 1950s, to the support of insurrectionary sabotage and finally armed struggle in the aftermath of the government's actions following Sharpeville. The change to a mass protest movement reflected the ascension in the ANC of the new generation of lawyers and profes-

---

or revolutionary methods? The early ANC, founded in 1912, was cosmopolitan and reformist. Indeed, some of the men who founded the ANC were admirers of Booker T. Washington and his doctrine of black self-help and accommodation to white authority.

17 The Sharpeville incident marked a turning point in South African politics. In March 1960 the Pan-Africanist Congress launched a campaign of civil disobedience against the pass laws. A confrontation in the township of Sharpeville resulted in the police massacre of 69 unarmed protesters. Another 180 were wounded. The ANC called a one-day stay-at-home in sympathy with the victims and in solidarity with the PAC. Sharpeville signaled a new, more repressive phase on the part of the state. The government declared a state of emergency and arrested over 1,500 people. It soon banned the black liberation organizations and detained on the order of 11,500 people. In Tom Lodge's (1983: 225–226) estimation, Sharpeville also represented a turning point in the history of African nationalism, when protest finally hardened into resistance and when African politicians were forced to begin thinking in terms of a revolutionary strategy. Nonviolent protest no longer seemed a viable strategy.

sionals active in the ANC Youth League, the starting place of Nelson Mandela, Walter Sisulu, and Oliver Tambo. And though the ANC was an organization of many proclivities (including the ethnocentric Africanism of the ANC Youth League), the congress's central document, the 1955 Freedom Charter, affirmed the multiracial character of South African society. The charter promised equal status for all national groups and argued for the transfer of the nation's wealth and industry to "the people as a whole." By the 1950s the Communist Party gained influence in the congress alliance, and this was seen in the non- or multiracialism of the congress and its basic orientation of class over race. The importance of the Freedom Charter is such that the ANC and its allies are referred to as "Charterists." The Pan-Africanist Congress (PAC) was the product of a 1959 breakaway from the ANC primarily over the issue of multiracialism. These young Africanists, led by Robert Sobukwe, felt that multiracialism served to perpetuate the psychological subservience and dependency on whites upon which minority domination rested. For the PAC, race was the fundamental category, and the organization rejected alliance with whites. The PAC's Africanism also displayed a kind of political voluntarism. If the principal shackles inhibiting popular resistance were psychological, the PAC believed that if its leaders showed the light the masses would find the way to liberation. Both organizations were banned after Sharpeville, and many of their leaders were imprisoned. Both operated from exile and established armed units to engage in sabotage in South Africa (Umkhonto we Sizwe for the ANC and Poqo for the PAC). However, the government was so successful in suppressing the liberation organizations in the 1960s and early 1970s, that their presence and direct influence was limited, known to younger Africans largely as legend.

The Black Consciousness (BC) movement emerged among the students of the new segregated universities in the late 1960s and early 1970s. Though drawing on the same intellectual tradition as the Africanists, and taking some cues from African-American black power writings (which, to complete a circle, had relied on some pan-Africanist liberation writing, particularly that of Frantz Fanon), BC focused on the psychological level rather than the overtly political. Black Consciousness was a product of the new black urban intelligentsia, fed by a rising literate clerical stratum and university students, but percolating deeply to the African populace generally. It was concerned with black autonomy and with ridding blacks of the feelings engendered by subservience. Black Consciousness saw

South Africa as a black country, but unlike the Africanists and the PAC, BC involved Indians and Coloureds as well as Africans. The 1976 Soweto uprising, which began with student protests against government efforts to require instruction in the hated oppressor language of Afrikaans, was in part inspired by the Black Consciousness movement. The Azanian Peoples' Organisation (Azapo) was founded in April 1978, but was more overtly political and oriented toward the black working class. Many BC leaders who were imprisoned on Robben Island came over to Charterism through political debate with longtime imprisoned ANC leaders. Indeed, Robben Island was nicknamed "the university." The large number of student rebels who fled South Africa after 1976 wound up paradoxically in ANC training camps, largely because the PAC by then was organizationally defunct. The Inkatha Freedom Party (IFP) began as a Zulu cultural organization revived by Chief Mangosuthu Buthelezi in the early 1970s. In 1975 it began to structure itself as a mass organization. Buthelezi used the political structure of the homeland system to fashion an effective political power base in KwaZulu. Inkatha has been both anti-apartheid and, at times, anti-ANC, countering the ANC's multiracialism with a sometimes virulent Zulu-based nationalism (see, among others, Biko, 1978; Lodge, 1983; Marx, 1992; Mandela, 1994b; Fredrickson, 1997).

Alongside the resistance press grew a white-owned commercial press oriented to black readers. The Argus Group became involved with a venture known as the Bantu Press in the early 1930s. The Bantu Press operated several newspapers in South Africa, edited and staffed primarily by Africans but whose copy was tightly supervised by white overseers and owners. The most important of these was *Bantu World* (later just *World*), which articulated a modernist, often depoliticized vision of black South African life. *Bantu World* was founded in 1932 by a white liberal segregationist who sought to create a forum for Africans, and brought in black investors to the general-interest weekly. According to Switzer (1997a), the newspaper became by far the most important medium of mass communication for the literate African community, providing a Western modernist model of what was considered permissible and relevant for Africans to buy and read. With 11,000 readers in 1959, *World* circulation increased to 90,000 in 1968 when it was transformed into a daily with a Sunday edition, and to 145,000 in 1976 (Tomaselli and Tomaselli, 1987: 47). *World* epitomized what Tom Lodge calls the "prevalent intellectually lightweight tone of African journalism" – oriented primarily to crime, sport, and human interest reportage (Lodge, 1983: 356). Yet even *World* was banned in 1977 after covering the Soweto uprising and moving toward a Black Consciousness viewpoint. Two other black publications owned by Jim Bailey (son of SAAN's Sir Abe Bailey), *Drum* (a monthly) and *Golden City Post* (a tabloid), begun in the 1950s, also reached large readerships by observing and recording the conditions of life and work in black South Africa. *Drum* was probably the most important outlet for black creative writing in the 1950s, and, though far less political than the resistance press, did occasionally run exposés on a number of contentious issues. After 1961 *Drum's* editorial policy became increasingly subject to commercial considerations. The Soweto-based *Golden City Post* was bought out by the Argus in 1964. The *Post* became a daily with a Sunday edition in the late 1960s, and this opened it up to some political dissent. It ran a "release Mandela" petition form in its columns for several months in 1980 as well as editorials helping to popularize the Freedom Charter (Lodge, 1983: 341). The *Post* was banned after its journalists went on strike in 1980. The Argus launched the *Sowetan* in its place, which would become the largest circulation black daily in the country. The editorial proclivity of the Argus Group's black publications since the 1970s was Black Consciousness as opposed to the Charterist tradition of the ANC (P. Louw, 1993). In general, between the time of the banning of the early resistance press and the Soweto uprising in 1976, the orientation of black newspapers was aimed toward the coverage of sports, society, and crime, and, although anti-apartheid in general orientation, they were cautious in the coverage of politics. The Afrikaans press also moved into the African market, for instance countering *Drum* with *Bona*, an educational magazine published in Zulu, Xhosa, and Sotho. Naspers bought *City Press*, *Drum*, and *True Love* in 1984.

A second phase of resistance press – most often referred to as the "alternative" press – arrived in the 1970s with the Black Consciousness movement, particularly after the Soweto uprising. Still largely aimed at segregated black and/or white audiences, the alternative press also encompassed progressive academic journals and student publications from historically white universities, as well as a variety of literary, musical, and performance texts generated mainly in segregated black settings. What made the "alternative" press alternative was the adoption of an engaged stance in favor of the black liberation struggle and the destruction of apartheid. The *Weekly Mail*, for example, considered itself a publication of the United Democratic Front (UDF), the key anti-apartheid political organization of the 1980s (Harber, 1997). Some of the alternative publications were commercial and accepted advertising, but their primary orientation was in getting out the message rather than profits. Most were understaffed and underresourced, supported financially by foreign anti-apartheid organizations and donor agencies (primarily from Holland, Sweden, Germany, and Canada). It was the alternative press that was the main target of the antipress actions of the government in the 1980s (Switzer and Switzer, 1979; S. Johnson, 1991; Manoim, 1996; Switzer, 1997a,b).[18]

The Newspaper Press Union, to which the mainstream English newspapers belonged, was the instrument facilitating the give and take between government and the English language press. No such accommodation was reached with the alternative press. The Publications and Entertainments Act provided for control of all newspapers and periodicals that were not members of the Newspaper Press Union. An appointed Publications Control Board exercised supervisory control over these publications, with power to deem any of them "undesirable" and therefore prohibited. The board could also refer an undesirable publication to the attorney-general for prosecution (Hepple, 1974: 20). The government set upon the alternative press in the mid-1980s. The Botha government declared a state of emergency beginning in 1985 to confront the UDF-inspired grassroots rebellion. Among other things the government put strict press regulations into effect, augmenting already existing legal restrictions. The central aim was to suppress or contain information about the civil unrest.

Because most of the coverage of unrest tended to be in the alternative press, it was those publications and black journalists in particular that were the focus of the antipress provisions of the State of Emergency. The June 12, 1986 order, for example, banned journalists from areas of unrest, which could be so designated by the police at their discretion. The order prohibited the announcement, dissemination, distribution, taking or sending within or from the Republic of

18 Alternative media in the 1980s included newspapers such as *New Nation, Vrye Weekblad, South, Weekly Mail,* and *New African,* a range of magazines that included *Learn & Teach, Speak, Challenge, Shopsteward, Work in Progress, SA Labour Bulletin, Upbeat, Die Suid-Afrikaan, Exit,* and *New Ground,* and community-based newspapers such as *Grassroots, Saamstaan, Numaqua Nuus,* and the *Grahamstown Voice.* The alternative papers, particularly the white ones, grew out of the generational politics spurred by opposition to the draft and the war in Namibia and the proxy war in Angola, as well as identification with the black struggle against apartheid. The student activism of the early 1980s engendered a mood of defiance and of law breaking, and constituted some of the sociocultural sources of the alternative press (Harber, 1997).

any comment that reflected poorly on any government official or member of the police or armed forces or that might incite anyone to take part in any unlawful strike, boycott, form of unlawful protest, civil disobedience, or statement that might engender feelings of hostility or weaken confidence in the government. The government impounded entire runs of some newspapers. The alternative press, including *New Nation, Saamstaan, South*, and the *Weekly Mail*, and the more mainstream black press, such as the *Sowetan* and *City Press*, were especially hard hit by censorship, inasmuch as their coverage and constituencies focused on the UDF and the anti-apartheid struggle (see South African Institute of Race Relations, 1987/88: 813–849). Offending journalists were detained by the police or occasionally expelled if they were foreign correspondents. It is frightful to read through the innumerable accounts of intimidation, arrests, fines, bannings, and murders of journalists (particularly black journalists), not to mention the systematic suppression of the black press and "undesirable" literature, as reported over many years in the London-based journal, *Index on Censorship* (see, e.g., Marcus, 1984; Hatchten and Giffard, 1984; Switzer, 1997a,b; Chimutengwende, 1978; Nix, 1997). While the attacks on the press during the states of emergency fell hardest on the alternative press, they affected the English language establishment press, as well (Finnegan, 1988; Heard, 1992).

SABC: THE EARLY HISTORY OF A MOST PECULIAR PUBLIC BROADCASTER

The early history of South African broadcasting, like most of white South African history, was rooted in and around the conflicts between Afrikaans and English speakers. Broadcasting, an important site for the production of culture, identity, and nation building – and entailing often zero-sum decisions on language choice – was therefore a major terrain of struggle. Issues around language had been a flashpoint for Afrikaners ever since the Anglicization policies pursued by British governors from the time of Sir John Craddock and Lord Charles Somerset at the beginning of the nineteenth century, and particularly the campaign to suppress the Afrikaans language by the hated Lord Alfred Milner at the beginning of the twentieth. The terms of the struggle between the two white language groups shaped the structure of the broadcast sector's main institution, the South African Broadcasting Corporation (SABC). Broadcasting's crucial role in constructing an appeal to the nation, in helping define the very idea of the relevant collective, and as an agent of social control was clearly not lost on either of the white partners. Notwithstanding their often bitter differences, the two white language groups crafted an ideological consensus to share the medium for purposes of maintaining their cultural and linguistic identities and, in so doing, to use broadcasting to maintain their dominance over nonwhites.

The SABC was established as South Africa's national broadcaster in 1936 along the model of the British Broadcasting Corporation – except that it was to serve dominant white interests. As stipulated in its inaugurating act from Parliament, SABC broadcast service was to be conducted in Afrikaans and English, and was to advance the cultures rooted in those languages. The domination of nonwhites was so much taken for granted that any nonwhite presence in early broadcast debates is incidental. Only later did the SABC establish a network of African language radio services. Both "native" radio and television were consciously designed to fit the ideological necessities of maintaining white domination and apartheid. It took a while to reach this consensus. Early broadcasting in South Africa reflected both the geographic and income split between English and Afrikaanse communities. English speakers lived in cities and largely dominated business and the leisure industry. Afrikaner capital, with the exception of the Western Cape, was located mainly in rural areas. Those Afrikaners able to afford radio receivers tended to be successful farmers. Yet many of these were not connected to the electricity grid, and even for those that were, the reception of the medium-wave signal was poor. Rural-based Afrikaners were dependent on short-wave service. Battery receiving sets were available, but battery life was short, hence the sets were relatively expensive. Radio, then, in the 1920s and early 1930s was primarily an urban and English phenomenon, both linguistically and culturally. Enough amateurs engaged in broadcasting in the early 1920s so that the government, through the office of the Postmaster General, issued licensing regulations in August 1923 (Orlick, 1974). Three separate organizations located in the major cities of Johannesburg, Cape Town, and Durban were the main licensees. Because there was no adequate means of funding, all three stations ran into financial difficulties. A license fee from listeners did not generate much revenue for the stations. Station JB, in Johannesburg, run by the Associated Scientific and Technical Society, announced its closing in January 1927. With some reluctant facilitation by the government, I. W. Schlesinger, an American émigré whose wealth was in entertainment (particular film) holdings, was permitted to amalgamate the failing broadcast organizations into the African Broadcasting Company (ABC) in June 1927 (Rosenthal, 1974).

Schlesinger called for government support of his ABC radio venture, but was for the most part unsuccessful in this endeavor. The government merely made a regulation that every wireless dealer was required to furnish a monthly list of receiving-set purchasers. This regulation was designed to increase the payment of license fees, but it was only marginally successful. Schlesinger was compelled to turn to market-oriented schemes to finance the ABC. He contracted with retailers of domestic radio receivers to conduct competitions over ABC in return for a portion of the sale price of receivers (Rosenthal, 1974: 113–126). His "Blue Free Voucher" plan succeeded in spurring listenership and the sale of receivers, but its commercial orientation was offensive to important sections of both the Afrikaner and English communities. Schlesinger's proto-American commercial model demanded a maximization of the audience through concentration on the most popular programs. This meant that radio shied away from programming to the Afrikaans speaking community – a fact that caused great resentment among Afrikaners and their politicians (Orlick, 1974). Commercialism also bothered many English speakers, because it tended to go against British hierarchical and elite notions of culture. South African English speakers tended to exhibit that typical colonial expatriate emulation of the mother country, its institutions, its culture, its mores. They automatically looked to Britain in many spheres of life. The British Broadcasting Corporation thus was taken as the model for broadcasting.

The separate dissatisfactions of both English and Afrikaans speaking constituences, combined with the ongoing financial difficulties of Schlesinger's ABC, were behind the move in 1936 to place broadcasting under the broad aegis of the state. Prime Minister Hertzog invited John Reith, noted director-general of the British Broadcasting Corporation, to South Africa in 1934 to recommend a new structure for broadcasting. Not surprisingly, Reith recommended that the service be taken over by a public corporation funded by the national treasury (Union of South Africa, 1934). In the subsequent Parliamentary debate, English speakers (belonging to the newly formed United Party) supported the proposal because of general support of the BBC model and their distrust of advertising. Afrikaners in the United Party and in the opposition Gesuiwerde National Party supported the proposal in large part to gain a stronger foothold for Afrikaans language programming. The BBC claims of objectivity and impartiality would have been attractive to both English and Afrikaans speakers as a form of protection against each other (Hayman and Tomaselli, 1989; Rosenthal, 1974: 150–158).

The newly constituted SABC bought out the operations of ABC for £150,000 and began broadcasting in August 1936. The Broadcasting Act of 1936 gave the governor-general the authority to appoint members of the SABC Board of Control, the board of directors charged with setting general policy. The board was to be comprised of nine members, roughly half English, half Afrikaans speakers.[19] The SABC would be financed through license fees collected by the Post Office. The Corporation was to "frame and carry out its broadcasting programmes with due regard to the interests of both English and Afrikaans culture." No other license to broadcast would be given to any other body without the consent of the SABC (Union of South Africa, 1936). Hayman and Tomaselli (1989: 35–37) argue that the importation of the BBC model did not fully take into account the deep antagonism between English and Afrikaans speakers, and hence the early attempt to equalize programming on the single medium-wave channel, particularly given the poor reception in rural areas, proved problematic. The license fee could not support two separate language medium-wave *channels*; it could only support English and Afrikaans *services* sharing the same channel. And, even though the amount of Afrikaans language programming did increase, the BBC-style hierarchical cultural model prevailed and the bulk of programming reflected the urban, English, elite norm. The initial division of time on the medium-wave channel was 4:1 English to Afrikaans. The content ruffled Afrikaner sensibilities. A short-wave receiving station was used to rebroadcast chiefly British programs, including BBC news – a source of much unhappiness among many Afrikaner listeners, particularly during World War II. Against the backdrop of Afrikaner nationalist antipathy toward the British Commonwealth (which manifested itself among the more extreme with pro-Nazi support) and the formal policy of the SABC to avoid political broadcasts and controversial material in religious programs, the SABC relay of British programming was considered unwarranted propaganda

19 A new version of the broadcasting act was passed in 1976 to deal with the advent of television. That legislation mandated the prime minister to appoint a board for the SABC, of between 21 to 25 members, a chairperson of the board and a director-general of the broadcaster (Republic of South Africa, 1976).

by many Afrikaners. The relay of BBC news ceased in 1950, and the SABC established its own news section. Press opposition prevented SABC news from using material from the South African Press Agency (SAPA) and other news agencies. The board attempted to deal with the problem of the low amount of Afrikaans language programming by devoting short-wave transmitters to such programming. Fidelity, however, was poor.

The inability of the license fee to finance a separate Afrikaans channel led the SABC to announce plans in 1946 for a commercial channel. In the usual manner of South African policy making, the government appointed a commission to investigate the matter. After much gnashing of teeth, the commission, under the chairmanship of A. A. Schoch, approved the decision to establish a commercial channel, but advised that it be provided by an independent organization, outside the SABC. The commission considered SABC a public utility and did not want the public broadcaster to become involved in a commercial-type venture (Union of South Africa, 1948: 42). The government, in turn, accepted the advice, but soft-pedalled the commission's anxiety and awarded the right to introduce the commercial channel to the SABC. Springbok Radio, funded by advertising, began broadcasting in English and Afrikaans in 1950 (though because advertisers were overwhelmingly English, the station still retained an overall English character) and thus introduced an uneasy mix of American and British models of broadcasting to the SABC. Revenues from Springbok Radio did allow the SABC to expand and by 1957 the three services – the English and Afrikaans services and Springbok Radio – received an equal share of the seventy daily broadcast hours over fifty-two transmitters (Orlick, 1974: 142–143).

The Schoch Commission also recommended the reintroduction of a "rediffusion" or cable service for "Natives." In cooperation with the Department of Native Affairs, during World War II the SABC had established a single-channel service via wire and loudspeakers to compounds, hostels, and residences in some black townships, but the service was shut down in 1945 when the Department of Native Affairs withdrew its support. The purpose of the cable service was clear: entertainment, education, and social control. In the words of the Schoch Commission Report:

> Others again who are concerned about the developing trend of
> political, sociological and economic thought among Natives, and

whose views deserve serious consideration, have urged the desire-
ability of a broadcasting service for Natives in order to counteract
the warped and dangerous doctrines which are being propagated
assiduously by agitators among Natives throughout the country
and particularly in urban areas, and in order to enlighten and
educate Natives generally. (Union of South Africa, 1948: 59)

The cable service was designed to orient the emergent urban black
labor force to the dominant ideology. It was revived in 1952, beginning
in Orlando Township, outside Johannesburg. A brief program in
Xhosa, Zulu, and Sotho, called "Radio Bantu," also was transmitted on
the medium-wave English and Afrikaans service beginning in 1949.
Great stress was laid on traditional customs and rituals, although
the musical programming was chiefly American jazz. The 1952
SABC *Annual Report* was candid in defining the role of the service: "The
SABC has a dual purpose with this new service: in the first place to
provide the Native with entertainment in his own home and in this way
to contribute towards the prevention of crime; and secondly to contribute towards the education of the Bantu" (SABC *Annual Report*,
1952: 36).

In contrast to the private nature of the white press, broadcasting was
historically located within the ambit of the state and hence directly open
to nationalist mobilization. Broadcasting's historical status as a state-
run corporation enabled its capture by Afrikaner nationalism, but even
this is too strong a judgment, and the process requires explanation.
Following its 1948 electoral victory, the National Party began to move
Broederbonders into the SABC Board and key management positions.[20]

20 In their 1978 book on the Afrikaner Broederbond, Ivor Wilkins and Hans Strydom calculate
that at least forty-nine identifiable Broederbonders were involved in broadcasting, mostly at
high managerial and board levels. Piet Meyer, longtime chairman of the SABC Board of
Control, also served as chairman of the Broederbond from 1960 to 1972 and earlier as information director of the Afrikaner pro-Nazi organization, Ossewa-Brandwag. Wilkins and
Strydom (1978: 10–12) cite a secret Broederbond document, "Masterplan for a White Country:
The Strategy," as evidence of the importance with which the Broederbond saw broadcasting.
Peter Orlick (1974: 142) quotes interview sources indicating that another, somewhat less conspiratorial factor accounted for the increasing complement of Afrikaners working at the SABC,
at least in the period before the National Party's 1948 rise to power. World War II had already
brought a subtle transformation of SABC personnel. As English-stock SABC employees vol-
unteered for military service, their places were taken by Afrikaners set on rectifying the imbal-
ance between the English and Afrikaans services. Orlick's source (identified as an
English-speaking actor long affiliated with the SABC) claims that "gradually key administrative posts were filled by Afrikaans-speaking and/or sympathetic individuals . . . the ground was
thoroughly prepared for an Afrikaner take-over in Broadcasting."

This was a pattern found throughout the parastatals. In the view of informed observers, it took about ten years to erode the old British civil service ethos after the Nationalists came to power in 1948. Then followed years of promoting people according to principles of ethnicity and ethnic loyalty. Traditional parastatal culture embodied the archetypical mode of National Party decision making. Issues and policies tended to be measured less on grounds of economic or administrative rationality, but rather, "How does this or that policy affect the Afrikaner? What will this do to or for the Afrikaner?" This culture created a hierarchy of people in the parastatal managements, many of whom were there for reasons of ethnic loyalty and personal security, not primarily to serve the public or even carry out the job. At the same time, the culture did not permit or encourage debate. Decisions typically were made in an old-boys fashion behind closed doors. Underlings were expected to obey. The system tended to marginalize inquisitive, innovative managers, and departments tended to grow like topsy. The parastatals were characterized by a caricature of bureaucratic procedure: dozens, scores, hundreds of enormously complicated, picayune rules and regulations that had little economic rationality in and of themselves but whose formulation and application functioned to provide work for the surfeit of employees (Bester, 1995a; Botha, 1996; B. Clark, 1996; also Trapido, 1963; Enloe, 1980; Seegers, 1994).

As Keyan and Ruth Tomaselli argue, however, it is not correct that the SABC was the tool, pure and simple, of the National Party after 1948. Again, because South Africa was nominally a political democracy for whites within the broad confines of racial dominance, state broadcasting allowed some debate and some veneer of non-partisanship – although the agenda setting and hidden publicity for the party in power were considerable, particularly with the advent of television (K. Tomaselli and R. Tomaselli, 1989). Hayman and Tomaselli (1989: 54–55) describe the process whereby the long-standing SABC practice of airing informative talks by impartial experts was only gradually displaced after 1948 by programs oriented toward Afrikaner nationalism, particularly programs promoting and defending the government's apartheid policy. Even the BBC legacy meant something. During the first decade after the National Party victory, the relative independence of the SABC from government was due largely to the fact that the SABC was led by a liberal Cape Afrikaner, Gideon Roos, who believed in the Reithian credo of impartiality. He clashed frequently with the Broederbond-dominated board as it endeavored to transform broadcast programming. But the SABC suffered financially for Roos' independence. The SABC appeals for government assistance (primarily permission to raise the license fee) failed – even as it embarked on an expansion of broadcast service. It was only after the consolidation of power by Piet Meyer, SABC Board of Control Chair, and the ouster of Roos after 1960, and the subsequent closer relation between the SABC and the National Party government, that the financial fortunes of the state broadcaster improved. Government paid for the installation of a VHF/FM system, permitting the creation of a flexible network of six high fidelity channels. Government also granted a long-term loan to SABC and authorized the collection of license fees on second and third radio receivers.

In keeping with the consolidation of grand apartheid, the 1960 Broadcasting Amendment created an "equal but separate" structure for the administration of black programs. Government began paying a subsidy for the production of programs for Radio Bantu, which was placed under a separate administrative structure with some thirty-five white supervisors (linguists or anthropologists) controlling output. The three original white services became national FM channels with the Post Office's completion of a carrier link system in 1959. Three additional white FM channels, carrying advertising, were introduced on a regional basis: Radio Highveld for the Transvaal highveld, Orange Free State, and part of the northeastern Cape went on the air in 1964; Radio Good Hope for the western Cape, in 1965; Radio Port Natal for the Natal coastal area, in 1967. As the FM "native" network expanded, the inclusion of black programs on medium-wave services was phased out, as was the old rediffusion system. By 1964 Radio Bantu had expanded to seven separate African language services on the FM: a Xhosa service in Cape Province; a South Sotho service in the Orange Free State; a Tswana service in the northern Cape and western Transvaal; a North Sotho service in central Transvaal; a Zulu service in Natal and southeastern Transvaal; Tsonga and Venda services in northeastern Transvaal.

Under Meyer's leadership, and consequent to new political tensions in the wake of the 1960 Sharpeville massacre, news and current affairs moved more explicitly toward propounding the interests of the hegemonic white alliance. As the chairman of the Board of Governors wrote in 1961:

In respect of broadcasts on contentious matters, the Board of Governors has laid down the policy that Radio South Africa should constantly supply exhaustive, balanced and truthful information to the best of its ability and discretion and furthermore take care that the broadcasting service is not abused to undermine the safety and the interests of the country or promote revolutionary intentions inside or outside the country's borders. It was further decided that Radio South Africa should by means of positive contributions in its own sphere, promote the survival and bounteous heritage of the White people of the RSA whilst at the same time enouraging the development and self-realisation of the non-White population groups in their own spheres. (SABC *Annual Report*, 1961: 6)

Thus SABC's role was seen as defender of the apartheid state and propagator of its separate development policies. In line with Verwoerdian doctrine, this meant the maintenance of racial discrimination presented as "ethnic self-determination." In Roos' vision of the SABC (following Reith), the corporation could abandon its objectivity and impartiality only during wartime and in times of crisis. After Sharpeville, Meyer simply inflated the sense of crisis to mean hostility to the Republic (Hayman and Tomaselli, 1989: 63–67). The SABC programming became increasingly characterized by anti-Communist propaganda, the promotion of Afrikaner nationalism, and the concept of separate development (Group of Thirteen, 1994b: 11–12). The 1961 SABC *Annual Report*'s articulation of the corporation's policy on news coverage represented a bizarre refusal to cover any politics other than recognized party politics and at the same time a pledge to keep the coverage noncontroversial. This was no doubt in reaction to Sharpeville.

Political reports are regarded as contentious and are only broadcast when they are of a factual and/or authoritative nature, or if they consist of a positive policy statement by a political party represented in Parliament and do not contain comparisons with, or comment on, the declared policy or conduct of other South African political parties. (SABC *Annual Report*, 1961: 8)

Anecdotal evidence shows that the SABC aired many attacks on English institutions and the English press over the years, including attacks on the World Council of Churches, the Christian Institute, and newspapers including the East London *Daily Dispatch*, the *Star*, the

Rand Daily Mail, among others. Personal denigration of figures identified as hostile to the government was frequent. Requests of reply were
never granted (see South African Institute of Race Relations, 1964, 1965,
1966). Modest studies of SABC political coverage showed massive bias,
even at the level of time allotments. A survey of the 1977 Parliamentary
election campaign by the Journalism Department at Rhodes University,
for example, found that SABC television devoted more than 80 percent
of its coverage to government or National Party viewpoints. A month-
long content analysis found that 32 percent of news time was given over
to political representation, that is, reports pertaining to policies or principles of political parties in South Africa. Of this time, 47 percent was
devoted to coverage of government and National Party figures. In the
1981 election campaign, a survey of the first two weeks of coverage
showed that the NP received 1,200 percent more air time than the opposition Progressive Federal Party. The other parties – New Republic Party
and Herstigte Nasionale Party – each received less than one minute of
television news time during the two-week period (cited in Hachten and
Giffard, 1984: 218–219).

The uneasy mixture of American and British models of broadcasting was paradoxically well-suited to apartheid ideology. The white
national channels reflected a steady didactic effort at restating and reca-
pitulating the terms of the hegemonic white alliance. Some of this was
done in seeming apolitical fashion, through extensive religious programming – accounting for some six percent of broadcast time on the
English and Afrikaans services (K. Tomaselli and R. Tomaselli, 1989:
104). The SABC always was heavily influenced in its style and sexual
conservatism by the Calvinism of the Dutch Reformed Church. The
black and white regional channels in contrast programmed an Ameri-
can-style all-day music–advertising–news format (though they were to
avoid the wilder forms of popular music), tied together by disc-jockey
chatter. Most of the content of Radio Bantu was aimed at the maintenance and the renaissance of traditional tribal values and social institutions. In the words of the 1967 SABC *Annual Report,* "During the past
year, Radio Bantu has again helped to bring home to the Bantu population that separate development is, in the first place, self-development
through the medium of their own language" (SABC *Annual Report,*
1967: 10).[21] Among other programs Radio Bantu featured the *Radio*

---

21 As the Tomasellis argue, this had a second dimension in that, by strengthening affiliations to
   tribal authorities, the South African state was able to exert control in a disguised manner. Tribal
   chiefs were "paid functionaries of the State and are thereby incorporated into the State, while

Bantu Schools Service, whose educational orientation lay in passing along vocational information in keeping with preconceived expectations of black occupational possibilities, as well as seeking to instill "a sense of responsibility, obedience to authority and respectfulness" (SABC *Annual Report*, 1981: 88). The Bantu Programme Advisory Board, appointed by the SABC Board to determine programming for blacks, consisted almost entirely of white men. Unlike the Reithian model of a single national broadcaster that unifies and exposes parts of the nation to other parts, the South African model was designed to isolate and reinforce racial-linguistic differences in their own broadcast services.

Verwoerdian language policies rested on the belief that different peoples could only develop to full maturity if, among other things, their languages were assisted to acquire full dignity. This was one of the lessons Afrikaners had drawn from their own struggles against British colonialism and the post–Anglo-Boer War Anglicization schemes of Lord Milner.[22] And this, among other reasons, is why so many Afrikaner intellectuals defended apartheid policies as humane and caring. The intellectual pedigree is the Counter-Enlightenment's recognition of the uniqueness of cultures and their maintenance in the face of colonialism and the rampaging modernist universalism of certain applications of the Enlightenment legacy (see Berlin, 1980). The application of this lesson, even if genuinely held, to Bantu education and media, however, became a means to imprison African language speakers in their ethnic cultures – the terms and authenticity of which were determined externally, by the dominant white social power. Language policy, couched in the rhetoric of self-determination, could be used to fragment and subjugate black people along largely externally imposed ethnic lines. This coincidentally would curb the growth of African and more generally black nationalism (Alexander, 1989).[23]

seemingly representing 'genuine' tribal values" (K. Tomaselli and R. Tomaselli, 1989: 96). Although this analysis begs the question of what is "genuine" culture, the Tomasellis are surely correct regarding the regime's mobilization of ethnicity for conservative ends (see Maré, 1993; Mamdani, 1996).

22 For an account of the "invention" of Afrikanerdom through words and symbols, in the spirit of Eric Hobsbawm and Terence Ranger (1983), see Hofmeyr (1987) and Vail (1991).

23 This is not to argue that ethnic or "tribal" identity is false or foreign, imposed from without. The point, rather, is that the kinds of strong ethnic or tribal allegiances that characterize some African nations apply less to South Africa. As Robert Price (1994) has argued, the nineteenth century wars of dispossession, the so-called *mfecane*, resulted not only in a loss of sovereignty for the traditional African political communities of the South African interior, but also in the wholesale displacement of communities from their indigenous habitats, and in extensive land

A paradox should be noted as regards apartheid media policy. As Hachten and Giffard observe, notwithstanding the overwhelming paternalism of Radio Bantu and its utilization for purposes of ideological control (particularly successful with regard to older Africans, according to one survey), the SABC was preserving and encouraging the language, traditional music, drama, legends, and folklore of African cultures – at a time when critics of Western broadcasting decried that institution's destructive influence on the traditional cultures of the Third World (Hachten and Giffard, 1984: 221). A related paradox rests in the fact that in the West, part of the intellectual assault on the public broadcasting system (especially television) was that the public service broadcaster tended to impose one particular kind of (class-based) culture as *the* national culture. The BBC in particular, with its Oxbridge management and staff and dedication to a particular set of production values, demarcated "culture" and national identity and hence fenced off from other groups and sensibilities the imagined community depicted, and in turn partly created, by public broadcasting. In John Keane's (1991: 122) formulation, "the public service claim to representativeness is a

alienation. The alienation of most African land by the end of the nineteenth century undermined the usufruct land tenure system, the material basis for kinship and village solidarity. The traditional system of land tenure lay at the basis of the traditional sociopolitical system. Africans in South Africa, unlike most of Africa, were forced into a process of proletarianization and urbanization, processes that also tended to weaken traditional ethnic loyalties. The Land Act of 1913 added to the destruction of the traditional basis of land tenure, which further undermined old kinship networks of communalism, the building blocks of ethnic politics. Finally, apartheid itself substantially delegitimized traditional identities and ethnicity as a basis for political organization and mobilization. The opposition to apartheid and separate development policy tended to generate a *civic* political identity as opposed to an ethnic one, in large part because apartheid's intention was to retribalize. The white minority state essentially delegitimized ethnic identification as a mode of political organization. For a comprehensive treatment of the *mfecane* and the scholarly disputes over its interpretation, see Hamilton (1995). That ethnic identification can become *mobilized* in political organization is another matter, as the emergence of Inkatha makes clear (see Maré, 1993). Inkatha's mobilized ethnic politics underscores the political legacy of late colonialism and its consolidation in apartheid doctrine: In establishing a bifurcated power that mediated racial domination through tribally organized local authorities, colonial political practice laid the foundation for the reproduction of racial identity in citizens and ethnic identity in subjects. In other words, ethnicity was a form of power whose institutional underpinning – the Native Authority and customary law – was crafted under the colonial state. This construct was as central as race to implementing the double political project of apartheid: to unify its beneficiaries around a racialized identity and to fragment its victims through ethnicized identities (see Mamdani, 1996, 1997). Again, attributing such ethnic politics to the legacy of colonialism does not magically sweep away its existence or impact. But it is important to consider African ethnic politics as historically situated rather than as a timeless essence. And it is important to highlight that in contemporary South Africa, such ethnic politics appear to be the exception rather than the rule, also for concrete historical reasons.

defence of *virtual* representation of a fictive whole, a resort to programming which *simulates* the actual opinions and tastes of *some* of
those to whom it is directed" (see also Curran and Seaton, 1985:
125–250). Opening up such systems to competitive market entry would
presumably permit the diversity of cultures to be depicted on the air.
South African broadcasting, in a bizarre inversion and paradoxical complement to the postmodern critique of public service broadcasting,
featured an imposed version of cultural diversity and engaged in no
attempt whatever at imagining a "national" culture. Or, rather perhaps,
parallel to other colonial societies, South African broadcasting did
picture a national culture – but one in which some members of the
nation (in this case the majority) were seen as in a state of perpetual
childhood.

This is not to say the broadcast media were controlled, lock, stock,
and barrel. No communications system can ever be completely controlled; all communication is "leaky" to some degree, at both encoding
and decoding levels (see Hall, 1980). A prime example of leakiness was
Radio Today, a $2^1/_2$ hour weekday morning actuality program begun in
1974 on the English service, which displayed a relative independence
from the National Party line. And, occasionally, black announcers on
the Radio Bantu services could sneak through some antigovernment
commentary, as could liberal religious figures through allegory during
the religious programs. But these were the exceptions that underscored
the general condition, and in the case of *Radio Today*, functioned also
as ideological legitimation insofar as the state broadcaster could point
to the program as evidence of the SABC's nonpartisanship. Alongside
and consequent to the heavy Broederbond presence in management and
its overt set of controls and censorship, including denial of funding for
the production of certain kinds of documentaries, the SABC system
worked by means of self-censorship (see K. Tomaselli and H. Tomaselli,
1989; Kevin Harris Productions, 1996).

If there was a certain degree of space for debate and differing views
in radio, there was far less in television, though even in television there
was resistance, particularly from a group of English language producers. But because the advent of television coincided temporally with
the rise of internal insurrection (the Soweto uprising and television
both began in 1976), SABC television tended to be enlisted whole-hog
into the NP's so-called total strategy against apartheid's opponents.
Hence straying from the correct line in television was kept within
extremely tight margins. Television in fact had been resisted for many

years, largely because of fears by the Afrikaner right wing that television could overwhelm Afrikaner language and culture. The J. Arthur Rank organization was ready to introduce television into South Africa as early as 1953, but the government blocked the attempt. The National Party saw only disadvantages in television, especially the compromising of Afrikaner cultural independence through creeping Anglicization. Worries about the psychological effects of television on urban blacks (in particular worries about unleashing black male sexuality) also entered into the calculus of resistance to the medium. The government also blocked a plan led by the Anglo-American Corporation to introduce television in the mid-1960s (see Orlick, 1970). By the early 1970s, however, Piet Meyer won over the opposition. The Meyer Commission of Inquiry on television (consisting of twelve members of whom seven were Broederbonders) recognized that international satellite broadcasting could, in principle, permit South Africans to receive foreign television signals from backyard receiving dishes and hence bypass South African communications prerogatives altogether. The best way to counter the potential incursion of foreign broadcast material was to establish a South African television service (Republic of South Africa, 1971).

More was at stake in television than glossing over the possible threat to Afrikaner culture, of course. The Meyer Commission recommended the introduction of television also because of the impetus to and multiplier effect it might bestow on the local electronics industry, with spin-offs for the growing armaments industry (Republic of South Africa, 1971: 43). The initial television service, TV1, commenced in January 1976, broadcasting for five hours in the evening, divided equally between Afrikaans and English and targeted at a white audience. The Meyer Commission advised that South African television should "give direct and unequivocal expression to the established Christian, Western set of norms and values that are valid for South African society in all spheres of life, in order to strengthen and enrich our own religious and spiritual life" (Republic of South Africa, 1971: 16). In keeping with apartheid practice, a second television service, TV2, aimed at blacks, was launched at the end of December 1981. The service was expanded a year later into two separate, ethnically based services (TV2 and TV3) serving the Nguni and Sotho language families, broadcasting each for 27 hours per week on one shared channel and called TV2/3. TV4 began in March 1985 on the existing TV2/3 channel after those services signed off at 9:30 P.M. TV4 aired sports and imported entertainment programming; in just a year, it outpaced TV1 in late night popularity (SABC *Annual Report*, 1986). In the Pretoria–Witwatersrand–Vereeniging (PWV) Province there was some extra, unused transmission infrastructure. SABC began using this to air sport programming in the early 1990s, in effect creating another white channel, known as TopSport Surplus (TSS). By 1986 the SABC was leasing a transponder on an Intelsat satellite for national redistribution of five radio channels and TV1.

SABC television was to be financially self-supporting. It could rely on just two revenue sources: the license fee, which it set, and advertising, beginning in 1978. Because SABC endeavored to avoid the politically unpopular step of increasing license fees, it moved to capitalize on its position as a national advertiser and quickly relied on commercial sponsorship for the bulk of its revenues. The rapid movement of advertising to television was said to be a significant factor in the financial difficulties of the print media, and, as a consequence, of government approval in the mid-1980s of M-Net (discussed in Chapter 4), a subscription television service owned by the press consortium (D. de Villiers, 1983; Jackson, 1993: 84–87).

Programming on TV2/3 tended to cover similar themes as did Radio Bantu, but unlike radio, the projected television audience was urban and upwardly mobile. This 1982 description of TV2/3 programs is typical:

> Several South African-produced drama series were broadcast. These included "USenzekile" (TV2), the story of a young girl from Zululand who takes a job in the city as the housekeeper of a wealthy Black man with a devious past, while TV3 transmitted, among others, "Le tla Mpona" in Tswana. It told the story of a man who loses a considerable inheritance through poor management. "Incutshe," in Xhosa (TV2) was the story of a talented and successful musician who is at the same time a top-class soccer player, faced with the dilemma of having to choose between a career in music or soccer. "Mmampodi," in South Sotho (TV3) told the story of a young man who used his boxing skills to pay for his medical studies. (SABC *Annual Report*, 1982: 56)

TV2/3 programming also tended to reflect separate development policy and the exigencies of South African politics in the 1980s. One of TV2/3's biggest original programming projects, *Shaka Zulu*, a ten-part series on the history of Shaka and the "Zulu nation" that began airing in October

1986, fit the ideological interests of both the apartheid government and Mangosuthu Buthelezi's Inkatha organization. In depicting the history of the Zulu kingdom *as* the history of the Zulu royal family, and in portraying that kingdom as having been politically and socially united, the series reinforced Buthelezi's claim that the Zulu royal house (to which he claimed legacy) was the unquestioned "traditional" ruler of a united Zulu people today. While Zulu ethnicity is a fact, its understanding and meaning has been a matter of intense debate and conflicting mobilization over the past two decades, responsible in part for the virtual civil war in the early 1990s in what is now KwaZulu-Natal Province (Maré, 1993: 80–82). By asserting the unity and historical integrity of the "Zulu nation," SABC's *Shaka Zulu* series played directly into the hands of Inkatha, which by 1986 had positioned itself as the Inkatha Freedom Party, a black opponent of the ANC and the other Charterist organizations. The SABC's extension of apartheid policy to separate, racially based broadcast channels thus paradoxically reflected, in a fashion, the postmodern critique of classical public service broadcasting.

In the sometimes "doublethink"-sounding language of apartheid, the SABC described its news coverage as "reflecting the South African debate," but without "offer[ing] itself as a platform for those who would instigate confrontation and revolution" (SABC *Annual Report*, 1983: 7–8). In this regard, the SABC duplicitously engaged the critique of "sensationalist" Western news-gathering practices to justify the pro-apartheid new bias evident in its own coverage of the internal insurrection.[24] Typically, foreign broadcasts were filled with footage of violence and unrest during the 1980s. But South Africans saw and heard only police assurances that everything was under control on SABC TV and radio. In but one example, the SABC legitimized its slanted coverage of the Soweto uprising as a way to avoid "falling into the trap – as has happened so often in other parts of the world – of being an instrument for promoting unrest and panic" (SABC *Annual Report*, 1976: 15).

The SABC was to support the state's national security policies, particularly through its news coverage and current affairs programming. In the words of the 1976 *Annual Report*, "Because of the dangerous times in which we live the television services made a point of stressing the need for spiritual, economic and military preparedness,

---

24 The Kerner Commission Report (United States, 1968) on U.S. media coverage of the Detroit race riots determined that the reportage had fanned the flames of civil unrest.

of promoting understanding and cooperation between the various national groups and of stimulating a spirit of optimism and belief in the future of the country" (SABC *Annual Report*, 1976: 17). Accordingly, the SABC aired several documentaries on different divisions of the armed forces in the late 1970s, allegedly modeled after the Frank Capra *Why We Fight* U.S. series of the 1940s (SABC *Annual Report*, 1977: 53; K. Tomaselli and R. Tomaselli, 1989: 132–134). Sampie Terreblanche, an SABC Board member in the 1970s and 1980s, attested in 1992 that the security forces were inside the SABC (cited in Carver, 1995: 78). When they were covered at all, black organizations were typically portrayed as leaderless, rudderless groups, whose only aim was to destroy civil order and legitimate government. Such coverage further legitimized the security forces and their actions. Opposition figures, such as Anglican Archbishop Desmond Tutu, were demonized in SABC reports. News commentary in the black languages was patronizing and formulated to coopt dissent. News and public affairs programs would go black at times because a government minister would call at the last moment and demand that a clip, a statement, an interview not be aired.

Anecdotal accounts of government intervention in the SABC-TV newsroom are legion. One particularly egregious incident occurred in 1987, when Alan Hendrickse, the leader of the Labour Party, a Coloured political party, took a defiant plunge at a whites-only beach in Port Elizabeth. For this he was fired from the tricameral Cabinet by an outraged President P. W. Botha. A television news report of the incident that evening so angered Botha that he called the then director-general of the SABC, and, after the weather report, Botha's view on the Hendrikse incident was aired at great length (P. Naidoo, 1997). According to SABC producers, management screened most programs and demanded cuts or changes as they saw fit (Kevin Harris Productions, 1996). One of the best known, and perhaps apocryphal incidents, involved producer Kevin Harris' documentary, *Bara*, a look at Soweto's famous Baragwanath Hospital. *Bara* was a fairly straightforward treatment of the workings of the hospital. The documentary's introduction, however, showed some of the squalid conditions of everyday life in Soweto. A National Party official objected to the introduction because it belied the view of the townships the NP wanted to foster, and Harris was asked to cut it. Harris assured SABC management the cuts were made, but aired the original version instead. He was fired within 24 hours (Kevin Harris Productions, 1996). Other examples of control are described by Keyan

Tomaselli and Ruth Tomaselli (1989: 118–132). In addition to out-right censorship, SABC management created conditions for self-censorship. "You can present anything you want, but you must show both sides of the story," was the operative line. But both sides of the story meant that any criticism of government policy had to be so watered down that the criticism became a whitewash (Kevin Harris Productions, 1996). As Johan Pretorius (1992), editor-in-chief of SABC-TV news, summed it up in 1992, "It would be naive to deny that the Corporation followed a fairly strict government of the day line."

In sum, South African broadcasting was a strange mix of models, and the SABC a very strange beast. Ostensibly a public broadcaster, it was more or less understood as under the sway of the National Party, if not the NP's outright tool for pursuing ideological and social control. The SABC was part of what J. I. K. Gagiano (1986) labeled the *Boereplaas*, as belonging to Afrikanerdom. The vast major-ity of Afrikaners allied with the National Party and Conservative Party tended to regard the state as an Afrikaner state and state symbols as Afrikaner symbols. Since 1948 the Broederbond was a major pres-ence in the governing and management echelons of the SABC, exercis-ing latent and manifest control over program content – particularly in television. Still, the white hegemonic bloc had to be acknowledged and kept intact. The separate white broadcast services were oriented, in effect, to mediate the antagonisms between Afrikaans and English speakers. The nonwhite services were oriented toward the apartheid doctrine of separate development and were expected to facilitate social control. Overseen by whites, Radio Bantu aired programs essen-tially to remind the various African language groups of their African-ness. TV2/3, oriented toward coopting black political animus, largely emphasized urban-oriented consumption and the possibility of class mobility. After all, the percentage of Africans with television sets was limited to those electrified urban dwellers with enough income to afford a set – precisely those who might be seduced into a politically moder-ate middle class.

THE SOUTH AFRICAN INFORMATION BUREAU

What the SABC aimed to accomplish internally the South African Infor-mation Bureau worked to facilitate internationally. This organization came into being during World War II to serve as a clearinghouse for official information within South Africa. The bureau was designed to keep the press and broadcasting services adequately supplied with information within the limits of wartime security. With the 1948 NP victory, the bureau was expanded as a self-accounting subdepartment of the Department of External Affairs, under the title "State Information Office." Its main function now was to disseminate information about South Africa abroad, to massage the image and undermine criticism of the apartheid state in the international media. Its tasks included the distribution of written, televisual, and cinematic informational materials in overseas countries. Such materials typically defended apartheid and government actions (Hepple, 1960: 57–60). Although its official responsibilities and names changed over the years, the bureau's function as the government's information/communication/public relations agency remained essentially the same over the years. The service worked hand in hand with the SABC in the operation of an External Service, Radio RSA, on a very powerful set of transmitters designed as a broadcast counteroffensive to criticism of the apartheid regime (Magnusson, 1976).

By the 1970s the government's information function had coalesced into a Department of Information that amalgamated the liaison sections of the departments of Foreign Affairs and Bantu Affairs. Both had worked to legitimize apartheid – one outside the country, the other inside. Among other things, the Department of Information kept dossiers on journalists, particularly foreign journalists. In conjunction with the Department of Home Affairs it would assess the political proclivities of foreign journalists and decide whether to grant visas to reporters. If a foreign journalist was given a visa, department personnel would shepherd that journalist during his or her time in South Africa, orchestrating the visit in order to shape the story (Kotane, 1997). The department did not confine itself to massaging the image of South Africa in the international sphere. Indeed, it was the department's actions, particularly on the domestic front, that precipitated the media scandal known as "Muldergate," a scandal that changed the course of Afrikaner nationalism.

Muldergate involved the covert effort of the government to bankroll an "independent" newspaper, the *Citizen*, in order to ensure favorable government coverage in the English language press and to reduce the circulation and revenues of the government's most vocal media critic, the *Rand Daily Mail*. The surreptitious financing of the *Citizen* was the basis of the 1977–79 scandal, named after the brainchild of the scheme,

Minister of Information and the Interior Cornelius (Connie) Mulder (see, among others, Rees and Day, 1980; Hachten and Giffard, 1984: 229–261; O'Meara, 1996: 210–249). The secret activities conducted under Mulder's watch encompassed far more than just the government's covert establishment of the *Citizen*. Mulder and Eschel Rhoodie, his director-general of the Department of Information, orchestrated attempts to purchase leading South African, British, French, and American newspapers and magazines, secretly to subsidize pro–South African programs on international television networks, and to fund the production of pro–South African movies. Efforts extended to the offer of bribes to various political leaders to recognize the independence of the Bantustans and to other capers that subsidized political parties and candidates friendly to the South African government. Prior to bankrolling the *Citizen*, Mulder's department had tried unsuccessfully to buy out South African Associated Newspapers, owners of the *Rand Daily Mail*. These covert operations were conducted through scores of front companies using slush funds of state monies without any oversight, accounting, or control. About R64 million was removed from the defense budget for the Department of Information's special projects (Schrire, 1991: 33). The activities, and the bureaucratic arrogance that underlay them, were brought to light through investigative reporting, assisted by leaks arising from National Party infighting. According to the Mostert and Erasmus judicial commissions set up to investigate the scandal, the Department of Information had written the *Citizen*'s operating charter and was funding its monthly losses of R400,000. The department eventually gave R32 million to the newspaper or its putative "owner," frontman Louis Luyt. In the aftermath of the scandal, Perskor bought the *Citizen* and ran it at a loss for years.

The revelations of corruption, deceit, and dirty tricks rocked the National Party establishment and played a direct role in the triumph of the Cape *verligte* wing of the party. Mulder, leader of the Transvaal *verkramptes*, had been expected to win the NP leadership election after John Vorster stepped down in 1978. The scandal doomed Mulder's chances, however, and P. W. Botha, head of the Cape NP, won the September 1978 NP leadership election. This was a political watershed. In Dan O'Meara's words,

The long campaign of press revelations and judicial inquiry around the Department of Information had fatally undermined the political credibility of the most prominent representative of the NP right wing at a crucial moment in the factional struggle for dominance both within the NP and the government. It led directly to Mulder's humiliating defeat which then marked a significant shift in the balance of class forces organised by the Nationalist party qua party under the banner of Afrikaner nationalism. Through the victory of PW Botha, Afrikaner business effectively consolidated and now institutionalised its position as the dominant force in the nationalist alliance. Through Botha it announced its intention to modify some of the hallowed policies of this alliance, policies which went to the heart of the support for the Afrikaner nationalist alliance from white labour and certain strata of the petty bourgeoisie. The election of Botha broke the log jam in the NP and enabled the cautious introduction of policies for which Afrikaner business, together with all sections of monopoly capital, had long been pressing. (O'Meara, 1996: 248)

The impact of the election of P. W. Botha and the ascendance of "reform apartheid" will be taken up in Chapter 3.

THE SOUTH AFRICAN POST OFFICE AND THE "ANCIEN TELECOMMUNICATIONS RÉGIME"

The final link in the ancien South African communications chain was the South African Posts and Telecommunications (SAPT). Otherwise known as the Post Office, the SAPT was one of the original parastatals. It was in most respects a classic post, telegraph, and telephone (PTT) monopoly, legally monopolizing postal and telecommunications services and operating a system characterized by internal cross-subsidies (Union of South Africa, 1958). As a state-owned monopoly the Post Office realized economies of scale and scope through vertical integration, interconnection, and technical standardization. Its monopsony buying power assisted in the creation of a national equipment supply industry. Thus the SAPT not only built out a sophisticated telephone infrastructure, it also was responsible for helping establish an infant electronics industry and constituted a permanent market for it. Because the telephone monopoly managed a complete system, it could engage in the cross-subsidization of tariffs to expand service to particular constituencies.

Table 1. *Number of Telephones per 100 Residences*

Year	Whites	Asians	Coloureds	Africans Metropolitan	Rural
1978	71.5	36.1	19.3	3.3	1.8
1982	83.3	61.5	46.2	24.0	8.3
1987	83.9	72.2	53.2	38.0	13.7

Source: Republic of South Africa, 1989: 3.

Like many traditional telecommunications regimes, the SAPT utilized value-of-service pricing and cost-averaging schemes, among others, to effect cross-subsidies: typically, from business users to residential users, from long-distance (especially international) to local, from urban to rural.[25]

What was different about telecommunications in South Africa was, of course, apartheid. The historical operation of telecommunications, like all South African state services, was inscribed within the apartheid system, and the inequitable distribution of infrastructure and access to service reflected this fact. The disparities in telephone penetration by race were (and remain) striking. The policy of separate development meant that there was inadequate infrastructure in the black townships and virtually none in black rural areas. For example, 1989 figures showed telephone penetration per 100 blacks at 2.4 compared with 25 for whites (Coopers & Lybrand, 1992: 8). Table 1 provides a more datailed picture of penetration, showing telephone density per 100 residences by population group between 1978 and 1987.

The teledensity disparity was not simply a matter of skewed income levels. As a comprehensive report on the sector written by Coopers & Lybrand in 1992 noted that, although the white and black communities showed levels of telephone penetration broadly consistent with the normally observed relationship between telephone penetration and per capita income, there were a number of countries with similar per capita incomes to those of the black community in the Republic of South Africa but with much higher telephone penetration. The report con-

---

25 Value-of-service pricing means that those who value the service more and hence willing to pay more, are charged more. Cost-averaging means that similar kinds of calls will be charged the same, even if the actual routing on a particular call would cost more than would a similar call going by a different route.

cluded, neutrally, that there was considerable "suppressed demand" in the black population (Coopers & Lybrand, 1992: 9). Thus, whereas in many countries the traditional state-owned monopoly model constituted a kind of social democratic bargain to provide universal service, in South Africa the model was marshaled to provide service primarily to whites and to business (see Horwitz, 1989).

The question whether or not the SAPT itself practiced apartheid – that is, extending or withholding telephone service on the basis of race – is only partly relevant. Former Deputy Postmaster General W. J. Taylor (1997) attests that, to his knowledge, apartheid never played a role in the provision of telephone services. Demonstrated demand and the availability of capital determined where and how the network would be expanded. However, stories circulated about how SAPT application takers would tear up "frivolous" applications, that is, applications from blacks, who were judged to have no need for a telephone (White, 1991). Regardless, a "demonstrated demand" policy in the context of the broader configuration of apartheid, with its resultant income skew and geographic strictures, meant that service was not extended to black areas. Apartheid's legacy to infrastructure development can be seen in the fact that, while telephone service was virtually unavailable to rural blacks, it was extended to white farmers – and on a highly subsidized basis. Because of the historic economic and political power of the white, overwhelmingly Afrikaner, farming community, the average white farmer had access to health, education, electricity, transport networks, and a telephone as a result of a commitment from the state to provide whites with such services through public sector provision. According to one 1991 account, if tariffs for telephone service to the farming community were levied on a cost-related basis, the basic rental would have been R114 per month, not the R24 that was charged at the time (Preiss, 1991).

Historically, service was relatively good to those favored constituencies. The network in 1991, the year telecommunications was separated from posts, consisted of 3.3 million main lines, 48 percent of which terminated on digital equipment. Digital transmission was 100 percent in the large metropolitan areas and 78 percent outside of those areas (Lachenicht, 1991). Originally served by some twenty high-frequency circuits and two telegraph cables prior to 1969, international connectivity improved greatly with the completion of a submarine coaxial cable between Cape Town and Portugal (known as SAT-1) that year. It was supplemented by a satellite Earth station in December 1975. A second undersea cable, the fiber-optic SAT-2, commissioned in

1994, carries a 565 megabits per second transmission – providing the equivalent of 7,680 voice channels with nodes in Madeira and the Canary Isles. A modern telex service with over 30,000 connections linked all the major population centers in South Africa – although, as in all nations, facsimile has displaced telex and, hence, telex investments became a major loss. By the 1980s the SAPT began offering a wide array of value-added network services, sometimes in advance of a number of industrialized countries. It was one of the first telecommunications operators to introduce a public videotex service (Beltel). The X.400 protocol electronic message handling service has been available since the 1980s. An international X.25 packet switching network (Saponet-P) replaced an analogue network in 1983. A digital point-to-point service (Diginet) was introduced in 1986 for companies that need to transfer large volumes of data at high speeds. Businesses could lease lines, including high-capacity 2 megabits per second lines. SAPT introduced a pilot ISDN system in the late 1980s (see Telkom, 1991).

Service quality, while not quite up to European standards, was exceptional in comparison with African telecommunication operators and compared favorably to other operators in the developing world. International price comparisons of a basket of telephone services with industrialized countries (based on 1989 tariffs and exchange rates) indicated the SAPT's tariffs for both business and residential customers to be low by international standards. Residential line rental and connection charges were also comparatively low by these standards. Unlike many countries, business customers were not charged higher prices than residential customers. Therefore business line rental and connection charges in South Africa were even lower by international standards than those for residential customers. On the other hand, its international long-distance tariffs were comparatively rather high. For instance, charges for calls to the United States by the late 1980s were typically some 30 to 40 percent greater than a U.S.-originated call to South Africa (*Financial Mail*, 1993a). National long-distance charges were in line with the range found in industrialized countries. Call charges accounted for approximately 50 percent of the SAPT's total revenue (Coopers & Lybrand, 1992: 11–17). Cross-subsidies historically can be understood as follows: international and to a lesser degree national long-distance charges subsidized local service (but this is not directly business subsidizing residential service); calls greatly subsidized rentals.

Perhaps the clearest cross-subsidy was that from telecommunications to posts. With the entire operation statutorily forbidden to make profit or loss, profitable telecommunications services balanced out large operating losses on the postal side. Classified a "state business enterprise," the Post Office was run as a government department in a Cabinet ministry. The postmaster general (PMG) was the head of department; deputy PMGs ran the postal and telecommunications operations. Post Office finances were controlled by the Treasury. Post Office revenue was paid into the Exchequer and all Post Office expenditure came from the Exchequer. Because it operated directly out of a government ministry and hence was tied to Parliament's annual budgetary planning cycle, the SAPT budget went directly through Parliament. SAPT generally experienced close financial oversight. It was obliged to submit detailed annual reports on its budgets, accounts, and proposed capital expenditure to the auditor-general (an instrument of Parliament), who then wrote a report on the parastatal. The postmaster general would have to testify before the parliamentary committees on Post Office Affairs in response to the auditor-general's report. The Post Office was required to obtain authorization from the State Tender Board for equipment purchases, though really large expenditure orders would go directly to the minister (Taylor, 1992).

Under this system of oversight the SAPT as a rule experienced little outright corruption or gross overspending, but it generally suffered from a shortage of capital inasmuch as it had to compete for funds with other central government capital projects. Close government oversight also meant that SAPT could not set tariffs according to standard marginal costing principles. Tariffs were set below a level that would have enabled the SAPT to meet demand expediently. If upward tariffs were thought to contribute to inflation or prove politically difficult for the minister, they typically would be adjusted downward. According to former Deputy Postmaster General Taylor (1992, 1997), proposals to raise tariffs to ensure an economic return on investment were frustrated by government's attitude that as a state undertaking SAPT should set an example by keeping increases below the official inflation rate. The SAPT was always in trouble with the business community because the parastatal could not keep up with the extent of business demand. But when SAPT went to the Treasury for more funds, typically it would be rebuffed. The 1977–78 South African Posts and Telecommunications *Annual Report* illustrates the point. After describing the weakening of key financial measures such as return on assets, the ratio between

Table 2. *Annual Rate Increases, ESKOM and South African Posts and Telecommunications*

	1986	1987	1988	1989	1990
Consumer					
Price Index rise	18.6%	16.1%	12.9%	14.7%	14.4%
ESKOM increase	15.0%	12.0%	12.9%	10.0%	14.0%
SAPT increase	15.0%	9.6%	0%	4.1%	4.3%

Source: Republic of South Africa, 1991a: cols. 2153–2154.

operating surplus and operating expenditure, and the ratio between long-term debt and net fixed assets, the report states that "in the national interest, it was decided to postpone rate increases for a further period," making it nearly five years since rates were last increased. Contrast, for example, Post Office tariff increases with those of the electricity parastatal, ESKOM, between 1986 and 1990 (see Table 2). ESKOM, though a monopolistic parastatal, was *not* run directly out of a government ministry.

Ministerial control inhibited the development of a coherent planning horizon. The yearly politics of tariff setting meant it was impossible for the SAPT to calculate its finances on a long-term basis (Bets, 1992). The system of financing changed to some degree in 1968, when the finances of the Post Office were separated by law from the Exchequer and placed under its own control. Yet, while SAPT controlled its revenues, and was expected to use "profits" for the expansion of services, it was still dependent on Treasury loans to finance capital expenditure. As in many nations, the SAPT operated a savings bank that provided for some of its loan requirements. The Post Office Savings Bank was taken over from the Treasury for the SAPT's own account in 1974. It was only in 1972 that SAPT was empowered to negotiate its own foreign loans (*Financial Mail*, 1986). Overseas loans required approval by the South African Reserve Bank and SAPT's annual budget still had to be approved by Parliament (Taylor, 1997).

If the Post Office's status as a state business enterprise entailed a relatively close oversight of its finances, it did not mean the parastatal was particularly efficient. Judging by comparative productivity indices, one could reasonably conclude that the SAPT functioned as a repository for public employment. For instance, on the telecommunications side, access lines in service per employee measured a low 45.4 as late as

1989.[26] The SAPT's low productivity must be understood in the broad context of the expansion of parastatal organizations and the job reservation system. The combination of parastatal growth and job reservation policy meant the expansion of the white public sector workforce. As the apartheid policy of white uplift succeeded, Afrikaners moved into technical and managerial ranks, and nonwhites began to occupy the lower job grades of the parastatals. A gradual shortage of white labor meant corresponding increases in the employment of blacks.[27] Black public sector employment grew from 5.47 percent of economically active blacks in 1946 to 10.55 percent by 1980 (Standish, 1987: 12–13). The ratio of black to white employment in the Post Office rose from 0.38 in 1968 out of a workforce of 51,140 to 0.68 in 1980 out of a workforce of 75,490 (Standish, 1987: 45). But this increase was not a matter of course. At the SAPT it required agreement by the white staff associations (the name for the postal trade unions) over the number of nonwhites who could be taken into service for training each year (Taylor, 1997). The SAPT also participated in the job reservation system indirectly, through the contracts the Post Office fashioned with domestic equipment manufacturing companies. Particularly in the early years, the equipment manufacturers were under mandate to hire whites, Afrikaners in particular (Kaplan, 1990: 31–32).

The relationship between SAPT and domestic equipment suppliers functioned in the manner of an industrial policy, with local purchasing obligations and high domestic content requirements. And in the main, the policy succeeded rather well, to a point. The manufacture of telecommunications equipment grew to become the largest part of the South African electronics sector but with all the eventual drawbacks of import substitution industrialization policy. Before 1958, SAPT's equipment was supplied by the principal contractors to the British Post Office: Automatic Telephone Electric Company, Siemens U.K., and

---

26 By way of contrast, in South Korea there were 226.3 lines; in the United States, 130.6; in Mexico, 95.6. Even Turkey outperformed South Africa at 65.9 access lines in service per employee, according to 1989 data (Coopers & Lybrand, 1992: 16). The South African figure improved to 70 in 1996, though the absorption of the TBVC telephone network and workforce effectively lowered the figure to 66.5 (Telkom *Annual Report*, 1996). The average cost of a new line, another indicator of productivity and efficiency, amounted to $4,798 in 1992 in South Africa, compared to a developing country average cost of $1,485 (International Telecommunication Union, 1994: 3).

27 Whites constituted 20% of the population from Union in 1910 until 1960. After 1960 the white demographic base started to shrink. The proportion of whites to the total population fell to 15% by 1985. As a result, an acute shortage of white manpower manifested itself in both the public and private sectors (Giliomee and Schlemmer, 1989: 115).

Standard Telephones and Cables. With military and strategic considerations in mind, in late 1957 the government utilized the monopsonistic power of SAPT to stimulate the local production of telecommunication equipment. Following the British example, SAPT signed a series of ten-year contracts (officially known as the Manufacture and Supply Agreements) with several local telecommunications equipment companies. The agreements were extended for another ten years in 1968 and then at the end of 1979, with the advent of digital technology, for a further fifteen years. The agreements embodied national goals on local content. SAPT purchases accounted for 74 percent of the demand for telecommunications equipment in the mid-1980s, according to one estimate (Kaplan, 1990: 27–31, 79–85).

The four main companies (down from the original five due to a merger) were the Altech Group, Siemens, Telephone Manufacturers of South Africa (TMSA), and Plessey. Other companies, including ATC, Aberdare, and Grinaker Electronics, carved out niches in local equipment provision as well. The production of telecommunications equipment in South Africa tended to be highly concentrated, frequently with a single local producer for a particular technology: Altech subsidiary companies in transmission equipment; Siemens and Altech in digital exchanges (with Siemens having two-thirds market share); Siemens in telex and teletex terminals, automatic telegraph exchanges, and telephone exchange power supply equipment; TMSA in telephone instruments and, with Telkor (now part of the TMSA operation), public telephones; Plessey supplied switchboards for test and maintenance centers as well as manual exchanges, and was sole supplier of small business telephone systems to SAPT; Philips, Siemens, and Plessey in analogue mobile telephones. Plessey originally was responsible for providing private branch exchanges but that market opened to competition in 1987–88. Aberdare and ATC were selected to produce cable for the national transmission network. ATC was the only manufacturer of optical fiber cable in South Africa. The import substitution model resulted in vertically integrated telecommunications companies making a wide range of products for the local market. All the principal local producers of telecommunications equipment and components had a significant part of their equity held by one of the large local corporate groups. As we saw in the case of the press, this is in keeping with the larger historic patterns of the South African economy. The five conglomerates were well represented in the telecommunications equipment industry (see Table 3).

Table 3. *Corporate Shareholding in the Major South African Telecommunications Companies*

Firm	Local Shareholding	Foreign Shareholding
Altech	20% Anglo-American	12.5% Alcatel (France)
Siemens	16% Sankorp	
	16% General Mining (Gencor)	52% Siemens (Zurich)
	16% IDC	
Plessey S.A.	26% Sanlam	74% Plessey U.K.
TMSA	50% Plessey S.A.	
	50% GEC S.A. (Reunert)	

Source: Kaplan, 1990: 84.

The rapid and progressive substitution of lower-paid black labor for white males allowed the industry to grow and be profitable during the period of electromechanical technology. With digitalization, telecommunications technology became more complex, and production and research and development more capital intensive. The local South African telecommunications equipment industry could not adjust to these changes. As a result, the local South African companies became essentially licensees of First World companies. SAPT's decision in the late 1970s to digitize the network resulted from both an increasing demand and the fact that the British-based electromechanical switching system had begun to develop technical problems. SAPT management faced a crossroads on the switching system because existing switching could not handle the new demand. But small nations cannot easily amass the capital and expertise to create and manufacture highly advanced, general (as opposed to niche) telecommunication devices. As a result, South African equipment companies entered into licensing arrangements to assemble foreign-designed telecommunications equipment in South Africa. Siemens licensed TMSA to manufacture the German EWSD digital exchange; Teltech (part of the Altech group) was licensed to manufacture the French Alcatel E-10 digital exchange (designated locally as the SA 128E). The choice of suppliers was limited inasmuch as these were the early days of digital technology, and only a few companies could present viable digital equipment offerings at that time. The decision to authorize two different foreign suppliers was largely a political one. Given the threat of economic sanctions and the possibility of a supplier cutoff, dependence on a single source of foreign technology was thought to entail considerable risk. The government believed that any difficulties of meshing two different digital exchange systems were outweighed by the political slack offered by two different foreign suppliers (Kaplan, 1990: 41–42). As a result of these historic relationships, foreign owners had significant percentages of shareholding in most of the major South African telecommunications equipment companies (see Table 3).[28]

Originally the Manufacture and Supply Agreements were for a ten-year term. The equipment suppliers persuaded the SAPT to increase the term to fifteen years because of the high investment in plant and technological transfer from overseas principals, particularly for digital equipment. Under the terms of the agreements, SAPT was obliged to purchase its equipment from the domestic companies when feasible, depending upon the percentage of local content and the comparison of local with international equipment prices. SAPT would generally purchase South African–made equipment if there were a reasonable degree of local content so long as the price did not exceed the international price by more than 25 percent. But in many instances the price premium was far higher, ranging from 32 percent for standard telecommunications equipment to 60 percent for electronic components (Kaplan, 1990: 106–126). Whereas the Manufacture and Supply Agreements worked well to ensconce viable equipment firms and establish coherent standards and specifications, the pricing structures may have acted to replicate the famous Averch-Johnson-Wellisz effect (Averch and Johnson, 1962; Wellisz, 1963). As a rule SAPT would take back a percentage of high supplier margins as a kind of rebate or "profit sharing." Designed to give suppliers incentives to enhance efficiency, the rebate arrangement instead gave suppliers incentives to reinvest in their own plants (such investment being part of the overall cost structure) in order to reduce the amount that SAPT would take back (Hartyani, 1992; P. Schulze, 1992). Intended also to foster innovation and product development, the supply agreements paradoxically may have hindered them. According to Kaplan (1990: 99–101), the supply agreements functioned

---

28 There have been considerable recent ownership changes in the manufacturing companies, reflecting a general rationalization and a specific regrouping in the advent of a sharp decline in orders from Telkom in the early 1990s. TMSA is now held by GEC South Africa with a 66.66% stake (GEC S.A. is 50% owned by GEC U.K. and 50% by Reunert, a Barlow Rand company [ultimately SA Mutual]); Siemens holds 33.33%. In January 1993, Alcatel boosted its stake to 50% in Altech and allowed Altech to buy a stake in Alcatel as well, thus integrating the companies more fully (Kaplan, 1999).

to exclude the entry of new smaller companies that might be highly innovative. These agreements provided alternative and less risky routes to achieving high levels of profitability.

Even before Kaplan published his inquiry into the equipment supply industry, the SAPT itself conducted an investigation of Altech and other equipment suppliers in the mid 1980s. The SAPT Components Committee had to threaten the reopening of the Manufacture and Supply Agreements to get the supply companies to release data. The committee discovered a pyramid system, whereby internal companies were set up to import equipment that they, in turn, sold as locally produced and with considerable markup to another internal company, and so on. In an interview, a Telkom general manager who declined to be identified indicated that each transaction succeeded in padding the overall cost to the Post Office (also Klok, 1996). As if to underscore the weakness of South African telecommunications equipment manufacturing, the South African Board of Trade and Industry reported that telecommunications manufacturers exported only 1.5 percent of their products in 1985 (Kaplan, 1992). The Manufacture and Supply Agreements expired in September 1994 and were replaced by an open tender system for equipment purchases.

The fact that the Post Office was a parastatal run by a line function government department meant that historically it not only constituted a cog in the job reservation and Afrikaner uplift systems but also tended to be imbued with the political culture of National Party administration and Afrikaner nationalism. Bureaucratic excess was endemic. In sum, the old SAPT served whites and business relatively well, functioned as a repository for white employment, and wasn't particularly efficient vis-à-vis standard measures of lines per employee. Though it facilitated the growth of a domestic equipment supply industry through a classic import substitution industrial policy, those very arrangements over time led to high equipment costs because of declining economies of scale and contracts prone to corruption. Because telephony was a service dear to customer–voters, political pressure was salient. The responsible Cabinet minister felt political heat to keep the Post Office's tariffs low, set according to political rather than economic criteria. One consequence of low tariffs was that SAPT was often short of capital to finance expansion, and the politics of tariff-setting made it difficult for SAPT to engage in anything resembling a normal business plan. The internal culture of the Post Office, particularly at management level, reflected Afrikaner nationalism's concern for ethnic loyalty above merit and performance – which also comported with the predominance of an apartheid political logic over economic or administrative rationality.

Broadcasting, the state information service, and telecommunications were institutions ensconced within apartheid structures and apartheid goals. The print press was relatively contained within the tense accommodation between the hegemonic white groups. But the ancien régime in the sector came under challenge, particularly in telecommunications. Notwithstanding the general historic success of the Post Office in providing telecommunications service within its apartheid purview, the status quo could not, or did not, endure, for two sets of distinct but intersecting reasons: first, changes internal to telecommunications in particular and state-owned enterprises in general; and, second, a shift in National Party politics. State-owned enterprises worldwide had begun to come under scrutiny regarding their economic efficiency in the 1980s. Perhaps the leading sector in this scrutiny was telecommunications, which had undergone something of a technological revolution, and which had been cut loose of many government controls in the United States and the United Kingdom. In South Africa, the election of P. W. Botha to National Party leader marked the victory of the *verligte* faction of the party and its attempt to reform apartheid. "Reform apartheid," responding to huge problems in the South African economy, set in motion the political struggle that eventuated in the negotiated transition of 1990. One feature of reform apartheid was the move to transform the parastatals, including the SAPT and the SABC. The reform of the parastatals placed them within the vortex of the political struggles of the 1980s.

CHAPTER 3

"Sharing Power without Losing Control": Reform Apartheid and the New Politics of Resistance

Parastatal reform was part of the government's broader project to modify the apartheid system. Apartheid may have been a multifaceted, systemic method of political oppression along racial lines, but, at bottom and in origin, it was a system for the control of labor. "Reform apartheid," inaugurated by P. W. Botha's *verligte* faction of the National Party, represented the recognition that that system of control had become dysfunctional, that many of the structures guaranteeing white privilege were now incompatible with the demands of a modern economy. Reform apartheid comprised a contradictory set of strategies: the improvement of the basic conditions of black life but the lessening of state intervention in the economy; devolution of political power to local areas but maintainence of the prohibition against African participation in national political life. With respect to the parastatals, reform apartheid resulted in both their expansion and the attempt to privatize them. Reform apartheid's aim was to end formal apartheid but reconsolidate white supremacy through the market and a restricted political franchise. This propelled, in classic dialectical fashion, the emergence of a broad, coherent internal opposition movement against the government's top–down reforms. The violent conflict over the reform of apartheid in the 1980s set the stage for February 1990 and structured the political struggles over the parastatals in the democratic transition period. In the activist anti-apartheid civil society organizations lay the groundwork for the political culture of consultation and transparency characteristic of the post–February 1990 democratic transition period.

Apartheid was a success for whites. Economic growth was impressive through the 1970s. A cheap labor economy and import substitution behind protectionist trade barriers combined to bring unusually high rates of return on capital. White workers were virtually guaranteed access to jobs, and they experienced rising wages and amenities. The cold war, and South Africa's geopolitical position as a Western ally situated at the intersection of important global trading routes and access to the Atlantic and Indian oceans, brought the apartheid state political stability and support from the West, notwithstanding international condemnation over the Sharpeville massacre. But by the mid-1970s South Africa entered into a different set of mutually reinforcing political and economic dynamics. The Soweto uprising of 1976 ended the years of relative political quiescence on the part of the black majority. Black labor had already become partially organized and militant, beginning with a series of successful strikes in 1973 in Durban. The tensions between apartheid policies and the capitalist economy had become more visible, particularly as they began to intersect broader developments in an increasingly interdependent international economy. With the exception of mining, South Africa's protected companies were largely uncompetitive in international markets (see Joffe et al., 1995). Its economic profile as exporter of minerals and agricultural products and importer of capital equipment, technology, and oil no longer favored the country – especially as a more hostile international political climate began to threaten South Africa's export markets and jeopardize its access to international financial markets.[1] For years surrounded by neutral or friendly states, by the mid-1970s South Africa began to confront hostile, if weak neighbors, as Portuguese colonialism collapsed in Mozambique and Angola, and white supremacy was under attack in Rhodesia. The Muldergate scandal heightened, and unexpectedly resolved, at least for the short term, the *verligte–verkrampte* struggle within the ruling National Party in favor of the moderates. This development, too, was rooted in a set of larger historical forces, namely the change in Afrikaner class composition as a result of the success of Afrikaner uplift. A consequence of these forces and events was reform apartheid. This chapter briefly examines a sequence of events and sets of forces and structures that have been presented

1 As Dan O'Meara (1996: 477) suggests, the United Nations system, while hardly replacing bilateral diplomacy, did alter the terrain of diplomacy, especially after the emergence of postcolonial states by the end of the 1960s. A new set of transgovernmental arenas of diplomacy emerged to reshape the issue areas of world politics. In this reshaping, apartheid and South Africa came to be vilified. This new diplomatic terrain permitted the freezing out of South Africa from international political forums, and paved the way for the eventual boycotts, sanctions, and disinvestment campaigns.

much more fully elsewhere (see Saul and Gelb, 1981; P. Frankel, Pines, and Swilling, 1988; Price, 1991).

The immediate spark for the 1976 Soweto uprising was the imposition by educational authorities of a rule requiring instruction in the Afrikaans language in arithmetic and social studies curricula.[2] The backdrop to the uprising was the percolation of Black Consciousness ideas through the African townships, particularly among students and student organizations such as the South African Students' Organisation. The assertion of black identity, of black resistance that was central to Black Consciousness ideology was there in the student revolt, as it was in the emerging militance of black workers. Both the new student and worker activism reflected broader changes in the material conditions of the black population by the early 1970s, to wit, the emergence, relatively speaking, of a rising literate clerical stratum and the movement of blacks into more semiskilled and skilled jobs in the growing manufacturing sector. At the same time, apartheid urban policy meant that while more Africans were brought into the formal economy, the construction of housing in the townships had been frozen and expenditure on urban services reduced. These measures resulted in a qualitative decline in the living conditions of urban Africans (see Swilling, 1988a).

Student demonstrations against the Afrikaans language requirement were met by police violence and led to rioting. The unrest spread to other townships and escalated with a series of widespread stay-at-home actions between June and October 1976. Conservative figures estimated at least 575 were killed and 2,389 wounded, thousands imprisoned and thousands more leaving the country to join the black resistance in exile (Republic of South Africa, 1980: Vol. 1: 523–525). Although a powerful display of black rage, the Soweto uprising could not have been successful as a revolt against the state. As Tom Lodge (1983: 336) argues, at no stage in the uprising "would it have been conceivable to have mounted a challenge which the forces at the disposal of the state could not have overcome." Rather, the effects of the uprising were, one, to stimulate the growth of black resistance movements and organizations inside the country and, two, to amplify in government and business policy-making circles pressures for reforms in the legal status and economic position of urban Africans.

---

2 The Afrikaans language policy itself had roots in the Afrikaner–English conflict. A *verkrampte* faction of bureaucrats led by Education Minister Andries Treurnicht insisted on compulsory Afrikaans in the African school curriculum as part of a strategy to ensure the survival of Afrikaner culture (Rich, 1996: 52).

Pressures for reform were already there. The steady growth of manufacturing and the relative shrinkage of the white population through the 1960s led to shortages of skilled labor in many areas of manufacturing (Republic of South Africa, 1979a). For decades the white population constituted 20 percent of the total population, but after 1960 the white demographic base started to shrink, falling to 15 percent by 1985 (Giliomee and Schlemmer, 1989: 115). Manufacturing, constituting 16.5 percent of the GDP in 1950, accounted for 19.1 percent in 1960, 21.2 percent in 1970, and 25.6 percent in 1980 (Giliomee and Schlemmer, 1989: 117). The apartheid policies of influx control and job reservation, and Bantu education that trained Africans only for menial work, exacerbated the labor problem. Many employers had begun to ignore job reservation and other job color bars, and big companies were negotiating with white unions to loosen job restrictions so that blacks could fill vacant positions previously reserved for whites (Mufson, 1990: 135–136). The combination of extremely low wages, inflation, and the new leverage available to black workers in more skilled positions underlay the 1973 Durban strikes. These apparently spontaneous, leaderless work stoppages aroused black workers across the nation and led to a strike wave after 1973. Workers resorted to the strike in part because there were no mechanisms to express grievances. But because black unions were for the most part illegal, and black labor leaders were summarily fired or arrested as agitators, there were no union leaders with whom factory managers and business executives could negotiate.[3] These conditions led some employers to begin to press for a rationalization of black labor relations. Anglo-American Corporation in particular played a role in moving to liberalize the thinking about labor relations (Friedman, 1987: 37–68). There had been union movements in earlier decades, characterized by a broad industrial mass movement approach with ties to the political organizations. But they suffered under political repression and were unsuccessful in turning worker support into a permanent source of power (Friedman, 1987: 11–36).

In the aftermath of the Soweto uprising, the calls for some kind of reform in the legal status and economic position of Africans grew louder and more widespread. Representative bodies for Transvaal's

---

3 Africans were excluded from trade union rights by the Industrial Conciliation Act of 1956. African workers' relations with employers were governed by the Native Labour Settlement of Disputes Act of 1953, which limited the workers' opportunities for dispute settlement to plant-level works committees, only 24 of which existed by 1973 (Maree, 1985).

commerce and industry, for example, produced memoranda in favor of improving the legal and economic security of township residents through ameliorating influx control, improving wages and job opportunities, providing more and better housing with land-ownership rights, and encouraging the development of a black middle class. The business-based Urban Foundation, established in late 1976, concentrated on improving the quality of African housing. Foreign-based companies, under political pressure at home, added their voices to the call for reform (Lodge, 1983: 336; Friedman, 1987: 112–148). The government appointed two high-level commissions in 1977 to study labor and manpower legislation. By the time these commissions published their reports in 1979, P. W. Botha's *verligte* wing had assumed leadership of the National Party.

After decades of leadership by the hard-line traditional *verkrampte* wing of the party, P. W. Botha rose to party leader and prime minister in 1978 in the aftermath of the Muldergate scandal. Botha brought to a head the long-simmering friction between *verkrampte* and *verligte* factions, that is, between those who continued to champion undiluted Afrikaner domination and racial exclusiveness and those who had come to advocate broader white unity and easier race relations through, among other things, mixed sport and the abolition of petty apartheid measures. The *verkramptes* in effect upheld the National Party as a politically mobilized ethnic movement; the *verligtes* represented an effort to push the NP to become a bona fide national political party, characterized by a set of values and policies that would attract supporters beyond ethnic Afrikaners. To be sure, the contemplated *verligte* reforms were still firmly rooted in the Nationalist conception of the group, not the individual, as the basis of any political arrangement (Giliomee, 1979a: 217–218). The *verligte* vision was based largely on a recognition that the South African economy could no longer function under the conditions of traditional apartheid. Botha publicly courted the corporate elite. In 1978, as prime minister he began to implement the reform agenda. His famous "adapt or die" speech to the 1979 National Party Congress warned that apartheid was a recipe for permanent conflict. "The world does not remain the same," Botha intoned, "and if we as government want to act in the best interests of the country in a changing world, then we have to be prepared to adapt our policy to those things that make adjustment necessary, otherwise we die" (cited in Schrire, 1991: 29). In Robert Schrire's (1991: 47–49) interpretation, Botha believed that the unrestrained pursuit of white interests through policies of privilege and prejudice was neither moral nor sustainable. As it evolved, the ideological move of the reform strategy was to separate apartheid, now identified as a set of mechanisms that had outlived its functions, from white dominance, which was always the goal. The Botha government's broad hope, seemingly in a page taken from Seymour Martin Lipset's (1960) playbook, was to cultivate a nonwhite middle class whose political moderation would undermine the opposition to continued white domination. Or, as a prominent business leader put it in a revealing quotation presented by Giliomee and Schlemmer (1989: 132), "We Afrikaners must try to find the secret of sharing power without losing control." The relaxation of traditional state intervention into the economy would, it was hoped, facilitate the economic growth to ensure political reform. Political reform thus made alliance with business (see, among others, P. Frankel, 1980; Mann, 1988; Price, 1991).

The publication of the weighty reports from three key government commissions in 1979 laid the technical groundwork for the National Party's ideological and policy shifts. At bottom, the reports dealt with the ramifications of apartheid policies on the South African economy. The de Kock Commission (Republic of South Africa, 1978) examined monetary policy and the exchange rate system. The Riekert (Republic of South Africa, 1979a) and Wiehahn (Republic of South Africa, 1979b) Commissions investigated labor and manpower legislation and their implementation. All three reports, produced by the usual cream of Afrikaner intelligentsia, emphasized that the time had come for the state to play a less dominant role in shaping the economy.[4] The private sector should play a very much larger part in economic policy making and the market should be left to operate as freely as possible. The de Kock Commission Report recommended that exchange rates be allowed to float against other currencies under a quasi-protective umbrella. Wiehahn proposed that African trade unions, through a system of formal registration, be incorporated into the officially sanctioned collective bargaining process. Statutory job reservation

---

4 Interestingly, the Wiehahn Commission, already politically balanced to include representatives from the national employer associations and the white labor unions, also included one African, one Coloured, and one Indian. As Steven Friedman (1987: 151) argues, it seemed that the commission was not an inquiry at all, but rather a vehicle for testing the acceptability of reforms to key labor interest groups. In this regard, the Wiehahn Commission represented a new feature in the South African political landscape, a kind of quasi-corporatism, in which capital and labor were brought together for policy advisory purposes (L. Pretorius, 1996).

should be abolished. Whereas the Wiehahn Commission argued in favor of the extension of an interlocking system of privilege and control for African industrial workers, the Riekert Commission proposed, complementarily, to isolate this group – together with the urban African middle class – from the growing numbers of the unemployed. African industrial workers would be given the legal status of permanent urban residents, and could live in cities with their families. More and better quality family housing would be constructed in the townships and township residents could purchase their own homes. The Riekert proposals would also remove restrictions on the development of an African business class. At the same time, Riekert recommended tightening influx controls on *migrant* labor through a variety of measures, including stiff fines imposed on employers who hired illegal migrants. Migrant and contract workers could not join registered unions. In other words, the combination of the Wiehahn and Riekert reports aimed at ending several time-honored features of apartheid, but with the intention of creating a more tempered, presumably controllable black labor movement and a black middle class within a more informal system of white dominance. The commissions seemed to have rejected *formal* white supremacy, arguing that the continuation of apartheid would undermine the continued success of the private enterprise system. Indeed, tied to the Wiehahn recommendation that both trade union organizations and individuals "be afforded full freedom of association in that individuals should be free to join any appropriate trade union of their choice," was the premise that "full involvement, participation and sharing in the system of free enterprise by all population groups with as little Government intervention as possible would not only give all groups a stake in the system but would also ensure a common loyalty to both the system and the country" (Republic of South Africa, 1979b: 44, 4).

Reform apartheid essentially acknowledged that the old system of labor and residential controls had become dysfunctional. The demands of a modern economy were increasingly at odds with the policies of white privilege. Educated black workers possessing skills were essential now that manufacturing had displaced mining as the single most important component of the economy. But reforming apartheid provoked fundamental contradictions. In order to fulfill the goal of improving the conditions of urban Africans the state's role would have to expand and public expenditure increase. Yet the *ideology* of reform entailed a move in the opposite direction. It is important to note that as the National Party under Botha's leadership began its move *away*

Table 4. *Ratio of Income of Afrikaners*
to English, 1946–1976

Year	Personal Income	Per Capita Income
1946	40:60	100:211
1960	47:53	100:156
1976	50:50	100:141

Source: Giliomee, 1979b: 174.

from grand apartheid, it also began moving *toward* classical market economics and monetarism. Reform apartheid not only entailed a new political logic, but also a sometimes hesitant, yet genuine embrace of the market now that the historical project of Afrikaner uplift had succeeded. Particularly relevant to the National Party's dance away from its long-standing policy of strong state interventionism was the essential realization that the long coddling period for Afrikaner capital was no longer necessary. In the National Party's reform thinking, now that Afrikaner capital was on reasonably strong footing and Afrikaners had finally joined their English-speaking white confederates at the top end of the economic structure, the abstract and "natural" workings of the market (presumably reinforced by social mores) could be trusted to safeguard effective white dominance. The ascendence of the *verligte* tendency was rooted in the emergence of a class of self-confident Afrikaner capitalists whose interests now went beyond those of the relatively narrow class alliance of farmers, white workers, and Afrikaner petty bourgeoisie out of which they had emerged (O'Meara, 1983: 251–254). (The rising fortunes of Afrikaners are shown in Table 4.) The point is that between Afrikaner economic gains and a broader concern about apartheid's increasingly negative impact on the economy, the dominant wing of the National Party moved closer to the traditional economic concerns of business and English-speaking whites in general. As its core Afrikaner constituency had become more urbanized, affluent, and bourgeois, the *verligte* wing seemed willing to risk losing the National Party's traditional farmer, petty bourgeois, and working class Afrikaner base to attempt to forge alliance with business and English speakers. The recognition of black trade unions and elimination of job reservation in 1979 signaled the end of the government's formal protection of white workers and the emergence of the National Party as essentially a bourgeois political party. And although the policy of separate development still held sway, it too would give way, in fits and starts, to one of national economic growth.[5]

This strategy entailed political risks. Ideological conflicts between hard-liners and moderates had caused various splits of the Nationalist movement previously. Leading members of the *verkrampte* wing had been expelled from the National Party in 1969. Led by Albert Hertzog, they formed the Herstigte (reconstituted) National Party, based on the traditional "pure" Afrikaner principles, and garnered a small share of the Afrikaner vote in subsequent elections. In the general election of 1981, as the NP initiated its reform agenda, the party lost support to both its right and left. The party drew just 63 percent of the Afrikaner vote, dropping from a 83–85 percent share in the 1970, 1974, and 1977 elections. Most of the falloff (i.e., 33%) went to the far-right parties, which had received only 7 percent of the Afrikaner vote in 1977. Four percent of the Afrikaner vote went to the liberal Progressive Federal Party (identified with English speakers), compared with 1 percent in 1977. In mid-1981 Prime Minister Botha faced a censure debate in Parliament mounted by the increasingly powerful right wing. The bureaucracy had effectively thwarted some of Botha's proposals, particularly those aimed at setting up economic cooperation ventures that would ignore the borders between South Africa proper and the black homelands. Conflict over the question of incorporating Coloureds into Parliament prompted a formal split in the National Party in early 1982. The *verkrampte* wing of the Transvaal NP, led by Andries Treurnicht, was pushed out of the NP and became the Conservative Party.

Reforming apartheid would also require putting in motion a set of changes with manifold fiscal and economic, as well as political, ramifications. In addition to rescinding many apartheid laws, reform would require the expansion of public expenditure to deal with the appalling education, training, and living conditions of the black majority. For instance, spending on African education, which stood at just R27 million in 1972–73, rose to R566 million by 1981–82 and R1.2 billion by 1988–89 (South African Institute of Race Relations, various years). This reform-induced expansion of the state accelerated a trend that had been in place for many years. Particularly noticeable was the growth of the main infrastructure parastatals – the institutions that would be largely responsible

5 In his first four years of power, Botha tried to make the homelands system work, encouraging the Bantustans to become "independent" and attempting to strengthen them economically through territorial consolidation, land transfers, and the decentralization of industry. Botha himself acknowledged the policy was a failure (Schrire, 1991: 51–56).

for the extension of public services to blacks. The percentage of the economy accounted for by the public corporations (*not* including the state business enterprises, such as the Post Office) had risen steadily through the years, and jumped rapidly between 1975 and 1985, from 4.1 percent of GDP in 1975 to 7.7 percent of GDP in 1985 (South African Reserve Bank, cited in Nattrass, 1988: 234). This pattern is pretty much in keeping with the practices of most developing nations during this period of time. International borrowing was easy; large loans (primarily from banks recycling petrodollars) went to developing country governments, which invested them in state-owned firms (Stallings, 1992). The South African state had long followed a standard developing country import-substitution industrialization strategy, with heavy protectionism and high tariff walls (Joffe et al., 1995). The basic inward-oriented economic policy was reinforced by a feeling among National Party leaders that South Africa was a country under political siege.

It should be apparent that reform apartheid embodied contradictory tendencies. Its policies were subject both to ongoing internal political battles within Afrikaner nationalism and to external pressures, particularly the loss of foreign capital and, later, international sanctions. On the one hand the strategy entailed increased services to black communities, in part through expansion of the parastatals. The task of raising black levels of education and training would be expensive. Reform would thus require continuation of a strong centralized state. The sense that South Africa was under siege – a combination of the international disapproval of apartheid, internal unrest, and the success of anticolonial movements in neighboring states – stoked the old tendency of inward industrialization. Public investment in "strategic" industries, such as oil from coal (Sasol), natural gas (Mossgas), and military armaments (Armscor), was an important consequence of seige mentality, as was increased expenditure on security. On the other hand reform apartheid called for a devolution of political and economic power, the first through the creation of "own-area" political authority for South Africa's various ethnic groups, the latter through marketization and even privatization. Yet whatever actual reforms were implemented, they would have to be bounded. Reform measures would be countenanced only to the degree that they did not fundamentally challenge white hegemony.

Reform apartheid's crowning political dimension – the creation of a tricameral Parliament, allowing for Coloured and Indian, but not African, political representation – was in keeping with these constraints. Trumpeted as a progressive move and a serious concession from whites, the new system of political representation was firmly in keeping with basic apartheid doctrine. Elections were to be race elections, the legislative chambers were to be segregated, and the white Parliament could overrule the (Coloured) House of Representatives and the (Indian) House of Delegates. Whites were given a built-in majority over Coloureds and Indians by a ratio of 4 : 2 : 1 in the size of their respective chambers, the election of the state president (to replace the office of prime minister), and the composition of the President's Council, which would mediate disputes between the chambers. The constitutional changes were intended to incorporate Coloureds and Indians into a delimited consociational central government structure without threatening the autonomy of the white parliamentary system. This consociational, or power-sharing structure[6] was seen as a component of a larger overarching confederal structure that would link the various Bantustan and South African governments (Swilling, 1988a: 6).

The other major element of political reform, the Black Local Authorities Act of 1982, constitutionalized apartheid in the sense that it allocated control over education, health, and "group areas" to the relevant "own affairs" authority. This represented another element of the reform strategy, an attempt to substitute central state control of the black population with indirect and decentralized means. The Black Local Authorities Act gave highly unpopular and frequently corrupt township governments a range of new powers and responsibilities. As Robert Price (1991: 133) puts it, the aim of devolution was "indirect rule – blacks controlling blacks . . . [to] substitute for the coercive fist of the white state." At the same time, in a move designed to retain overall control, President Botha greatly expanded the role of the State Security Council (SSC) as an "inner Cabinet" in which certain senior Cabinet ministers, administrative heads of some state departments, and the top officers in the army, police, and intelligence services deliberated upon security matters and monitored the administration of the state. The SSC fashioned decisions on issues prior to their discussion at Cabinet meetings. It was the key decision-making body in the fields of security and foreign policy under Botha (Schrire, 1991: 36–42).

6 Arend Lijphart, the leading scholar on consociationalism or consociational democracy, defines it as government by a grand coalition of the political leaders of all significant segments of a plural society. The other basic elements are (1) the mutual veto or "concurrent majority" rule, which serves as an additional protection of vital minority interests, (2) proportionality as the principal standard of political representation, civil service appointments, and allocation of public funds, and (3) a high degree of autonomy for each segment to run its own internal affairs (Lijphart, 1977: 25).

Reform thus entailed three processes: (1) educating and training blacks and allowing them upward economic mobility, with the hope of producing a black middle class loyal to the status quo; (2) regional development aimed at alleviating the poverty of the Bantustans to lead to a devolution of power to the regions where mechanisms of consultation between the races would be built from the ground up; (3) granting political representation to Coloureds and Indians, and erecting the organizational structures of a confederation of states, beginning with the President's Council (see Giliomee, 1982: 34–42, 136). The state's so-called Total Strategy thus was an effort at a kind of technocratic revolution from above, entailing initiatives in four areas: urban policy, industrial relations, the creation of a consociational/confederal constitutional framework to reorder the institutions of political representation, and the reorganization of the security and intelligence apparatuses.

THE RISE OF BLACK CIVIL SOCIETY RESISTANCE

Contrary to the government's hopes, the reform strategy served to reawaken black opposition. The Soweto uprising had repoliticized urban blacks; the resurgent labor movement taught previously powerless people that through organization and collective action, they could make real gains. As Steven Friedman (1987: 8–9) writes, perhaps a bit romantically but not inaccurately,

> It is because they have won rights in the factories that workers are demanding them in the townships. . . . This is why all those 'humdrum', 'routine' battles in the factories are so important, why they are so political and why they have affected politics in the black townships. . . . It is because they have controlled their own organisations that they are demanding that community groups also allow their members to control decisions. . . . The battle in the factories has not only strengthened the movement for change, but has also given birth to a type of politics which has been rarely seen among the powerless here: a grassroots politics which stresses the ability of ordinary men and women, rather than 'great leaders', to act to change their world.

The trade unions successfully opposed the government's plan to exclude migrant workers from the unions. Unions affiliated with the Federation of South African Trade Unions (FOSATU), established in

1978–79, not only insisted on seeking registration for unions with migrant workers, but also on a nonracial basis. By 1983 new independent unions had an organizing presence in 756 workplaces and had signed formal agreements with management in 420 of these. By 1985 the number of workplaces in which organizing was occurring reached 3,400. "Man"-days of labor lost to strike activity in 1985 were over ten times greater than the annual average in the immediate pre–Wiehahn era (Webster, 1988; Price, 1991: 163–164). Migrant workers, the backbone of the new unions, began to organize and mobilize alongside urban insiders, thus undermining the Riekert strategy that attempted to divide the working classes along urban–rural lines (Swilling, 1988a: 8). The economic collapse of the Bantustans and the shortage of land there spurred migrant interest in unions, because to return to homelands meant to starve. Dismissal or retrenchment meant loss of job and loss of access to urban areas. Some individual unions extended activities beyond the shop floor, by way of the creation of shop steward councils in the townships and alliances with community and political organizations (Webster, 1988; Maree, 1985). In the aftermath of the Soweto uprising through 1983, hundreds of community organizations formed to address the everyday concerns of township residents, from wretched and insufficient housing, forced removals, rent hikes, bus fares, and the like. These were informal associations of civic, church, and youth groups that took up community grievances with local officials and businessmen, that orchestrated rent strikes and boycotts, and that battled the government-aligned Community Councils (and later the Black Local Authorities). In the black townships of the Transvaal, these organizations included the Evaton Ratepayers Association, the Soweto Civic Association, the Vaal Civic Association, the Krugersdorp Residents Organisation, the Duduza Civic, the East Rand People's Organisation, to name but a few. Perhaps the most effective civic nationwide was the Port Elizabeth Black Civic Organisation, better known as Pebco (see, among others, Cooper and Ensor, 1981; Seekings, 1988; McCarthy and Swilling, 1984; Grest and Hughes, 1984; Shubane, 1991).

The government's constitutional reforms galvanized the widespread, but splintered black opposition into forming a national political organization, the United Democratic Front (UDF), in 1983. The UDF, organized primarily at the local level and embracing a deliberately vague nonracialism, described itself as a loose alliance of almost 600 community organizations and trade unions of varying sizes.

As Mark Swilling (1988b) shows, the UDF was multiclass and multirace, its leadership drawn from almost all factions of black liberation politics and spanning four generations of political protest. The front began with a high profile campaign to oppose municipal elections in townships in November 1983 and the Coloured and Indian parliamentary elections in August 1984. It progressed to campaigns to oppose black town councils, to orchestrate boycotts, and, finally, to make the townships "ungovernable." The overall rallying cry during the campaign against the constitution and tricameral Parliament was a defense of nonracial democracy, and, though there was an inchoate nature to UDF ideology, its Charterist and socialist orientations were clear.[7] Yet this was not top–down movement. Momentum for the struggle came from township civic organizations, most of which had originated in the local indigenous struggles against rent and fare increases and the effort to undermine township councillors. In fact, according to Jeremy Seekings, early on the UDF was relatively uninvolved in township struggles. The UDF focused most of its attention to the national issue of the tricameral parliamentary elections. It was only by 1985, when it was clear that township struggles were the key element in internal opposition politics, that the UDF gave greater representation to civics.

Police repression escalated the new politics of protest into broad insurrections in the black townships, provoking a further centralization

---

7 As Martin Legassick (1998) argues, though the ANC was only marginally involved in the formation of the mass organizations of the 1980s, the *idea* of the congress was invoked. The ANC was conceived of as standing for revolutionary social transformation, and the Freedom Charter was understood as a program for socialism. In a kind of revisionist history, the ANC contends now that the UDF was actually the ANC's internal wing, that the community organizations established from 1980 onward were consciously organized by the ANC (see G. Mbeki, 1996: 45–47, 53–55, 69; African National Congress, 1996a: 54–55). But this flies in the face of most of the evidence. While much united the UDF and ANC, their resonance was largely in spirit, rather than in direct operational fact. The community organizations developed as mass organizations out of a response to local grievances, encouraged by the militancy of the youth and the resilience of trade union organization. The switch from Black Consciousness to Charterist politics, Legassick maintains, took place through a gradual internal recognition among trade union and youth activists of the significance of the black working class and of class struggle – as a solution to national as well as social grievances – rather than through direct intervention from outside. Where the ANC did exercise influence was at the ideological and symbolic levels, and this powerfully colored the overall terms in which internal resistance actions were couched – hence the formidable resonance of the ANC's calls for "ungovernability" and a "people's war" (Marais, 1998: 54). Still, the ANC's calls for "ungovernability" *followed*, rather than anticipated or directed, the internal insurrection. Indeed, the internal insurrection pushed the ANC to change its official position on the anti-apartheid struggle from one of guerrilla warfare to that of mass insurrection.

of power in the state and military through the declaration of martial law. Reform apartheid thus meant reform and repression (see, among others, Collinge, 1986; Mufson, 1990; Lodge et al., 1991; Marx, 1992). Two "states of emergency" were declared: one from July 1985 to March 1986, the second from June 1986 to December 1986. Mainline troops of the South African Defence Force became occupying armies in many townships, particularly those in which the UDF was most active. Nearly 8,000 people were detained under the first State of Emergency; almost 30,000 were detained under the second. Many hundreds of activists were murdered (Republic of South Africa, 1998e). The government banned numerous UDF-affiliated organizations and eventually the UDF itself (Price, 1991: 258–263).

The township civic organizations must be understood within the concrete South African political context of the resistance to white rule and later the transition to democracy and majority rule. As discussed in Chapter 1, the civics had functioned as loci both for opposition to apartheid and local self-help in the context of making the townships ungovernable during the liberation struggle. As part of this opposition to white rule, many civics inaugurated participatory, consultative mechanisms for deciding upon political strategies, rent and service boycotts, etc. The UDF formulated a strategy of linking the destruction of apartheid to the positive tactic of township residents taking control of their own communities. Some UDF affiliates started to position themselves as alternatives to the official government. In townships where rent and consumer boycotts were particularly successful, civics became involved in negotiations with local businessmen and local government officials. In a few townships, mainly in the Eastern Cape but also in large Pretoria–Witwatersrand–Vereeniging townships such as Alexandra, civics developed loosely subordinate hierarchies of area and street committees that performed many local government functions, including refuse collection, policing, and dispute resolution through people's courts. Such organization was instrumental in obtaining consensus for mounting consumer boycotts and other actions. In some areas, such as Port Elizabeth, the efforts at self-governance and particularly effective consumer boycotts induced local white leaders to call for a nonracial municipality. On the other hand, in areas where grassroots organization was weak, physical force, particularly from youth, was more frequent. Indeed, according to Seekings, the impetus of civic activities during 1985–86 was aimed at restoring some order in response to youth militancy and violence (Swilling, 1988b; Mufson, 1990: 104–133, 240–245; Seekings, 1992).[8]

The youth congresses and civic associations eventually took their cue from the black trade union experience, attempting to practice a form of direct democracy in which leaders and representatives functioned as bearers of public mandates (see Baskin, 1991). The black unions that arose after the 1973 Durban strikes developed a very strong practice of representative accountability, centering on the role and responsibilities of the shop steward. The new unions sought to avoid the example of the earlier South African Congress of Trade Unions (SACTU), which had been a "political" union federation closely identified with the ANC in the 1950s and which did not possess much organization or power on the shop floor. The state repression that banned the ANC and sent its leaders into prison and exile in the 1960s also destroyed SACTU. The new independent unions of the 1970s devoted their attention to building democratic shop-floor structures around the principles of worker control, accountability, the mandating of worker representatives, and to developing a working class leadership in the factories (Webster, 1988). Shop stewards were expected to consult with the membership heavily in a system of organization described as "relentless participatory democracy" (MacShane, Plaut, and Ward, 1984; Webster, 1984). The Federation of South African Trade Unions (FOSATU), created in 1978, concentrated on bread and butter trade union issues and on establishing strong, internal structures and shop-floor organization. FOSATU unions thus tended to be politically tentative, wary of compromising their nascent internal democratic and disciplined structures of accountability by allying with politically inchoate groups. FOSATU unions were leery of participating with activist organizations, which, in the unionists' view, had no structures of mandating and accountability. During the early UDF period, FOSATU was challenged by "community unions," including the General and Allied Workers Union, the South African

8 Township youth organizations vacillated between community protection and simple criminal violence, legitimated by political ideology. Though the communal organizations of the 1980s changed popular attitudes to unjust authority, altered popular expectations from government, and instilled more egalitarian values, they often did not acknowledge the moral legitimacy of political differences. As Tom Lodge (1996) explains, their pyramidal structure reflected a view of the community as an organic unity. A somewhat parallel gap between theory and practice was true of the UDF. The UDF did have a strong ideological commitment to grounding its decision making in "community-wide consultation," a doctrine taken over from the trade union movement, but its leaders did not always practice what they preached (Lodge, 1992; also Seekings, 1993; Friedman and Reitzes, 1995).

Allied Workers Union, the National Federation of Workers, which were more political and which were affiliated with the UDF. Among other things, these latter unions organized parallel consumer boycotts of companies under strike.

By 1984, the crisis in the townships and the general level of nationwide political mobilization were forcing unions to take an appropriate stand. FOSATU locals began to meet with student and youth organizations to exchange views. A successful two-day stayaway in the Transvaal in November 1984 involved coordinated action between trade unions and political organizations. Other coordinated actions followed. Association with the trade unions produced organizational effects within many civic associations and UDF, particularly at the level of adopting the labor-derived mechanisms of local popular empowerment and accountability. As a "UDF Message" put it the February 1986 edition of *Grassroots*, one of the most successful community newspapers at the time, "Our structures must become organs of peoples' power . . . Ordinary people [must] increasingly take part in all the decisions . . . Few people making all the decisions must end" (cited in Lodge, 1996: 193). There was a great emphasis on the requirement that leaders of civics and political organizations receive a popular mandate through continuous mass meetings and "report backs" (Price, 1991: 182). This is not to paint an overly rosy picture. The scope of internal democracy and accountability was very uneven. The "ungovernability" campaign encompassed an element of violence and rage that often escaped the control of UDF and civic organization structures and principles. Despite the ideal of people's democracy, there were limits on differences of opinion within the UDF or its constituent organizations. Notwithstanding, starting out as a reactive politics of protest, the UDF evolved to encompass a politics of transformation parallel to the trade union movement, where internal democracy and rigorous procedures of accountability began to replace loose elitist committees (Ritchken, 1989).

The trade union movement wasn't just a model for civic and UDF practices. Like the unions, the mass organizations of the 1980s articulated a socialist ideology. As Tom Lodge (Lodge et al., 1991: 134) has written, "Working-class identity and a socialist understanding of exploitation were two constant themes in the public rhetoric and personal perceptions of [UDF] rank-and-file activists. . . . Evidence suggests a substantial proportion of the UDF's working-class following was inspired by a socialist vision." Labor itself provided leadership of the popular struggle after the establishment of the Congress of South

African Trade Unions (COSATU) in 1985 and in the wake of the repression from the government's state of emergency. In November 1985 the two union groups joined forces with a third, the National Union of Mineworkers (which had broken from the Black Consciousness–based Council of Unions of South Africa federation [CUSA]) to establish COSATU, a nonracial union federation with 450,000 dues-paying members.[9] COSATU issued a manifesto to the effect that the struggle for workers' rights on the shop floor was inseparable from the broader political struggle. At its second national conference in 1987 COSATU adopted the ANC's Freedom Charter and acknowledged the ANC as the leading force in the liberation struggle.[10] The labor federation also finally resolved in favor of constructive "disciplined alliances" with mass-based, democratic and nonracial community organizations. On May Day 1986 COSATU brought out 1.5 million workers to the streets. Especially after the banning of the UDF and sixteen other organizations in February 1988, the trade unions took on the responsibility of continuing the anti-apartheid struggle. COSATU helped reassert mass politics with the February 1989 Defiance Campaign, in which 3 million workers participated in a national stayaway in protest of segregated government-controlled facilities such as hospitals and schools, and in response to police shootings (Lodge et al., 1991: 84–112). Meanwhile, the banned UDF constituent groups regrouped into the Mass Democratic Movement (MDM), with labor playing a leading role.

THE ECONOMY

Reform apartheid and the resistance to it magnified existing economic troubles. New programs contributed to the expansion of public expenditure. These included not just expenditures for the improvement of black housing and education, but the "own affairs–own areas" policy meant a profusion of new bureaucracies. Martial law and military

---

9 The unionization of mineworkers (the National Union of Mineworkers was founded in 1982) structurally began to bridge the divide between FOSATU and the community unions, between the shop-floor orientation and a broader political stance. Mineworkers were migrant workers, living in hostels, with problems and grievances that transcended narrow shop-floor union activities. A widening of the scope of union action beyond production moved the shop-floor unions closer to the community unions and the political organizations generally.

10 COSATU's loyalty to the ANC was qualified in some respects. COSATU highlighted that the Freedom Charter provided only a set of "minimum democratic demands" that did not diminish the federation's commitment to "economic transformation based on working class interests" (see Marx, 1992: 205).

actions in neighboring countries required significant expenses for policing and the deployment of the Defence Force (see Savage, 1986).[11] When experienced in tandem with a virtual cessation of foreign investment and a debt crisis (both tied to international reaction to the state's repression), these generated highly undesirable economic effects. Real average economic growth rates slowed to about 1 percent per year in the 1980s. Taking population growth into account, this meant a decline of 1.3 percent per year in GDP. In contrast, the growth rate of South African GDP had been an average of 5.6 percent per annum during 1964–1971; 4.6 percent for the period 1967–1974; and 3.2 percent for the period 1974–1982 (Republic of South Africa, 1984a: 123). Inflation in the 1980s, although it did not approach the hyperinflation of many Latin American countries, was considerable, running at an average of 14 percent from 1977, the year after Soweto, through 1990 (cited in South African Institute of Race Relations, 1992: 412). The rand lost $3^1/_2$ times its value during the same period, from U.S. $1.15 to 31 cents (cited in South African Institute of Race Relations, 1992: 410). Job creation dropped from 157,000 per year between 1960 and 1974, to 57,000 per year between 1974 and 1985 (Gelb, 1991: 6). Foreign capital influx changed from more than 10 percent of the total investment during the period 1946–1976 to a net outflow after 1976 (cited in Republic of South Africa, 1984a: 139–146). Between 1984 and 1988, more than R25 billion flowed out of the country (cited in Price, 1991: 228).[12]

The fall in the value of the rand from 1980 meant that South Africa's real foreign debt escalated dramatically. External debt as a proportion of GDP grew from 20.3 to 45.7 percent between 1980 and 1984. Because foreign exchange inflows had slowed to a trickle, servicing the debt had to be paid out of whatever trade surpluses could be achieved in the face of international sanctions and out of the country's declining foreign reserves (O'Meara, 1996: 355). Although South Africa was considered an "underborrowed" country, the pressure of debt repayment and the need for continuing large surpluses on the current account of the balance of payments constituted a major constraint on South Africa's overall economic policy. The economic strains from accelerated debt

11 The real costs for police and defense forces were mostly hidden. The *Weekly Mail* put a conservative estimate of spending for security at 25% to 30% of the 1987–88 budget or at 8% to 9% of GDP (*Weekly Mail*, March 11, 1988, cited in O'Meara, 1996: 354).

12 To be sure, some of the poor economic performance reflected the fall in the price of gold, still a major export. The price of gold peaked in 1980 at U.S. $612.94 per ounce and fell to an average of $375.85 in 1982 and $317.29 in 1985 (cited in South African Institute of Race Relations, 1992: 409).

repayment, combined with blocked access to new foreign capital, were exacerbated by trade sanctions (Economist Intelligence Unit, 1992: 51–52; Lewis, Jr., 1990: 111). International sanctions, dismissed by many as an insignificant symbolic gesture, did indeed have a variety of effects on the South African economy. When foreign companies left South Africa they sold their operations to domestic conglomerates, which then consolidated operations and reduced the workforce. This led to a significant loss of jobs and a drain on the economy generally. It also concentrated the economy even further (Clarke, 1991). A good portion of the foreign debt was generated by the parastatals, which had borrowed on international capital markets to finance extensive growth in the 1970s and early 1980s. The Reserve Bank had provided them with forward exchange cover for periods of up to ten years. According to Ewald Wessels (1995, 1996a,b), a member of the executive of the Cape Chamber of Commerce and Industry, that practice incurred a loss of some R15 billion in the 1980s. It also generated another set of consequences: The cost of parastatal debt subsidies, among other things, meant that domestic consumption had to be cut back by means of high interest rates; these interest rates would also reduce imports, the aim of which was to generate surpluses in the balance of trade; and the surpluses would then provide the billions of rand in foreign exchange the bank had underwritten for the parastatals. The result was even less available capital for the private economy.[13] In this context, the complaint of the business community that government spending – officially rising to about 30 percent of GDP (and not counting the often hidden allocations to police and defense) – was crowding out the private sector, no longer fell on deaf ears (see Republic of South Africa, 1979c, 1985c). During the period 1977–1982, for example, R2.897 billion flowed out of the country: R5.178 billion flowed out of the private sector and R2.281 billion flowed into the public sector. In the decade 1971–1980 approximately two-thirds of all capital available for investment was gobbled up by the public sector, in particular by the three main infrastructure parastatals – ESCOM, SAPT, and the South African Transport Services, formerly known as SAR&H (Republic of South Africa, 1984a: 140–143).

---

13 One indication of the lack of capital can be seen in the ratio of gross domestic fixed investment to GDP, which fell from 27.7% in 1982 to 18.7% in 1987. Real domestic fixed investment declined by 31%. By 1987 gross fixed investment had shrunk back to the level it had been in 1973 (South African Reserve Bank, *Quarterly Bulletin*, June 1988, cited in O'Meara, 1996: 354).

Economic decline had political effects. Government debt, worsened by international financial sanctions and the absence of investment capital, strengthened arguments for "rolling back the state" in the economic sphere. Murmurings of privatization were discussed in the press and Parliament as early as the mid-1980s. In his 1984 address to the House of Assembly, Finance Minister B. J. du Plessis for the first time raised the issue of the possible privatization of public services (Republic of South Africa, 1984b). He introduced the concept of deregulation in a 1985 budget speech (Republic of South Africa, 1985a). From then on one finds a good deal of public discourse about government monopolies and privatization, about the need to stimulate economic activity through deregulation (see, e.g., Republic of South Africa, 1985b: Vol. 4, cols. 6687–6688). A confidential 1986 report of the Economic Advisory Council of the State President on Proposed Long-Term Economic Strategy (Republic of South Africa, 1986b) and a 1987 White Paper on Privatisation and Deregulation (Republic of South Africa, 1987) recommended privatization. The Postmaster General, for example, referred to the mention of the Post Office's possible privatization in the 1984–85 SAPT *Annual Report.* Discussions of privatization began to filter out into scholarly and popular forums as well (see, e.g., Wassenaar, 1977; Brand, 1988; Truu, 1988). Here the example of the West, and of the United Kingdom in particular, with the dramatic monetarism of the Thatcher government, and the privatizations of British Telecom and British Gas, had real influence. For, despite the long contentious relationship between Afrikaans and English speakers, and between the National Party and the English Commonwealth, the United Kingdom has remained something of a model for white South Africa. In the context of the National Party's reform strategy and attempts at class realignment, the diffusion of the new, emerging international economic orthodoxy to South Africa does not seem surprising. Privatization was adopted as part of the government's long-term economic strategy in 1987 (Republic of South Africa, 1987).

To be sure, South Africa's economic decline could not in any simple way be laid at the door of reform apartheid and black resistance. The economic problems were already there. One comprehensive study of manufacturing concluded that South Africa's poor manufacturing performance since the mid-1970s was attributable to low investment and low productivity. And, though several factors underlay these, a major reason was the negative impact on productive efficiency rooted in the highly centralized and inegalitarian character of South

African industrial organization (Joffe et al., 1995). The South African economy, as we have seen, was characterized by a high degree of concentrated, conglomerated ownership and a wide array of key commodities being produced in highly concentrated markets. As David Lewis explains,

> [W]hilst oligopolistic markets may be reflected in intense competition between their participants, this all too frequently gives rise to cosy collusion; in particular, domination at key points in the productive chain and ubiquitous vertical integration underpins the weakness of SMEs [small and medium sized enterprises]; and while concentrated corporate control may accord shareholders an unusual degree of authority over operational managers, it drastically narrows the entrepreneurial base of the society – the incentives that derive from a share of effective ownership are extremely narrowly focused. (Lewis, 1995: 135)

Concentrated markets and conglomerated ownership structures have the consequence of undermining small and medium-size enterprises domestically (widely understood to be key elements of a modern, competitive manufacturing sector) *and* of raising barriers for prospective imports of both commodities and capital. Moreover and counterintuitively, they also underpin the persistent inability of large, long-standing, and well-resourced South African manufacturers to penetrate international markets, as they induce an inward orientation and lack of dynamism (Lewis, 1995: 143–145).

The industrial policies of the apartheid government exacerbated these structural tendencies. Here lies one connection between the expansive parastatals and the concentrated, inefficient, and underinvested private economy. Government policies systematically raised domestic prices of semiprocessed raw materials to levels far higher than their international equivalents, contributing more than anything else, according to Ewald Wessels (1996b), to the high cost of manufacturing in South Africa. A two-tier manufacturing economy was created with inefficient, hugely capital-intensive, subsidized, and protected mineral beneficiation industries extracting high prices from the more labor-intensive downstream industries. A good example of this was steel. In that industry, the parastatal ISCOR used its influence over distributors to restrict free trade in steel, thereby maintaining premium prices on the domestic market. With government blessing, ISCOR's average domestic price was far higher than its average export price (as much as 67% in some years). Such policy may have served to protect ISCOR and, with the exports created by the mineral beneficiation strategy of steel, paper, aluminum, and other products, to help maintain the rand exchange rate. But the result was to raise the input costs to downstream companies significantly, in many instances causing them to shrink, depress wages, or go out of business altogether. Yet the number of people employed in the downstream manufacture and assembly of components for machinery and various other products out of a ton of steel is far higher than the number of people employed in the manufacture of the steel itself. The consequence was that domestic employment opportunities were destroyed as a result of the decline of downstream South African companies. The numbers employed in the steel and engineering industries have dropped more than 40 percent since 1980, representing a loss of more than 180,000 jobs, even though exports of steel have grown.

THE DE VILLIERS INVESTIGATIONS

The arguments to reduce state intervention found a particular target in the parastatals. State President Botha appointed W. J. (Wim) de Villiers, a former Sanlam vice-chairman and executive director of Gencor, its massive mining subsidiary, to investigate the practices and management of the main parastatals. Known as a tough capitalist of high integrity, de Villiers personified the political evolution of the Cape Afrikaner business community that had moved toward the principles of reform apartheid. He published various books in the early 1970s arguing that the crisis of South Africa was a crisis of skills shortage – though in his view, this was largely a function of the nature of black culture rather than due to apartheid structures. At the same time, de Villiers favored the movement of blacks into formerly white-reserved jobs because it was the only way to maintain the existing order of South Africa's apartheid society. Considered radical at the time, de Villiers' thinking essentially anticipated the tenets of reform apartheid. He said in defense of black advancement, "It represents the alternative to drastic and radical change, and is in reality a reformist process which leaves existing values intact" (cited in Jones, 1995: 148).

Apparently much esteemed by President Botha, de Villiers functioned in the mode of what John Waterbury (1992) has identified as a technocratic "change team," whose ability to induce economic policy reform – particularly the liberalization of state-owned enterprises – derives largely from insulation from normal bureaucratic decision-making channels and distributive claims. De Villiers went first to the Electricity Supply Commission (ESCOM). His investigation found that ESCOM had overforecast the demand for electricity and consequently had grossly overinvested in power-generating equipment and power stations in the 1970s and early 1980s. ESCOM invested enormous amounts of capital into new fixed assets that would be grossly under-utilized, possibly for decades to come. De Villiers slammed ESCOM's accounting methods as archaic and incomprehensible, and noted a 25 percent productivity decline in power station employees despite an increase in economies of scale. He recommended a two-tier control structure that would separate the ESCOM board of control from its management board. De Villiers also strongly argued that ESCOM scale back its construction plans and adopt an orientation of financial prudence via energy efficiency, including assuming a leading role in energy conservation. At the same time, his report recommended that the old parastatal principle of operating neither at a profit nor at a loss be discarded in favor of a sound assets and income structure. In concert with this, de Villiers endorsed a complete revamp of ESCOM's antiquated fund accounting system. Many of de Villiers' recommendations were adopted in a 1985 restructuring of ESCOM (Republic of South Africa, 1984a; Horwitz, 1994a).

At de Villiers' next stop, the South African Transport Services (SATS, the renamed and amalgamated Railways and Harbors parastatal, since renamed Transnet), the investigation unearthed similar problems. De Villiers determined that, like ESCOM, SATS had overforecast demand. The gradual migration of goods and passenger traffic from the rails to the roads generated a high percentage of trains running under capacity. And despite a decline in traffic and newer rolling stock, SATS had not trimmed employment at its vast rolling-stock workshops and still employed hundreds of thousands of people. Of all the parastatals, SATS had absorbed the greatest number, by a wide margin, of poor whites under job reservation (Abedian and Standish, 1985). Among de Villiers' key recommendations was that SATS reorganize itself into quasi-independent operating entities with hard budget constraints, price and cost breakouts, and bottom lines (Republic of South Africa, 1986a).

When de Villiers got to the Post Office in 1988, his reputation preceded him. Having found all kinds of problems and ineptitude at ESCOM and SATS, de Villiers fully expected to find the same at SAPT.

Among SAPT management, de Villiers was widely suspected of being simply a hatchet man. As a consequence, some managers refused to cooperate with the investigation. They withheld requested information and even on occasion offered false data. De Villiers was able to gain access by exploiting rifts within SAPT management. Some of the younger managers on the telecommunications side, with business as well as engineering training, and with enough international exposure to see that the international telecommunications environment was changing, cooperated with de Villiers. These managers, most prominent among them Senior Manager Ben Bets, hoped to use de Villiers' expected criticisms to launch the kinds of changes that had begun to liberalize telecommunications parastatals in other parts of the world.

As expected, de Villiers found much to criticize at SAPT. Roughly consonant with the thrust of reform apartheid, the SAPT had begun to expand telephone service to nonwhite areas in the late 1970s (discussed in more detail in Chapter 5). The costs of the new service expansion program were magnified by decisions that had to be made on the switching system. As the SAPT moved to expand service, it faced the problem whether to augment a problematic electromechanical switching system or go digital. It decided to pursue the digital option, which was expensive but appropriate (Taylor, 1992). Together, these projects required a vast infusion of capital, which, as a result of the reforms on Post Office financing, the SAPT was permitted to obtain in loans on the international capital market. The annual capital expenditure on telecommunications equipment increased fivefold over the seven years from 1980–81 to 1986–87, from R340.4 million to R1.7 billion, an average annual rate of 23.5 percent from 1978 to 1987 (Republic of South Africa, 1989: 55; SAPT *Annual Report*, 1987/88). Because expansion had been financed largely through foreign borrowing, the subsequent fall of the rand was a disaster with regard to the SAPT debt. The total loan commitment at March 1988 exchange rates was R4.577 billion, of which R3.25 billion was foreign. Because of exchange rate losses, SAPT's finance costs were 14.5 percent in 1986–87, expected to rise to 27.2 percent in 1990–91 (Republic of South Africa, 1989: 55–57, 62–63). As borrowing became impossible by the mid-1980s, the cost of further service expansion could only be financed by placing a greater burden on existing telephone subscribers.

The costs of cross-subsidization were borne largely by the business sector. According to the de Villiers Report, the actual cost of telephone rental per month in 1987–88 was about R28, though the actual rental charge was R15. Thus telephone rentals were heavily subsidized by higher call tariffs. But a large proportion of subscribers (particularly new, usually nonwhite subscribers) made very few calls per day. In fact, consumer resistance to rising rental and call rates was reflected in the increased use of pay phones and considerably limited the demand for services and call traffic after 1982, leading to lower annual growth rates. As a result SAPT telephone revenues rested on a narrow base of subscribers. Six percent of subscribers (of whom about 78% were business and 22% residential telephone subscribers) contributed 50 percent of the total telephone revenue (Republic of South Africa, 1989: 7, 25).

As a consequence of these factors, de Villiers found that the system was characterized not only by heavy debt but also by a rise in unused capacity – a function, he asserted, of a too rapid conversion to digital technology and an overestimation of demand. De Villiers questioned whether the digital upgrading was justified, given the balance of regular telephone users to value-added users. In other words, de Villiers leveled the now-familiar judgment that SAPT, like ESCOM and SATS, had overforecast demand, but in the context of a more damaging charge that the upgrading of the network was unnecessary – particularly the installation of infrastructure capable of accommodating value-added services to users (for the most part, black) who were barely using the basic telephone service. As a result of the technical improvements to the network and low usage by blacks, de Villiers found the traditional average capacity utilization level of the routes connecting the nine largest cities had dropped to 53 percent. Indeed, de Villiers was quite critical of SAPT estimation of demand for services and in call traffic, calling the forecasts "completely over-estimated" (Republic of South Africa, 1989: 7, 48). In short, de Villiers deemed what he saw as a too rapid conversion to digital technology as goldplating, pure and simple.[14]

14 While the SAPT may not have been a particularly efficient parastatal, de Villiers' condemnation of the decision to digitalize the network was the product of faulty reasoning. Because of the flexibility and long-term economies of digital technologies, de Villiers' judgment on digitalization was understood by most informed telecommunications observers as nonsensical. On a visit to London as he was conducting his investigation, de Villiers was told, in a conversation about digitalization, by Sir John Clark, chairman of Plessey, "Dr. Wim, you are now talking absolute bloody balls" (recounted with great mirth by W. J. Taylor [1992]). Taylor argued that de Villiers' charge of overcapacity was a red herring because with digital exchanges and transmission, a telecommunications operator can provide access lines when needed. Indeed, the evidence is that demand follows the implementation of digital exchanges. This was clearly borne out by the data on the mid-1980s expansion. Despite rapid expansion, the wait list actually *increased* during this time, indicating large pent-up demand for telephone service.

Whereas de Villiers averred that the telecommunications administration of the Post Office should retain its monopoly on the ownership and operation of the network, his report argued strenuously that SAPT be reorganized "to bring the undertaking in line with business principles similar to those applying in the private sector, and more specifically those geared to the norms of return on capital and cost-related rates" (Republic of South Africa, 1989: 84). The report recommended that SAPT significantly revise its schedule of further digitalization of the network and sharply cut back annual capital expenditure. Annual expenditure must be limited to economically justifiable expenditure based only on cost-related rates. Staff appointments should be frozen. The introduction of new control structures should be linked to a gradual elimination of cross-subsidization as far as possible and to the introduction of cost-related rates for all kinds of service. The most consequential recommendations of the report called for the separation of telecommunications from posts and for legislation creating a profit-oriented and tax-paying telecommunications company that would, after a transition period, be privatized.

The various de Villiers reports gave the reform wing of the National Party the intellectual ammunition it needed to proceed toward statutory changes in the organization of the parastatals. In 1985 the government adopted the recommendations of de Villiers' report on the Electricity Supply Commission. It pushed through Parliament an amendment to the Electricity Act to restructure ESCOM (including a new spelling, ESKOM) with an eye toward its future privatization. A similar dynamic yielded the Legal Succession of the South African Transport Services Act of 1989, which in turn created the Transnet group as a public company in April 1991 in accordance with the Companies Act. In his February 1988 address to Parliament, State President Botha devoted a considerable amount of time promoting the benefits of privatization and discussing the government's plans to privatize the major parastatals. He declared:

> The government has already decided in principle to table [in South African idiom, "to table" means to "bring to the table"] the necessary legislative amendments in Parliament for the conversion of Eskom, the South African Transport Services and Posts and Telecommunications into tax-paying profit-seeking enterprises, either in their entirety or after subdivision into appropriate business undertakings. . . . Given the successful reorganisation

achieved in respect of Eskom, the necessary investigations aimed at listing on the Stock Exchange will be undertaken first in its case. (Republic of South Africa, 1988: cols. 7–8)

Accordingly, a "privatisation portfolio" was created in the Cabinet in March 1988 to constitute a new Ministry of Administration and Privatisation. Supporters advocated privatization for the usual reasons: to reduce the involvement of the state in the economy generally; to increase the size of the tax base thereby reducing the individual tax burden; to encourage private share holding; to raise higher allocational and operational efficiency by exposing an artificially protected state monopoly to the discipline of a competitive market. More specifically, proponents sought to promote organizational and managerial reforms in particular economic sectors, to align prices according to actual costs, and to raise the level of investment capital (see Brand, 1988; Truu, 1988; also Taylor, 1990). Government moved toward the privatization option with ISCOR, the iron and steel parastatal. Facing large losses after iron and steel were added to the U.S. embargo on South Africa in 1986, ISCOR was privatized beginning in October 1989, by way of a listing on the Johannesburg Stock Exchange. Over 150,000 investors participated, raising R3 billion for the Treasury. Government had earlier initiated the privatization of Sasol, the state-owned oil and gas parastatal, in three tranches: The holding company Sasol Ltd. was floated in 1979; in 1983 Sasol II was privatized; and Sasol III was privatized in 1991.

In other words, the government's Total Strategy of the mid-1980s – the attempt at a technocratic revolution from above – included a key feature not normally identified by students of recent South African history, that is, the privatization of the parastatals and the general effort to remove or transfer state assets from state control.[15] The commitment of the National Party to parastatal reform did not falter with the change of leadership from P. W. Botha to F. W. de Klerk in 1989. In an often

---

15 The government's late land transfers to the Bantustans can be understood within this rubric, as well. In November 1991 the government announced the transfer of land still held by the South African Development Trust to the homeland of Bophuthatswana. Just before the 1994 election President de Klerk announced the decision to hand over 3 million hectares of land to King Zwelithini under the KwaZulu Ingonyama Trust Act. As Paul B. Rich argues, the motive behind these actions was less the consolidation of the Bantustans, which were doomed as serious political entities, than the preemption of land reform by an ANC-led government. In the Ingonyama case, an added consideration was the need to ensure the Inkatha Freedom Party's participation in the election (Rich, 1996: 54).

ignored part of the famous speech of February 1990, in which he announced the unbanning of the ANC and other liberation organizations, President de Klerk declared his government would continue on the path toward economic reform and privatization. "By means of restricting capital expenditure in parastatal institutions, privatisation, deregulation and curtailing government expenditure, substantial progress has been made already towards reducing the role of the authorities in the economy. We shall persist with this in a well-considered way" (Republic of South Africa, 1990).

The original goal coming out of the various de Villiers investigations was that the parastatals be privatized, with "commercialization" as an interim step (Republic of South Africa, 1988; van Rensburg, 1992). Commercialization was identified as a process whereby a public corporation or state business enterprise would be reoriented according to market principles while still under state control, a sort of way station to prepare market-inexperienced managers for the rigors of competition. In the case of the Post Office, the first step would entail the separation of telecommunications from posts, and the separation of both from the line responsibilities of the ministry. Legislation was introduced to this effect in 1990. But large-scale state reforms are not politically easy, as they reconfigure the balance of beneficiaries and threaten to disrupt electoral coalitions. As previously noted, reform apartheid represented a shift of the National Party from the longtime support of its traditional constituencies of Afrikaner farmers and working class toward urban, middle class Afrikaners and reaching seriously toward business, English-speaking whites, and beyond to Coloured and Indian communities as well. The National Party could manage the political difficulties of reform as long as the overall political situation remained subject to the government's military coercion and the franchise remained limited to whites and hence essentially under NP electoral hegemony. With the unbanning of the ANC in February 1990, the equation changed dramatically. Although it had set in motion a powerful economic reform impulse, the NP could no longer control its outcome. The government set the agenda, but the ANC alliance had the ability (perhaps its only real power at this point in the transition process) to vet policy decisions through its control of the streets and workplaces, and looming in the uncertain future, the vote. On its other flank, the NP now risked further defections of the white electorate to the right wing. In the 1989 election, the NP lost ground to both the Conservative and Democratic parties, receiving just 48 percent of the vote as opposed to 31 percent for the CP and 20-plus percent for the DP.[16] Thus after 1990 the government had to contend with a new balance of political forces and needed to move with some delicacy on the economic policy front.

Privatization was a flashpoint. Reflecting the political sensitivity to privatization, the recently formed Ministry of Administration and Privatisation quickly changed its name to the Ministry of Administration and Economic Coordination on March 15, 1990. Dr. W. J. de Villiers himself – of the various de Villiers Reports – was named minister. The privatization portfolio was transferred to another amalgamated ministry, now called the Ministry for Minerals and Energy Affairs and Public Enterprises.[17] The privatization option was not dropped, just made less visible: It was now embodied as the Policy Unit of that ministry. Significantly, the ministerial control of the commercialized parastatals was transferred to this ministry, as "guardian" of the government's shareholding. Whereas many of the *functions* of the parastatals were still overseen by line ministries, the control of the parastatals themselves now was housed within a separate ministry, that of Public Enterprises. So, for example, jurisdiction over roads, traffic, civil aviation, and airports continued to be exercised by the Ministry of Transport. But SATS, the huge transportation parastatal, was now made the responsibility of the Ministry for Public Enterprises. In the view of the ANC, the change in ministerial control was in preparation for parastatal privatization (Jordan, 1995a).[18]

16 The Conservative Party had broken away from the NP in 1982. The Democratic Party was launched in 1989 out of a merger between the Progressive Federal Party (the party of "English-speaking liberalism") and two very minor political parties of dissident Nationalists who had abandoned the NP in 1987.

17 An unfortunate overlap of names of ministers and name changes of ministries causes confusion here. The original Ministry of Administration and Privatisation was given to Dawie de Villiers. When it changed to the Ministry of Administration and Economic Coordination in March 1990, the portfolio was given to Dr. W. J. (Wim) de Villiers. Dawie de Villiers became minister of Minerals and Energy Affairs and Public Enterprises, within which was housed the Office of Privatisation. Following the death less than a year later of Dr. W. J. de Villiers, Dawie de Villiers became the minister of a further amalgamated portfolio, the Ministry of Economic Coordination and Public Enterprises, in April 1991. In this role, Dawie de Villiers had responsibility for the Office of Privatisation (now renamed the Policy Unit), the Competition Board, the Central Economic Advisory Service, and oversight of Transnet, ESKOM, and Posts and Telecommunications.

18 According to Jordan (1995a), SAPT was on the list to be transferred to Public Enterprises before the process was halted. Then Public Enterprises Minister Dawie de Villiers had actually begun to move his offices into the top floor of the Telkom Towers in Pretoria. But it could be there was another dimension to this, separable from the direct political dimension but inexorably

Soon after it was unbanned the African National Congress exercised its veto power in the matter of parastatal reform. The congress publicly warned that, though it was no longer wed to nationalization as a matter of general policy, public sector corporations and parastatals that were privatized prior to political accommodation would be prime candidates for (re)nationalization (Mandela, 1990; Battersby, 1990). The ANC interpreted the National Party's privatization strategy as a way to take key state apparatuses out of the hands of a future black government, to preempt the future use of state power for purposes of redistribution and patronage. The ANC's pronouncement took the wind out of the sails of the privatization gambit. No one will risk purchasing a privatized parastatal when the potential government-to-be (with a history of espousing theories of command economics) threatens to renationalize it.

The big industrial parastatals such as SATS, ESKOM, and SAPT were not the only state-owned enterprises to be considered for transformation and privatization. The South African Broadcasting Corporation had not been part of the government's proposal to privatize the parastatals in the 1987 *White Paper on Privatisation and Deregulation in the Republic of South Africa* (Republic of South Africa, 1987) – presumably because the broadcaster was seen as too important to the government's Total Strategy against black insurrection. The SABC however did become enmeshed in the ambiguous, suspicious politics of restructuring of the late 1980s, early 1990s. Just a month after de Klerk's February 1990 speech unbanning the black liberation organizations, the Minister of Home Affairs, Gene Louw, appointed a Task Group on Broadcasting in South and Southern Africa, to investigate what should be done with the state broadcaster. Even before the Task Force's recommendations, the SABC had instituted broad changes to television and initiated an internal reorganization along business lines. Amidst the argument that the SABC was inefficient and bloated, TV2/3 and TV4 were consolidated into one multilingual African channel, Contemporary Community Values Television (CCV) in January 1992. The SABC's

intertwined with it. Surely the parastatals were seen by the old regime as state apparatuses to hive off to the private sector in advance of a new political dispensation. But it is also the case that by this point in time, as we have seen, the parastatals were widely perceived by the NP government as being grossly inefficient and a serious fiscal drain on the state. In principle, one way to reform the parastatals would be to seek to eliminate the built-in conflict of responsibilities of a minister having to run a parastatal, safeguard the state's investments, and serve the parastatal's customers at the same time. This could in part explain separating the state's shareholding interest from its line functions, by housing each in different ministries.

1991/92 *Annual Report* speaks of transforming the TopSport Surplus "network" (TSS) into a full-fledged noncommercial channel for airing specialized programs for minority audiences during prime time. The SABC's request for government permission to do so was granted and TSS eventually became National Network Television (NNTV) in February 1994 – a noncommercial educational and public service channel along the lines of the American Public Broadcasting System, operating under a temporary license and with a limited geographical distribution (SABC *Annual Report*, 1990/91, 1991/92; Republic of South Africa, 1995d: 36).

In short, the government's and SABC's attempts at restructuring envisioned moving South African state television toward a commercial white channel (TV1), a commercial black channel (CCV), and a poorly accessible noncommercial public service channel in the American PBS mold (NNTV). Internally, the SABC was reorganized into five business units, each with separate financial responsibility as a profit-making entity. This included the restructuring of its internal production capacity and the establishment of new units to take back production from private producers, allegedly to reduce production costs (Teer-Tomaselli, 1995; SABC, 1994a). The central feature of the structural changes, according to the SABC, was "a desire for market orientation and cost efficiency" (SABC *Annual Report*, 1991/92: 14).

Many read the moves to restructure the SABC as much more than a simple efficiency-driven strategy. Rather, the restructuring thrust was considered entirely "in line with state strategy of privatising parastatals to secure political and economic interests in the private sector" (Republic of South Africa, 1995d: 36). Indeed, the changes contemplated for the broadcast sector were broadly consonant with the reform apartheid strategy of privatizing the parastatals as a subtle, largely hidden market-driven means of entrenching white dominance. On the one hand, a commercial white television channel would guarantee the continued protection and dissemination of the languages and cultures of the white alliance, as well as provide lucrative business opportunities. A black commercial channel, by virtue of the pull of market forces in television, would likely be drawn toward entertainment and away from politics. Any rationale for the retention of state ownership of commercialized channels already fully supported by advertising would fall away. Their privatization could be expected both to bring much-needed revenue into government coffers and provide an attractive vehicle for a safe version of black empowerment. On the other hand, the proposed public service channel, constituted as essentially a minority program transmitter, would be overwhelmed by the commercial channels, and, if the American example held, would have to fight for adequate funding.

What the television and other parastatal restructurings seemed to reflect was a general reform apartheid logic that white interests could be protected by the seemingly natural and impersonal workings of the market and a strong neutral state. State-enforced racial domination would be replaced by the far more subtle and fluid system of domination based on class. Of course, if the existing division of wealth, income, and employment were largely preserved, whites would effectively retain power. This concept, no doubt, in part underlay the impressive ideological shift of the *verligte* or reform wing of the National Party toward bona fide market capitalism and away from state intervention in the 1980s. The *verligte* wing's commencement of negotiations with the ANC did not, of course, contemplate a naive confidence in the ability of the market to safeguard Afrikaner survival and white dominance. This is why in constitutional negotiations the NP was so adamant in its rejection of simple majority rule, the protection of existing property rights and the civil and military bureaucracies, and the insistence on the retention of Afrikaans as an official language (see, among others, Greenberg, 1987; Giliomee, 1992).

Essentially derailed by the black insurrection, reform apartheid's failure highlighted the stalemated situation that afforded F. W. de Klerk, who became National Party leader in February 1989, the room for a new initiative. Notwithstanding the overall failure of reform apartheid, individual aspects of it, such as the transformation of parastatals, continued apace. The next chapter takes up the struggle of the transformation of broadcasting.

CHAPTER 4

"Control Will Not Pass to Us": The Reform Process in Broadcasting

The political dynamic of the first couple of years after February 1990 consisted of the government positioning itself for negotiations and moving ahead in "reform" efforts that would alter the nature of the relationship between the economy and the state, while the ANC found itself in catch-up mode, trying to make a rapid transition from an exiled liberation movement to a functioning political party. The general political situation was, of course, more complicated than this. From 1990 to 1992 the Afrikaner hard-line and shadowy movement of military operatives (called by observers the "Third Force") engaged in a largely successful effort to disturb the path of negotiations by killing key political persons, fueling civil strife, and exacerbating the hostility between the ANC and the Inkatha Freedom Party. But in most of the issues of the 1990–94 transition period, the main protagonists were the National Party and the ANC. This was particularly true in the media policy arena. The Democratic Party was occasionally active in the debate, particularly when broadcast issues entered the CODESA constitutional negotiations, but in the end was a minor player. The Conservative Party, the Pan-Africanist Congress, and the Inkatha Freedom Party were virtually invisible in the media policy arena.

The National Party's various policy thrusts – particularly those concerning the parastatals – were ensconced within a stealthy bit of politics that amalgamated a needed transformation of old apartheid state-owned enterprises with a stratagem to secure white dominance by establishing market-oriented structures for these institutions. With the ANC returning from exile, it fell to the United Democratic Front/Mass Democratic Movement to organize the anti-apartheid alliance's opposition. The MDM began to counter the government's various policy efforts by creating the stakeholder forums described in Chapter 1. The forums, whose principles, mechanisms, and culture derived largely from the township civic organizations and the black trade union movement, were constituted both to prevent the government from making decisions unilaterally and to open up the policy agenda in keeping with the culture of democratic consultation and transparency.

The government's early policy initiatives included the reform of broadcasting. This is not surprising, given broadcasting's importance for the control and dissemination of ideology, and in view of the deep-rooted anxiety concerning the perpetuation of Afrikaans language and culture. What complicates the story is that the SABC really *did* face serious problems, for reasons logically separate from, though bound up with, its apartheid design. The SABC was an organization that had grown too large for its traditional structure of centralized control. The expansion brought by the introduction of television, in conjunction with the typical pattern of white employment growth in the parastatals, had led to large staff increases in the 1980s, with some managers building mini-empires, according to Neel Smuts (1996), former member of the SABC Management Board. In Smuts's judgment, top appointments to the SABC always suffered because they were made with a view toward politics and factional compromises within the National Party, rather than on the basis of actual managerial competence. SABC staff numbers rose to a high of 7,033 in 1984 and began to decrease slowly thereafter until 1989 (SABC *Annual Reports*, 1984–1987). And notwithstanding a bloated staff component, much television production – particularly programming in Afrikaans – was commissioned out. Commissioning editors gave work to favored producers, often extending the Broeder-bond connection throughout the television production industry. According to one account, an association of production houses and producers, including INTV, Pro-Five, Fanie van der Merwe, and J. P. Niemand, with links to the best Afrikaner families, got the biggest contracts (Haffajee, 1998b). The SABC budget deficits, compounded by inflation and the decline of the rand, rose as a consequence of staff expansion and commissioned production. SABC posted losses of R27.1 million in 1985, R27.9 million in 1986, and R13.2 million in 1987. From the mid-1980s onward, the SABC was an institution continually trying to reorganize itself. Every year the annual report described this or that consultant's analysis, announced this or that organizational restructuring. Indeed, in keeping with the government's early forays into privatization policy, the SABC 1986 *Annual Report* mentioned the possibility of privatization as one mode of restructuring.

The internal organizational changes the SABC had begun to put into effect in the early 1990s – including the creation of separate business units and the consolidation of television services – were designed to deal with the problems of financial losses and lack of control. They were engineered by Quentin Green, a businessman originally brought over from Sasol (the coal and oil parastatal) to take on the financial portfolio of the SABC Management Board. Green became chief executive of SABC Television. According to Neel Smuts (1996), Green was less of a political man than a businessman; he brought a strong emphasis on commercial activity. Green may not have been a political appointment, but his commercial orientation was very much in keeping with the *verligte* wing of the National Party. Hence the SABC's internal reorganization was parallel to the commercialization process that had been brought to other parastatals such as the South African Posts and Telecommunications and the South African Transport Services (see Group of Thirteen, 1994b: 44).

Intimately bound up with the SABC's organizational difficulties was the problem of financing, particularly as both domestic and international competition were coming to bear on South African broadcasting. Domestic competition had a paradoxical source. As part of the progression of the apartheid policy of separate development, the Bantu radio stations in the "independent" homelands, Radios Transkei, Bophuthatswana, Venda, and Ciskei (TBVC), had been transferred to the homeland authorities as they became "independent states." Capital Radio, a station launched from Transkei in 1979, tried to transmit its commercial, top-40 popular music format into South Africa's PWV Province. But Capital was dependent on permission from South Africa for access to the airwaves and on the SABC for technical assistance. According to a Capital Radio manager, the independent nature of Capital Radio's news kept South Africa from granting Capital the necessary transmission facilities (Group of Thirteen, 1994b: 17). Bophuthatswana broadcasting was the main source of competition for the SABC and of peculiar political difficulties for the South African government. Geographically, Bophuthatswana was spread over large parts of the Transvaal in discrete and discontinuous clumps. Radio Bophuthatswana, which broadcasts in English, began in 1978, grew steadily, and could be picked up in various parts of the PWV. A second signal, operated by Bophuthatswana Commercial Radio, began broadcasting on medium wave in June 1980 under the name of Channel

702.[1] Its rapid rise in popularity prompted SABC to launch Radio Metro in 1986 to compete with it. In the mid-to-late 1980s, 702 adopted a predominantly talk format and became 702 Talk Radio. By 1989 it had a million listeners. Both 702 and Capital Radio gave a limited amount of wiggle room for anti-apartheid views during the 1980s' states of emergency. Radio 702 in particular became a forum for real news, if only because it was able to practice something approximating liberal journalism during the states of emergency. After airing official South African government press releases, 702 would typically air other perspectives, which included those of the United Democratic Front. The talk radio format also opened up cultural avenues that had no existence within the closed world of SABC broadcasting.[2]

Bophuthatswana television, or Bop-TV, took to the airwaves in 1984. To reach its "citizens," Bop-TV had an agreement with SABC to use the latter's Johannesburg, Krugersdorp, and Pretoria transmitters, providing that Bop-TV comply with certain content restrictions – namely, not to broadcast material that "undermines law and order in South Africa." Bop-TV's signal could not be easily contained, and it spilled not only into Soweto but into some white parts of Johannesburg as well. It quickly attracted a large audience. Equally as quickly, the SABC erected a new aerial system on its Brixton Tower to cut down on the spillage into white areas, an action that prompted a broad, though unsuccessful petition campaign. Whereas for the most part Bop-TV was the mouthpiece of the homeland chief, Lucas Mangope, it too occasionally offered a delimited avenue for a certain amount of media resistance. Bop-TV interviewed banned South African opposition figures, such as ANC leaders Oliver Tambo and Winnie Mandela in 1984, and later aired an interview with South African Communist Party head, Joe Slovo. Bop-TV began leasing a satellite transponder in 1988 to relay its signal, one result of which, in principle, was the reception of its signal free of South African control (Group of Thirteen, 1994b: 18).

1 Channel 702 was owned and controlled by Kirsh Industries, a private South African company, with a 40% stake, and the Bophuthatswana Government through its holdings in the Yabeng Company (20%), and Sunbop (20%). The remaining shares were held by the four South African press groups with a 5% stake each. Kirsh ran the station from studios in downtown Johannesburg, relaying its signal via SAPT microwave links to its transmitters in Bophuthatswana (Republic of South Africa, 1991d: 48).

2 For example, one of the 702 talk DJs, a former Irish rugby player, was adept at hearing the hidden racist assumptions in South African speech. A caller into a program might preface his perspective with the preamble, "I'm not a racist," and the DJ would interject quickly and loudly, "BUT," the effect of which would underscore the hidden racist construction.

The TBVC broadcasters thus brought some competition to the SABC. But the real competition to SABC came from within the white power structure itself. Casino resort mogul Sol Kerzner approached the government in 1982 with a proposal to set up a pay television channel. Cabinet demurred, but was receptive shortly afterward when approached by the management of Nasionale Pers, the Afrikaans press conglomerate. Despite resistance from the SABC, the government appointed a task group in 1985 to investigate the desirability of permitting subscription television and quickly awarded the concession to the Electronic Media Network (M-Net) – the proposal of the press consortium. Nasionale Pers, fronted by Naspers Chairman and Broederbonder Ton Vosloo, was awarded the largest ownership stake (at 26 percent) along with responsibility for managing the new subscription television license. The Argus Group, Times Media Limited, and Perskor each took 23 percent ownership, with Dispatch Media and the Natal Witness receiving the remaining 5 percent. Because of the pyramid holding schemes of the press conglomerates in South Africa, this meant that ownership and control of M-Net was effectively Sanlam and Anglo-American (Group of Thirteen, 1994b: 21; Dison, 1996).[3]

In effect the state had given particular private parties an immensely valuable privilege – a monopoly on a new media form. The overt rationale for the award was to halt the erosion of newspaper advertising revenue, particularly from the Afrikaans language press, to television. The conspiratorial interpretation is that the creation of M-Net was part of a deal the government struck with the press groups to close the *Rand Daily Mail* and the *Sunday Express*, the most critical establishment newspapers. That deal underscored the mid-1980s attempt to forge a rapprochement between big business and the government. The quid pro quo, crudely, was that big English business would silence the government's most vocal establishment press voices and the government would move forward with economic reform. In this view, no other scenario can explain the government's surprising sustenance of the English language press groups, toward which it had been historically so hostile (see R. Tomaselli and K. Tomaselli, 1987: 79–86; Harber, 1997; R. Louw, 1997). The closing of the *RDM* was thus one element of Botha's efforts to align business with his reform apartheid initiatives. Just to be safe

---

3 In 1990 M-Net went semipublic, with a listing on the Johannesburg Stock Exchange. Twenty-two percent of the ownership was floated. Nasionale Pers retained its 26% stake, the Argus Group and Times Media Limited dropped to 18% each, Perskor to 12%, Dispatch Media and the Natal Witness 2% each.

politically, however, Naspers, historically tied to the National Party and its *verligte* wing, was guaranteed the M-Net management contract in perpetuity.[4]

M-Net began its subscription broadcast service via an encrypted signal on terrestrial frequencies in October 1986, airing primarily American feature films, soap operas, and international sporting events. It was not permitted to air news. M-Net expanded its footprint by adding satellite distribution in 1991. Notwithstanding its effective control by Naspers, an Afrikaans company, M-Net's programming is overwhelmingly in English. Its local program content and Afrikaans language requirements have been changed several times in favor of giving flexibility to the company. Cabinet even approved an arrangement in 1987 whereby SABC was obliged to make available its TV4 channel to M-Net between 6 and 7 P.M. so that M-Net could relay its programs during an "open time" on an SABC channel. This arrangement lasted a year (SABC *Annual Report*, 1987). There is little clarity over M-Net's actual "license." There are apparently several licenses, some of which, in the words of Alison Gillwald (1996), Independent Broadcasting Authority (IBA) manager of policy development, "are little more than typescripts composed by a minister after hastily agreeing to changes requested by his M-Net friends."[5] As part of the continuing story of back-channel deals between M-Net and the apartheid government, just months before the passage of the Independent Broadcasting Authority Act in 1993, M-Net secured a second channel as part

4 The "rapprochement" between big business and the government must not be exaggerated. Business clearly supported some aspects of reform apartheid, notably the ability of blacks to unionize and the intention of the government to improve the conditions of the townships. But business generally opposed the government's military efforts – both within and outside of South Africa. Some businesses suffered under divestment and economic sanctions. Stephan Haggard and Robert R. Kaufman (1995: 30) suggest that if business believes that authoritarian governments are unwilling or unable to change policies detrimental to business's individual and collective interests, it can quickly recalculate the costs associated with democratization – particularly where there are opportunities to ally with "moderate" oppositions. In keeping with this observation, by late 1985 major industrialists began the first of several visits to Lusaka to meet with the exiled ANC in Zambia (R. Price, 1991: 240).

5 Even the Viljoen Task Group, the group appointed by the government in 1990 to investigate broadcast policy, and on which M-Net's Ton Vosloo served as vice-chair, intimated that M-Net's various renegotiated licenses were not quite on the up and up. In the report's exceptionally careful prose, "M-Net's license conditions have been modified on three occasions since then [the original], each time several matters were addressed. Some of M-Net's requests were granted and some were refused. This follows a similar pattern overseas, in countries that have no long-term broadcasting policy and no independent regulatory authority with standard licensing conditions" (Republic of South Africa, 1991d: 46).

of the renewal of its license. M-Net also is allowed to broadcast a decoded signal between 5 and 7 P.M. every day, known as "Open Time." According to SABC calculations (hotly disputed by M-Net [Bierbaum, 1995]), 70 percent to M-Net's R430 million in 1994 advertising revenue was earned during Open Time (SABC, 1995b). Aimed at urban whites with discretionary income, M-Net grew to over a million subscribers as of May 1996 (Scholtz, 1996).

Thus when SABC Board Chairman Christo Viljoen announced the corporation's restructuring in January 1991, to foster, in his words, "a greater degree of decentralization, greater emphasis on the SABC's clients, and preparation of the SABC for a more competitive environment" (SABC *Annual Report*, 1991), he was in many respects responding to real needs on behalf of the corporation. The 1990 SABC *Annual Report* reflected a well-informed concern about the future of the SABC in the emerging global broadcast environment. Given the long-standing organizational problems of the SABC and the emerging funding crunch, some moves toward restructuring were probably inevitable. But the moves to restructure the SABC were also clearly congruent with, and widely perceived to be part of, the National Party's strategy of protecting its control in broadcasting under the guise of market-based reforms. Recall that in the early 1990s the SABC engineered a revamp of its television channels, establishing TV1 as a commercial white channel, TV2/3 as a commercial black channel renamed Contemporary Community Values television (CCV), and creating a public service channel (National Network Television, NNTV) out of the old TopSport Surplus (TSS) "network." NNTV seemed to have been designed to ghettoize public service television in one channel, enabling the eventual privatization certainly of TV1 and possibly of CCV as well. As the 1991/92 SABC *Annual Report* averred, a revamped TSS (into a public service station) could be

> ... a solution to the SABC's dilemma of reconciling its role as public service broadcaster in television with its commercial financing structure. The SABC's dependence mainly on advertising for its income, coupled with its duty to satisfy target audiences, makes it impossible for the two existing channels, TV1 and CCV, to show specialized programmes or programmes for minority audiences in prime time. There is simply not enough air time for them at practical times without incurring a considerable loss of income. There is, therefore, a great need in South Africa for a

channel that could carry educational and cultural programmes, and programmes of general interest to minority groups. (SABC *Annual Report*, 1992: 5)

THE VILJOEN TASK GROUP AND ITS OPPONENTS

The SABC's internal restructuring was independent of, but broadly connected to the Viljoen Task Group, which was created by the government in 1990 to investigate the future of broadcasting in South Africa. Consisting of thirteen white men, including, among others, representatives from the South African Defence Force, the Bureau of National Intelligence, Bureau of Information, the South African Posts and Telecommunications ministry, and the Department of Foreign Affairs, the Task Group's composition underscored how important the government considered broadcasting and accented the nature of the constituencies the government believed had a stake in broadcasting's reform. Viljoen, the Task Group chair, came from the SABC Board. Responding to public criticism, Minister of Home Affairs Louw (in whose bailiwick broadcasting was then lodged) added two English-speaking white men and Aggrey Klaaste, the black editor of the *Sowetan*. But Minister Louw later also added Ton Vosloo, the head of M-Net, as vice-chair, and Professor J. P. de Lange, head of the Broederbond, as well. The Task Group took up the kinds of problems and options that had been debated by many countries in this period of new technologies and decline of old broadcast structures and rationales, to wit, deregulation and various configurations of competition and privatization. The Task Group must be seen as the National Party's main reformist thrust in media policy in the new period after February 1990.

Mobilizing to counter the NP move was a coalition of the civil society–based media organizations that had formed during the UDF period, various journalist organizations, and labor (primarily the Post & Telecommunications Workers Association). As would be expected, these organizations often connected to political tendencies. The South African Society of Journalists (SASJ) was composed primarily of liberal whites from the mainstream English language press. Media Workers Association of South Africa (MWASA) was a Black Consciousness organization of journalists and nonjournalists in media positions with some ties to Azapo, led originally by Zwelakhe Sisulu (son of ANC stalwarts Walter and Albertina Sisulu, and who, after 1994, was named chief group officer of the SABC). The MWASA had declined to affiliate with the UDF. The Association of Democratic Journalists (ADJ) was racially mixed but primarily black, drawing its membership largely from the alternative press and associated with the UDF. The Film and Allied Workers Organisation (FAWO) joined together independent film and video producers with academics in media studies. The Community Radio Working Group and its affiliates represented independent radio producers. Various media and journalism departments at some of the South African universities were active, including the Centre for Cultural and Media Studies at the University of Natal, the Journalism Department at Rhodes University, and Media Studies at the University of the Witwatersrand (Armstrong, 1987; Phelan, 1987: 29–45; Raubenheimer, 1991; K. Tomaselli and Louw, 1991b; Matisonn, 1996; Niddrie, 1996). One manifestation of the broad coalition formed by civil society media organizations during the UDF period was the Save the Press Campaign. Launched in 1988 by journalists largely from the alternative press, the campaign was designed to draw attention to government restrictions on the press and the targeting of journalists during the states of emergency.

Within the ANC, responsibility for media issues rested with the Department of Information and Publicity (DIP). At the time the Viljoen Task Group began its work, however, the ANC was still largely in exile, and DIP's principal concern was with publicity. The MDM civil society media groups in effect mobilized media policy on behalf of the tripartite alliance. They also galvanized thinking about media within the ANC itself. The ANC National Executive Committee, the congress's central leadership caucus, was well behind the curve on media matters. The mass media were far down on the ANC's set of priorities in its "constitutional guidelines" blueprint for a transition to a post-apartheid South Africa, drawn up in Lusaka in 1988 (Teer-Tomaselli, 1993). Indeed, it could be said that the ANC had scarcely any developed media policy, besides an inchoate aim to take over the SABC and break up the white press conglomerates. And, in the short term, the congress was concerned mainly with obtaining mass media voice for itself. The leaders of the ANC's DIP were another matter. Pallo Jordan, Joel Netshitenzhe, Gill Marcus, and Carl Niehaus formed a strong nucleus within the DIP in support of the principles of a free press and a public broadcaster separate from government.

The Campaign for Open Media (COM) grew from the earlier Save the Press Campaign. The COM was MDM's umbrella organization for the struggle against both the SABC's commercial restructuring and the

Viljoen Task Group. The COM was chaired by prominent liberal and former *Rand Daily Mail* editor, Raymond Louw, and assisted by radio journalist (and former U.S. National Public Radio South Africa correspondent) John Matisonn. Under the COM umbrella the FAWO led the broadcast debate, organizing workshops and conferences. The Post & Telecommunications Workers Association provided the street muscle, the pinnacle of which was a 2,000-person march on the SABC headquarters on August 25, 1990. The COM became the main forum for talking about democratizing the South African mass media, and four conferences, largely organized under COM auspices, the Rhodes University Media Policy Conference in September 1990, the Jabulani! Freedom of the Airwaves Conference in the Netherlands in August 1991, the ANC DIP meeting in November 1991, and the Free, Fair and Open Conference in Cape Town in January 1992, became the principal venues for the discussion and eventual formulation of ANC-alliance media policy. Jabulani! was of particular importance. Because it was convened and financed by Omroep voor Radio Freedom, an antiapartheid Dutch coalition openly supportive of the ANC, the Jabulani! conference bestowed legitimacy on the South African civil society media groups.

The groups under the COM umbrella posted a fundamental procedural objection to the Viljoen Task Group: Any restructuring of South African broadcasting could not be considered under the conditions of old-style secret deliberations by an elite white commission. Policy issues in other sectors were being taken up in the context of stakeholder forums, and broadcasting should be no exception to the emerging practice of broad political consultation. The MDM was deeply suspicious of the SABC's internal restructuring and the work of the Task Group. As Willie Currie, then secretary-general of the Film and Allied Workers Organisation, put it at the Jabulani! Freedom of the Airwaves Conference (August 1991) in the Netherlands:

> The strategies of the State and big business aim at restructuring broadcasting before a new government comes to power or a new constitution comes into force. The aim is to change the economic environment to limit local access. The SABC has pulled most production inside for its own production unit and there is limited local content on M-Net/Bop-TV. The SABC will be restructured into business units, which could be sold to the private sector or which could operate as de facto private companies in a relation of

unfair competition to independent film production companies. Moreover, it would allow the concentration of power in M-Net by press companies and big business. (Currie, 1991: 9–10)

By the middle of 1990, many groups under the general rubric of the MDM were moving away from defining politics as full-fledged confrontation with the apartheid government, which had been typical of the politics of the UDF period, and instead toward a politics that strategically combined confrontation and engagement. This was represented as a change from a Gramscian "war of maneuver" (a frontal, military attack on the state apparatus) to a "war of position" (political struggle in the realm of ideas, culture, education, and public policy) (Gramsci, 1971; Currie, 1995a). The change was in large part due to a recognition that the South African political situation had changed fundamentally with de Klerk's February 1990 speech and that the political "game" now revolved around strategic negotiation and accommodation. In the broadcast arena this movement was given additional impetus from an unexpected quarter. Larry Schwartz, information officer at the U.S. Embassy, began attending meetings of both the MDM media groups and the government. His modus operandi was to buttonhole respective leaders and challenge them to engage with each other, explaining that policy disagreements in the United States were discussed transparently, in the open. Schwartz effectively became a broker between the MDM media groups and the government (Currie, 1996b). He also brought in Brian Fontes from the U.S. Federal Communications Commission, who also met with the various parties and encouraged openness and engagement.[6] With the assistance provided by this brokering, the mass democratic opposition and the Viljoen Task Group engaged in some degree of intellectual interaction, albeit mediated and strained. One manifestation was a decision of the Task Group to hold an open meeting, on November 28, 1990. Government commissions had never held open meetings in the past. The ANC declined to make submissions to the Task Group for fear of legitimizing it. But FAWO did make a presentation, in which it articulated the congress alliance's opposition to the government's restructuring plans. Another key instance of interaction was when Viljoen himself consented to an interrogation at the Jabulani! Conference in the

6 The process of bringing outside expertise also encompassed the visit of Erwin Krasnow, a former head of the U.S. National Association of Broadcasters (NAB), who was brought to South Africa to help establish a South African NAB.

Netherlands. Answering criticism of the unrepresentative and non-consultative nature of the Task Group, Viljoen defended the commission, saying he could either have disbanded it or tried to promote things he believed in, including the democratization of the airwaves. ANC DIP representative Carl Niehaus argued there was a third option – to recommend the Task Group's report not go to the undemocratic authority that would implement it and, instead, hold public hearings. Niehaus explained:

> The problem is that in the interim period there can also be an underlying hidden agenda, that you want to move as fast as possible and change the landscape of broadcasting in order to make it very difficult for a democratically-elected government to implement really what the people want, rather than what a small group wants. Our concern is to prevent that situation. (*Jabulani!*, 1991: 60)

In fact the Task Group's report reflected a liberalism in policy rather unusual for an apartheid government document. Indeed, as a testament to how far and how quickly the political winds had shifted, the Viljoen Task Group articulated its mission in the final version of the report upon its publication in August 1991 thus: "To ensure that broadcasting in South Africa serves the public in such a way that the ideals of a democratic, non-racial, non-sexist and prosperous society are pursued and advanced" (Republic of South Africa, 1991d: xii).[7]

The Jabulani! Conference underscored the differing political tendencies within the ANC and the Mass Democratic Movement on broadcast policy. There was a clear pluralist force, arguing for the existence of a public service broadcaster (PSB), but, informed by evident distrust

7 The report was a relatively progressive and farsighted document. Many of its constituent components – on the need for local content obligations for all broadcasters, on the problem of funding the SABC, on the need for new broadcasters, on the need to separate the signal distribution function from the SABC, and on the requirement for independent regulation – mirrored the arguments and recommendations of the civil society media groups and the eventual Independent Broadcast Authority itself. On the other hand, the report's brief history of broadcasting in South Africa entirely elided the history of apartheid and white power. Its recommendation that new broadcasters use the medium wave only served to reveal its bias toward the SABC, which would not be required to move from the much better FM frequencies. Its refusal to grandfather 702 Radio and Capital Radio revealed both its pro-SABC bias and its antipathy to those few broadcasters who historically had managed to break the SABC's conservative lock on the medium. And because the report adopted no clearcut cross-media limitations, it could be interpreted as entrenching white power in the broadcast medium. See the Task Group Report (Republic of South Africa, 1991d) and its critique by Currie (1993).

of the experience of state broadcasting both in South Africa and the Soviet bloc, also championed that adequate room be made for commercial and community broadcasting. Within the pluralist camp, there were differences over the extent and scope of commercial broadcasting. On the left were advocates of public service broadcasting – but of a new kind, at odds with the old monopoly orientation of the traditional PSB rationale. Public service was to be spread through all the constituents of a mixed broadcast system. This faction wanted a commercial presence in the post-apartheid South African broadcast environment, but not one that would skew the broadcast system toward an American model of broadcasting. Suspicious of both the state and an unfettered market, their basic idea was to build in as much nonstate, noncommodified broadcast presence as possible. It is perhaps most accurate to describe this approach as post–social democratic. Its vision called for a mixed system of broadcasting, the anchor of which would be a strong and independent public service broadcaster. But the public broadcaster would not be permitted to monopolize the medium. A monopolistic PSB was seen as too close to state broadcasting and too likely to engage in cultural hegemony.

Existing commercial broadcasters, such as Capital Radio and 702 Radio, carved out a conservative pluralist position. They put forward an anti-authoritarian argument tied to a thesis about consumer sovereignty, articulating a vision in support of broad deregulation and a reduced role for a public service broadcaster. In a manner typical of market liberalism, they tied the political battle of freedom of the press to the workings of the market, and sought implicitly to redefine civil society and the mass media in terms of commodity production and exchange.

Although it was not articulated extensively, there was clearly a centralist, state broadcaster orientation among some at the Jabulani! Conference and within the ANC generally. The sentiment that the SABC should be taken over by the liberation forces was shared by many ANC rank and file and even among members of the ANC National Executive Committee. The view was conveyed at Jabulani! in comments during the discussion of community radio to the effect that community radio was all fine and good, but real power remained with the SABC: The anti-apartheid forces must go after the SABC and take control (*Jabulani!*, 1991: 20–22). The most visible proponents of the state centralist model were ANC cadre associated with Radio Freedom, the ANC's exile broadcast organization.

In the end, the post–social democratic coalition seemed to have won the day at Jabulani!. The conference released a series of recommendations recognizing three levels of broadcasting: public service, commercial, and community. The public service broadcaster must cater to all tastes and be independent of the government of the day, the conference report declared. Advertising must be cut back and the "Christian National" bias of the SABC must be removed. All indigenous South African languages must have access to broadcasting, and education must become a genuine orientation of South African broadcasting. The key problem was how to get from here to there, what to do during the transition period. Jabulani! called for a democratically accountable commission of inquiry to be appointed by an All Party Conference to survey public opinion on the regulation of broadcasting. The All Party Conference should appoint an Interim Broadcasting Commission to make sure that there is fair and impartial reporting during the transition period (*Jabulani!*, 1991: 67–69).

Jabulani! was an important gathering. The recommendations coming out of the conference effectively set the terms of the public debate for the next few rounds. This was especially critical with regard to internal ANC discussions, in particular for the ANC's Department of Information and Publicity National Media Seminar a few months later in November 1991, attended by some 300 delegates. The MDM media groups (particularly those of the post–social democratic tendency) had effectively situated themselves as key players in the internal ANC debate, and the resolutions of the DIP National Media Seminar essentially reiterated the main themes articulated at Jabulani!. This was a turning point in ANC media policy. The meeting endorsed the principle that a public service broadcaster be independent of the ruling party, governed by structures representative of all sectors of South African society. In the interim period, DIP asserted that the National Party could not be player, referee, and programmer of an the airwaves during the process of party negotiations. Rather, the control of state media must be placed under appropriate mechanisms of an interim government. DIP denounced the unilateral attempt of the government to restructure broadcasting and reiterated the Jabulani! call for the control and regulation of broadcasting to be placed on the agenda of an All Party Congress (African National Congress, 1991). These resolutions were formalized into an ANC draft Media Charter, which identified freedom of communication at the core of democracy and called for the establishment of independent, representative structures to "promote and monitor the realisation of these freedoms" (see African National Congress, 1992a: 67–71).

Ruth Teer-Tomaselli (1993), drawing upon Tom Lodge's analysis of how ANC policy is typically shaped, argues that an effective alliance between ANC-elected leaders in the DIP and the appointed specialists from the MDM media groups won over (or outmaneuvered) the ANC rank-and-file faction that supported a partisan media. That faction soon found itself excluded from the main locus of power within DIP structures. Pragmatism won out, insinuates Teer-Tomaselli, because, under post–February 1990 political circumstances, characterized by negotiations and compromise at every level of policy, the ANC pragmatists realized the congress could not hope to achieve control of the SABC. They believed that advocating an impartial broadcaster was the only viable, though second best, option. No doubt this is true of some, perhaps many, within the ANC-DIP. But others viewed the independence of broadcasting as a matter of principle, including, notably, DIP head Pallo Jordan (Matisonn, 1996).

EXCURSUS: THE RELATIONSHIP BETWEEN THE ANC AND THE UDF/MDM

Highlighting the differences within the anti-apartheid alliance over broadcast policy is not to create an artificial separation between the MDM media groups and the ANC. Many of the key players in the civil society organizations were, in fact, ANC members, or, if not card-carrying members, fellow travelers deeply committed to the anti-apartheid struggle. These were groups and individuals sympathetic to, though not necessarily directly aligned with, the ANC. The point is rather that the civil society groups were generally born in the UDF and, hence, had greater allegiance to participatory structures and mechanisms, and a more principled commitment to democratic deliberation and pluralism in policy debates. They were steeped in a strong ideological commitment to grounding their decision making in community-wide consultation, a doctrine taken over from the trade union movement and the civic associations. This commitment manifested itself not only in the process of public deliberation over broadcast policy, but also in the substantive vision of the structure of post-apartheid broadcasting. In this respect they were intensely wary of any state control of media. In contrast, many ANC exiles, returning to South Africa and assuming leadership positions in the tripartite alliance, came from the more top–down, "commandist" political culture engendered by the years underground and in armed struggle with the apartheid state. Among a large faction of the exiled ANC leadership, thinking about post-apartheid media was essentially summed up by the idiom "free but responsible." This idiom was articulated early on by Aziz Pahad, then from the ANC's Department of Information and Publicity (later deputy foreign minister), at a Johannesburg meeting of journalists and ANC officials in early 1990. In John Matisonn's (1998) retelling of the meeting, Pahad's explanation of a "free but responsible" press – that the press must be part of the ANC alliance's post-apartheid democratic nation-building process – reminded some journalists of the kind of journalism the outgoing white government had demanded on behalf of the apartheid state. Indeed, in pre-election discussions within the alliance on the subject of Cabinet portfolios, for instance, serious consideration was given to creating a Ministry of Information, reflecting a vision of communications in keeping with the authoritarianism of the exiles' former Soviet bloc and African nationalist sponsors.

The "broad church" metaphor for the ANC is more apt in some historical periods than others. The 1955 "Freedom Charter" is, for example, an expansive and catholic document, with broad enough general principles drawn from classic Enlightenment theory to accommodate many ideological tendencies under its umbrella (see Frederikse, 1990). The destruction of the apartheid state was the central principle and goal. Any ideological tendency that supported the goal was more or less welcome. After 1960 the ANC became less tolerant of ideological diversity, as the congress was forced underground and many members were jailed or went into exile. Guerrilla warfare in the 1980s served to militarize the ANC's approach to political and strategic questions. As an exiled insurgent body, the ANC necessarily acquired a rather disciplined and autocratic character. This fact had important consequences after 1990. As Tom Lodge (1996) argues, the ANC exiles returned home with a well-developed set of authoritarian and bureaucratic reflexes. The ANC exiles had not passed through the experience of the UDF/MDM participatory democratic politics of the 1980s, and they brought different discursive frameworks and different political instincts to the post–February 1990 situation. The political reflexes, particularly of those exiles who had spent decades living in Africa or Eastern Europe, were rooted in Africanist, anticolonialist discourses or reflected their patrons' Stalinist intellectual models. As a result, notwithstanding the ANC's formal ideology of democracy and nonracialism, significant sections of the congress returning from exile touted a mixture of a black nationalism and neo-Stalinism. These cadres were comfortable practicing a top–down, leaders-know-best approach to politics typical of a centralist, hierarchical culture of decision making (Lodge, 1992; P. Louw, 1994). The political culture of those imprisoned on Robben Island may have been somewhat different from those of the exiles, but the leadership styles were fully compatible. In Lodge's words, "The Robben Islanders brought back from their prison experience an especially rigid and exclusive hierarchical form of authority which critics likened to a system of chieftaincy" (Lodge, 1992: 53).

The reunification of the Charterist groups after February 1990 thus papered over important ideological differences. The UDF may have operated, in effect, as the internal proxy of the ANC during the 1980s, but it was a movement that had developed its own distinctive politics. This was in part because ANC leadership and cadres *had* largely been imprisoned or in exile, and the ANC structures inside the country were relatively weak. The struggles of the 1980s brought new organizations such as the civics, the trade unions, and the UDF to the fore with new strategies, theoretical understandings, and organizational principles. Toward the end of the 1980s the leadership of the anti-apartheid struggle essentially rested with organized labor, which brought its strong conceptions of internal democracy, consultation, and accountability to the struggle. The need to counter reform apartheid's efforts to co-opt Coloured and Indian communities, particularly the tricameral Parliament gambit, meant a deliberate downplaying of the language of black nationalism and an explicit articulation of nonracialism. As has been discussed, the UDF and the civic associations also put a great deal of emphasis on popular grassroots democracy both as an organizing principle and as an important part of the call for a future nonracial democracy. As a consequence the UDF attracted an impressive number of Coloureds, Indians, and whites, and hence the anti-apartheid struggle inside South Africa during the 1980s did not take the form of a black–white struggle (see P. Louw, 1989).

Upon becoming unbanned, the ANC reasserted its organizational and ideological hegemony over the radical and precocious grassroots social movements that emerged during the insurrectionary period of the 1980s. Elements of the ANC feared that the UDF could be used as a base for some activists to undermine the ANC. Indeed, some ANC leaders dismissed the notion of independent civil society organizations and argued that the civics must not be separate from ANC mass structures. The notion that civic organizations might serve as local organs for the articulation of local needs and act as watchdogs for democracy when the ANC becomes government, was dismissed as an abandonment of the central goal of building of a mass and democratic ANC (see Nkwinti, 1991; Nzimande and Sikhosana, 1991, 1992). The UDF resolved to remove itself from the political center stage in favor of the ANC. But in the words of one account, the UDF was "unceremoniously disbanded" in 1991. Even though many UDF/MDM activists joined the ANC, a large number withdrew from political activism and were lost to the movement (Ginsburg, Webster, et al., 1995: 7). As South African Communist Party Deputy General Secretary Jeremy Cronin observed in 1994, "People abandoned their organisations and joined the main political organisation. The real experience and worth of the popular movements was not understood; they were seen as a kind of 'B-team', a substitute until the 'A-team' [the ANC] could enter the playing field" (cited in Marais, 1998: 73). The UDF's parting effort was to promote the formation of a national civic body. In May 1991 the UDF hosted a national consultative conference in Bloemfontein to plan for the organization that became SANCO, the South African National Civic Organisation (Seekings, 1992).

The tripartite alliance of ANC, COSATU, and the South African Communist Party (SACP), often thought to be a commodious political coalition, in fact was and remains a somewhat fractious one united by the baseline anti-apartheid stance. The ANC stayed organizationally coherent over the decades by articulating a relatively vague program of nationalist democratic revolution, a politics capable of accommodating many ideological tendencies under its banner. COSATU, strongly identified with its labor constituency, advocated a union-dominated democratic socialism. It frequently clashed with the ANC over the latter's economic policies and class politics. The SACP was able to legitimate its close relationship to the ANC by articulating a two-stage theory of revolution (the national democratic phase followed by a socialist phase). In contrast to the ANC's broad nationalist orientation, the SACP championed the poor and unemployed under the rubric of socialist revolution (see, among others, Lodge, 1983; Fredrickson, 1995; Eidelberg, 2000).

BROADCAST REFORM ENTERS CODESA

Another key conference in the formation of ANC alliance broadcast policy was the Free, Fair and Open Conference, organized by the

Campaign for Open Media and the Centre for Development Studies. This conference brought together a wide range of political and media groups in Cape Town to formulate a consensus proposal on how to deal with media during the political transition. Various speakers denounced the status quo and put forward their views of a democratic media system. The lineup of speakers included former SABC officials, who confirmed the extent of suspected political control of the SABC by the National Party. Sheila Camerer, National Party MP and Director of its Information Service, claimed that the new National Party was committed to the free flow of information, a free press, and free, independent, and impartial broadcast organizations. Privatization was the principal means to achieve this end. On the other end of the spectrum, Neil Coleman, COSATU information officer, argued that the lack of representivity in South African media wasn't due simply to National Party control. The control and ownership of the print press by a handful of large corporations was also a major problem, he argued, and a prime reason why the mainstream print media lacked credibility for the majority of the population. Coleman advocated the democratization and restructuring of commercial media, as well as creation of a system of state subsidies for independent and community papers (Free, Fair and Open, 1992). Publicly, there was a convergence on the part of all groups: There must be an nonpartisan broadcasting system overseen by an independent regulator. Again, the problem was how to get from here to there, particularly in light of the announcement by the minister of Home Affairs that legislation embodying the recommendations of the Viljoen Task Group would be submitted to Parliament during the 1992 session. Home Affairs was also quietly handing out radio licenses to certain preferred constituencies, and, in 1993, a second license to M-Net. To counter this, the Free, Fair and Open Conference proposed that broadcast policy be brought directly into the CODESA negotiations (and in so doing in effect calling for CODESA to act in the capacity as an interim government). Bringing broadcasting into CODESA meant that government could not do anything unilaterally to change the broadcast environment (Currie, 1993: 58). The Free, Fair and Open Conference called on CODESA to facilitate the appointment of new Boards of Control for the public broadcasting services (the SABC and the TBVC equivalents). It also called for the creation of an Interim Independent Communication Authority, accountable not to the government but to CODESA, to normalize the position of existing broadcasters and to ensure the establishment of a broadcast sector whose impartiality and fairness are broadly recognized (Free, Fair and Open, 1992; Matisonn, 1996).

These calls were successful, and broadcasting *was* included at CODESA, in large part because all political parties were concerned about the control of media as the possibility of elections approached. Broadcasting was placed within the terms of reference of CODESA Working Group 1, Subgroup 3, which was mandated to examine the creation of "a climate and opportunity for free political participation," including the political neutrality of, and fair access to, the state-controlled media (Friedman, 1993: 36). Negotiations within the CODESA subgroup were difficult. At an early meeting the National Party/government adopted a stance suggesting that changes were not now necessary and the SABC's new code of conduct and present editorial policy met the requirement for political neutrality (Friedman, 1993: 53; see also National Party, 1992). This was unacceptable to the ANC negotiators, but they were relatively uninformed on broad questions of media policy, and still tended to focus not so much on any future structure of broadcasting as obtaining a political voice in the mass media. FAWO coordinated a Joint Submission to CODESA from nine civil society media organizations, in large part to educate the ANC alliance negotiators at CODESA (Organisations Which Form Part of the Independent Broadcasting and Film Industry, no date).

In the meantime major players in the telecommunications industry realized that CODESA was now taking up broadcast policy in ways that were likely to affect telecommunications. Key telecommunications players lobbied government to propose a single regulatory authority over both broadcast and telecoms. The National Party negotiators did so, along with a proposal for a Broadcast Complaints Commission, which was offered to resist the demand to change the SABC Board. An agreement was reached in principle to establish an independent communications regulatory authority, tentatively named the South African Independent Telecommunications Authority (SAITA). The logic was that an independent body should license broadcasters, break the government's monopoly of the airwaves, guarantee diverse access to broadcasting, and regulate telecommunications. But agreement in principle on a SAITA did not necessarily mean agreement on the question of the SABC Board. As far as the ANC was concerned, the SABC continued to function as an arm of the National Party. The ANC alliance thus insisted on immediate changes to the composition of the SABC Board. This was opposed by the government. According to Friedman (1993), the negotiations were murky with regard to SAITA and the SABC Board. The ANC alliance representatives often appeared to speak of the two as one and to assume that agreement on SAITA implied consensus on a nonpartisan SABC Board. The final Working Group 1 documentation is also imprecise with regard to the SABC. Although it implies agreement on "reconstitution" of the board, reconstitution, in the eyes of the government, meant only that more people would be brought onto the board to join the incumbents and that it would not be entirely independent from government. There is evidence that the members of the ANC alliance in the CODESA Working Group had little understanding of the technical and economic issues involved in telecommunications or how broadcasting and telecommunications interact. And the lack of clarity on the question of the reconstitution of the SABC Board was, in the eyes of the Mass Democratic Movement (MDM) media groups, a disaster waiting to happen. They were actually relieved when CODESA fell apart in June 1992 and the initial broadcasting agreements came undone.[8]

The ANC suspended talks after the Boipatong massacre. With the breakdown of CODESA, the government reverted to unilateral action and tabled before Parliament a draft of the communications bill that Pierre Pretorius, adviser to the minister of Transport and Posts & Telecommunications, had been writing. The bill would establish a South African Telecommunications Commission (SATCOM), headed by the postmaster general and staffed by his department. The MDM media groups saw this as a regression from even the limited agreements for an independent body that had been reached in CODESA. The bill would allow the state president to appoint SATCOM commissioners without a public process. But the proposed legislation didn't go anywhere. Apart from the outcry against unilateral government action, the telecommunications sector was hopelessly split over how to transform that sector and could not organize a national stakeholder forum to discuss the issues confronting it. Concern was voiced in the business community

---

8 This point was made by Michael Markovitz of the Film and Allied Workers Organisation. FAWO had been commissioned by the ANC to comment on the government's communications regulation proposals. Markovitz voiced the opinion that the breakdown in CODESA talks may have been a blessing in disguise. In his estimation, the ANC alliance ran a serious risk of agreeing to things it did not fully understand and might well regret later. As for the actual content of the government's first proposals on the regulatory body at CODESA, Markovitz claims that 60%–70% dealt with the problem of pensions (Markovitz, 1992). This surprising feature of the CODESA discussions underscores the fact that a good part of the political negotiations revolved around the National Party's very concrete concerns to protect its own.

and by Telkom itself that telecommunications issues would be given short shrift by SATCOM. That same concern, albeit perhaps animated by different aims, was shared by POTWA, the powerful black Post & Telecommunications Workers Association (*Financial Mail,* 1992; Post & Telecommunications Workers Association, 1992). Eventually, when political negotiations began again, in the Multi-Party talks at Kempton Park, telecommunications were dropped from the discussions on broadcasting. Minister of Transport and Posts & Telecommunications Piet Welgemoed himself resisted all attempts to bring telecommunications to the Multi-Party negotiations, according to David Dison, an important player in the ANC-aligned media groups (Dison, 1997a). Because of the immediate importance of broadcasting for the future elections and the absence of consultative negotiations or much movement in telecommunications, the political parties agreed to move ahead just on broadcasting. An Independent Broadcasting Authority was agreed to in principle by the Multi-Party Negotiating Council, and legislation was drafted by a technical committee of outside representative experts.

In the final analysis, the establishment of independent broadcasting commanded consensus because, for their own strategic reasons (as well as genuine ideological agreement in some cases, to be sure), every political party could see the danger if its opponent obtained control of the medium. It was thus politically expedient to agree to a nonpartisan SABC and an independent regulator. The convergence of the National Party and the ANC was rather simple: the ANC was fearful of continued NP control of broadcasting *before* the election; the NP was fearful of the possibility of ANC control of broadcasting *after* the election. Thus it was essential for both that the SABC be reconstituted as an independent broadcaster. Even ANC alliance "commandists," those supporting the centralized power of the ANC, backed this (Dison, 1996; Markovitz, 1996). Essop Pahad, one of the ANC's negotiators in Working Group 1, Sub-Group 3 (who at the Rhodes University Media Policy Conference in 1990 had offered rather ambiguous statements about how independent the broadcast system should be in a post-apartheid South Africa), made a telling comment about the political compromise on broadcasting: "I still think it is a bloody good agreement," Pahad declared. "And not enough is made of the fact that the ANC is being very magnanimous; control [of broadcasting] will not pass to us" (cited in Friedman, 1993: 55; see also Pahad, 1993).

The relationship between the MDM civil society groups and the CODESA/Multi-Party Negotiating Council processes was complex. On the one hand, the civil society groups, and particularly labor, were called upon to provide evidence of the allegiance of the masses to the ANC alliance, when necessary, by taking to the streets and shutting down the country. This was used to strengthen the negotiating hand of the ANC alliance vis-à-vis the National Party, demonstrating to the government that the ANC retained the capacity to mobilize its following against the government. (In fact, it may be that the ultimate function of the mass action campaigns was to keep alive the bonds between the ANC rank and file and their leaders and create a connection of the rank and file to the negotiating processes.) On the other hand, constituent civil society groups had interests, and especially expertise, well beyond the alliance negotiators in CODESA and later at the Multi-Party Negotiating Council at Kempton Park. This discrepancy in large part explains the high profile, but behind the scenes role of people like Willie Currie, Michael Markovitz, David Niddrie, and Raymond Louw. Because they possessed crucial expertise, knowledge of international practices, and a legitimacy born of leadership in the MDM civil society groups, they became media advisers to the Department of Information and Publicity after the ANC was unbanned. (Pierre Pretorius performed much the same function for the National Party.) Hence some of the action outside the negotiating forums was designed to educate and cajole the alliance politicians as much as it was to keep up pressure on the NP. As Tom Lodge (1992: 70) has written, "The chief importance of the activists (and indirectly perhaps, 'the masses') is not so much supplying the pavement protest during crucial altercations over the negotiation table, but in maintaining pressure on ANC leadership to hold firm to those policy essentials which would constitute a programme of radical socio-economic reform." Again, too much can be made of this tension. The interaction between civil society media groups and ANC leadership was productive and often two-way. Joel Netshitenzhe, the ANC's chief negotiator on broadcast issues at Kempton Park, made it a practice to report back to the executive committee of the key civil society media umbrella. But, clearly, there were serious differences between the civil society organizations and the ANC leadership on media policy and political strategy.

CIB AND THE SABC BOARD

With the idea of an impartial SABC presumably settled, the MDM media groups mobilized outside the political negotiations over the question of the reconstitution of the SABC Board. For this a new umbrella group was formed in November 1992: the Campaign for Independent Broadcasting (CIB), a coalition made up of some 37 groups, among others, COM, South African Union of Journalists, Media Workers Association of South Africa, FAWO, Congress of South African Writers (COSAW), the Paper and Allied Workers Union, as well as the ANC, the main labor federations, the SACP, and the South African Council of Churches. The CIB agitated for the appointment of a new SABC Board that would be more representative of the demographic and political diversity of South African society (Emdon, 1993; Republic of South Africa, 1995d: 36). In the wake of the perceived failings of the political negotiators, CIB declared that civil society, rather than the political parties, should take the lead in broadcast reform. The term of the fourteen-member SABC Board was due to expire in March 1993, and the CIB generated as much pressure as it could for a public process in the appointment of a new board. In the face of a labor threat to shut down the SABC, Home Affairs Minister Danie Schutte assented to the CIB proposals.[9] The two main political parties agreed that a panel of eight jurists would conduct public hearings to select a new SABC Board, with some role reserved for the state president. Under guidelines agreed to by the government and CIB, candidates to the SABC Board would be interviewed in public hearings. An independent interviewing panel, chaired by the only sitting nonwhite judge, Ismail Mohamed, would make recommendations to President de Klerk, who would have limited powers to refer the names of nominees back to the panel. Under the political circumstances, the composition of the selection panel could not be anything else but an attempt at balancing among various interests, hence the main guarantee to the legitimacy of the process was transparency and public involvement.

---

9 According to David Niddrie (an activist in COM and the CIB and later to become Group Manager of SABC's Strategic Planning Unit), Marcel Golding, then a leader of the National Union of Mineworkers, on pure bluff told Minister of Home Affairs Danie Schutte that labor would shut down the SABC unless independent selection of the SABC Board was agreed to (Niddrie, 1996). The success of the strike of MWASA against the SABC in May-June of 1992 gave the threat some teeth.

Candidates could be nominated by anyone, but criteria for appointment were set out in general guidelines that, among other things, disqualified employees in government structures and persons who held political office in any political organization. But the guidelines stipulated that the SABC Board had to reflect society as a whole, taking into account its gender, geographic, and social composition. As it happened, the panel's 25 nominees were weighted toward the ANC. President de Klerk vetted 7 of the panel's recommended nominees, including Professor Njabulo Ndebele, its nominee for the chair. The appointment guidelines gave de Klerk no such clear veto power, but, according to David Niddrie (1996), there were too many other deals between the NP and the ANC hanging in the balance, and fighting de Klerk on this could jeopardize the others. Moreover, challenging de Klerk would delay the seating of a new board and forging ahead with an independent SABC. Whatever the explanation, the judicial panel did not object to de Klerk's intervention. De Klerk nominated Dr. Frederik van Zyl Slabbert as chair. Notwithstanding de Klerk's dubious interference, a few pluralists were pleased with the nomination of Slabbert, a widely respected, thoughtful liberal and former head of the Progressive Federal Party (precursor to the Democratic Party) – and a "can-do guy," in David Dison's phrase. But the controversy over de Klerk's interference in the nomination process doomed Slabbert's candidacy. Dr. Ivy Matsepe-Casaburri, an ANC member, but hardly a prominent party activist, was nominated chairperson of the board. The new board was finally appointed on May 31, 1993. Dison, who would coauthor the draft legislation for an Independent Broadcasting Authority, asserts that he then understood the new politics of the situation. An anti-apartheid human rights lawyer with longtime connections to the liberation movement and a strong pluralist in the broadcast debate, Dison felt at battle with commandist tendencies in both the NP and ANC camps. He was not the only person to point out the paradoxical affinities between the NP and elements of the ANC with regard to centralized structures. Because of the perception of having lost the battle of the SABC Board to the commandists of both the dominant parties, Dison endeavored to write a "radical" IBA Act (Dison, 1996). Dison and Michael Markovitz, principal drafters of the act, had remarkable leeway in writing, a circumstance which stemmed from the facts that very few people in South Africa had much knowledge about broadcast regulation and that the ANC and NP leaderships had large numbers of crucial issues to negotiate, and hence left the drafting of legislation to others.

THE INDEPENDENT BROADCASTING AUTHORITY ACT
AND THE TRIPLE INQUIRY

The IBA Act *was*, in some respects, a radical piece of legislation. Its general provisions called for the regulation of broadcasting in the public interest to promote the provision of a diverse range of sound and television broadcast services on national, regional, and local levels, "which when viewed collectively, cater for all language and cultural groups and provide entertainment, education, and information" (Republic of South Africa, 1993b: sect. 2). The legislation established an independent regulatory authority to ensure the development of three levels of broadcasting: public (the public service broadcaster), private (commercial), and community (nonprofit and locally rooted). It encouraged ownership and control of broadcasting services by persons from historically disadvantaged groups. To facilitate the protection and viability of public broadcasting, the act directed the Independent Broadcasting Authority to convene an inquiry into the matter. As part of that brief the IBA was authorized to investigate financing options and the proper balance between the three levels of broadcasting (sect. 45). Recognizing the importance of developing local South African program content, and the difficulty of doing so with cheap foreign programs flooding the market, the act also bid the IBA to convene an inquiry on local content and independent production requirements (sect. 53).

The act is also, fundamentally, an antitrust document. It statutorily limits persons to the control of one private television broadcast license; it limits persons to the control of two private FM or two AM radio licenses, and does not permit anyone to control two private FM or two AM radio licenses in the same or substantially overlapping license areas (sect. 49). It places a 20 percent cap on foreign control of financial or voting interests. Cognizant of conglomerated power in the print media, the act directed the IBA to convene a third inquiry in order to determine proper limitations on cross-media ownership and control (sect. 50). To ensure the independence of broadcasting from political control, the act forbids granting a license to "any party, movement, organization, body or alliance which is of a party political nature" (sect. 51). It prohibits party election broadcasts and political advertisements except during election periods, and specifies the conditions under which they can be aired during those periods (sect. 58–60). The act's call for investigations into the viability of public broadcasting, cross-media ownership rules, and local content provisions led to the "Triple Inquiry." No

145

new licenses could be granted until the Triple Inquiry Report was completed, except for temporary licenses to community radio broadcasters. The IBA granted approximately eighty of those temporary licenses at the time of the report's publication (Republic of South Africa, 1995d: 10).[10] Dison and Markovitz encoded into the act various elements of the better international models: the treatment of local music from the Canadian broadcast law; the categorization of licensing from Australian law; procedural safeguards from the U.S. Federal Communications Commission; and the concept of provincial public broadcasting from the German system (Markovitz, 1996).

In other respects, the act is less radical than it appears. The negotiated transition between the National Party and the ANC required the ANC to agree to protect vested property rights. In broadcasting, this meant that the Independent Broadcasting Authority Act included a grandfather clause protecting the M-Net license "under existing conditions" for a period of eight years from the date the IBA was established (March 1994). This limited the IBA's actions in any comprehensive effort to restructure South African broadcasting. M-Net's occupation of scarce terrestrial frequencies precluded the IBA from using those frequencies for policy-determined broadcast uses. It is highly unusual for

10 One reason the IBA began licensing community radio stations in advance of the Triple Inquiry was to deal with Radio Pretoria. Radio Pretoria was a pirate station of right-wing Afrikaners, who began broadcasting without a license in protest against the coming political dispensation. The IBA was determined to soft-pedal this issue so as not to inflame the right-wing, but needed authority to grant any temporary license. Parliament passed an amendment to the act that allowed the IBA to grant temporary community radio licenses in advance of the Triple Inquiry (Republic of South Africa, 1994a). The IBA accepted four distinct groups of community radio stations: ethnic, religious, student, and development-oriented. Communities of interest were also granted licenses for classical music and jazz, or for specific purposes such as an agricultural show, or a peace radio in specific geographic areas (Emdon, 1996). The community radio licenses were considered a great success. But there are problems, in large part because the IBA saddled these stations with some handicaps. Some community stations broadcast at such low power that their signals are difficult to pick up. Some share frequencies, a consequence of which is that it is difficult for a station to establish an identity. And finally, the IBA did not pay much attention to financial viability. There was no government support for community radio. It is difficult to get much advertising in township and rural stations where there are few businesses large enough to advertise and the target audience is beset by very high unemployment. In the estimation of William Siemering (1996), an important historical figure in U.S. public radio brought to South Africa by IBA Councillor John Matisonn to help community radio groups, "It is amazing that the stations are doing as well as they are. Radio Atlantis is performing a remarkable community service as is Radio Zibonele in Khyelitsha and others as well, but hanging on by a very thin thread." Despite difficulties, community radio is perceived as being largely successful in providing important development information and as constituting an access point for public discussion in local communities (see Siemering, Fairbairn, and Rangana, 1998).

a subscription television service to use terrestrial channels, and spectrum availability in South Africa is very limited. Two other factors lessened the efficacy of the act: the divided leadership of the IBA Council and the ambiguity of the scope of the IBA's authority. Both derived from the IBA's having been founded as the product of political negotiations as opposed to the result of a considered mandate from a democratically elected government.

Because the IBA was born in the heat and suspicion of rough and tumble political negotiations, the negotiators required that the leadership of the IBA Council be shared between an NP and an ANC appointee. The ANC's chair was an ANC-aligned communications academic who had spent years in exile teaching in the United States, Dr. Sebiletso Mokone-Matabane. Peter de Klerk, a former executive in the white-dominated South African advertising industry, was the NP's chair. The other original councillors included William Lane, a respected Johannesburg newspaper lawyer, Lyndall Shope-Mafole, a Cuban-trained engineer from a prominent ANC family, former SABC Board Chairman Christo Viljoen, and John Matisonn. While politically expedient, the compromise of cochairpersons hampered the IBA's actions. In the estimation of many observers, it meant *no* leadership. The problem was magnified by another underlying the weakness of the IBA. With the exception of John Matisonn, the IBA Council lacked activists who either had been directly involved in the political processes to transform broadcasting or who had participated in the drafting of IBA legislation. This meant that the councillors required a long time to get up to speed and had a less intimate understanding of the politics of the issues at stake. And the overall political climate of suspicion that made it difficult to appoint media activists to the IBA Council also induced a general wariness of placing trust in any single administrative or political structure. No doubt, too, a factor here was the historical experience by black people of the unchecked and arbitrary power of the apartheid bureaucracies. These factors translated into a limited scope of authority for the IBA. Indeed, because the act neglected to provide the IBA certain powers the act had to be amended on a few occasions not long after it was passed.

The IBA's limited authority was most evident in respect to the outcome of the Triple Inquiry. Although the IBA was directed to convene the Triple Inquiry, it was not authorized to make policy from the investigation. Rather, the IBA was to furnish its recommendations on the protection and viability of public broadcasting services and cross-media control of broadcasting services to Parliament. Parliament would determine policy. (Local content was considered to fall solely within the IBA's regulatory mandate, hence the results of that inquiry did not require parliamentary approval.) Neel Smuts confirms that oversight of the IBA's Triple Inquiry by Parliament was part of the general political compromise at Kempton Park. The Multi-Party Negotiating Council wrote this oversight into the act "due to mutual suspicion. Too much detail written into the act tended to tie the IBA's hands" (Smuts, 1996).[11]

Passage of the IBA Act had been undertaken in the pressure-cooker environment of the political negotiations to ensure the impartiality of the state broadcaster for the upcoming election. Indeed, the impression was that something had gone amiss in the drafting process. The original call from the Campaign for Open Media had been for the creation of an *interim* Independent Communications Authority, to engineer an impartial SABC for the election and to make sure the National Party could not move forward with privatization in advance of the democractic dispensation. In this view, legislation creating a *permanent* IBA was inappropriate because there was not yet a democratic political framework upon which to base regulatory authority. There had not been an open public discussion regarding the type of broadcasting system the country desired. IBA councillors had been appointed not by a duly elected democratic government but by a set of negotiations between warring political parties (Niddrie, 1996; Moeti, 1997). There is something to this view, and in an indirect way Michael Markovitz's (1996) marveling at the leeway the legislative drafters possessed, confirms it. On the other hand, the IBA's Triple Inquiry clearly approxi-

---

11 Parliamentary authority over Triple Inquiry recommendations was justified in terms of a separation between regulation and policy making: The IBA was to attend to regulating the broadcast sector; Parliament was to make policy for it. In the usual scheme of things, however, a regulatory body always engages in policy making – the distinction some make between regulation and policy is so murky as to be essentially spurious at the end of the day. But regulatory policy making *is* typically guided by a broad policy mandate given it through legislation, and the latter was largely lacking in the South African case. Of course, a related issue was likely the unfamiliarity of the regulatory agency in the South African context, a context in which political suspicion would naturally fester. The transition from ministerial control to independent regulation was uncharted and complicated. How much independence or autonomy is optimal? Autonomy from whom? Should the regulatory agency engage in both regulation and policy? After all, these issues have never really left even the American regulatory debate. To some, the fact that the American independent regulatory bodies mix legislative, executive, and judicial functions is their beauty; to others that same mix is evidence of their unconstitutionality (see Horwitz, 1994b).

mated the features of the open and consultative public deliberations that would characterize the later Green Paper/White Paper processes. Indeed, the Triple Inquiry can be said to have been among the first of the official consultative stakeholder policy processes.

The IBA commenced the Triple Inquiry with publication of notice in the *Government Gazette* on April 15, 1994. A first round of written submissions was summarized in three "issues papers" written by the IBA staff. The papers were widely distributed. They framed a series of public hearings and discussions held between November 1994 and June 1995. Despite widespread publicity on the process, most of the participants in the public hearings were those individuals and organizations long involved in the broadcast debate or with pecuniary interests at stake. Most hearings were held in greater Johannesburg, but the IBA took the hearings on the road to each of the provinces as well. Attendance in the provinces was spotty other than participation from a provincial premier or by a senior member of the provincial government. Nonetheless, the IBA Council heard 180 hours of oral testimony and received 130 written submissions (Republic of South Africa, 1995c: Appendix J). Because questions regarding costs and revenues in broadcasting arose regularly, the IBA contracted the accounting and consulting firm Deloitte & Touche to provide an independent analysis of scenarios. This had the benefit of providing an expert check on SABC claims and numbers. The IBA also commissioned the Community Agency for Social Enquiry (CASE) to conduct focus groups on a range of issues on which there was either highly controversial or no research, notably including people's language and programming preferences (Republic of South Africa, 1995d: 7–8).

The relative absence of civil society media activists from the IBA Council had an impact on the understanding of the political stakes of the Triple Inquiry. The IBA's "Summary of Submissions to the Triple Inquiry on the Protection and Viability of Public Broadcasting" is perhaps a case in point. The summary characterizes the major division in the submissions as between those who "saw the provision of public broadcasting services as the sole domain of a single or number of public institutions and those who envisaged public broadcasting as the responsibility of all broadcasters" (Republic of South Africa, 1995c: Appendix I, 1). Indeed, there *was* an important split between those parties who wanted to construct a broadcast system along what could be characterized generally as a broad public service model, and those who advocated what approximated an American commercial model. The groups arguing for public service broadcasting as a shared responsibility envisaged a dominant public service broadcaster providing a mix of educational, informative, and entertainment programming in a tiered system where *all* broadcasters would have some public service responsibilities. They insisted that broadcasting in the public interest in the new South Africa – especially under the new conditions of the emerging global broadcast marketplace – could work only if the public service load, so to speak, were spread to all broadcast players. Those groups pushing the American model saw a smaller, narrowly public broadcaster amidst a far more deregulated commercial broadcast system. In the latter model, the public service broadcaster would provide educational and informational programming, but be fenced off from the provision of more "commercial" programming fare.

But there was an equally serious split, however, only indirectly acknowledged and dimly understood in the IBA summary, between a centralistic, maximalist SABC and the post–social democratic, civil society media groups over how much of the broadcast market the public service broadcaster should control, and on the need for provincial, as opposed to just national, public service television broadcasting. Backing the SABC were those more commandist ANC players who viewed the SABC as an old-style (near-monopoly) public service broadcaster that might still effectively be controlled by the (new) government.

Excursus: The Political Economy of Broadcasting

An important backdrop to the debate over the structure of South African broadcasting was the changing international political economy of the sector. Market forces and technologies as simple as audio recordings and external radio broadcasting (such as the BBC World Service and Voice of America) and as complex and expensive as direct broadcast satellite and cable TV had pried open various states' monopoly over what citizens were permitted to listen to or view. In the authoritarian political systems of Eastern and Central Europe the expansion of broadcasting was a blow for democracy, as it had served to force state-controlled media to provide at least some information that was made available from external broadcast sources (see Splichal, 1994; also Ash, 1990). But the same forces of technical and market expansion in broadcasting also posed a severe challenge to public service broadcasting in the liberal capitalist democracies, particularly because the expansion of broadcasting coincided with the crisis of social democracy in those nations. The combination of tight budget constraints and change in the political commitment to public institutions forced public broadcasters in the liberal capitalist democracies to defend their budgets and justify their missions. The legitimacy of the market-based attack on public service broadcasting was elevated because it came accompanied by a revival of the old language of freedom of the press and raised genuine questions regarding the kind of cultural representation secured by monopoly public service broadcasters (see Pool, 1983; Keane, 1991; Noam, 1991). In the face of new technologies and delivery options, the resultant proliferation of channels, and the accompanying drop in the salience of the technological scarcity/natural monopoly rationale, governments have tended to lessen their support for public service broadcasting (see, among others, Garnham, 1986; Dyson and Humphreys, 1990; Blumler and Nossiter, 1991; Hoynes, 1994; M. Price, 1995).

The combination of these economic and political forces has created a very strong dynamic toward commercialism and globalization in broadcasting. The economics of commercial broadcasting have long been understood. The major investment lies in the initial cost of program production, and, according to American studies, 80 percent of programs do not earn back their production costs. The high costs of production and high failure rate lead, at the creative level, to a reliance on tried and true strategies; at the marketing level, to expansionism and multiple markets; and on organizational and ownership levels, to vertical integration (see Gitlin, 1983; Le Duc, 1987; Blumler, 1989). High costs and high risks lead producers and buyers to exhibit strong preference for concepts reminiscent of past program success. Programs are tailored for their acceptability in multiple markets. Because so much depends on promotion for success in these venues, programs tend to be produced for their promotional qualities. This favors programs based on a simple idea, with exciting action and familiar stars, able to be described in a brief ad blurb. Internationally, as a result, the focus is on drama productions in which violence is a staple, because violence, in the argot, "has legs." The dynamics of competition also encourage media organizations to integrate vertically, for example, for production companies to control distribution outlets and vice versa. Media companies integrate backward and forward: They acquire publishing houses, magazines, and newspapers; film studios and television stations; and program packagers, cable systems, and satellite systems. Vertical integration spreads out risks and accumulates buying power, because it facilitates efficient use of resources in various media sectors. The ability to retransmit a successful program to additional national audiences brings the large profits that enable the system to cope with manifold risks. As a result of these forces, amidst globalization tendencies generally, there has been a marked trend toward the merger and consolidation of media companies worldwide (see Bagdikian, 1997; Herman and McChesney, 1997).

The economies of scale of the large entertainment companies, and their ability and willingness to discount programs for certain markets, means that local production is usually swamped by the global products. In South Africa, the broadcasting rights to imported television programs in 1994 cost about R400 per minute, dubbed dramas cost almost R1,000 per minute, local studio dramas cost about R4,000 per minute, and outside production of local dramas cost about R8,000 per minute (SABC, 1994a: 32). The disparity between the low cost of imported programs and high cost of indigenous production makes it difficult to sustain the ideal of a national broadcasting system as a mainstay of national culture. Indeed, expansion has created a disjuncture in national broadcasting between the national identity, and (in principle) public citizenship orientation of the traditional public service broadcaster, and the transnational consumerist orientation of the new multinational entertainment giants. Competition in broadcasting does not bring down production costs, which seem to be ever rising. Rather, competition increases imports (particularly of American films and television programs), often leading to a decline of locally produced programming. Because it is the result of economies of scale, the foreign film or television product tends not only to be cheaper, but often displays higher production values on account of its institutional creators' longer experience and greater capital backing. On another level, the advent of new broadcast technologies and additional television outlets tends to undermine the special position of the public service broadcaster, inasmuch as commercially successful cultural, even quasi-educational programming can, in theory, be filled by niche programmers – without the public subsidies traditionally commandeered by public broadcaster. Finally, the multichannel environment has challenged the legal rationale of the public service broadcaster, as traditional arguments of spectrum scarcity are easily dispatched (Horwitz, 1991). In the liberal ideological environment of the market, public service broadcasting corporations appear not just as bloodsuckers on the public purse but as retrograde inhibitors of media freedom and cultural diversity. Many governments have reduced funding levels and/or have forced their public broadcasters to commercialize some of their services (see Dyson and Humphreys, 1990; Noam, 1991; Blumler, 1992). The inclusion of broadcasting, however cautious and constrained the eventual agreements, in the General Agreement on Tariffs and Trade (1994) served notice that the relatively stable world of the public service broadcaster had forever changed (see, among others, Commission of the European Communities, 1984; Dyson and Humphreys, 1990; Blumler, 1992; Collins, 1993).

THE STRUGGLE OF VISIONS: SABC AND ANC COMMANDISTS VERSUS CIVIL SOCIETY MEDIA GROUPS

In its submissions to the IBA's Triple Inquiry, the SABC drew on this backdrop of the new political economy of broadcasting and the near ubiquitous view that the public service broadcaster must be a major player in nation-building. South Africa found itself post–February 1990 in the unique situation of engaging in what appears to be an old-fashioned, nineteenth-century nation-building exercise. While so many societies seem engulfed by issues of difference, identity politics, and the centripetal forces of ethnic mobilization, South Africa, which experienced a particularly corrupt version of these, found itself in the anomalous position of striving to create a national polity, identity, and culture. To do this in the nonracialist, nonsexist manner befitting the new post-apartheid polity, the public service broadcaster must broadcast in all eleven official languages (see Crawhall, 1993), cater to all cultures (even as it helps redefine cultural identity generally), do its part in cultivating an informed citizenry, and perform as a vehicle for the education of the previously disenfranchised majority. The SABC argued that it was a transformed organization able to take on this noble task, pointing to its impartial coverage during the 1994 election (see Silke and Schrire, 1994), its reconstituted and broadly representative Board of Control, its own consultative endeavor at internal transformation, and a new commitment to efficiency. But in order to fulfill its new role, the SABC argued that its financial viability must be preserved in the face of international trends. Financial viability became the crux of the broadcast debate, often overshadowing the broader debate about vision and structure. In a series of documents called "Delivering Value," the SABC advanced a set of proposals to address the issue.

In "Delivering Value" part 1, the SABC (1994a) put forward its general case as to the importance of a public service broadcaster and the need to protect its revenues. In many respects it was a general introductory document. Essentially assuming a status quo with regard to its structure and lineup of broadcast channels, SABC explained that it expected to lose R260–380 million per annum to competition and that new revenue sources would have to be found. The best options, it suggested, were a collection through the tax system, as an add-on to personal income tax or VAT, and/or contributions for specific services. But between the June 1994 release of "Delivering Value" and December, when it came out with part 2 (SABC, 1994b), many serious submissions had come in to the IBA's Triple Inquiry, several of which advocated reducing the role of the SABC and prohibiting it from deriving revenue from advertising. The most important submission to the Triple Inquiry in this regard came from the Group of Thirteen.

The Group of Thirteen was the new umbrella for the key post–social democratic civil society groups pushing for a pluralistic and progressive broadcast system. The consortium of groups filing together included numerous community media organizations and arts associations, human rights and church groups. Its documents, "The Joint Submission to the Independent Broadcasting Authority's Inquiry into the Protection and Viability of Public Broadcasting Services in a Democratic South Africa" (Group of Thirteen, 1994b) and "The Submission on Local Television Content and Independent Production" (Film and Television Federation, 1994), would deeply inform and underlay much of the logic of the eventual IBA Triple Inquiry Report (Republic of South Africa, 1995d). Authored largely by Willie Currie, the submission on public broadcasting provided a brief history of South African broadcasting and a trenchant socioeconomic description of the international context in broadcasting. The document argued that the international dynamic of media globalization could not be wished away, but that national broadcasting systems could prove resilient – especially in South Africa where broadcasting was expected to participate in nation-building and the construction of norms of citizenship – particularly if they countered globalization by allying with an emerging regionalist countertrend. To reach all kinds of cultures and markets, global media commodities tend toward homogeneity and typically picture an abstract audience of consumers. In contrast, national public broadcasters typically operate on a national level and picture the audience as citizens. Yet national broadcasters have tended to be metropolitan-centered, often slighting regions and the local. Regional broadcasting had emerged in some European markets as a response to globalization and, to a lesser degree, the decline of the national public broadcaster. "The homogenizing dynamic of globalisation has produced a reaction in local and regional cultures, that has stimulated a search for new kinds of identification with place . . . and political community." Media can be and are used at the regional and local levels to explore cultural identities and smaller political communities, and local film and television production companies have become economically viable in some areas (Group of Thirteen, 1994b: 32). Though "regionalism" in South Africa can conjure the old apartheid group areas and separate development, the Group of Thirteen document argued that the trend of regionalism must be addressed:

> [P]rovincial powers need to be taken into account when considering the restructuring of public broadcasting services in South Africa as a whole. The international counter-trend to globalisation, regionalism, should be seen as a positive rather than a negative feature that automatically undermines the national level, as some people think. In the contemporary world, people live their lives through multiple identities. Any individual human being is in a continual process of negotiating their identity as the resident of a suburb or a township, a city or a town, a province, a country, a continent as well as the world in addition to negotiating identity across race and ethnicity, gender, class, language, age or sexual orientation. This is an ongoing process of negotiating difference at the same time as commonality. One can be different in terms of any of these factors and yet share a common identity as a citizen of the PWV region and a citizen of South Africa. One of the keys to the success of nation-building in the 1990s will be the degree to which nation-building does not repress difference. This was partly captured in the slogan at the President's inauguration: One Nation – Many Cultures. (Group of Thirteen, 1994b: 39)

In the South African political context this demands a mixed, or tiered system, anchored by a strong public service broadcaster but which avoids the centralization of broadcast power. The Group of Thirteen submission proposed that the SABC consolidate itself as an effective national broadcaster, operating just two national television channels, with regional windows for provincial news or other locally oriented programs. The SABC should operate between five and nine national radio stations in the most utilized languages of the country, with at least

one of the stations dedicated to the delivery of educational programming. Each provincial government should facilitate the establishment of a provincial public broadcasting corporation, which could offer
public radio and television services. The regional SABC and TBVC radio
services could then be transferred to the provinces. The vacated third
television channel should be open to commercial exploitation – but not
at a national level. Private licenses should be awarded for five to nine
provincially based television broadcasting entities, which, however,
could link together in a network. Importantly, though private, these new
licensees would also have some public service obligations, that is, to
share the public service load so as to protect the financial viability of
the public broadcaster. If the public broadcaster has all the public
service obligations and the commercial broadcasters none, the public
broadcaster would be at a disadvantage in getting an adequate share of
the audience and the funds that follow, whether through public funding
or through advertising.

Radio could be treated somewhat differently, according to the Group
of Thirteen. Because of the lower entry barriers, adequate spectrum
space, and the potential diversity of voices, there should be no preconceived limits on the number of commercial radio stations, and regulation should be far less stringent. Community broadcasting should
be strongly encouraged, but limited to nonprofit organizations. Finally,
the document recommended that public broadcasting should not be
funded through advertising, because such a funding source skews programming toward delivering audiences to sponsors rather than delivering quality programming to citizens or communities. The primary
sources of public finance for public broadcasting should come from
taxation and license fees, perhaps gathered through electricity rates.
Advertising should be phased out over a five-year period, to allow
both the SABC and the advertising industry time to adjust (Group of
Thirteen, 1994b: 46).

Combined with its parallel proposal for strong local content requirements for all broadcasters (60% of the schedule of programming on
public television, unencoded commercial, and community television
should consist of local content, and 40% of the total schedule [i.e.,
two-thirds of local content] should consist of independent television
production), the Group of Thirteen put forward a South African
approximation of a BBC model of broadcasting, but also went beyond
it (Film and Television Federation, 1994). Given the submission's
understanding of the new economics of public television, the recom-

mendations against advertising were considered more a negotiating position than an absolute principle (Currie, 1996a).

In the face of these and other powerful parallel submissions, the SABC returned with part 2 of "Delivering Value" in December, a much more pointed submission.[12] Part 1 had made a general case for the SABC retaining primary responsibility for public broadcasting. It even averred, "This argument should not be confused with a claim that the Corporation should forever retain its existing number and range of broadcast outlets. (The SABC does not so claim – but this is a separate matter for argument)" (SABC, 1994a: 46). In its next presentation to the IBA, however, that is precisely what the SABC did claim. An SABC proposal floated in October 1994 by SABC-TV head Quentin Green called for retention of the three television channels. But the meaning of this proposal was the subject of struggle within the SABC – which, like all South African public institutions, was dealing with the confusion and stress of melding a new set of managers (the largely black Transformation Unit, led by Group Chief Executive Zwelakhe Sisulu) with the old (whites who were protected by virtue of the transition negotiations and the Interim Constitution). Tension within SABC management between

12 Reiterating many aspects of the Group of Thirteen document were submissions from the Reconstruction and Development Council, the Electronic Media in Education Forum (representing many educational organizations and NGOs), and the Freedom of Expression Institute (the successor to COM, under the leadership of Raymond Louw). The Reconstruction and Development Council was a broad front of extra-governmental, mass-based membership organizations, including the ANC, COSATU, SA National Civic Organization, SACP, Black Sash, National Arts Coalition, South African Council of Churches (SACC), Black Management Forum, National African Federated Chambers of Commerce (NAFCOC), S.A. Democratic Teachers Union, and Congress of South African Students, among others. Its submission came under the signature of SACP heavy, Jeremy Cronin (Reconstruction and Development Council, 1994). These submissions called for a strong public broadcaster, committed to education and nation-building and with far less reliance (if any) on advertising. The state should meet the financial requirements of the public broadcaster. In contrast, the Association of Marketers, M-Net, the Independent Broadcasters' Committee, and 702 Radio argued that the public broadcasting system be styled more along the U.S. model. These parties, however, agreed that the public broadcaster should not rely on advertising (largely because advertising on public television would clearly cut into their own potential advertising share). A few submissions emphasized regional broadcasting and proposed using the Bophuthatswana Broadcasting Corporation facilities to develop such regional experiments. Bop Broadcasting itself came out strongly in support of its becoming a regional broadcaster and at one time could claim the support of several provincial authorities. The Media Workers Association of South Africa (MWASA), representing several thousand journalists, technicians, and other media workers, on the other hand, called for the immediate reintegration of the former TBVC broadcasters into the national broadcaster. The broadcast union essentially cast its lot with its parastatal. It argued strongly that the SABC be allowed to collect revenue from advertising (submissions to IBA Triple Inquiry, held in the IBA Library, Johannesburg, in 1994).

old and new guard at this time was widely known, and the new staff were clearly irked both by Green's nonconsultative manner and the rehashed television scenario (Gevisser, 1994). Green's proposal essentially replicated the old TV-1, CCV, NNTV structure: a purely market-driven commercial channel (broadcasting in English), a mixed public broadcaster/commercial channel, and a public service channel providing exclusively information and education in all language groups. At about this time David Niddrie was appointed head of the Strategic Planning Unit at SABC. Niddrie, a veteran journalist of the 1980s and of broadcast policy politics, who, according to some, tended toward the commandist side of the policy debates, took charge of the SABC submissions to the IBA's Triple Inquiry. Quentin Green left the corporation.

Representing an odd, strategic accommodation among the SABC old guard, returning exiles with experience in British television, and the ANC commandist tendency, "Delivering Value" (part 2) released in December, defended the SABC's three television and multiple radio portfolio. This version, however, altered the rhetorical discourse of the commercial orientation championed by Quentin Green. The document discussed the SABC stations in terms of public service broadcasting, with a strong focus on the language issue. The SABC suggested there were but four real options in the structure-funding complex: (1) full state funding; (2) reduced portfolio; (3) revenue diversification; (4) competition. It considered option one so unlikely as to be almost inconceivable, and spent little energy on option four, probably because there was no support for it anywhere in the debate. The corporation targeted most of its firepower against option two. Reducing SABC's portfolio, the document argued, would signficantly increase the difficulty of the corporation in meeting the public need in terms of diversified language and regional and provincial programming. Option two would decrease the cost efficiency of the remaining services because fixed costs would be borne over a smaller number of units, claimed the SABC. It would undermine the system of cross-subsidization, from which African language services benefitted most. And it would remove the SABC's primary income generator, TV1, with no clear alternative revenue source. The SABC favored option three, revenue diversification. The corporation promised to reduce its dependence on advertising revenue to 55 percent. The plan called for increasing the efficiency of its license fee collection such that it would contribute 25 percent of total funding, and asked the government to fund a 15 percent contribution, approximately R234 million per annum. (This figure did not include additional state funding for educational broadcasting to the tune of R147 million.) The final few percent would be captured by increasing the value of other revenue through initiatives like co-productions, program sales, facilities and service hire, and merchandising (SABC, 1994b: 21–22).

With regard to radio, the SABC argued for the retention of the eleven national language-based radio networks, creating an additional multi-lingual national youth station, and retaining Radio Lotus (which serves the Indian community) – leaving the SABC with thirteen national radio channels. (The list would eventually also include a request to retain Good Hope Stereo, which serves the Coloured community.) As regards television, the SABC proposed that it retain the three television channels in order to meet language, regional, and educational needs. Without the three channels, the corporation argued, it would not have the available minutes to fulfill its central public service obligation of providing for viewable, accessible programming in the eleven official languages. Channel identity and programming mix would be based on audience preference and the segmentation of audiences on the basis of those preferences, structured along the lines of a tripartite division into commercial, "rainbow," and PSB channels, with the first cross-subsidizing the other two (cited in Republic of South Africa, 1995c: Appendix I, 6; SABC, 1995a).

At this point the two main policy issues coalesced. The SABC's maximalist plans made certain sense if the broadcast system were to be relatively commercial and if new, private broadcast entrants had few or no public service obligations. Both the SABC plans and its underlying assumptions of a commercial system were challenged vociferously by the civil society media groups when it came time for the IBA public hearings. Michael Markovitz and David Dison, presenting the position of the Group of Thirteen, specifically referred to the SABC's proposed radio portfolio and language policy as being based on an "expansionist mindset" and "incorrect assumptions" about the structure of the broadcast industry. Because other broadcasters would be obliged to contribute to public service broadcasting, in their estimation the SABC needed only eight national radio licenses. The remaining language-based stations should be given over to provincial broadcasting author-ities – independent of the SABC – and the commercial stations be privatized (Group of Thirteen, 1994a). John van Zyl, professor and head of media studies at the University of the Witwatersrand and presenter of the Group of Thirteen's stance on television matters, rejected SABC's tripartite division of television into commercial, rainbow, and PSB channels. By promoting a commercial framework, he argued, the SABC was perpetuating the problem of market censorship. Free market television would never find a place for minority tastes, controversial subjects, long-term, expensive investigative journalism, education, or prestige cultural programs. Instead, the Group of Thirteen proposed that SABC be restricted to two channels for public service television broadcasting, funded by means other than advertising. The logic was rather straightforward: A leaner SABC could concentrate on its public service mandate and require less revenue to do so. Vacating a channel would free up the spectrum for new voices, particularly at the regional or provincial level. Thus, a third channel should be an open commercial channel with some public broadcasting commitments at a regional level, and tied into a national network where commercially appropriate. A fourth channel, if there was room in the spectrum, could be a "publisher" channel along the lines of Britain's Channel 4, that is, a commercial channel owned by a consortium (notably including civil society organizations) that would commission programs produced and owned by others (cited in Republic of South Africa, 1995c: Appendix I, 7).

Another set of interrelated debates ensued on cross-media ownership and local content. These debates took predictable form. The civil society media groups and several of the independent producer organizations argued for high local content regulations to embody South African identity and life experiences, foster local production, and as a means to resist the maw of global programming (bolstered with research data showing locally produced programming to be popular with audiences). Without local content requirements there would be nothing to prevent the massive importation of cheap foreign programming, and the entire system of public broadcasting would collapse. The civil society media groups also argued for tough cross-media limitations in order to facilitate a multiplicity of ownership and the diversity of voices. The opposing parties, including existing and prospective private broadcasters, the Association of Marketers, the National Association of Broadcasters, M-Net on the local content issue, and the newspaper conglomerates on the cross-media limitations issue, framed their submissions in the rhetorical manner, "we support the inclination, but . . ." M-Net, for example, claimed that high local content requirements don't work, and highlighted the travails of the French Canal Plus as evidence. The NAB argued that local music quotas were premature, as record companies had not yet committed themselves to the development of the South African music industry. Many put forward the concept of consumer sovereignty. The newspaper conglomerates argued strongly that they should not be boxed out of broadcasting by unreasonable cross-media limitations, particularly inasmuch as the communication revolution means the erosion of previously separate modes for the delivery of information. Survival of the press may depend on the freedom to move into other sectors of the information business. Moreover, they argued, the print press could bring all kinds of skills, approaches, and synergies to broadcasting, particularly in joint ventures with disadvantaged groups.[13] Finally, the newspaper groups raised the spectre that unreasonable limitations infringed on their constitutional rights to freedom of speech and intimated darkly that they might challenge the limitations in court (Republic of South Africa, 1995d: 108–111; Republic of South Africa, 1995c: Appendix K).

THE TRIPLE INQUIRY REPORT AND ITS AFTERMATH

The IBA Triple Inquiry Report (Republic of South Africa, 1995d) reflected much of the logic of the Group of Thirteen submissions, even if the actual recommendations fell somewhat short of what the civil society media groups had proposed. The report called for trimming the SABC's radio and television station portfolio and for government to fund a sizable chunk of SABC's budget. Also notable were the report's recommendations for strong cross-media limitations and substantial local content obligations for all broadcasters.

RADIO

The IBA recommended giving SABC the eleven full-spectrum language stations and the two national commercial stations, Metro and 5FM (see Table 5 for a compendium of SABC radio stations). Radio Lotus and the seven regional stations should be sold. This, it was argued, would open up the airwaves and stimulate the growth of private radio. SABC would be a national broadcaster only. SABC's retention of Metro Radio and 5FM was designed to protect the corporation's financial viability in the face of competition from the soon-to-be privatized regional

13 Indeed, the joint venture route to "black empowerment" would emerge as one of the central mechanisms of white corporations to spread some wealth and protect the status quo. And it was the press and other media industries in which a large portion of the early empowerment deals were undertaken. This issue is discussed in Chapters 6 and 7.

Table 5. *SABC Radio Stations and Audiences*
(in millions)

Radio Goudveld	0.012	Radio South Africa	0.454
BRFM Stereo	0.023	Radio Swazi	0.468
Radio Venda	0.116	Radio Tsonga	0.519
Radio Algoa	0.199	Good Hope Stereo	0.610
Radio KFM	0.273	Afrikaans Stereo	0.695
Radio Lotus	0.276	5FM	0.899
Radio 2000	0.283	Setswana Stereo	1.032
RPN Stereo	0.302	Sesotho Stereo	1.516
Radioranje	0.330	Radio Metro	1.530
Radio Ndebele	0.351	Radio Xhosa	1.656
Highveld Stereo	0.367	Radio Zulu	3.356
Jacaranda Stereo	0.424		

Source: SABC *Annual Report*, 1994: 26.

SABC commercial stations. The IBA accepted the SABC's proposal for a national, multilingual youth station. In pursuit of a nonracial society, the report argued, ethnically based or identified stations should not be encouraged – hence even the naming of the services by the language in which they broadcast should be prohibited.

TELEVISION

The IBA report recommended reducing the SABC's portfolio to two terrestrial channels, giving the corporation until 1998 (and possibly another year) to effect the transition. The two stations would both be public service television stations, required to provide a full range of entertaining, informative, and educative programming across the schedule as a whole and during prime time. The SABC was encouraged to open a satellite-delivered television service as well. In January 1998 a new private television channel would be licensed with substantive public service, language, and local content obligations. The IBA expressed preference, but not a hard and fast recommendation, that the new private channel consist of a network of regional stations rather than a single national license. This reticence was due to questions about the financial viability of regional stations. A second private channel would also be considered, but the IBA, relying on financial analysis from Deloitte & Touche, doubted whether there was enough "adspend" in the South African economy to support four television channels (in addition to M-Net). Along with the IBA's proclivity to have the SABC reduce its portfolio and concentrate on its public service obligations, the perceived adspend shortfall cemented the case for two SABC channels and one private channel. Research also indicated a three SABC channel scenario would deliver only fractionally more local content than a two SABC channel option (Deloitte & Touche, 1995).

Funding

Public broadcasting services should be funded through a mix of advertising and sponsorship, license fees, government grant, and other income such as merchandising their products and leasing facilities. The IBA came to the conclusion that eliminating advertising from the public service broadcaster's revenue mix was not feasible, but it hoped the advertising component could be reduced to about 50 percent of SABC's total revenue. Parliament should provide funding on a triennial basis.

TBVC Broadcasters

The assets in the former TBVC states (homelands) should be regarded as national assets and should not be used to favor the development of broadcasting in any individual province. Thus the IBA recommended that all TBVC television facilities be integrated into the SABC as follows: Radio Ciskei and Radio Transkei be merged with Radio Xhosa of the SABC to provide a single, principally IsiXhosa language service; Radio Venda and Radio Thohoyandou be merged into a single, principally Tshivenda language radio service; a full-spectrum, principally Setswana language service be formed from Radio Mmabatho and Setswana Stereo; Radio Bop and Capital Radio be sold; Radio Sunshine be closed and the frequency be considered for a community license. Oddly, the report did not mention Bop-TV.

Sentech

Signal distribution, now known as Sentech, should be separated from the SABC and be converted to a public company in which the shares are transferred from the SABC to the government, under accountability of the Ministry of Posts, Telecommunications and Broadcasting. Signal distribution facilities of the former TBVC states and staff should transfer to Sentech. Sentech would become a common carrier responsible for signal distribution for the SABC and the new broadcasters.

CROSS-MEDIA LIMITATIONS

Here the IBA held fast. It recommended that no person who controls a newspaper may acquire or retain a controlling interest in both a radio and a television license. No person who is in a position to control a newspaper may be in a position to control a radio or television license in an area where the newspaper has an average issue readership of more than 15 percent of the total newspaper readership in that area if the license area of the radio licensee overlaps substantially with the said circulation area of the newspaper. Substantial overlap was interpreted to mean an overlap by 50 percent or more. This would permit some newspaper investment in broadcasting properties, but would forbid control. "Control" was interpreted as 15 percent shareholding.

Not requiring parliamentary approval were broadcasting license conditions regarding local content and South African music. Here the IBA was rather bold.

MUSIC

The relevant broadcasting services must ensure that at least 20 percent of the musical works broadcast between 5 A.M. and 11 P.M. consist of South African music and must be spread reasonably throughout the time period. By the year 2000, private broadcasters and music format stations should achieve a South African music quota of 40 percent; full spectrum national public radio stations and community radio stations should achieve 55 percent.

FREE-TO-AIR TERRESTRIAL TELEVISION

The IBA required broadcasters to provide a full range of informative, entertaining, and educative local television programming throughout the schedule and at prime time. Broadcasters could be required to provide programming in a number of South African languages. Higher local content quotas will be set for public and community stations than for private stations. Within three years, the national public broadcaster must air 50 percent local content between 5 A.M. and 11 P.M., broken down into minimums of specific program categories:

- Drama – 20%
- Current affairs – 80%
- Documentary and informal knowledge building – 50%
- Educational – 60%
- Children – 50%

Private terrestrial free-to-air stations must achieve a local television content quota of 30 percent, with minimum quotas within the following program categories:

- Drama – 15%
- Current affairs – 70%
- Documentary and informal knowledge building – 40%
- Children – 30%

Compliance with the local television content quota would be measured weekly.

SUBSCRIPTION TELEVISION

Even subscription broadcasters were expected to make a contribution to national development, though less than the other broadcasters. Nonterrestrial subscription broadcasters should air local content or have a financial obligation. Terrestrial subscription broadcasters, to wit, M-Net, must ensure either that at least 5 percent of its programming consist of local television content or that it expends a specified sum of money per year, determined by the IBA, on local television content. If a portion of its service is unencoded time, the broadcaster must, for the purposes of that portion, fulfill local content obligations at least equal to those of other free-to-air private terrestrial broadcasters (30 percent). In effect, the IBA proposed that M-Net keep its two-hour daily Open Time, but with an increased local content obligation in these broadcasts.

INDEPENDENT PRODUCTION

Television broadcasters must ensure that at least 40 percent of their local television content programs are commissioned to independent producers.

In the public launch of the Triple Inquiry Report, Minister Jordan indicated his basic overall support of the IBA's recommendations. He asserted that a market approach to broadcasting was out of the question, inasmuch as it would condemn South Africa to "electronic serfdom ... to half-a-dozen multinational media corporations who have no interest in nation-building and whose sole raison d'être is the maximisation of profit by selling their TV programmes at one-tenth of the price at which small countries are able to produce them." Neither unbridled market freedom nor protectionism was appropriate. The proper way forward, Jordan argued, rather, was "regulated competition." But Jordan indicated his unease with two IBA recommendations. He was unsure about limiting the SABC to just two terrestrial television channels. Conversely, he expressed concern that waiting until 1998 to introduce the private terrestrial channel might "overprotect" the SABC and "defeat the disciplinary aims of regulated competition to improve the quality and range of both public and private TV" (Jordan, 1995b).

Minister Jordan's public uncertainty concerning the future of the SABC's portfolio set the stage for further skirmishes. The IBA Triple Inquiry Report would seem to have settled the struggle between commandists and pluralists on the question of the balance between public and private broadcasting, largely in favor of the pluralists. But recall that the IBA did not itself make policy; the Triple Inquiry Report represented only a set of recommendations to Parliament. Parliament's ultimate determination of policy and the IBA's weaknesses allowed the SABC another avenue to pursue its case. Here the IBA Council's inexplicable inattention to its relations with the Parliamentary Portfolio Committee on Communications was a key factor. According to Alison Gillwald (1996), IBA Manager of Policy Development, the Parliamentary Committee indicated it intended to write its own report, using the IBA Triple Inquiry Report only as a guide. Gillwald repeatedly approached the IBA Council, suggesting it send her or someone to Cape Town to educate the Parliamentary Committee about the principles, trade-offs, and logic underlying the Triple Inquiry Report. But the IBA Council did not act on these suggestions. It also appeared that Minister Jordan did not engage in much shepherding of the IBA Report through the Parliamentary Committee. In contrast, the SABC did send representatives to Cape Town, submitted an extensive written commentary on the Triple Inquiry Report to the Committee (SABC, 1995c), and also engaged in the usual lobbying niceties, such as sponsoring parties for the Committee. M-Net did much the same.

In its analysis of the Triple Inquiry Report to the Parliamentary Committee on Communications, the SABC essentially tied the IBA's recommendations on public broadcasting to the funding questions. The SABC made two fundamental assertions: (1) It could not fulfill its public service obligations in eleven official languages on just two television channels, and (2) the IBA erred in its analysis of the future state of the advertising revenue pool. SABC representatives claimed that the IBA's analysis was far too conservative. The "adspend" would be there to

support four television channels. South Africa's adspend as a proportion of GDP is low, they asserted, largely as a consequence of the
country's isolation and the resultant protection of local manufacturers
and marketers from international competition. As the South African
economy normalizes and becomes more competitive, its adspend of
0.91 percent of GDP will move toward the European norm of 1.6
percent – increasing the total. The entry of several international competitors in consumer products was set to precipitate sharp competition
for South African markets, and the major beneficiary would likely be
television ad revenue (SABC, 1995a: 10). Moreover, argued the SABC,
many of the IBA Report's recommendations flowed from the question-
able assumption that the national government would finance a sizable
portion of the public service broadcaster's activities. The SABC proposed to Parliament that the IBA recommendation for a reduction of
its television portfolio be amended to provide for retention of the status
quo, subject to a review once a clearer picture of the total available
revenue pool emerged – at the end of 1997 (SABC, 1995d). In the same
document, the SABC argued in favor of retaining Radio Lotus and
Good Hope Stereo on the basis that these stations "provide unique services to sizeable minorities (Indian and Coloured, respectively) whose
interests are not specifically met by any other public service radio stations." The SABC objected to the M-Net's retention of Open Time, even
if the pay-TV operator had to increase the local content. And the SABC
objected to the IBA's proposal that local content percentage be calcu-
lated during high viewing times only (SABC, 1995c).

The Parliamentary Portfolio Committee on Communications held a
week of public hearings on the Triple Inquiry Report in Pretoria in the
second week of November 1995. The SABC floated its now familiar
arguments about retaining the third television channel, along with a
more seriously articulated commitment to engage in provincial television broadcasting, beginning with regular "break-aways" on Channel
2 (CCV) to the provinces for news. Various MPs voiced reservations
about any statutory government contribution to the SABC outside the
license fee. African National Congress MP Carl Niehaus foreshadowed
the government's eventual position, responding to SABC management
that its case for retaining the third channel was convincing, but he
foresaw a problem with money forthcoming from government, given
its other development obligations. SABC managers played their cards
intelligently, arguing that if government wanted the SABC to fulfill a
broad public service mandate, it would have to find a way of financing

it.[14] A grant from government was essential, SABC argued, but one other way of helping the public service broadcaster would be to close M-Net's Open Time window. Shutting down Open Time would not only halt an inequitable practice but would free a significant amount of adspend for the SABC and the new commercial channel (SABC, 1995b).

The parliamentary committee met on February 6, 1996, to discuss the IBA Triple Inquiry Report. The committee's changes to the report in some ways were to be expected, given the comments of various MPs during the November public hearings (Republic of South Africa, 1996u). On the whole, though the changes effected by the committee seemed modest, they altered the structure of broadcasting considerably from the model proposed in the IBA's report. The committee voted to restore the SABC's third television channel and to speed up the licensing of a private television channel by six months, to mid-1997. It amended the IBA's language on funding so as to limit the government's responsibility. With the National Party and the Freedom Front dissenting, the committee did, however, approve the paragraph committing Parliament to funding on a triennial basis for the cost of provincial split time on radio stations, the cost of increasing African language and local content television programming on the SABC, and the cost of funding the previously determined Education Ministry/SABC Task Group recommendations on educational broadcasting.

Consequentially, the committee deleted a paragraph (3, sect. 4.1.2) in which the IBA suggested *how* the SABC should reduce its three television channels to two. The language of the original paragraph directed the SABC to absorb NNTV's public service and documentary programming on *both* the remaining channels. This was deliberately phrased by IBA drafters to prevent the SABC from loading the public service programming onto one channel to make the other available for primarily commercial fare. Inasmuch as the parliamentary committee restored the SABC's television portfolio to three television stations, it may be that the paragraph was moot. But the deletion of the language gave the SABC room to configure its channel lineup in a paradoxic

---

14 The IBA had recommended state funding to the SABC of R639 million in 1998 – for two channels; the SABC itself was asking government for only R496 million – for *three*. The IBA insisted that a three television channel SABC portfolio would require government funding of R1 billion per year. Notwithstanding the SABC's positioning of its funding needs as, in a sense, a bargain in comparison with the IBA numbers, the joke at the hearings was the committee's fear that the SABC would be like Oliver Twist, always coming back to ask for more (SABC, 1995b).

approximation of the model proposed by the old apartheid government in its original restructuring moves of the early 1990s. The committee did let stand paragraph 5, that "the public broadcaster will be required to provide a full range of entertaining, informative and educative programming across the schedule as a whole and at prime time." But not enshrining the structure of the public channels in legislation gave the SABC that much more wiggle room on this key issue in the future. Interacting with that change was the committee's other deletion in the television area. It deleted a paragraph (1, sect. 4.5) in which the IBA had proposed that "private terrestrial free-to-air television services should be full spectrum services offering a wide range of programming with *substantial* public service and local content obligations." In its place the committee added a watered down version of the obligation: "New private channels [will] be licensed with *some* public service, language and local content obligations" (emphasis added). The committee also eliminated the IBA's preference that the private channel be regional. The channel could be regional or national.[15]

The combination of these changes – a three channel SABC without guarantees of state funding alongside a private commercial television channel with reduced and ambiguous public service obligations – had the potential to create a commercializing juggernaut in South African television the consequence of which will severely test the public service nature of the system. Without "substantial" public service obligations, the private channel will undoubtedly import global programming cheaply and attract heavy ad revenue. The SABC, straining under its high local content obligations and inadequate funding for three channels, will be compelled to compete with the private channel in

---

15 The removal of the regional preference for the new private television channel may have been due in part to skepticism that regional channels would be economically viable. The IBA itself indicated that the issue required serious attention (Republic of South Africa, 1995c: Appendix I, 18). However, a more politically based explanation seems equally valid. Regionalism, or federalism, had become an enormously fraught political issue. It was the official linchpin of the intense and violent conflict between the ethnically mobilized nationalism of the Inkatha Freedom Party and the ANC's Enlightenment-based, politically centralized nonracialism. Notwithstanding the possible benefit of more locally based television, the ANC may have decided to resist regional licenses because of, one, how it might color the broader struggle over federalism and, two, how regional channels might be used by "retrograde" regional politicians in Kwazulu-Natal (IFP) and Western Cape (NP). The federalism issue bedevils the ANC. There is evidence that ANC provincial leaders are frustrated because they have so little authority and budgets to deal with complex regional and local issues. They themselves would like some central governmental authority devolved to the provincial level. But they cannot publicly so advocate due to the overweening political conflict with the IFP.

delivering audiences to advertisers, thus moving toward a commercial orientation in one if not two of its channels and ghettoizing its public service offerings on the third channel. The question, of course, is whether the modifier on the local content provision, "some," comes attached with hard and fast measures. The IBA did so attach in the Triple Inquiry Report. It is not clear whether the Parliamentary Committee did so, and there is no indication from the transcript of committee proceedings. It is true that the IBA controls licensing and through that authority can conceivably mold the overall structure of program content. But in the absence of statutory language, the extent of the IBA's discretion on the matter is unclear. The Parliamentary Committee's deliberations were not extensive and the amendments to the IBA Triple Inquiry were undertaken without a great deal of discussion.

Politics explain the ANC policy decisions on the Triple Inquiry Report. Because the National Party had consistently tried to whittle down the power of the SABC and create more space for private broadcasters, the ANC's natural response was to bolster the SABC's portfolio. According to one highly placed ANC committee member, the NP believed that a genuine public service broadcaster in all languages was inimical to its interests. Hence the NP members of the Portfolio Committee on Communications, particularly caucus leader Marthinus van Schalkvyk, continually cast doubt on the independence of the SABC and publicly denigrated it as the mouthpiece of the ANC, and challenged the competence of the SABC Board.[16] The restoration of the third television channel and the disputed radio channels thus was a political decision related to the tasks of broadcasting in the eleven languages and to maintain the strength of the SABC as the national public broadcaster. But, as a high-ranking ANC MP later privately admitted, the ANC "misjudged the size of the funding cake," and regretted the vote to restore the third television channel to the SABC.

THE IBA: TOO WEAK OR TOO INDEPENDENT?

An independent regulatory body, the IBA was an unfamiliar entity in the South African political scene. And because it oversaw the sensitive and contentious broadcast sector, the IBA was subject to harsh, often

16 In addition to slowing down the parliamentary committee's work and stoking anxiety among Afrikaners about the fate of Afrikaans language programming on the SABC, this strategy had the added benefit of building up van Schalkvyk's position within the National Party hierarchy. Van Schalkvyk became NP leader following the retirement of F. W. de Klerk in 1997.

contradictory criticism. Some, including the act's drafters, judged the IBA a "captured" agency, taking too literally its mandate to protect the public broadcasting services and being overly tentative in general (Dison, 1996; Markovitz, 1996). The IBA's reaction to the SABC's "relaunch" of its three television stations in February 1996 was a case in point. The relaunch altered features of the existing licenses of the stations, including their language percentages. The IBA determined that these changes were illegal and that the SABC was obliged to hold public hearings. After threats to shut down the SABC, some face-saving gestures were offered on both sides, and the SABC was permitted to proceed (to the intense dissatisfaction of the Afrikaans lobby, inasmuch as it was the percentage of programming in Afrikaans that would be most diminished in the new station lineup). Selling the six SABC radio stations slated for commercial acquisition was another purported instance of the IBA's needless tentativeness. In Dison's view, after the Triple Inquiry Report the IBA presumably could have demanded control of the frequencies held by the SABC (after all, the authority has jurisdiction over the broadcast portion of the electromagnetic spectrum) and begun the process of making some available to private bidders. Yet, two years after its creation the IBA still had not licensed a private radio broadcaster (see Republic of South Africa, 1996h).

Paradoxically, the disposition of the six SABC stations designated for commercial acquisition prompted Minister of Posts, Telecommunications and Broadcasting Jay Naidoo to conclude that the IBA was, in fact, too independent. When his ministry tried to take control of the process it was rebuffed because the IBA Act stipulated that any transfer of a sound broadcasting license must be carried out in terms of section 74 of the act, which in turn required that the full notice-and-comment and public hearing procedures in sections 41–42 be observed. The fact that the IBA was singled out for criticism in the press in March 1996 for exorbitantly high salaries and staff generally "on the gravy train" also contributed to Minister Naidoo's judgment. He saw the IBA as too independent, a runaway agency answerable to no one, and announced that his department would take over the framing of broadcast policy and scale down the IBA to the status of a "normal" regulatory body (Powell, 1996).

Between charges of being too weak and too independent, the IBA's tentativeness was perhaps understandable in light of the absence of a clear public process that provided an unambiguous mandate for a permanent regulatory body. Recall that the IBA was established only within the CODESA framework, and it was only in the drafting process that an interim oversight body became transformed into a permanent one. The IBA's authority was challenged from all sides. A telling feature of the disposition of the SABC radio properties struggle was that not just the Ministry of Posts, Telecommunications and Broadcasting tried to assert jurisdiction, but Cabinet and the SABC tried as well (Salgado, 1996).

The question of the IBA's authority and the limits of its independence were underscored by the denouement of the licensing of commercial radio and television. The SABC, hoping to pocket the proceeds of the radio station sales, wanted the criteria for selection to be primarily the highest bidder. The IBA, hanging tough, interpreted its requirement to "encourage ownership and control of broadcasting services by persons from historically disadvantaged groups," as essentially an affirmative action set-aside (Republic of South Africa, 1996e, 1996f: sect. 7). Applicants for the SABC and new licenses would have to show:

- the extent to which the financial interests in the application reflect inclusion of the historically disadvantaged;
- the nature and extent of decision making by the historically disadvantaged in the business venture; and
- the empowering of historically disadvantaged staff through training and development programs as well as the extent to which such staff are included in senior managerial, administrative and editorial decision-making positions.

The category "historically disadvantaged South Africans" was understood by the IBA as those against whom the apartheid system had discriminated and those who were discriminated against by reason of their gender. As a result of the IBA's insistence on empowerment criteria, a high percentage of the assets of private radio is now held by blacks – by one 1998 estimate, 63 percent (Janisch and Kotlowitz, 1998: 29). The IBA held fast to its empowerment criteria and did not always choose the highest bidder (the case in KFM, East Coast Radio, and Radio Jacaranda), but some of the license awards reflected ANC political influence peddling and cronyism.

The commercial license awards thus highlighted the IBA's success in transforming South African broadcasting and the limits of its independence. The awards also reveal the pattern of black economic empowerment in the post-election period. Radio Jacaranda, a Pretoria-based station, was awarded to Newshelf 71, a consortium of New Africa Investments Ltd. (NAIL), at 65.1 percent, and the French European Development International (EDI), even though its R70 million bid was R20 million lower than that of the main competitor, National Labour and Economic Development Institute. NALEDI had a lower empowerment stake (at 45 percent), but its black shareholding was arguably more widespread than NAIL's. The IBA indicated that EDI's experience also was a factor in the award (Republic of South Africa, 1996g). NAIL, of course, has strong links to the ANC leadership. The award was successfully challenged in court because the IBA's decision was made without a proper quorum of councillors. There were also allegations that one of the IBA councillors had improper connections to EDI. Eventually the matter was settled when the two contending bidders agreed to split the station between them, and the combined applicant was awarded the license in August 1997.

Highveld Stereo was the most attractive asset in the SABC portfolio, largely because its area of signal reception included Johannesburg's affluent white suburbs. Africa On Air's bid of R320 million dwarfed the nearest competing bid by R190 million and was awarded the license. But many were unhappy about the arrangement. Zerilda, Africa On Air's empowerment consortium, consisting of the Mineworkers Investment Company, South African Clothing and Textile Workers Union (SACTWU) Investment Group, and the Women's Investment Portfolio, held 60 percent of Africa On Air, but would not have effective control for at least ten years. Primedia Broadcasting, the money behind the consortium and the 40 percent partner, would effectively control Highveld. Given its control of the already powerful Radio 702, Primedia effectively held two of the most desirable radio stations in South Africa. Even if Africa On Air's bid could not be turned down because of the empowerment promise and the high offer, the IBA's award clearly did not do much to increase diversity of ownership in South African radio.

In another case, a viable jazz station applicant with 85 percent empowerment proportion of shareholding (Jazz FM Consortium) lost to a poorly structured Youth Radio Consortium that had inside backing from former Radio Freedom cadre. Indeed, Mopani Media, the Y-FM applicant, submitted a very thin document as its initial application. The submission did not address many key questions. The IBA hearings on the license took place in early February 1997, and the official announcement of the award was March 15. Mopani Media submitted the full application document only on March 12, three days before the license was awarded (see Republic of South Africa, 1997a). The popular Y-FM station is considered one of the sucess stories of the radio privatizations, but the license award procedures were suspicious.

Finally, the largest prize of all, the new commercial television channel, went to Midi Television, a consortium of Hosken Consolidated Investments (the company owned by the investment arms of the SACTWU and the National Union of Mineworkers) with participation from the U.S. media giant, Time-Warner, and smaller stakes held, among others, by the National African Federated Chambers of Commerce (NAFCOC) and the Disabled Employment Concerns Trust. This ownership scheme, and the fact that the channel was to be managed by people with local broadcast experience (from Bop-TV), convinced the IBA to award Midi the license. Midi won out over six other bids, all of which featured various percentages and mixes of black participation (Republic of South Africa, 1998c).

Several conclusions can be drawn from the IBA radio license awards. The IBA's insistence on empowerment criteria for license applicants forcefully transformed the ownership complexion of private broadcasting in South Africa. The IBA stood fast in rejecting the traditional centers of media power, particularly the license applications that included the traditional press groups. The authority was largely successful in creating a regulated pluralism in South African broadcasting. This was no small accomplishment. At the same time, its decisions in three of the commercial radio awards seemed to favor certain big black business consortia and old comrades. Finally, the license awards did little to address the urban–rural gap. Audiences reached by the new commercial stations are overwhelmingly urban-based, and the stations have a strong inclination to target more affluent audiences that can be sold to advertisers. The IBA thus ran into the very real limitations of trying to inculcate, in a market-based broadcast structure, programming diversity via ownership diversity. In this regard, the IBA's supposed weakness and tentativeness was also a function of the pragmatic difficulties of regulation itself, of formulating intricate strictures and incentives for players in a fluid and largely untested environment.

CONCLUSION

South Africa finds itself in many respects in the rather unique situation of engaging in an old-fashioned exercise of nation-building, needing to construct a national identity and culture after decades of apartheid and separate development. That is why the broadcast debates are so important, as broadcasting is understood to be an essential institution in that exercise. Broadcasting, of course, is also acknowledged as a key medium of the public sphere and hence crucial to the transition to democracy and the ongoing process of democratization. The public service model, in spite of its shortcomings, is still the foundation (though, pointedly, only the foundation) of imagining a national culture through the medium of broadcasting, because it addresses the audience as citizens of a unitary social formation. But the ability of broadcasting to fulfill these tasks is complicated by the fact that broadcasting is no longer the stable, confinable medium it was even twenty years ago. Public service broadcasting can barely hold its own in the rush of the multichannel environment and the market power of the global entertainment consortia.

The political negotiations and subsequent actions of the Independent Broadcasting Authority managed to establish a three-tiered broadcast system that embodied a post–social democratic politics. But this was a fragile victory. The IBA's ability to transform South African broadcasting was constrained at the outset by the protection of established property rights agreed upon as part of the negotiations of the political transition. The political requirement that the IBA Council and leadership be shared between the NP and ANC may have preserved an important patina of impartiality, but it increased the difficulty, time, and expense in determining and coordinating broadcast policy. The political balancing of the IBA's independent status and South Africa's unfamiliarity with regulatory bodies induced suspicion of the IBA among ANC parliamentarians. These factors (along with probable financial improprieties among some IBA councillors) undermined the perception of the IBA's effectiveness and limited its scope of authority. They set the stage for further weakening its powers by the minister of Posts, Telecommunications and Broadcasting. Although the IBA put out a smart report (the Triple Inquiry), its weak structural position in the policy-determination process and its neglect in shepherding its policy recommendations meant that Parliament – for a variety of political reasons – scaled back the post–social democratic broadcast vision and set in motion economic forces that may well track South African broadcasting closer toward an American commercial model. The weakness of the IBA in the context of evolving party politics, the lobbying strength of a "transformed" SABC – as well as the weight of the argument that SABC had a mandate to broadcast in all eleven languages, and, finally, the untouchability of M-Net, altered the broadcast structure enough to threaten the delicate balance of the post–social democratic vision.

In effect, SABC and its allies in government won the battle but lost the war. By keeping the three television channels and additional radio stations without expectation of government funding, the SABC added to its responsibilities without adding to its financial viability, and, hence, greatly complicated and perhaps undermined its public service mission. There was no evidence that government would ever allocate the necessary funds to the SABC. Indeed, the proceeds from the sale of the SABC radio stations, in excess of R500 million, went, with Minister Naidoo's acquiescence, to the central fiscus, not to the SABC. Without adequate financing to program three television channels, the SABC's triumph jeopardized its long run viability as a public broadcaster. SABC, as a public broadcaster, is a weak giant. It posted a R21 million loss in 1996, the result of dwindling advertising and license revenues, and increased public broadcasting commitments. Projected shortfalls for 1997 were R77 million. To stem its losses, SABC implemented the recommendations of a report conducted by the McKinsey consulting company, shedding thousands of jobs, outsourcing much of its programming, and buying into the idea of cross-subsidizing its public service offerings by commercial ones. In short, the relative absence of public funding and corresponding reliance on advertising, combined with SABC's extensive brief, in principle set in motion the commercializing dynamic that bedevils the American Public Broadcast System. On the one hand, the SABC will have to devote time and money to fulfill its mandated public service programming, which will probably not attract sufficient advertising, thus forcing SABC to try to skimp on these programs. On the other hand, in order to bring in revenue, the SABC will sink lots of money into entertainment programs it believes will compete with M-Net and the commercial broadcasters. At the same time, those who hoped that a big SABC could act to convey the government's message will likely be disappointed. When there are broadcast alternatives, audiences invariably desert didactic program offerings.

Although sobering, this outcome should not overshadow what was, in most respects, a successful transformation. Like the South African transition to democracy itself, the new South African broadcasting was born of the pressure-cooker environment of negotiations between intensely suspicious parties. Notwithstanding centralist tendencies in both the National Party and the ANC, their mutual suspicion favored the compromise solution of an independent broadcaster, formally separate from state and political parties. The strong and continuing presence of post–social democratic civil society media groups substantially aligned with the ANC (but also wary of its centralist tendencies) was a major factor both in the general compromise and in fashioning a new structure for the sector. The presence of these groups effectively derailed the apartheid government's strategy to begin reforming and privatizing South African broadcasting prior to the general democratic dispensation. And they essentially won the battle of vision: the three-tiered broadcast system anchored by a strong public broadcaster, prodded substantially by competition from a limited private commercial broadcast presence, and augmented by community broadcasters, particularly in local radio, all supervised by an independent broadcast regulator. The paring back of the SABC's portfolio, as limited as it was, did launch the private radio and television broadcast licenses that opened up the airwaves to new voices as well as establishing a condition of contestability to the SABC. Moreover, the new private licenses represented the first genuine, if modest, effort in the restructuring of state assets in post-apartheid South Africa, creating an early avenue for black economic empowerment.

CHAPTER 5

"All Shall Call": The Telecommunications
Reform Process

As was the case with broadcasting, reform apartheid set in motion a complex process in which an inescapable reform of the South African telecommunications sector became tied to the subtle politics of the government's effort to maintain white dominance in a post-apartheid dispensation. Even more than with broadcasting, internal sectoral dynamics set the reform process in motion in telecommunications. Recall that in the effort to meet the needs of business and begin to extend service to black neighborhoods, the South African Posts and Telecommunications had borrowed heavily to digitalize its network and expand its infrastructure in the 1980s. Despite, or perhaps as a consequence of, this effort, the SAPT came open to criticism for its alleged goldplating, inefficiency, bloated workforce, and considerable debt. Trashed in the de Villiers Report (Republic of South Africa, 1989) and facing competition from prospective new entrants deploying new technologies by the end of the decade, the SAPT looked to be a parastatal ripe for change in a sector badly in need of reform. The SAPT was the subject of a legislative effort in 1990 to separate telecommunications from posts, to remove both from the line responsibilities of the ministry, and to prepare the parastatal for privatization.

A good chunk of the South African telecommunications story is little different from those of other countries in the past several years. South African telecommunications were affected by the same forces that challenged traditional telecommunications regimes in other nations: the erosion of monopoly boundaries by technology and demand from large corporate users, the interrelated damage to the cross-subsidy system and attacks on the natural monopoly rationale. And as *other* nations transformed their telecommunications regimes in the 1980s, asymmetric deregulation constituted an exogenous factor with consequences for traditional post, telegraph, and telephone (PTT) systems, including South Africa's. Newly deregulated international telecommunications operators were now scouring the globe looking for opportunities to serve the communication needs of large business users in any country (see, among several others, Cowhey and Aronson, 1988; Duch, 1991; Foster, 1992; Drake, 1994). And those operators and their host governments began lobbying bilateral and multilateral forums to break down the exclusivity of national monopoly structures. Indirect pressures for liberalization and privatization, often orchestrated by the United States, were constant in the South African telecommunications reform process.

At the broader, macroeconomic level, the structural changes in the telecommunications regimes of developing countries can be viewed as part of the large trends in those political economies triggered by the debt crisis of the 1980s: the sea change toward more orthodox economic policies of monetarism and budget deficit reduction and the retreat from state-led development strategies (see, among others, Kahler, 1986; Nelson, 1990; Haggard and Kaufman, 1992). It should be understood, however, that local political dynamics played a crucial, if not controlling role in the transformation of South African telecommunications. It is perhaps more accurate to say that the general forces underlying the transformation of global telecommunications ran through and were focused by the political events of reform apartheid and the subsequent transition to democracy. The exogenous forces of change in telecommunications and the external influences at the level of general economic policy were necessary conditions for the transformation of South African telecommunications. They set the stage and created pressures, opportunities, and constraints. But they were insufficient in and of themselves to account for change or its particular direction. Domestic politics, conditioned by external factors, are the key. The politics of the transformation of South African telecommunications are intimately bound up in the politics of the transition to democracy.

In a previous chapter, I argued that telecommunications services in South Africa were fully ensconced within the apartheid political calculus. Service was not extended to black townships because, among other reasons, the policy of separate development stipulated that blacks were temporary residents of South Africa who would one day be repatriated to their appropriate tribal homelands. Because, in the ideological register of Verwoerdian grand apartheid, the black townships surrounding the white South African cities were understood as transient urban formations, any expenditure on them was deemed inherently wasteful. And any attempt to make them better places to live would have the unwanted consequence of encouraging further African influx to the cities. As the policies of grand apartheid fell into place, the South African Post Office could not officially extend telecommunications infrastructure to the homelands because the parastatal had no formal jurisdiction outside true South Africa. Each homeland was supposed to be responsible for providing services to "its" people. Hence where telecommunications infrastructure existed in the TBVC areas, it was nominally under the control of homeland parastatals. This general state of affairs changed in the late 1970s to early 1980s, as the SAPT began to extend telephone service to Indian and Coloured areas and, later, to some African areas. The change was due to a number of interconnected factors, the most important of which was that the white telephone market was essentially saturated.[1] But it was also the case that some high Post Office civil servants actually subscribed to the public service ethos found in many classic PTTs (Taylor, 1992).[2] At the broader level, the expansion of telecommunications to blacks also reflected and embodied the general, if desultory, set of government policies characteristic of reform apartheid.

Recall that, notwithstanding the essential error in condemning SAPT's digitalization program, the de Villiers investigation of the SAPT

---

1 While the white market was essentially saturated, there was clear evidence of unmet demand. The wait list hovered around the 100,000 figure since at least the mid-1970s. This amounted to a wait of several years for service (Taylor, 1992). As the Post Office began its expansion of service to nonwhite areas, the wait list actually increased, in some years dramatically so, registering 141,166 in 1981 to over 225,000 for each of the three years following (South African Posts and Telecommunications, *Annual Reports*, various years). And it is assumed that the official wait list understated actual demand.

2 The expansive vision of SAPT leadership is a factor of some importance in the decision to grow beyond white and business customers. In an interview, Telkom Senior General Manager Ben Bets attributed the expansion of service in the late 1970s, early 1980s in part to marketing, in part to the vision of Jimmy Taylor (Bets, 1992). Taylor was somewhat of an anomaly in the South African parastatal universe. An English-speaking engineer from Natal who spoke fluent Zulu, Taylor was not the typical South African parastatal bureaucrat. He believed in state monopolies, public service, and universal telephone service to all. With typical modesty, Taylor attributed the SAPT expansion program to his predecessor, Louis Rive. Taylor recalled that Rive would agonize over the difficulty of extending service to blacks; he wanted to expand the telephone infrastructure but despaired over finding the capital (Taylor, 1992). The existence of a public service ethos underscores the fact that the Post Office (and by extrapolation, other South African parastatals) was a complicated organization that cannot be characterized as either a simple pork barrel for the apartheid regime or as a simple tool of capital. It suggests that the notion of a monolithic, ethnically loyal parastatal culture must be jettisoned for something more complex. See N. Clark (1994) for an elucidation of this position.

underscored a host of problems faced by the parastatal. These problems were typical of most PTTs at this time. The ideal typical PTT or regulated private telephone monopoly entailed a de facto or explicit grant of an exclusive franchise or monopoly status that protected the carrier from the anarchy of competition. Monopoly control of the network and monopsony equipment purchasing solved the problems of standards, interconnection, and easy access to (cheaper) capital for the massive expense of wiring and constructing a network. Typically, equipment purchasing functioned in the manner of industrial policy, since the PTT would purchase from domestic equipment supply companies. A stable and secure telephone service and domestic equipment supply capability were often seen as matters of national defense as well. A central feature of traditional infrastructure parastatals and regulated monopolies in the developed world is that they came to function – or at least came to be legitimated – as a kind of social democratic industrial policy, generally consonant with Keynesian macroeconomics. During the period of regulated infrastructure growth, efficiency tended to be balanced with equity, development with forms of redistribution. In principle, direct state control or regulated monopoly established a mandate for the communications carrier to expand service universally and generally to keep basic prices relatively low. It often also meant the broad unionization of labor in those industries. In the United States, monopoly status for privately owned telephone companies entailed a series of public interest quids pro quo. In exchange for monopoly status, a telephone company had to fulfill certain obligations as a "common carrier": an obligation to serve all who request service, nondiscrimination, and the provision of service at relatively cheap rates. Regulation, in theory, would protect consumers from monopoly abuses.

The goal, particularly in the United States, was universal service, service to everybody. This was secured through regulatory oversight of tariffs and a system of cross-subsidies whereby, generally, long-distance and business tariffs subsidized residential and rural service. The expected consequence was the so-called network externality, that more people could and would connect into the network, making the network as a whole more valuable to everyone. State-sanctioned monopoly control meant that areas left unwired (because of low profit potential) would be wired, because costs would be spread through the system generally by means of value-of-service pricing and cost averaging. Equipment was amortized over a very long period, constituting another way of spreading out costs to make rates cheap and connections more likely.

For the most part this arrangement worked. By the 1970s, telephone penetration had grown in the United States to over 92 percent. (For a challenge to the American story, see Mueller, 1997, and a response by Horrigan, 1998.) Roughly similar stories can be told of the European and other developed nation PTTs, though it should be understood that in many, if not most nations, the old telecommunications model worked better in theory than in practice. Even France and Germany made their most significant strides toward the expansion of telephone service only in the 1970s – after many decades of supposed commitment to the goal. Indeed, talk of a universal service "obligation" surfaced in European countries only when the PTTs came under liberalization pressure. In a survey of Organization for Economic Cooperation and Development countries, Nicholas Garnham (OECD, 1991: 28–29) found that universal service was an implicit rather than explicit goal of telecommunications policy in the sense that individual citizens possessed no legal right to telephone service on demand, or that, conversely, telecommunications administrations were under no legal obligation to provide service. Thus the way in which universal service provision was interpreted was essentially voluntarist on the part of either the government or the telecommunications administration or both – a matter of changing political and/or administrative priorities and perceptions (see also Hills, 1993).

Despite its apparent success, there were problems with the traditional model. Something of a consensus emerged among economists in the 1970s that regulation had engendered many unwanted outcomes, including sheltered inefficiency, the suppression of innovation, and misallocation of resources (see A. Kahn, 1988, Vol. II: 1–46, 172–250; Horwitz, 1989). Under rate-of-return regulation, which was the formula applied to regulated privately owned monopoly utilities, there is no clear relation between costs and prices. Prices are set according to general goals in a process of quasi-political accommodation. Costs are largely irrelevant because they are internal to what was usually a vertically integrated system.[3] Rate-of-return regulation gave the regulated

---

3 The way it worked in the United States was to make a vertically integrated American Telephone & Telegraph Company (AT&T) the network manager of the entire telephone system (made up of AT&T-affiliated local service monopolies along with many, far smaller independent local service monopolies). AT&T's vertical integration meant that the company controlled local and long distance services, provided for its own equipment through manufacturing subsidiaries, and engaged in its own research and development. Telephone companies were guaranteed a fair rate of return on investment. The companies would submit their costs of providing service to the regulator, who would determine the percentage of profit that would be factored into tariffs.

company a reasonable rate of profit on top of its stated costs of doing business. In most cases, however, the regulatory body is dependent on the information provided by the regulated company. The incentive of the firm under rate-of-return regulation is to inflate its rate base by overbuilding its plant or by increasing equipment stocks and fixed capital more than would be the case under the normal cost-minimizing pressures of the market – a practice sometimes called "goldplating" or the Averch-Johnson-Wellisz effect (Averch and Johnson, 1962; Wellisz, 1963). Indeed, there were long-standing allegations that, in addition to common goldplating, AT&T engaged in artificial boosting of the prices of its equipment in order to inflate further the base from which its rate of return was determined (United States, 1939).

Somewhat different, but parallel incentive mechanisms were said to push state-owned enterprises away from rational, cost-minimizing actions. Property rights theory suggested that, because they do not have access to shared information, governments face difficulties in providing appropriate incentives to public sector managers and in monitoring their performance. Managers are given less discretion than their private sector counterparts and so choose a relatively "quiet life." They will perform only to the level necessary to meet the performance standards set for them, and these may be modest compared with the potential of the firm or industry concerned (see Alchian, 1965; Demsetz, 1967; Levi, 1988). The theory explains differences in organizational behavior on the basis of the individual incentives created by the structure of property rights. Private ownership concentrates rights and rewards; public ownership dilutes them. The more individuals stand to gain from tending to their property, the better will it be tended. Conversely, the more attenuated and diluted their property rights, the less motivated individuals will be to use the property under their control efficiently. Unlike shareholders in a private corporation, customers of public enterprises have no property (shares) to sell if they are dissatisfied. Hence there is no check on the dissipation of value by the management of public enterprises. And under conditions of monopoly provision, dissatisfied customers cannot change providers.

Alternatively, public choice theory suggests that public managers act not in some abstract public interest, but rather according to their own self-interests, or in the lingo, "rent-seeking." Applying the logic of microeconomics to politics, public choice theorists find that whereas self-interest leads to good results in the marketplace, it produces nothing but pathology in political decisions. Public choice theory most often focuses on political actors in a democracy, but it also applies to the management of public enterprises. The managers of public enterprises seek to secure greater pay, power, and prestige by forming coalitions with civil servants in relevant ministries. The result is increased budgets. Budget maximization becomes an end in itself, and other objectives – both commercial and noncommercial – are conceded to achieve it. In other words, public managers' interests are the same as their private sector counterparts, but whereas self-interested behavior in the private sector supposedly secures cost-minimizing rationality, self-interested behavior in the public sector brings only economically inefficient action and higher government spending overall (Buchanan and Tullock, 1962; Niskanen, Jr., 1971). Both property rights and public choice theories primarily derive from the Chicago School of law and economics and the earlier work of Friedrich von Hayek (1935, 1940, 1960). Hayek argued that as long as a government cannot credibly commit itself to noninterference in the competitive process, managers will not be profit maximizers and economic inefficiency will result. Janos Kornai (1992) followed the argument into a sociology of the "soft budget constraint" under state socialism: Facing inefficiencies from state-owned enterprises, political authorities will grant loans, "soft" prices, and "soft" taxes to keep firms afloat which, without state intervention, would have failed. For an overview and critique of the general approaches, see Starr (1988), also Rose-Ackerman (1992) and Roemer (1994).

These and related theories tried to address why, for instance, telecommunications monopolies in developing countries were long plagued by persistent large unmet demand for service, call traffic congestion, poor service quality and reliability, and limited territorial coverage – even though in many developing nations the telecommunications parastatal was rather profitable. Very often, the culprit was identified as state ownership. Governments appropriated operating surpluses to the detriment of reinvestment within the sector, thus starving the parastatal for capital (Vickers and Yarrow, 1988; Saunders, Warford, and Wellenius, 1994). The conflicting pressures upon parastatal management to satisfy a number of constituencies, including government officials, were identified as a prime source of inefficiency. In some instances, different aspects of a parastatal's operation were accountable to, and in effect micro-managed by, different government ministries – creating cross-cutting pressures that tended to paralyze the parastatal's managers. In other instances, state-owned enterprises were said to identify output maximization as a management goal, but, because there was no possibility of bankruptcy, there was little incentive to minimize costs. A belief that deficits would be financed by the Treasury would lower incentives to cut costs and raise prices. Finally, because such enterprises generally were highly unionized, and because high government officials tended to consider the unions a key constituency to be placated, the regime would favor lower levels of productivity (see World Bank, 1995).

The SAPT exhibited some of these features within a South African register. Job reservation padded its workforce. For most of its existence, the SAPT was short of capital, even though telecommunications were quite profitable. Its tariffs were set according to political criteria. Like all large organizations, it was divided by various management factions. A large "traditionalist" faction valued the SAPT for its secure, "quiet" life. A quasi-public utility ethos could be found among the traditionalists, but wholly within an apartheid context. The ethos went only so far as to value the company as a big (white) family – a kind of friendly, cooperative work culture nicely reinforced by the classic civil service protection of jobs. When Dr. W. J. de Villiers came poking around in the late 1980s, the traditionalist faction was concerned that any major change would jeopardize managerial jobs and the settled ways of doing things. In contrast, a "modernizing" faction in the SAPT saw commercialization and privatization as a way to make employees and the company accountable. These managers experienced the chummy work environment as a way of hiding incompetence and sloth, the long-term contracts with equipment suppliers (the Manufacture and Supply Agreements) as economically irrational and a cesspool of protected corruption. Viewing a break from ministry control as a positive development, the modernizing faction believed that putting the company on a true business footing could enable expansion of basic services *and* accommodation of business needs. Registering SAPT under the Companies Act would force the company to operate by law according to normal, sound business practices – including establishing performance criteria at suitable intervals against predetermined policy and budget benchmarks. For, as a child of a ministry, SAPT did not have to conform to normal fiduciary or performance practice. Breaking from the ministry would also facilitate establishing better relations between SAPT and its labor force. Privatization thus was seen by modernizers as comporting with changes in technology and mirroring the liberalization of telecommunications under way in Europe. The odd faction out was the very small group that held to a genuine public service ethos, represented most clearly by the head of telecommunications, Deputy Postmaster General Jimmy Taylor. Taylor was perhaps the principal proponent of those espousing a nonracialist, traditional public service ethos and one of the architects of the early 1980s' plans for service expansion. He was highly suspicious of moving SAPT out from the ministry because he believed that without a traditional PTT mandate and cost structure, telephone service would never be extended to the black population.

A brief examination of the general forces behind liberalization in telecommunications is instructive to contextualize the events in South Africa. In the United States, the reasons for early policy experimentation outside the monopoly framework were innocuous enough, stemming from AT&T's inability to service certain kinds of business users adequately. The provision of services such as private lines were opened to alternate providers who utilized technologies outside AT&T's patent control, such as microwaves. Technological developments, first in microwaves, later to encompass satellites and digitalization still later, provided both entrepreneurial opportunities for would-be entrants and economic incentives to large users to bypass the regulated system. Together, these players pushed at regulatory boundaries, exposing flaws and contradictions in traditional policy, and winning small policy victories that produced still further tears in the broad policy fabric. These limited liberalization moves were *not* done in support of competition per se; they were undertaken because of AT&T's temporary incapacity. But, however small and limited were these new entrants, among which was MCI, they had secured a niche at the fringes of "Ma Bell's" monopoly. And with technology and a big legal effort, and a quiet alliance with some large users, the new entrants began to try to move from the fringes toward the Bell core. This dynamic, over time eventuated in the divestiture of AT&T and the deregulation of American telecommunications (see, among several others, Temin, 1987; Horwitz, 1989; Stone, 1989).

In a sense, the very success of the regulated monopoly or state-owned enterprise in establishing a universal network undermined the network's exclusivity. Once the network was rolled out and in place, the conditions supporting exclusivity became less salient. Competition over the network was not only possible, but, in telecommunications, perhaps inevitable, because of the flexibility afforded by new technologies.

However, competition was generally thwarted by the monopolist (often with the grudging support of the regulator) who argued that the system would suffer technically and economically if new entrants were permitted. The cross-subsidy burden, which tended to fall more heavily on large users, was perceived as increasingly onerous – especially when service options to large users were limited and those users were usually prevented from taking advantage of options outside the regulated system.

Deregulation in the United States set off an explosion of competition, manifested by a flood of entry. This disrupted business-as-usual and set off price wars, business failures and consolidations, along with significant labor retrenchment in the traditional telephone companies. Prices for individual services were realigned more closely with marginal costs, resulting in substantial price reductions in some areas and equally substantial price hikes in others. Competition induced companies to reduce their workforces and reduce wages, presumably thereby becoming more efficient. New entry offered consumers an increased variety of price, quality, and service options. Politically, the old regulated monopoly structure represented a coalition between small users, organized labor, and the state to spread fixed costs across many participants. The deregulated system broke up that coalition. More than just the liberalization of entry for suppliers, the new system also represented the liberalization of exit of (primarily large) users from a sharing coalition that had become confining (Noam, 1994).

The sea change in American and British telecommunications policy set in motion a powerful dynamic of asymmetric deregulation. Once the liberalization dynamic was unleashed, pressure was put on other PTT systems to open up – first in the industrialized countries and later in less developed nations. This pressure was due to several factors. Liberalized markets and market-determined pricing in equipment and services at an international market level tended to undermine the economic rationality of domestic cross-subsidy and internal equipment purchasing arrangements. Business users (domestic and multinational enterprises) learned that the telephone was no longer just a mundane cost of doing business. Rather, because of new technologies, telecommunications constituted a competitive tool for which services could be specifically crafted to meet specific needs and budgets. With new options available, business users both wanted to be relieved of subsidizing local services and wanted their PTTs either to provide sophisticated services or get out of the way of self-provision. Technology, and the flexibility it brought to large users, was crucial. The ability to capture, store, and transmit information over long distances – that is, data communications between and among large businesses – strained the traditional, largely analog, voice traffic–oriented PTTs. At the same time, large corporate users, building or utilizing private networks, now had the ability to bypass local PTTs using their own equipment or that of eager third parties to fulfill their specialized communication needs. And private data communication networks, originally built for carrying data, with digitalization proved equally capable of carrying traditional voice traffic.

In other words, once one key player opted out of the national monopoly model and its telecommunications system became governed by market-oriented principles, the inherent flexibility of the technology permitted the liberalized system's companies to poach or "cherrypick" business traffic from regulated systems. Private or deregulated carriers could offer more sophisticated services at cheaper rates than could the PTTs, whose tariff structures supported traditional imperatives. Because business and international traffic brought in the revenue that cross-subsidized other services, their loss threatened to undermine the entire traditional edifice. Traditional telecommunications enterprises found themselves in a situation of either adapting or losing crucial revenues.

The SAPT experienced local, South African variations of these forces. Chief among them were an erosion of SAPT's natural monopoly and the inability of the parastatal to keep apace of demand, business demand in particular. These two phenomena were, of course, interrelated. Feeling themselves restricted under a traditional, natural monopoly telecommunications structure, business users began to lobby for the liberalization of the enhanced and value-added services that were made possible by digital communications. This began, modestly enough, with private area branch exchanges (PABXs). Amidst heavy lobbying by PABX suppliers and users, SAPT finally agreed in 1987–88 to liberalize the PABX market. The market for the internal wiring of buildings was demonopolized as well. These relatively innocuous liberalizations created a competitive market – admittedly at the far edges of the SAPT's monopoly. This market, however, sowed the seeds for a series of tariff squabbles because it created a situation where SAPT was now just one supplier among several of competitively offered telecommunications services. Complaints began to reverberate about the SAPT's unfair cross-subsidization of its PABX and internal wiring offerings. Whether or not SAPT actually was engaging in such cross-subsidization was unknown, because as a traditional PTT that offered "bundled" services, it did not normally apportion costs (Taylor, 1992; Hartyani, 1992). But that was the point. The "bundling" of services only became a problem – indeed, even came to be identified – when specific services became subject to competitive offering. What's important is to see that the pressures for the SAPT to behave as a normal business had begun in earnest.

Other pressures pushed at the SAPT in this period of the late 1980s. Under Post Office rules, for example, it was illegal for an automobile dealer to tap electronically into the data network of his supplying company to obtain information – since this constituted transferring data through the telephone network outside of SAPT provision or control. The economic irrationality of such rules in an age of rapid and intensive information transfer, and the pressure brought by newly con-stituted user groups such as the National Telematics User Group (NTUG, founded in 1978), impelled SAPT to enter into negotiations to allow businesses to register value-added network services (VANS) com-panies. Whereas these agreements represented some degree of accom-modation on SAPT's part, they also generated a new set of problems and frustrations. They forced a VANS provider to become a separate company, whose network and revenues could be audited by SAPT to ensure that the VANS provider was just that and not an illegal telecom-munications operator in disguise (see Knott-Craig and Hanekom, 1990; National Telematics User Group, 1991). This put SAPT in the position of being both competitor and effective regulator – a situation bitterly resented by businesses. Other major complaints centered around the inability of businesses that leased data lines from SAPT to use them for carrying switched voice calls and around the inflexibility engendered by SAPT's refusal to permit tenants of an office building to use the major tenant's private network or PABX. Large industrial users with geo-graphically far-flung sites and intensive data communication require-ments found it nearly impossible to secure adequate backup network connections from SAPT. In general, large users chafed at SAPT bureau-cracy, service and fault-clearance delays, its inflexible, sometimes unob-tainable service offerings, and the perception that they were shouldering the lion's share of tariffs and thus were paying for SAPT's inefficiencies. In other words, all the typical problems of large, intensive telecommu-nication users confronting a voice-oriented monopoly telephone network could be found in the South African situation in the late 1980s.

The paradox was that just as the SAPT had begun to address the inequalities of apartheid by expanding the network to blacks, its cross-subsidized tariff structure came under threat by the complaints of business users and the opportunities for bypass afforded them by new technologies.

In the wake of the de Villiers Report, the SAPT was forced to give greater emphasis to ensuring that any extension of the network was "economical," that is to say, self-financing. Placing greater burdens on an already discontented, increasingly politically obstreperous, user community was unacceptable. Recall that de Villiers recommended the commercialization and eventual privatization of the SAPT, and the immediate application of "business principles" to network expansion. The application of business principles meant slowing, if not halting, the policies to expand the network where such expansion was not remunerative, thus commencing a transition toward cost-based pricing. Capital expenditure was cut back and the conversion to a fully digital network delayed following the recommendations of the de Villiers Report. Capital expenditure slowed to a 12.1 percent increase in the year after the report – lower than South Africa's rate of inflation (SAPT *Annual Report*, 1990/91).

THE 1991 POST OFFICE AMENDMENT ACT AND ITS AFTERMATH

The government's moves toward implementing de Villiers' recommendations entered into the broader political picture and were partly scuttled by the newly unbanned ANC's opposition to privatization. Just two months after the legalization of the ANC, the government reversed its earlier position and decreed that many state enterprises might not be privatized after all (*Financial Mail,* 1990). Under these new circumstances "commercialization," the status that had been viewed as merely a preparatory stage for privatization, assumed importance as privatization's substitute. Commercialization would entail separating telecommunications from the post office and the ministry and necessitate registering a new telecommunications operator under the South African Companies Act. This was a complex political process that required a good deal of political capital and will, both inside and outside of Parliament. Several full-scale parliamentary discussions were devoted to the reform proposals (see Republic of South Africa, 1991a,b,c).

According to Brian Clark (1996), who was Telkom chief executive officer and managing director from 1995 to 1997, W. J. de Villiers drove the political side of the process in his capacity as the minister of administration and economic coordination. It was a difficult task. Many in Parliament didn't understand what separation entailed, and many didn't like it – especially if it seemed like it would cost money. The Conservative Party opposed commercialization because it believed the policy would jeopardize the provision of cheap communication services to its traditional and rural Afrikaner constituencies. In the eyes of the CP, commercialization would also further accelerate the government's dismantling what job reservation had secured over the years, and worried that without the subsidy from telecommunications, a great many of the (Afrikaner) jobs on the postal side would be jeopardized. According to some National Party and Democratic Party parliamentarians, the CP representatives occasionally even referred to it as the "White" Post Office (Republic of South Africa, 1991a: col. 3026).[4] The CP saw Afrikaner Post Office workers and managers as their political constituents, and they were threatened by commercialization. This was not an idle concern. Apart from, or in addition to, all the other reasons to transform the parastatals, one covert aim of the *verligtes* may have been to break the power of the parastatal old guards, who, as longtime beneficiaries of state intervention, constituted a power base for the *verkramptes* and who could, and on occasion did, undermine policy initiatives even from the state president. This was particularly true of the South African Transport Services (SATS) and the ESKOM power plants (see Giliomee, 1982: 128–129; Davies, O'Meara, and Dlamini, 1984: 256–266). The CP saw commercialization as simply the stalking horse for privatization.

Outside of Parliament, in an odd but understandable parallel, POTWA, the powerful black Post & Telecommunications Workers Association, saw commercialization in similar terms and lobbied against the reform proposals. POTWA had vehemently opposed the original proposal to privatize SAPT. The union mobilized against the Post Office Amendment legislation because it felt labor had not been properly consulted. It harbored serious concerns about likely retrenchments in a marketized telecommunications company and doubted the new company's commitment to expanding service to disadvantaged

---

4 This wasn't too far off the mark. The racial breakdown of Post Office employees in 1991 was 53,491 whites, 27,617 Africans, 11,839 Coloureds, and 2,399 Indians (Republic of South Africa, 1991b: col. 2095).

communities under a commercialized regime. The concerns of both the CP and POTWA had basis in fact and history. The initial bill specifically envisaged a future stage in restructuring that could include privatization. And the bill's initial draft exempted the commercialized companies from falling under the terms of the Labour Relations Act for two years (see Republic of South Africa, 1991a). Both provisions were eliminated in the final bill.

These different sources of opposition underscore why, in the political maneuvering and horse-trading over the Post Office Amendment Act, Telkom, the successor telecommunications company to the SAPT, was prevailed upon to contribute such a large subsidy to posts for the first couple of years and to absorb on its own a serious shortfall in the pension fund. Telkom was obliged to contribute R367 million to the postal deficit as it became a company in 1991, with the expectation that it would be responsible for R500 million for each of the next five years, to be met through taxes and dividends paid to the government. The Pension Fund was found to be short R1.59 billion, and would have to be fully funded by the company, not by government (Telkom, 1993). The SAPT unions demanded and received a "no retrenchments from commercialization" agreement, and also demanded and received the continuation of a complex and arcane set of "allowances" that are added to the paycheck, and whose administrative irrationality still bedevils Telkom (Moholi, 1996). But the bill did pass, 93:23 in the House of Assembly, with the National and Democratic parties joining forces in approval, and the Conservative Party voting in opposition (Republic of South Africa, 1991c). The act separated posts from telecommunications effective October 1, 1991. It created Telkom as a company under Companies Act law, oriented toward making profits, responsible for paying taxes and dividends, securing its own financing, and taking care of its own pension plan. Telkom remained fully state-owned – its shareholder, to whom it pays dividends, is the state – but is overseen by a board of directors responsible for strategic direction and policy. The minister still retained ultimate control over tariffs. The old Department of Posts and Telecommunications relinquished its joint role as player and regulator, and a very small department was to act as interim regulator. About 100 people remained in the department, whereas 67,000 went to Telkom. In December 1991, a few months after the dissolution of SAPT, Telkom and the major staff associations signed an interim recognition agreement which for the first time included telecommunications workers under the ambit of the Labor Relations Act (Haffajee, 1992).

Commercialization did succeed in separating telecommunications from posts and in transforming the previously ministerial telecommunications functions into a public corporation. But despite large outpourings of ideological verbiage, the legislation did not quickly succeed in transforming parastatal culture. Some of this failure was, in effect, by design, a bow to the reality of material power in the new company. As Brian Clark (1996) put it, the South African telecommunications network "could be disabled by the noncooperation of 200 technical people." Any transformation of the parastatal had to accommodate this potentially disruptive old guard. Longtime SAPT manager Danie du Toit was brought in as Telkom's first managing director to effect the transition because he was seen as "old boy" enough to pull the old guard along. According to the account of some Telkom insiders, du Toit was *too* much the old boy, engaging in heavy cronyism and thus causing considerable dissatisfaction among the company's modernizers. At the managerial level, people continued to be promoted according to sub-rosa networks of ethnicity and personal loyalty. Competent managers, seeing their chances for advancement blocked, left the company (Bester, 1995a; Klok, 1997). This inside view of Telkom at the managerial level comports with Brian Clark's view from the board level. Notwithstanding the establishment of a bona fide board of directors in 1991, Clark, then a member of the board, felt the board was often kept in the dark by Telkom management. The chairman of Telkom's board, Jack Clarke, had good intentions, but, coming from the private sector (Clarke came from ISM, the leftover company when IBM pulled out of South Africa), he did not really understand parastatal culture. He was sandwiched between MD Danie du Toit and Minister of Transport and Posts & Telecommunications Piet Welgemoed. Telkom may have been officially separated from the line ministry, but Minister Welgemoed continued to act in an interventionist manner, and did nothing to encourage a new culture within Telkom. In spite of the new political environment, MD du Toit vilified outside critics like the ANC's Andile Ngcaba (B. Clark, 1996).[5]

5 Ngcaba, an official in the ANC's Department of Information Systems, was the ANC's resident telecommunications expert. By virtue of his education and knowledge, he assumed the leadership role for the ANC in telecommunications matters. In partial confirmation of Clark's assertion of the absence of contact between Telkom and the ANC, when I went to Telkom to interview managers in June 1992, more than two years after the ANC had been unbanned, Telkom had not yet been holding any discussions with the ANC. Telkom General Manager for Corporate Strategy Gabriele Celli (1992) somewhat embarrassingly admitted he had no idea if and when the company intended to begin discussions. A source of Andile Ngcaba's long reluctance to engage with Telkom except on equal terms was Telkom's incredibly contemptuous attitude

At the sectoral level, the Post Office Amendment Act did not resolve the outstanding questions regarding institutional and regulatory frameworks. The central questions confronting any transformation of a PTT system – that is, which services will remain monopolized, which will be competitive and to what degree, and how should tariffs be adjusted – were left unaddressed by legislation. Moreover, questions of governance, that is, how and who would decide the central policy matters, were also not settled. The 1991 act was vague and contradictory with regard to the structure of post-SAPT telecommunications. For example, on the one hand, section 34 struck the words "Postmaster-General" and put in its place the words "telecommunications company," stating that the successor telecommunications company (Telkom)

> shall have the exclusive privilege of constructing, maintaining or using, or of authorizing any person to construct, maintain or use, any telecommunications line for the sending, conveying, transmitting or receiving of sounds, images, signs, signals, communications or other information, and of transmitting telegrams over any such telecommunications line within the Republic or the territorial waters thereof. (Republic of South Africa, 1991c: 36)

On the other hand, section 43 stated that

> notwithstanding anything to the contrary contained in this Act, the Minister may, after consultation with the successor company concerned, and if it is in the public interest, by notice in the Gazette, also authorize any other person to exercise any power corresponding with any part of the exclusive power to conduct the postal service or the telecommunications service which has in terms of this Act been transferred to the postal company or the telecommunications company, respectively, on such conditions as the Minister may deem fit. (Republic of South Africa, 1991c: 44)

Thus while Telkom seemed to have an exclusive operating privilege and the sole authority to determine the network's use, there was room

toward him and other ANC telecommunications people. Other players in the telecommunications scene were not so politically obtuse. Some of the equipment suppliers had begun to cultivate Ngcaba and the ANC. The Telephone Manufacturers of South Africa, for example, sponsored Ngcaba's visit to the International Telecommunications Union in 1992. Several corporations and user associations helped bankroll Ngcaba's initiatives to put together ANC-sponsored telecommunications policy conferences and to establish an ANC-affiliated telecommunications think tank, the Centre for the Development of Information and Telecommunications Policy.

in the statute for the minister to undermine that privilege. Yet the statute did not clearly give the minister the power to compel interconnection into the Telkom network in the event another carrier was authorized to provide a telecommunications service. And the authority of the postmaster general vis-à-vis Telkom was at best unclear and at worst minimal. In short, the Post Office Amendment Act left a number of central questions unaddressed and an effective vacuum of direction.

After the 1991 act and creation of Telkom, South African telecommunications policy stalled. Telkom, users, potential competitors, and the Department of Posts and Telecommunications engaged in a series of frustrating, essentially unresolved disputes over the terms of market entry and operating boundaries. Indeed, the governance vacuum left Telkom in the position of licensing its own competitors in the value-added service area, to the great dismay of new entrants and business users (see National Telematics User Group, 1991; VANGUARD, 1992). Telkom itself, highly geared (net debt as a percentage of shareholders' funds), cut back on its capital expenditure and slowed its expansion of the network considerably. The number of main lines grew only 142,000 in the 18 months between the time Telkom became a company in October 1991 and the date of its first annual report on March 31, 1993. This brought the number of main lines to 3,524,000, with a wait list of 121,000 (Telkom, 1993).

Why was policy so inchoate? Part of the answer is parliamentary politics and the nature of legislation. It is unrealistic to expect that a technically complex sector like telecommunications can be restructured in specific ways by a general legislative body such as Parliament. Hence it is not surprising that the determination of many issues was deferred. The legislation accomplished a major structural task, and now it was the job of the bureaucracy to construct the nuts and bolts policies that would provide form and rule to the newly transformed sector. But who, now, was the bureaucracy? Here, the determination of nuts and bolts policy in telecommunications was drawn into the politics of the South African transition and the National Party's efforts to utilize the power of the state to position itself in the post-apartheid future. Transport and Posts & Telecommunications Minister Piet Welgemoed ran a two-sided process. He appointed Pierre Pretorius, a South African Transport Services attorney who had helped guide the transformation of that parastatal, as an adviser to write new communication legislation. Legislation would create a legal structure and establish a regulatory apparatus. At the same time, Welgemoed contracted Coopers & Lybrand Ltd., the international accounting and research firm, to conduct a study of the South African telecommunications sector. Coopers & Lybrand's brief was, in effect, to recommend policy directions on major questions such as competition, privatization, the future of Telkom, tariffs, and universal service. Both moves were set in motion without engaging the ANC alliance in any meaningful consultation. The lack of consultation doomed progress in the sector.

Whereas the consultative stakeholder forums had formed around hundreds of institutions, sectors, and functions after February 1990, the forum process did not gel in the telecommunications sector. Various efforts to convene a forum were attempted, but mutual suspicion, hostility from Telkom management and Minister Welgemoed, and the strong desire on the part of the ANC for a telecommunications forum to be seen as *its* initiative, undermined the efforts (Smit, 1993). This had serious repercussions. The absence of a consultative process in telecommunications led constitutional negotiators to annul a previous decision at CODESA to deal with broadcasting and telecommunications policy together, and instead to proceed with establishing a regulatory authority for broadcasting separately. Telecommunications policy was put on hold. The absence of pressure from a telecommunications forum permitted Minister Welgemoed a relatively free hand. A National Party right-winger, Welgemoed resisted all attempts to bring telecommunications into the political negotiations (Dison, 1997a). Instead, he angled to use telecommunications to the government's strategic political advantage. Hoping to reap the political benefits of fostering new telecommunications services, Welgemoed endeavored to revamp the structure and governance of the sector on his own. The first move in this regard was the ministry's decision to contract with Coopers & Lybrand for an analysis of Telkom and the South African telecommunications sector. Following that was the government's decision to license two cellular telephone network operators. The Coopers & Lybrand Report (1992) was the focus of political strife in 1992; the cellular tenders became a significant political battleground in 1993.

The Coopers & Lybrand Report was a comprehensive study of the sector. Drawing lessons from international experience, the consultants recommended separate and distinct institutional roles for Telkom and the ministry, and called for the establishment of an independent regulatory authority. The government's role as sector policy maker should be separated from its role as Telkom shareholder. Responsibility for sector policy making should remain with the Minister for Posts and Telecommunications, while the role of government-as-shareholder should be exercised by the Ministry of Finance (Coopers & Lybrand, 1992: 47–70).

The report gave support to the principles of competition and privatization in general and in the abstract but acknowledged that certain service monopolies were necessary, at least for several years. Specifically, the report recommended that Telkom retain the exclusive right to supply long-distance and international voice telephony for a period of at least five years. The consultants recognized that opening long-distance to competition would result in widespread creamskimming and thus necessitate Telkom's increasing charges for local service by a factor between two and three. Coopers & Lybrand understood that this would be politically unacceptable. The quid pro quo for retention of the long-distance monopoly was that increased network penetration be formalized in terms of a regulatory obligation on Telkom to meet specified targets for service expansion. A system of price caps should be established for those services in which Telkom retained a monopoly, and explicit regulatory controls on Telkom's prices be instituted. At the same time, the provision of *local* service by independent network operators (such as Transtel [the communications company of the revamped transport parastatal, now called Transnet] or ESKOM) should not be ruled out. But such provision would not be in competition with Telkom; rather it should be a supplement to the main network (Coopers & Lybrand, 1992: 20–26, 81–95).

In the area of enhanced services, the Coopers & Lybrand Report suggested that the then-current draft VANS license should be issued immediately, subject to negotiation with the industry for further liberalization. However, because of the danger of straight resale of network capacity, the resale of voice services should not be permitted for three to five years. The self-provision of short haul circuits should be allowed, subject to defined limits (the report suggested a limit of 500 meters). Very small aperture satellites (VSATs) should be liberalized but subject to a ban on interconnection with the public switched network. The report recommended that provision of the first telephone instrument should be liberalized and the local content manufacturing requirements be relaxed over three to five years. Technical standards would be supervised by an independent body with a move toward more open, international standards. In what would soon become the most consequential element of the report, Coopers & Lybrand recommended that consideration be given to licensing two competitive digital cellular networks, among which network sharing should be permitted to avoid unnecessary duplication of resources. Telkom should be allowed to participate in one of these network-operating franchises, either on its own or as part of a consortium, but only through a fully separate subsidiary. Cellular air time resellers should be introduced to act as intermediaries between the networks and the end users (Coopers & Lybrand, 1992: 71–80).

Thus, while the Coopers & Lybrand Report recommended some competition to sharpen the incentives for improved performance, and held out the goal of privatization as a means to introduce private sector capital into the industry, a close reading reveals that in the short run the report suggests protecting Telkom as the primary supplier of telecommunications services and using a mixed set of regulatory controls to push the company to behave in an efficient, public interested manner. The only recommendation at odds with this general advice was to license two competitive cellular operators. Even here the Coopers & Lybrand Report hedged a bit, advising a prohibition on providing connections from mobile to fixed terminal equipment (such as private branch exchanges) in order to protect Telkom (Coopers & Lybrand, 1992: 76–78).

Perhaps sensitive to the very real political-economic tension between the need to expand the basic network in the post-apartheid period and the need to liberalize value added network services, the Coopers & Lybrand Report plotted three potential scenarios describing alternative development paths for the telecommunications sector in South Africa.

SCENARIO 1, the "base case," essentially followed Telkom's five year plan for modest service expansion and investment, extended forward to 2002.

SCENARIO 2, labeled "network expansion," proposed to increase the availability of basic telephone service in an aggressive manner, increasing access lines to 19.6 per 100 urban population versus 14.1 in the base case, and 6.2 access lines per 100 rural population versus 3.5 in the base case. Although there would be an increase in both local and national call charges, access would be cross-subsidized mainly by business through higher rental and connection charges. International charges would decrease however. In this scenario Telkom would not face competition in voice telephony. However, its profitability is the least good of the three options, primarily due to the significantly higher levels of capital investment. Some financial restructuring would be necessary to carry out the aims of scenario 2. Indeed, in order for the network expansion scenario to work, the report suggested the necessity of a capital injection of R4 billion in 1993–94 to retire an equivalent amount of long-term debt. This cash could come from the government or by privatizing Telkom.

SCENARIO 3, the "competition" option, would rebalance all prices over five to seven years to reflect actual costs, after which competition in voice telephony is introduced and prices presumably decline thereafter. Under such circumstances, business prices decline furthest and fastest. To increase the availability of basic service, public pay-phone penetration would be increased substantially to nearly 300,000 by the year 2002 versus 82,600 in Telkom's base case. In the competition scenario, access-line penetration plots out to 13.5 per 100 urban population by year 2002 and to 3.5 per 100 rural population – quite a bit lower than the network expansion scenario. Competition in all services is assumed to be a spur to productivity gains. Telkom would be in best financial shape under this scenario.

To the extent that the Coopers & Lybrand Report offered an endorsement among the scenarios, it suggested that both the network expansion and competition scenarios were better than Telkom's base case plan. Telkom's plan was judged to lead to only a limited expansion of levels of access and even that depended on network utilization increases that approached operationally infeasible levels. It seems reasonable to conclude that the Coopers & Lybrand consultants addressed what they understood to be the two main political-economic policy positions with regard to telecommunications – and in their report framed these positions within the discourse of expertise. In this sense, the Coopers & Lybrand Report tried to represent a kind of generic, framed debate between the ANC alliance and the National Party over the future of South African telecommunications. And perhaps this was the report's real significance. It presented a version of the basic progressive demand for network expansion as the baseline objective and framed it within acceptable boundaries.

To no avail. The ANC issued a blistering attack on the Coopers & Lybrand Report, branding it as flawed and denouncing what the congress perceived as the government's determination to restructure South African telecommunications without consultation (African National Congress, 1992b). And the report's general observation that labor retrenchments would probably be necessary in Telkom greatly angered

COSATU, which had not been approached by the Coopers & Lybrand consultants (Fanaroff, 1993a). Efforts orchestrated by the equipment supply and telecommunications consulting companies to get representatives of the ANC and the unions and the government together came to nothing. In certain respects the Coopers & Lybrand Report reflected a wariness that resolving the conflicts in telecommunications would be a difficult political process. The report even suggested the establishment of a stakeholder consultative body. This wariness evidently was not shared by the government. Pierre Pretorius, charged by the minister with drafting the new enabling legislation for the sector, wanted to set the legal structure in place before specific policies were determined. Short of a legal structure, Pretorius (1993), too, favored a consultative process for the determination of policy. Though seemingly placed in a powerful position, Pretorius was essentially ignored. The government went ahead with a strategy to revamp the telecommunications sector without a legal structure in place and without a consultative process. The vehicle for the revamping was the decision to establish two cellular network operators and send these licenses out to tender. Cellular became the key battleground in 1993.

With expressions of investment interest from big-time foreign operators – reputed to represent the largest single foreign investment in post-sanctions South Africa – the Cabinet met in early 1993 to authorize two digital cellular licenses. Originally the Cabinet explored the option of authorizing just one new cellular service, to be offered by Telkom. (The SAPT had offered a mobile phone service based on a variant of the German C450 analogue system since 1986. But the service had only about 13,000 subscribers as late as 1993 because of extremely high handset prices and lack of available frequencies.) But in a crucial meeting of the Cabinet, Telkom Board Chairman Jack Clarke was unable to assure Cabinet ministers that the company could build the infrastructure. Here Telkom's inherited debt situation and inability to borrow doomed its chances, as the company could put up just R600 million for a capital investment estimated at R3 billion. Given Telkom's lack of capacity, the Cabinet decided to authorize two cellular licenses. Telkom could take a 50 percent position in one of the licenses. The licenses were put out to tender in April 1993, and Minister of Transport and Posts & Telecommunications Piet Welgemoed appointed Ters Oosthuizen, an advocate who had worked for ESKOM, as a "regulator" to administer the process. The ANC and COSATU, joined by a group called the Cellular Telephone Consultative Forum, immediately charged that this regulator had been appointed outside of legislation and outside the Multi-Party Negotiating Council. The ANC alliance contended that the licensing of cellular telephony represented a unilateral restructuring of the industry, a form of privatization through the back door (Fanaroff, 1993b). Some of the government's own pronouncements supported that interpretation. Public Enterprises Policy Unit Adviser Eugene van Rensburg (who, with Minister Welgemoed, drove the cellular process) said in a magazine interview that the cellular policy could be taken as clear indication that the government favored competition (*Finance Week*, 1993). A complementary explanation put the politics of transition at center stage. A senior government source was quoted as saying that the National Party government saw it had the opportunity to provide telephones to the masses quickly through cellular technology, and the NP had no intention of waiting and thereby permitting the ANC to reap the political benefits (Sergeant, 1993). Other observers invoked a political explanation of the more traditional kind, arguing that Transport and Posts & Telecommunications Minister Welgemoed was a politician "of the old school" – meaning of the imperious apartheid stripe, who would never permit "interlopers" to make policy or interfere with his authority.[6]

Whatever the full explanation of the government's actions, it proceeded to set the terms of application for the cellular licenses and appoint a tender review board to review the applications. A R50,000 tender application fee was assessed in order to discourage all but the most serious bidders. The basic terms of the fifteen-year license were that each operator had to pay an initial basic fee of R100 million, plus an ongoing license fee of 5 percent of its net revenue. Another R5 million in annual radio fees must be paid to the postmaster general, plus R1 million a year for each 10-megahertz channel granted to the operator. Some of these fees were designed to finance the regulator, but the R100 million basic fee went straight to the Treasury (*Financial Mail*, 1993b). Applicants had to specify the extent to which their choice of technology would lead to high volumes and low costs, how their technology choices would support South African

6 Whether this observation (made to me by a high-ranking official of an equipment supply company) was a comment on Welgemoed's racial politics or rather a comment on his sense of his duly constituted authority as minister of Transport and Posts & Telecommunications is hard to say. But Postmaster General Ters Oosthuizen (1993) clearly evinced at least the latter in an interview. He bristled when I suggested that the Multi-Party Negotiating Council at Kempton Park was now in effect an interim government and that making consequential decisions for the telecommunications sector outside the evolving constitutional discussions may not be a good idea.

industry, and how they would provide a service to poor communities. The license required a certain percentage of phones earmarked for underserved communities.

The politics of the cellular tenders became quite hot in September 1993. According to Andile Ngcaba, the ANC wanted cellular to be an autonomous, separate parastatal service offered by Telkom in a sector rationally planned to take advantage of all existing communications infrastructure. Such a structure, the ANC believed, would best provide universal service (Ngcaba, 1993a,b). Ironically, unbeknownst to Ngcaba, the government's original vision for cellular (a single service owned and operated by Telkom) was not far off from his own. Under Ngcaba's guiding hand as the ANC's resident telecommunications expert, the ANC alliance called for a moratorium on the tender process. The government responded that it could not and would not stop the tender process; that applicants had spent millions of rand in a good faith effort to apply for licenses, and that suspending the process would lead to a myriad of lawsuits. The government also argued that suspending the process would jeopardize foreign investment (*Business Day*, 1993b; Oosthuizen, 1993). COSATU threatened strikes, ANC President Mandela met with State President de Klerk about the cellular license controversy, and ANC Secretary General Cyril Ramaphosa was quoted as saying that a future government would immediately review and perhaps cancel the cellular licenses if the government went ahead and issued them (Makhanya, 1993; *Citizen*, 1993; Fanaroff, 1993a).

The controversy died down for two reasons. First, another brouhaha intervened. The government tabled a bill to amend the Posts and Telecommunications Act. Although much of this bill simply clarified the power of the postmaster general and dealt with the problem of Telkom's pensions, the ANC alliance again vehemently objected to the government's lack of consultation in what it charged was a bid to restructure South African telecommunications unilaterally. In exchange for the government's agreement to hold off on the bill, the ANC agreed to back down on its opposition to the granting of the cellular licenses. But the other factor prompting ANC acquiescence on cellular was much more important. With the threat of strikes bolstering their position, ANC alliance negotiators got the government to agree that all tender bidders for the second cellular license must support black economic empowerment by earmarking significant ownership percentages for black shareholding (*Business Day*, 1993a). Telkom was awarded half of the first license. In compliance with the Coopers & Lybrand recommendations, Telkom entered into a consortium with U.K.-based Vodafone and the Rembrandt Group to form a separate subsidiary, Vodacom. The second license was awarded to Mobile Telephone Network (MTN), a consortium of M-Net (the South African pay television provider), U.K.-based Cable and Wireless, Transtel (the communications arm of the Transnet, the transportation parastatal), and National African Telecommunications (Naftel), an association of black businessmen. Naftel became a basis of New Africa Investments Ltd. (NAIL), the earliest and premier black investment group, which has subsequently entered into many economic ventures, much leveraged initially by the stake in MTN. In effect, NAIL was built in part from the investment negotiated in the heat of the cellular brouhaha. In many respects the MTN license award set the pattern in post-apartheid business deals and in the general character of black economic empowerment. State contracts and tenders can only seem to be won if the tenderer includes a so-called empowerment partner, most often consisting of a small group of black businessmen whose stake may be underwritten by established white corporations.[7] In the meantime, cellular telephony has grown very rapidly, faster even than Coopers & Lybrand had predicted. In less than three years the number of cellular subscribers swelled to about 567,000, with Vodacom accounting for about 60 percent of the market, and MTN the remaining 40 percent (Telkom *Annual Report*, 1996). By mid-1997 South Africa's cell-phone industry signed up its millionth subscriber (*Business Day*, 1997b). Despite the heat of the politics of cellular licensing, the subsequent success of cellular telephony resulted in a widespread conclusion that competition had abetted service

7 New Africa Investments Ltd. began as a company called Methold. In an effort to stay ahead of political dynamics, the Afrikaans conglomerate Sanlam sold control of its Metropolitan Life subsidiary to a consortium of black businessmen headed by well-known Soweto community leader (and Nelson Mandela's physician), Nthato Motlana. This was Methold, which took a 10% holding in Metlife in 1993 with financial assistance from the Industrial Development Corporation (IDC). A five-year call option gave Methold access to another 20% of Metlife's equity held by Sankorp and Sanlam. Soon after its creation Methold acquired significant media and telecommunication interests – primarily the stake in MTN – changed its name to New Africa Investments Limited and got listed on the Johannesburg Stock Exchange. Like other South African conglomerates, NAIL, too, is ensconced within a corporate pyramiding structure, its control held by an unlisted company, Corporate Africa, in turn controlled by the consortium of black businessmen led by Motlana (see *McGregor's Who Owns Whom in South Africa*, various years; Gleason, 1997). NAIL's pyramid shareholder structure vested most power in the top directors, with the majority shareholders holding nonvoting shares. These nonvoting shares were essential to the inception of NAIL and later black empowerment groups. Nonvoting shares meant that the institutions that supplied the start-up capital could not take control.

expansion. The level of cell-phone use among the South African elite of any race is astonishingly high.

TELKOM'S FIRST YEARS: LITTLE GROWTH, LOOMING COMPETITION, AND POLICY INACTION

During this conflictual 1991–94 period both Telkom and the sector as a whole suffered. This is not to claim that the various stakeholder forums in other sectors were necessarily successful in coming to consensus and/or formulating concrete, implementable policies. In many instances they were not. But the forums were essential in getting parties previously virtually unknown to each other to comprehend the necessities and complexities of policy under the new political dispensation. And their symbolic importance, in bringing blacks to policy arenas as equals, was vital. The forums also functioned materially – they furnished the ANC alliance a mechanism with which to hem in the government's policy options during the transition period. In a certain respect they constituted mini forms of interim governance. The forums, in short, not only were essential in "doing politics" during the transition period, but also in laying a broad foundation for political dialogue and in constructing the basis for any policy decisions in the post-apartheid era.

Though commercialized and clearly the dominant player in South African telecommunications, Telkom was in poor financial shape, saddled with a heavy debt burden, a bloated work force racially divided by skill and rank, militant unions, a corporate culture still tied to the old ways, large underfunded pension liabilities, and little ability to borrow. According to data compiled in its first annual report, Telkom (1993) had a work force of about 65,000, total fixed assets of R13.8 billion, and a gross long-term debt of R10.3 billion. The Telkom pension fund, short R1.59 billion, would have to be fully funded. In 1990–91 Telkom was obliged to contribute R367 million to the postal deficit. Between 1991 and 1993, Telkom contributed R209 million to the postal deficit, R130 million to the pension fund deficit, and R529 million in taxes. (The rand was worth about 2.6 to the U.S. dollar in early 1991, and 3.14 in March 1993.) At the same time an outflow of funds from the Post Office Savings Bank had begun – a net amount of R521 million from 1989/90 to 1990/91 – representing a loss of access to cheap capital of which historically 64 percent had been invested in telecommunication assets (South African Posts & Telecommunications *Annual*

Report, 1991). Telkom's gearing was a very high 181 percent at the end of fiscal year 1993–94. Approximately 20 percent of its budget was allocated for debt service. Unable to borrow, Telkom's capital expenditure since commercialization was from internally generated funds only. The company spent R1.8 billion on capital programs in the 18 months to April 1993, representing just under 17 percent of turnover (revenues), and continuing a trend of low capital expenditure that had begun in 1987 (Telkom, 1993; Fleming Martin Ltd., 1995). In contrast, telecommunications investments as a percentage of revenue typically had averaged around 45 percent in the period of 1975 to 1986. Thus Telkom's poor financial situation translated into a significantly lower amount of capital investment – precisely at the moment when apartheid's end dictated a vast expansion of the network. Telkom added only 142,000 new lines in the 18 months to April 1993, and another 136,000 in 1993–94, a growth rate of less than 4 percent (Telkom *Annual Reports,* various years).

At the operational market level, Telkom faced the difficulties of a monopoly whose control was eroding. Its most lucrative services were being poached by private networks, resellers, and international call-back operators (whose rates were at least 30 percent below Telkom's [*Financial Mail,* 1993a]). Potential competitors in business services, particularly value-added network service providers and large users dissatisfied with Telkom's service, found themselves stymied by Telkom and without recourse inasmuch as there was no effective policy or regulatory authority. These were the areas of business where Telkom was potentially most vulnerable. In 1992, for example, telephone traffic accounted for over 92 percent of telecommunications income, and that traffic was growing at about 7.5 percent per annum. However, it was in leased circuits and enhanced services where the growth potential really lay. Leased circuit growth for 1991–92 was estimated to top the previous year by over 20 percent (Republic of South Africa, 1992: 11; International Telecommunications Union, 1992: 353). It is precisely the value-added markets where Telkom faces potential competitors. Large users want the freedom to carry third-party traffic and the freedom to supply all services (including internal voice traffic) in an economically centralized way. Telkom, essentially acknowledging this as inevitable, wanted time to establish what it believed was "fair competition" in value-added services and create what it called a "level playing field." In practice, Telkom used its position as arbiter of VANS licenses to hinder their growth. Telkom's difficulties with these actual and potential competitors in value-added services were compounded by Telkom depreciation rates, which, at an average of 4.7 percent between 1980–81 and 1990–91, were too low to continue the modernization of the network – particularly in those areas where the company faced competition. Especially in data and value-added services, equipment changes quickly. Without provision for replacement, Telkom cannot buy new equipment and easily keep business customers. Telkom went over to a fifteen-year depreciation schedule for transmission and switching equipment when it became a company in 1991, but some knowledgeable observers judged even the new depreciation rates as too low (Hainebach, 1993).

In addition, large users, such as banks and multi-unit industrial concerns such as ISCOR, South Africa's large iron and steel producer, were keen to have additional or redundant networks available because of the immense amount of data traffic they transfer every day. Such users had become leery of depending totally on the Telkom network. Sitting in the wings were two, perhaps three, organizations that already had capacity to provide alternative networks. ESKOM, the electricity supply monopoly, and Transtel, the now for-profit subsidiary of Transnet, the commercialized transportation monopoly, each have substantial internal networks, with transmission capability, that could be made available to third parties on a point-to-point basis. The South African Broadcast Corporation's signal distribution division (now a separate company, called Sentech) also, in theory, could evolve into a carrier of point-to-point third party traffic.

Transnet and ESKOM historically were given permission to operate internal telecommunications networks to provide critical operational support, so that the respective parastatals would have direct control over operations where safety was paramount and life at risk. ESKOM's concession came from the postmaster general. In a November 20, 1969 letter, the PMG granted the electricity parastatal the ability to own and operate a private telecommunications network "to provide the communications facilities which are necessary for the efficient operation of its power systems" (cited in Bester, 1995b). The South African Railways & Harbours, by way of contrast, had permission to provide telecommunications by an act of Parliament. At the time when these exceptions to the South African Posts and Telecommunications' monopoly were granted, it was believed the public telecommunications network could not provide the necessary level of reliability for critical operations in electricity and transport. Moreover, SAPT often did not have infrastructure in some geographic areas covered by electricity and train lines. The grounds for the concession also included the fact that the SAPT would not accept legal and financial responsibility for consequential damages arising from a failure of the telecommunications circuits. Having been permitted to establish their own telecommunications facilities for critical operations, ESKOM and Transnet were also allowed to use these for their own internal needs, so as to optimize their investments in these facilities. In practice they were allowed to self-provide the voice and data private networks that other organizations were permitted to obtain only from the SAPT/Telkom. (For the technical features of ESKOM's communication capacity, see Bester, 1995b; BMI-TechKnowledge, 1997: 117–123.)

ESKOM could easily rent excess transmission capacity, particularly to large private users, but the parastatal displayed no desire to become a telecommunications operator – until 1996. In that year, during the telecommunications White Paper process, it proposed providing a national long-distance service in competition with Telkom. Transtel, the communications company of the transportation parastatal Transnet, posed a more direct threat. Here was an instance where reform in one parastatal had impact on another. One of de Villiers' main recommendations on South African Transportation Services was to divide the transportation parastatal into internal business units that apportioned costs and charged other units for services. The SATS internal communications arm became Transtel, which was forced to compete (with SAPT/Telkom) for Transnet's business. This pushed Transtel to reorganize itself, apportion and reduce costs, install metering – in short to become entrepreneurial. Indeed, in the aftermath of the legislation responsible for reorienting Transnet toward the market (the Legal Succession to the South African Transport Services Act), the Transnet Group moved to inculcate an entrepreneurial corporate culture. It endeavored to reinvent itself as a company that didn't simply provide transportation but was in the business of providing "logistical services." Transtel thus tried to provide clients with all manner of telecommunications services under the logic that when such clients are within the transportation parastatal's ambit they are part of its private network. In the business lingo of one of its managers, Transtel seeks "to integrate Transnet's transport value chain," bringing Transnet's major clients directly into the company's information–communication–logistics network (Webb, 1993; A. Schulze, 1993). Although Transtel is not allowed to offer telecommunications services to the public, it has pushed the "private network" envelope quite broadly. For example, it removed Telkom phones in Transnet facilities, such as airports and railway stations. Looking to play MCI to Telkom's AT&T, Transtel engaged in a series of increasingly nasty skirmishes with Telkom throughout the 1990s.

Transtel's network is more extensive than is ESKOM's, and is more adaptable to private customer use. In fact, as primary supplier of telecommunications services to Transnet and its business units, Transtel owns and operates Africa's largest private telecommunications network. Its infrastructure includes national voice switching, data transmission, and radio networks, located mostly near the existing rail network. (For a technical description, see Transtel, 1995.) The company is anxious to utilize its excess capacity to end-users in competition to Telkom. A primary market for Transtel would be the provision of business services and redundant networks for large users. And where it has infrastructure in place, Transtel would like to provide telecommunications service to those without access to Telkom's network. Transtel's preferred goal is to be permitted to enter into a joint venture with an international operator and become one of South Africa's future public telecommunications operators (Webb, 1993).

THE 1994 ELECTION AND
THE NEW POLICY INITIATIVE

Three events consequent to the 1994 elections began to move telecommunications policy in the direction of resolution: the establishment of a National Telecommunications Forum (NTF); the Reconstruction and Development Programme (RDP), the ANC's macroeconomic policy plan, set goals for telecommunications development; and the new (ANC) Minister for Posts, Telecommunications and Broadcasting in the Government of National Unity, Z. Pallo Jordan, initiated changes in Telkom management and set in motion a Green Paper/White Paper process to develop telecommunications policy. The formation of the NTF finally engaged government, business, labor, user groups, and civic organizations in the consultative processes that stakeholders in other sectors had established years earlier. Various of the players began talking in 1993 and the fledgling NTF finalized a constitution in June 1994. The participating organizations in the NTF were envisioned to be interest groups and organizations representative of end-users, operators, manufacturers, and marketers of equipment, contractors, organized labor, professional institutions, the state and regulatory bodies. In this respect the NTF – typical of the stakeholder forums generally – departed from a strictly corporatist gathering of government, business, and labor. The forum recognized that it must somehow bring in the vast majority, the so-called previously disadvantaged. But the difficulty of including the unorganized and those who were not yet customers of telephone service meant that this crucial constituency would in effect be represented by the civic organizations and ANC-aligned civil society groups with an interest in telecommunications, and guarded by the political fact of an ANC victory of some 63 percent.[8] Representation to the NTF Plenary and membership on the Management Committee was to be balanced between the four main categories of labor, consumers, business, and government. Funding of the organization was primarily by Telkom, with additional contributions from the equipment supply companies. The NTF's mission statement reflected the balance between redistribution and growth typical of other forums: "to offer policy option proposals that would ensure the socioeconomic development of all the people of South Africa through universal service, as well as the economic development of the country through a well developed, technologically sound and appropriate telecommunications infrastructure." At the first plenary meeting in November 1994, NTF working groups presented position papers on everything from radio frequency spectrum reform to the role of telecommunications in industrial policy. The forum clearly was perceived as a long time coming, and the plenary was legitimated with the appearance, among others, of Minister of Posts, Telecommunications and Broadcasting Jordan, Pekka Tarjanne, secretary-general of the International Telecommunications Union, and Percy M. Mangoaela, director of the Southern Africa Transport and Communications Commission (National Telecommunications Forum, 1994).

---

8 The civics established a national organization, the South African National Civic Organisation (SANCO) during the transition period. In May 1991 the United Democratic Front hosted a national consultative conference in Bloemfontein to plan for the organization that became SANCO (Seekings, 1992). Together with COSATU, SANCO had important influence in the content of the RDP document. But after the 1994 election the civics went into a period of decline, in part because a large number of their most competent and dynamic leaders stood for election and went into Parliament or other governmental office on the ANC list. This depleted the civics of effective leaders and the organizations suffered for it – their remaining representatives were stretched thin. Once boasting a membership of 800,000, in mid-1997 SANCO reported just 5,000 paid-up subscriptions (Gumede, 1997). As a result, civic and SANCO participation in stakeholder forums was sporadic. In the telecommunications process, formal input from the civics was minimal.

The RDP White Paper set a specific goal that business plans be put in place to extend telephone service to all existing schools and health clinics within two years (Republic of South Africa, 1994c: 49). This provided Telkom with formal impetus to move toward expanding the network to the previously disenfranchised. Telkom had paid lip service to the idea of universal service in the intervening years but had devoted an extremely modest budget toward expanding service to unserved areas. The company's "Community Telephone" project received R40 million in 1992–93 (Telkom, 1993). Telkom forecast that it would need to borrow R6 billion over the next five years to fund its RDP obligations (Fleming Martin, 1995: 4). Changes were made in the management of Telkom after the 1994 elections. Jack Clarke retired as chairman of the board in September 1994 and was succeeded by Dikgang Moseneke, former deputy president of the Pan-Africanist Congress (PAC) and a principal in the leading black investment company, New Africa Investments Limited (NAIL). The board appointed Dr. Brian Clark, former head of the Council for Scientific and Industrial Research (CSIR), to take over as managing director of Telkom. Internal management changes were effected at Telkom to make the managing director a more powerful position. Early on Clark replaced Telkom's representatives to the NTF, presumably with the intention of facilitating a smoother, more cooperative relationship between Telkom and the forum.

Minister Jordan initiated a Green Paper/White Paper process *outside* his ministry, tying the politics of telecommunications reform to the forum structures generally and to the consultative mechanisms of the NTF in particular. The Green Paper/White Paper model followed the British style of policy making in name but added a South African twist of reliance on civil society, participatory democracy, and extensive public deliberation to determine the actual substance of the document. The usual Western Green Paper is often a first draft of government thinking on a matter. The South African telecommunications Green Paper, in contrast, was designed to be a consultative document, in which the nature of problems would be described and a series of questions or policy options asked. It would not indicate the government's position on any particular issue, presumably because the government was using the Green Paper process to determine a position. Initial drafts of the subsequent White Paper were to answer the questions posed in the Green Paper, and, following additional public discussion, would indicate the government's intentions and construct a blueprint for legislation. It would be a mistake, of course, to argue that the Green Paper had no pre-shaping. Underlying the entire telecommunications reform process was the demand to bring telecommunications to the disenfranchised masses. As Minister Jordan put it at the September 1994 Plenipotentiary of the International Telecommunications Union in Kyoto, "In our view, telecommunications is a right, not a privilege." Or, as he stated on another occasion, in what was to become the unofficial slogan of the reform process, "All shall call" (quoted in Andersson, 1996: 3, 10).

Jordan went the Green Paper/White Paper route because he did not trust the old guard of his own Department of Posts & Telecommunications. An ANC intellectual with an independent streak, Jordan had been sharply critical of the compromise (proffered by South African Communist Party Chairman Joe Slovo) that committed the ANC to a government of national unity and the retention of the existing military and civil service bureaucracies (Jordan, 1992; Slovo, 1992; African National Congress, 1992c). Jordan believed such an agreement would leave the old regime apparatchiks intact to sabotage transformation. As Jordan baldly articulated in an interview, "many of the parastatals are still largely controlled by the ancien régime" (Jordan, 1995a). Accordingly, as minister, Jordan instead established the National Telecommunications Policy Project (NTPP) to manage the policy reform process. The NTPP convened a "Technical Task Team" of local knowledgeable people broadly representative of the main players in the sector, assisted at punctuated intervals by a small international group and led by a trusted political player, Willie Currie. The members of the NTPP Technical Task Team were selected by Minister Jordan in consultation with the NTF executive and a steering committee appointed by the minister. The NTF was to have various points of input into the process. The Department of Posts & Telecommunications was treated as just another party to be consulted, though its name occasionally appeared on NTPP documents and it was called upon to fund certain NTPP expenses. The Canadian International Development Research Centre (IDRC) put up the vast bulk of the money for the NTPP, authorizing $746,550 (Canadian) for the project. Reliance on the IDRC for funding was designed to ensure the independence of the process – from the old government bureaucracy, from IMF/World Bank structures, and from powerful South African interest groups alike. The Department of Posts & Telecommunications in fact made a couple of moves to take the reform process over and, when it could not, placed roadblocks in the way. For example, the department had put forward a plan for a telecommunications regulator in January 1995, and went so far as to draft a bill, but Minister Jordan rejected this gambit. Postmaster General Oosthuizen had earlier tried to undermine the Independent Broadcasting Authority by refusing to release authority over broadcast frequencies to it (P. Pretorius, 1993).[9]

THE GREEN PAPER AND WHITE PAPER PROCESS

The NTPP Task Team put together the Green Paper, which was written in the spirit of consultation that had become the hallmark of the stakeholder forums. The process entailed a set of politically delicate visits by the Task Team to various key stakeholders, including, among others, Telkom, Sentech (the broadcast signal distribution parastatal), the Electronics Industries Federation (EIF, the trade association of the telecommunications equipment manufacturers), Congress of South African Trade Unions, MTN (the cellular network operator), Orbicom (a black-owned satellite venture), and the NTF itself. At these meetings task team members elicited input from stakeholders and offered a general sense of the team's understanding of its brief. The process hit an early, worrisome bump at the NTF. After most of a morning's discussion among the NTPP team and primarily the white business members of the NTF, black NTF members, under the leadership of Elias Monage (national organizer of the National Union of Metalworkers South Africa [NUMSA]), indicated they believed the entire process was already biased toward privatization and thus considered the Green Paper illegitimate. Some quick fence-mending was attempted, but things cooled only after a long meeting between some of the NTPP team and the National Labour & Economic Development Institute (NALEDI), a COSATU-aligned research unit, at

9 In typical fashion of the rule-bound and hidebound nature of the old guard in government bureaucracies, the department thwarted many of the initiatives designed to publicize the Telecommunications Green Paper and the effort to elicit public response to the document. For example, a plan to air a 30-second TV infomercial was effectively scotched by the acting postmaster general because its cost exceeded R75,000, and thus required State Tender Board approval in terms of Section 187 of the Constitution. The department failed to place copies of the Green Paper in every post office in the country. A planned M-Net telelink chat called the M-Net Business Conferencing Programme, targeted primarily at black business and the civics, for which the acting postmaster general had undertaken responsibility, never took place. An extensive radio campaign, planned to publicize the Green Paper to the black community, was continually delayed. The bottleneck in this case was identified as the South African Communication Service (SACS), which controlled government communications and was itself a grossly inefficient bastion of the old apartheid bureaucracy. (See Chapter 6.) The Government Printer moved very slowly, and some translations of the Green Paper were not released until after the September 15 deadline for submissions (Andersson, 1996: 49–52).

COSATU House. There, Willie Currie dropped some of his usual soft-spoken neutrality and spoke forcefully about the enormous pressure on the ANC component of the Government of National Unity. If NALEDI, the Centre for the Development of Information and Telecommunications Policy, and labor did not participate in the Green Paper effort, Currie argued, they would effectively hand the process over to the forces promoting privatization and to the international players preying upon Telkom, he warned. Currie stated that the ANC was not in favor of privatization per se, but did endorse the restructuring of the sector. The participants at NALEDI expressed a worry about the representativeness of the NTPP team, that it did not adequately reflect labor and blacks. Currie's response was that the team was not a representative body and Minister Jordan did not intend it as such. The Green Paper process was constructed to open the sector up to public debate; representivity and participation would be ensconced in the public forum. By the end of the meeting, some degree of trust was restored. And much of what the NALEDI participants articulated – that the Green Paper clearly pose questions regarding the basic vision of government toward the sector, that the document ask questions concerning *all* types of ownership and market structure scenarios – were prominently included in the Green Paper.

The experience of the NTPP Technical Task Team at the NTF and in its meeting with NALEDI underscored a phenomenon that was characteristic of the nature of participation in various reform processes. The NALEDI representatives were politically sophisticated and read a great deal into every nuance of the initial Green Paper framework and proposed outline. But, for the most part, and quite understandably, they were novices in the technical and often arcane, yet crucial, details of the telecommunications industry and issues around liberalization. This indirectly acknowledged "lack of capacity" engendered an atmosphere of suspicion and a feeling that malevolent policy provisions would be put in place by white bureaucrats and businessmen under the noses of the black majority. In other words, apartheid's freezing out of blacks from education, technical skills, and policy making would continue to have baleful consequences when it came to making policy for technically based sectors. This, in fact, shaped black participation in the NTF. According to one knowledgeable insider, all through the processes of the NTF, the black representatives felt themselves in the minority (even though they themselves represented the majority of the population), largely a function of the racially based distribution of relevant knowledge. There was a constant fear of a secret agenda, a dread of being manipulated or outmaneuvered by the more knowledgeable white bureaucrats and businessmen (Currie, 1995b).

The Green Paper, an 80 page document published in early July 1995 in four languages (eventually) and put on the World Wide Web, was written in a direct and relatively simple manner. It attempted to provide basic information, analysis, and the elucidation of trade-offs. Its mode was to pose a series of questions divided by themes into chapters: market structure, ownership, regulation, tariffs, human resource development, black economic empowerment, and the like (Republic of South Africa, 1995e). Parties were given about four months to respond with written submissions. By October, when the period for submissions closed, 131 submissions had been made, amounting to over 4,000 pages of commentary. The NTPP Task Team then divided into groups to analyze the submissions. The submissions in themselves were not surprising. What was interesting was how they accommodated the new politics of the new South Africa. Telkom, now commercialized and headed by a liberal technocrat, took on the mantle of speaking on behalf of those without service, claiming that only under traditional conditions of exclusivity and cross-subsidization could the network be expanded fairly and rapidly. Whatever liberalization might be undertaken must be gradual, several years in the future, and must not undermine the company's efforts at securing universal service. Post & Telecommunications Workers Association and National Union of Metalworkers South Africa, the lead labor unions in the sector, found themselves to a point strategically allied with Telkom. They denounced any consideration of equity sales or privatization, and lobbied vociferously on behalf of the maintenance of Telkom's network monopoly. But labor was also suspicious of Telkom, particularly of the internal reorganization efforts the company had put in motion earlier in the year and that promised to hive off "noncore" units from the parastatal.[10] For labor, only a continued strong state presence would protect jobs and safeguard that the state asset would be used to the benefit of the black majority. Indeed,

---

10 Telkom had instituted a R60 million internal restructuring and re-engineering program to make the company more "consumer oriented." The plan called for selling off noncore services such as restaurants, transport, workshops, construction, and security, which operated at approximately R1 billion per year and which would affect between 15,000 and 18,000 of Telkom's employees (*Financial Mail*, 1995b). Telkom's actions raised tensions and protest from its unions, which saw them as an instance of Telkom acting ahead of and independently of government – a process of privatization by stealth. The hiving off of noncore units would primarily affect African employees (Duffy, 1995; Monyokolo, 1996; Tyibilika, 1996).

labor's position was more status quo oriented than even Telkom's. Business, though internally divided according to position vis-à-vis Telkom (as supplier, potential competitor, or captive customer), kept up a steady drumbeat on the inoperability of old structures and the inevitability of competition. Many submissions, particularly those from large business users and prospective telecommunications operators but also from individual telephone customers fed up with Telkom's service, lobbied for quick privatization and early competition. These policies, too, were promoted as offering the best, quickest opportunity to expand the network to the disadvantaged and to keep the South African telecommunications sector competitive. Except for labor, nearly all submissions advocated either partial privatization of Telkom or Telkom taking on an equity partner. There was broad support for facilitating shareholding and the participation of historically disadvantaged South Africans in the existing telecommunications companies, through "unit trusts," employee share schemes, procurement policies or joint ventures aiding black entrepreneurship. All submissions supported the concept of an independent regulator (Republic of South Africa, 1995g).

The Task Team constructed a narrative summary from the submissions. The statistical data were also compiled as a separate report, showing how every grouping had answered every question. Answers were coded and submitters classified according to various salient categories, such as labor, equipment suppliers, network operators, or nongovernment organizations, to provide a way of grouping answers into meaningful sets. The Task Team condensed a confusing welter of answers in the area of market structure and ownership to five basic scenarios, differentiated by the degree of liberalization and timing. (See Table 6.)

Both reports were offered to stakeholders at a large public briefing at the Carlton Hotel in Johannesburg in early November 1995 at which Minister Jordan offered an upbeat assessment that there was opportunity for consensus to be reached (Republic of South Africa, 1995f,i). The NTPP script called for a broad sectoral discussion of the central issues at a colloquium, which would be followed by White Paper drafts, more public discussion, and finally legislation.

TENSIONS WITHIN THE ANC ALLIANCE OVER PRIVATIZATION AND GENERAL ECONOMIC POLICY

The telecommunications Green Paper/White Paper process was proceeding amidst other concomitant developments. Lurking behind all

Table 6. *The Green Paper Submissions*

• *Scenario 1.* Telkom's basic monopoly is maintained, with slight liberalization in the long term. This position was supported by labor, and to a lesser degree by the Centre for the Development of Information and Telecommunications Policy (CDITP), the National Community Media Forum, and the Federation for African Business and Consumer Services (FABCOS, the black business association).

• *Scenario 2.* Telkom's basic monopoly is retained in the medium term, with liberalization in the long term. This won the support of Telkom and other parastatal organizations, such as Sentech (the signal distribution parastatal) and Denel (the arms parastatal). It was also supported by the Society of Telkom Engineers and New Africa Communications (NAC), a prospective new entrant.

• *Scenario 3.* Liberalization of the sector in the medium term; full competition in the long term, including competition from other parastatal networks. Proponents of scenario 3 included the Department of Posts & Telecommunications, Transnet, Computer Society of South Africa, Gencor, Electronics Industries Federation (EIF), Standard Bank, the oil industry (including British Petroleum, Caltex, Shell, and Engen), and outside players Sprint and Merrill Lynch.

• *Scenario 4.* Break up Telkom and limit its monopoly to local service and the network backbone; full competition everywhere else as soon as possible. This variation on the American model won partial support primarily from prospective entrants, including Landela Telecommunications Ltd., Association of Licensed Maintenance Organisations (ALMO), Council for Scientific and Industrial Research (CSIR), ABSA Bank, Africa Growth Network, Specialised Electronic Research (SERCH).

• *Scenario 5.* Immediate liberalization, full competition in the medium term. This was supported by large prospective telecoms operators, such as Mobile Telephone Network (MTN), First National Bank, ESKOM, AT&T, New Zealand (NZ) Telecoms, South African Chamber of Business (SACOB), National Telematics User Group (NTUG), South African Value-Added Network Services Association, Telephone Action Group.

Source: Republic of South Africa, 1995f, 1995i.

the stakeholder reform processes was the problem of the public budget, specifically, how to pay for Reconstruction and Development Programme projects. Although a figure of R39 billion had been bandied about before the 1994 election, the cost of the projects promised in the RDP document ranged between R80 and R135 billion over five years (Segal, 1994; Economist Intelligence Unit, 1994: 15). As a point of comparison, the government's 1994 total budget was about R124 billion (Economist Intelligence Unit, 1998: 48). Given the scarcity of public resources, the Interim Constitution's protection of existing property rights, and the Government of National Unity's commitment to fiscal discipline, one route to advance RDP goals without breaking the public budget was the privatization of major parastatals. After all, according to a report from the Ministry of Public Enterprises, the infrastructure sector accounted on average for half of the government's investment, and for every rand spent on funding the RDP, four rand were spent on servicing the public debt (Republic of South Africa, 1995m: 5). The book value of assets of the parastatals, as of 1996, according to the Ministry of Public Enterprises, was over R138 billion (Lunsche, 1996b). Telecommunications, electricity, and transport were areas where infrastructural expansion could conceivably be undertaken via private investment, leaving the public budget better situated to tackle services such as health, education, and housing (see Appendix, Table B).

Privatization was clearly a very controversial item within the tripartite alliance. It was part of a broader debate on basic economic policy and underscored important fault lines within the alliance, where positions ranged from neoliberalism to visions of old Soviet-style command economics. Although difficult to categorize into coherent rubrics, at least two fault lines with important overlaps characterized the ANC alliance: one, a visible divide over economic strategy, and, two, a largely subterranean ideological divide between the top–down, leaders-know-best approach to politics, described in the previous chapter as "commandist" or "centralist" often associated with the ANC exiles, and the grassroots, participatory democracy tendency associated with the "internal" activism of the United Democratic Front. I use the modifier "associated" here in a deliberately loose way. Clearly, some UDF activists displayed commandist tendencies while some ANC exiles displayed consultative ones. The point is that the tendencies, as ideal types, seemed in the main to attach to the particular political processes experienced during the struggle against apartheid.

The stakeholder forums were a legacy of the participatory, consultative politics of the UDF/MDM period. The exiles and former political prisoners who came to dominate the leadership of the ANC after 1990 accommodated the freewheeling, participatory culture of the forums in part because the moral authority of participatory democracy at that time was unassailable. The commandist elements also accepted the "culture of consultation and transparency" because doing so was politically advantageous. The forums constituted a means for blacks to gain access to policy-making arenas and also functioned as a mechanism to vet government actions during the transition period. In rather marked contrast, participation, debate, and the devolution of authority *within* the ANC were problematic and caused much discontent within the ranks of the "internals." COSATU officials publicly complained that the top–down style of ANC decision making was very different from that of the Mass Democratic Movement. Even ANC President Nelson Mandela, whose serene, grandfatherly public persona celebrated inclusion and participation, practiced a very tough internal leadership style that bordered on the autocratic (Lodge, 1992). At the 1994 ANC national conference in Bloemfontein, for instance, Mandela attempted, in the end unsuccessfully, to set up a special committee to handpick a "balanced and representative" list of candidates to stand for the ANC in the election. As the 1994 election loomed near, a strain of ANC political discourse tended to move toward Africanism and away from nonracialism. To be sure, Mandela himself and most of the visible ANC leadership continued to espouse nonracialism and practiced a highly visible politics of reconciliation. But the Africanist tendency was clearly there behind the scenes and tended to be concentrated among that ANC faction most comfortable with the top–down, commandist-style leadership. Political expediency also played an important role in the move toward African nationalist positions, as it was the African constituency that would clearly be the key to ANC electoral prospects (P. Louw, 1994: 37, 42). The meaning of "Africanism" is frequently unclear and is the subject of confused and sometimes fearful debate. Thabo Mbeki's (1998a,b) embrace of Africanism, for example, does not appear to be racially or ethnically based. Rather, it is articulated at the level of commitment to a continental revival – seemingly fashioned after the "Asian renaissance" of the former, now imprisoned, Deputy Prime Minister of Malaysia, Anwar Ibrahim (see Ibrahim, 1996). On the other hand, there are clearly racially identified Africanists within the ANC leadership and rank-and-file membership, who, among other things, challenge the legitimacy of appointing non-Africans to public positions and who darkly intimate that there are too many Indians in top political positions. This is the Africanist ideology reminiscent of the Pan-Africanist Congress and the old ANC Youth League (see, e.g., Edmunds, 1997; Forrest, 1997).

This overlapping commandist versus participatory, Africanism versus nonracialism tension linked up to the other internal ANC policy divide, that is, on economic policy. The UDF/MDM politics, with its important labor and civics components, embraced an economic orientation that oscillated between social democratic and socialist. This was abundantly visible in the ANC's Reconstruction and Development Programme base document, which explicitly tied together participatory politics with a bold reorientation of the state to focus on the formerly disenfranchised and economically downtrodden. The RDP base document was an election manifesto located in a developmental economics framework. It represented an economic vision of inward industrialization based on rural and infrastructural development, with the state as a critical catalyst using budget and parastatal resources (Cronin, 1998). The document was informed by the work of the Macro-Economic Research Group (MERG), a network of South African researchers linked in to ANC, COSATU, and SANCO structures and assisted by progressive British, Canadian, American, and Australian economists, charged with formulating a new, post-apartheid macroeconomic policy (Macro Economic Research Group, 1993). The MERG proposals, in Freund and Padayachee's (1998: 1175) words, "were located in what may be termed a Cambridge tradition ([John Maynard] Keynes, [Michal] Kalecki, [Nicholas] Kaldor and [Joan] Robinson)," calling for a two-phased approach. The state would play a major role in the first phase, via social and physical infrastructural investment as a growth driver. A second, more sustainable growth phase would see private sector investment kick in more fully. But the RDP base document was, at bottom, a vision, an orientation; it never spelled out a real, detailed, workable economic strategy (Gelb, 1998a).

Pushed strongly by COSATU and SANCO, the RDP proposal was only accepted by the ANC leadership a month before the election after some intense behind the scenes struggles. Other elements of the alliance, particularly ANC ministers-to-be of economic Cabinet portfolios, taking a seemingly more hard-headed assessment of economic constraints, had moved toward a more cautious, orthodox vision that focused on reconstruction through a conservative, private-sector–driven economic policy. The legacy of apartheid would be addressed through the growth of the private sector and through strong affirmative action policies. Fiscal and monetary discipline and reliance on the private sector formed their watchwords. The RDP document itself reflects the tensions between economic visions. Alongside the many sections of the document that promise development and redistribution targets in various sectors (to "redistribute a substantial amount of land to landless people, build over one million houses, provide clean water and sanitation to all, electrify 2.5 million new homes and provide access for all to affordable health care and telecommunications" in the first five years) are paragraphs warning, for instance, that "in the process of raising new funds, the ratios [of the deficit, borrowing and taxation to Gross National Product] must be taken into account." The RDP document mentions both nationalization and privatization (African National Congress, 1994b: 8, 143).

The tripartite alliance thus included two overlapping ideological tendencies, each with a general political and economic orientation. One tendency favored broad popular consultation, participation, and inclusion (the logic of which embraced a practical nonracialism), and a socialist or social democratic economic policy that favored a strong interventionist state on behalf of the black working class and poor. The other featured a leadership-oriented if not elitist political bent (with a strain of Africanism) and an economic policy that veered toward orthodoxy or neoliberalism, initially stemming from a sense of sober recognition of economic constraint and the infeasibility of autarkic economic policies – but, as time passed, with growing ideological comfort.[11] The latter tendency became ascendant as the ANC assumed political power. As the key member of the Transitional Executive Council – effectively the caretaker government prior to the 1994 election – the ANC had already in November 1993 signed a letter of intent to the International Monetary Fund committing the congress to cutting government spend-

---

11 Two documents are of note, here. One, by former ANC Youth League principal and Deputy Minister of Tourism and Environmental Affairs, Peter Mokaba, entitled "On Leadership" (1997); the other entitled "The State and Social Transformation" (African National Congress, 1996b), without attribution but said to be written by Vusi Mavimbela, top political adviser to Deputy President Thabo Mbeki. Both were written as discussion papers for the December 1997 ANC National Conference. Mokaba suggests that the new South African state is a "State of National Democracy," whose social base is multiclass and whose economic base is capitalist. The state itself is conceived in both documents as neutral, almost technocratic, bringing in as partners all nonreactionary forces for the purposes of national betterment. In this regard, writes Mokaba, the ANC has a particular responsibility to create the conditions for the emergence and development of the black entrepreneur class. The principal opponent of this vision in Mokaba's view is the South African Communist Party. Its members must not be permitted to act in the capacity of ANC officeholders and then turn around to criticize those actions as members of the SACP, according to Mokaba. The document implicitly labels the SACP a "left-wing infantile disorder," and verges on urging socialists to leave the ANC. "The State and Social Transformation," while more focused on the economic constraints posed by globalization and more careful than Mokaba in its rhetoric, articulates much the same analysis of the state and its role. "The State and Social Transformation" was adopted by the ANC National Executive Committee (NEC). Mokaba's reference in "On Leadership" to an "African Renaissance" is vague and does not seem to be racially or ethnically based, but Mokaba was one of those intimating publicly that there were too many Indians in the ANC leadership. With Mokaba one discerns an ideological strain within the ANC that once again sees race over class and marries African nationalism to African capitalism.

ing and espousing the virtues of market forces over regulatory interventions (Republic of South Africa, 1993c). The letter helped secure
South Africa a $850 million IMF loan. And notwithstanding some inter-
nal dissent, the ANC leadership accepted the clause of the Interim Constitution guaranteeing the independence of the central bank. The clause
insulated the Reserve Bank from government and political "interference" (Republic of South Africa, 1993a: sect. 195–197). As Nelson
Mandela proclaimed publicly just before the 1994 election,

> We argued for the independence of the [Reserve] Bank when this
> issue was discussed at the constitutional negotiations. We did so
> not only because we are committed to the sound economic man-
> agement of the country, but also because we want to send out a
> strong signal to the international and local business and financial
> communities that we are serious about this commitment. (*Finance
> Week*, 1994)

The agreement gave the Reserve Bank both an overly narrow economic
mandate and great independence.[12]

The ANC economic orthodoxy developed in response to the combination of the dismal condition of the post-apartheid economy and
the perception that globalization had removed the ability to isolate an
economy so as to permit the application of classic Keynesian tech-
niques. Beyond the normal inefficiencies of apartheid economics, the
last white government had run up a large debt in the waning few years
of apartheid. By 1990 total government debt had increased to 38.6
percent of Gross Domestic Product; by 1995 it was 54.9 percent; by 1996
it climbed to 65.0 percent of GDP. In 1995–96 debt servicing costs
amounted to 18.6 percent of the budget and 5.8 percent of GDP (cited

12 Unlike the U.S. Federal Reserve Bank, for example, which is charged with protecting the value
of the currency and, in the words of its mission statement, "to promote the goals of maximum
employment, stable prices, and moderate long-term interest rates," the South African Reserve
Bank is charged with "protect[ing] the value of the currency in the interest of balanced and
sustainable economic growth in the Republic" only. It has interpreted its mandate very narrowly, trying to reduce inflation, apparently to zero, by sticking firmly to restrictive policies.
Notwithstanding the U.S. Federal Reserve Bank's independence (and bizarre public–private
structure), it is at least nominally accountable to Congress. Since 1975 the Fed chairman must
testify before Congress four times a year and justify the Fed's policies (see Clifford, 1965). South
Africa's constitution made the Reserve Bank virtually unaccountable. The South African
Reserve Bank is under no parallel requirement to testify before Parliament. The closest thing
to political accountability is that "there must be regular consultation between the Bank and
the Cabinet member responsible for national financial matters" (Republic of South Africa,
1996a: Chapter 13, paragraph 224).

in African National Congress, 1996c). The debt situation was compounded by a weak economy and by opposition from domestic business to any substantial program of state-led economic activity. One index of the weak economy – and evidence of the reluctance by business to invest – was the decline in the ratio of investment to GDP, from nearly 28 percent in 1983 to a low of 15.7 percent in 1994 (Economist Intelligence Unit, 1997: 14). These circumstances left the ANC-led government little to work with. Indeed, the RDP was to be funded largely by shifting state spending around. Parliament appropriated a very modest R2.5 billion in the 1994–95 budget for the RDP, and R5 billion in 1995–96 – the equivalent of approximately 2 percent of total government spending (Economist Intelligence Unit, 1994: 15). An RDP Fund was set up within the parameters of the announced government target of keeping its consumption expenditure constant in real terms. The approach was to cut line departments' budgets and force them to reapply for the funds to spend on RDP-oriented projects, rather than increasing total spending to make room for these projects.

The point is that the approach to the RDP Fund rested upon fiscal discipline. Because of the perceived need to build credibility in the eyes of domestic and foreign business, using government spending to help spur economic growth – a key element of the RDP base document vision – went out the window. The monetarist stabilization policies that the Reserve Bank had put into effect in the last years of the apartheid regime showed some success by the time the ANC joined the government in 1994. In effect, the ANC saw its hands as tied for fear of losing credibility and destroying private sector confidence. Thus, notwithstanding the RDP's social democratic pedigree and tenor, the program was implemented from the very beginning within a framework of fiscal restraint. The continuation of Derek Keys as the Government of National Unity finance minister, and his replacement by another businessman, Chris Liebenberg, were signals that the ANC had accepted the macroeconomic reforms carried out in the final years of apartheid (Gelb, 1998b).

The powerful pressure of the "Washington policy consensus" clearly had impact on the ANC leadership, as well. The "Washington consensus," a term coined by the political economist John Williamson (1994), emphasizes fiscal and monetary discipline, outward (export) economic orientation, tax reform, liberalization of product and financial markets, deregulation and privatization, and marketization of state activity. This set of policy proscriptions has become a talisman, a mantra, for virtually all key players in international economics, including the U.S. government, the International Monetary Fund, the World Bank, the big consulting agencies, the World Trade Organization. Here the kinds of pressures, expectations, and taken-for-granted understandings, typical of the epistemic community of economic policy makers and central bank officials in particular, has bearing (see Kahler, 1992; Wilensky, forthcoming). The ANC ministers confronted the epistemic community everywhere they turned, from meetings with European Union and World Bank representatives, in WTO negotiations, to the many corporate scenario planning exercises unleashed after 1990, such as the Mont Fleur scenario exercise conducted by Global Business Network and published in the *Weekly Mail & Guardian* in July 1992 (Marais, 1998: 146–176).[13]

The ANC's National Executive Committee concluded toward the end of 1995 that the RDP would not succeed without concentrating first on stimulating growth (R. Cameron, 1996). Expected levels of investment had not appeared. The Government of National Unity formally replaced the RDP in June 1996 with a new policy initiative called the Growth, Employment and Redistribution strategy. The GEAR was predicated upon the assumption that if the government demonstrated its "credibility," that is, its commitment to fiscal and monetary discipline, then private investment would materialize. Indeed, the GEAR logic was premised on the assumption that state spending impedes economic growth because it tends to "crowd out" private investment. The government presented GEAR as a set of tools to help achieve the RDP's objectives. It conspicuously featured tight fiscal discipline and investor-friendly policies. With GEAR the ANC leadership visualized an export-oriented economy characterized by expeditious fiscal deficit reduction (aiming at 4% of GDP in 1997–98 and at 3% by 1999–2000), relaxation of exchange controls and reduction of tariffs, moderate inflation, regulated flexibility in the labor market, an accelerated depreciation scheme for new investments in manufacturing, a limit of 25 percent on the share of GDP taken by tax revenue, and increased spending on infrastructure through privatization. The plan counted on about R5 to 6 billion per year by the turn of the century from

13 This is how power in a Gramscian or Foucauldian sense works. The Washington consensus is not "ideology," in the sense that it is simply the policy positions of the dominant that are imposed on less powerful actors. Rather it is a well-documented set of policies that, under certain conditions, seem to secure positive results over the medium term, and which are ensconced within networks of action that also correspond to and benefit the material and ideal interests of the powerful. Adherence to the formula becomes a kind of common sense. Deviating from it seems ill-considered and dangerous and often, precisely because of structures of power and networks of action, self-defeating.

the partial privatization of state assets to help reduce the government's borrowing requirements. The policies were expected to induce job creation, and GEAR posted a target of 400,000 new jobs a year by the year 2000, with a 6 percent rise in GDP.

Although it contained many neoliberal features, GEAR was not strictly a neoliberal policy. It tied possible privatization to extensive infrastructure development. GEAR even contained a social compact section that featured an incomes policy, to be secured by the possible implementation of wage and price controls (Republic of South Africa, 1996d). But in other respects GEAR was almost a textbook case of the conventional wisdom in the politics of economic reform. It was drawn up in somewhat secretive conditions by a small team of economists, published after only the most cursory consultation within the ANC and with the alliance partners in the trade unions and the Communist Party. There was no consultation with interest groups in civil society. The National Economic Development and Labour Council (NEDLAC), the statutory co-determinative policy-making body composed of business, labor, government, and civil society, was bypassed entirely.[14] Indeed, GEAR was presented as "nonnegotiable." In this respect it must be understood that the Washington consensus had powerful resonance with the reigning leadership-oriented style of the ascendant faction of the ANC. According to the adherents and students of contemporary economic reform, the most important prerequisite of successful economic reform is a coherent economic team backed by a political leadership willing and able to insulate the team from political pressures (see Waterbury, 1992; Williamson and Haggard, 1994; Haggard and Kaufman, 1995; Rodrik, 1996). This the ANC could do. Despite GEAR's great unpopularity among many in the tripartite alliance, the ANC leadership applied the requisite muscle: GEAR achieved full organizational support and was ratified at the ANC's National Congress in December 1997.

14 NEDLAC was the statutory co-determinative policy-making body consolidated from the institutions that had been instrumental in formulating and implementing labor market policy during the transition, namely the National Manpower Commission and the National Economic Forum. According to the RDP White Paper (Republic of South Africa, 1994c: 27), the main aim of NEDLAC is to address economic, labor, and development issues particularly with respect to the implementation of the RDP, and the council must be consulted on major development policy proposals that affect labor and the labor market. In other words, NEDLAC is a corporatist body and is supposed to institutionalize the linkage of civil society to public policy making. Like the stakeholder forums, NEDLAC marks an attempt to include more than the usual corporatist tripartite government-business-labor grouping. The "community" is represented in NEDLAC by the civic organizations and representatives from women's, youth, rural, and disabled constituencies.

The ANC's orthodox economic policy may have evolved from a sincere and hard-headed assessment of South Africa's options in the contemporary global economy. One member of the ANC National Executive Committee, who declined to be identified in an interview with the author, described the turn to GEAR as one of "no choice." The budget had been left a shambles by the apartheid government. The RDP office had not worked. And because investment and trade agreements were of utmost importance to the transformation of South Africa, the space within which South Africa could operate in the world economy was, in his estimation, "very narrow." This, of course, is the South African version of the argument that goes by the acronym "TINA," as in "there is no alternative" (see, among others, Offe, 1996). But economic orthodoxy must be understood within the broader political context of the conflicts within the tripartite alliance discussed previously. Not only had economic orthodoxy and GEAR in particular been decided in an insular manner, within the leaders-know-best rubric, it promised a key political outcome and benefit for an ANC contemplating its political future. Economic orthodoxy would produce an African middle class largely beholden to the ANC-led government for contracts and patronage. The creation of an African middle class is a necessary feature of post-apartheid economic justice. But it has emerged in the political context of an ANC-led government positioning itself as a patronage broker, perhaps practicing a kind of clientelist politics, particularly for ANC cadre now being "redeployed" throughout the society. Thus, beyond the well-intentioned hoped-for macroeconomic benefits of GEAR, economic orthodoxy promises particular political benefits very much in keeping with the ANC's elitism and party-building orientations.[15] In this scenario, African nationalism and black economic empowerment become an ideology that serves the interests of an

15 The ANC leadership talks about "redeploying" its people to the command posts of society. The most paranoid reaction to this phenomenon was fear of a conspiratorial "Africanbond," that is, an African version of the old secret Broederbond, whose purpose would be to use the power of the state to secure benefits for its members (*Sunday Times*, 1996). Paranoia aside, redeployment is precisely what political parties do. But the electoral power of the ANC does bring to mind the possible analogy of a future South Africa to the recent history of Mexico. The Party of the Institutional Revolution (PRI), which ruled Mexico for several decades, was able to do so by trading on its revolutionary credentials at the ballot box and by controlling the state, bureaucracy, and patronage in so tight a manner that there was virtually no civil society independent of the state. Groups, organizations, and civic life were in a real sense defined by their relation to the PRI and the PRI's distribution of funds and patronage (see Riding, 1984; Cornelius, 1996). The ANC could probably never be in quite that position of control, but the parallels to the PRI are noteworthy.

emerging African middle class and papers over the resultant social contradictions and tensions within the broader black constituency. Deputy Minister Peter Mokaba's (1997) "On Leadership" paper, referred to previously, provides a good glimpse of this tendency. The vision entails accommodating white capital and enforcing a strong affirmative action policy at the same time. White business supports this combination because it makes potential class allies of talented blacks. And, as everywhere else in the capitalist world, business considers conservative government budgets good for business. Finally, joint ventures with newly empowered black firms allow the old-line white companies the political legitimacy to bid on public contracts.

For the Congress of South African Trade Unions and South African Communist Party alliance partners, the danger of this combination of economic orthodoxy and a version of black economic empowerment is that the state essentially loses its character as a progressive developmental state bent on transformation. Instead it becomes a clientelist, technicist state arbiting between labor and capital in an economy that is accepted largely as is. COSATU and the SACP cannot abide the centrist, bourgeois economic strategy and have clashed with the ANC leadership at several junctures (see, e.g., Congress of South African Trade Unions, 1996a; South African Communist Party, 1997; Nzimande and Cronin, 1997). At the same time, COSATU often responds with rhetoric and policy proclamations that do not reflect the complexities of South Africa operating as a middle-income developing nation in an increasingly globalized political economy. Hence its espousal of full state ownership and other time-honored socialist policies can appear as featherbedding and a kind of labor aristocracy.

Internal Struggles over Privatization Policy

Given the tensions within the tripartite alliance over economic policy, and given the poor state of the budget combined with the extent of state holdings, it is hardly surprising that a key early battleground was the privatization of state assets. Privatization was an intensely touchy subject in South Africa. It conjured up the hidden politics of the National Party's gambit of the 1980s and violated the sense among the ANC rank and file that the new democratic state should be using its resources to provide service to the neglected majority. Here the old National Party was a model. It had used the state to benefit the Afrikaner; now the state must be used to elevate the black majority. Factions within the ANC alliance began early positioning on the privatization question after the 1994 elections. Announcing a Cabinet decision to transform the public sector, which included the possibility of privatization, Deputy President Thabo Mbeki (1994) released a statement in late October 1994 that

> the Government will consider full and partial privatisation of state assets and enterprises where appropriate to release funds for the reduction of debt and for use in the RDP Fund. Privatisation could also facilitate empowerment of disadvantaged sectors. This programme will focus on an overall evaluation to ensure that state assets are used as productively as possible and that their activities are in line with RDP objectives. This evaluation will also focus on development agencies and their role in the new intergovernmental structure.

Deputy Finance Minister Alec Erwin indicated that there were no sacred cows regarding privatization. At the same time, Jay Naidoo, former head of COSATU and now minister in charge of the RDP, countered publicly that "we will not sell off crown jewels such as electrification, the core of telecommunications and the public transport system" (Rumney, 1994). ANC officials aligned with the South African Communist Party and COSATU in particular were suspicious, if not outright opposed, to any privatization initiative. Many items in *The African Communist* (1995) and the *South African Labour Bulletin* (1995, 1996) were devoted to critical analysis of privatization during this period (see Makgetla, 1995a, 1995b; Bethlehem, 1995).

Mbeki's announcement set in motion a high-level discussion on the future of state assets. The ANC had assumed responsibility for all the Cabinet portfolios directly related to the privatization question, perhaps hoping to mute the expected ideological clang of the debate (Thomas, 1995).[16] Nevertheless, the importance, sensitivity, and contentiousness

16 It is hard to know whether this was deliberate, but it is telling that so many of the most important ANC politicians were given what in other countries would be seen as second- or third-level ministries. Kader Asmal took over Water Affairs and Forestry, Pallo Jordan went to Posts, Telecommunications and Broadcasting, Mac Maharaj went to Transport, Joe Slovo took on Housing. Stella Sigcau, not known as a particularly strong politician (indeed, her ministerial appointment was seen by some as the bone thrown to so-called traditional leaders who had lent political support to the ANC), nevertheless was ANC and was given Public Enterprises. The one infrastructure ministry given the National Party was Mineral and Energy Affairs (Pik Botha). However, that area not only was taken up by an unusually effective ANC Chair of the Parliamentary Portfolio Committee, Marcel Golding (former second in charge of the National Union of Mineworkers), but it was also an area where there were in place long-standing vigorous ANC- and COSATU-allied research and policy groups, namely

of the privatization question led early discussion drafts to be thrown out (B. Cameron, 1995). These early drafts looked at privatization within a predominantly neoliberal framework, as a policy to provide additional public revenue. A second draft on "Restructuring of State Owned Enterprises," one which jettisoned the strong neoliberal cast, was approved by the Cabinet in August (Republic of South Africa, 1995k). The document was pragmatic and cautious, sensitive to language, replacing the word "privatization" with a more neutral term, "restructuring of public assets." The document argued that private sector, and possibly foreign direct investment, must be considered in the future of the parastatals (Republic of South Africa, 1995m). This did not mean, however, that wholesale privatization would be likely. Rather, the draft endorsed public–private partnerships and joint ventures. In addition to fulfilling the goals set out by the RDP, the restructuring of parastatals could effect a large macroeconomic benefit as well – because such restructuring could in part provide an opportunity for more widely dispersed ownership, and, perhaps more important, bring in foreign investment capital. The final draft reflected a marked departure from the early drafts that conceived of privatization as primarily a method for garnering additional revenue. Instead, competition and the commitment to RDP goals shaped the document, and the categorization of the main parastatals as having a clear public interest seemed to forestall any full privatization of them (see Appendix, Table A).

The reorientation of the privatization discussion away from the neoliberal framework won some praise. Contingents of COSATU and SACP had marched to the Union Buildings in Pretoria in protest against privatization plans before the public enterprises paper was published. Eventually, the flexibility and pragmatism of the released document calmed, if not won over, some opponents. Jeff van Rooyen (1995), Special Adviser to the Ministry for Public Enterprises, said that the SACP sent a letter congratulating the ministry on a thoughtful document. But it was still a very divisive discussion, particularly as far as labor was concerned. The unions evinced a public hostility toward the initiative. At a November 1995 "Bosberaad" (Afrikaans for "meeting of chiefs"), attended by members of Parliament, industry executives, trade unionists, and senior executives of the state enterprises, the union rep-

the Energy for Development Research Centre and the Minerals and Energy Policy Centre. Indeed, it was Marcel Golding's committee that pushed the Green Paper/White Paper process in energy; the Ministry and Department of Mineral and Energy Affairs were led into the reform process with both feet dragging.

resentatives demanded a greater say in the process of the reorganization of state assets and an immediate suspension of any further measures aimed at commercializing state-owned companies. The union representatives asked why there was so much emphasis on the need for return on investments and not on social factors, such as employment. Seeking to mute such outcry, Minister of Public Enterprises Stella Sigcau asserted that the government would not be rushed into the restructuring of state enterprises, that "there will be no garage sale" (Republic of South Africa, 1995l: Vol. I, part 9).

Although the reform process in the telecommunications sector began late in comparison with other sectors, it had moved so quickly that telecommunications would likely be the first big test in the restructuring of state assets debate.[17] Minister Jordan was treading carefully through a political minefield, inching his way toward a viable public position. In February 1995 he stated in a news briefing:

We intend during the course of this year to actively pursue, with respect to telecommunication especially, the possibility of strategic partnerships. This will probably entail putting some of the shares of Telkom on the market so that they can be purchased both by

17 The privatization bridge had already in fact been crossed, though largely hidden, in water affairs. Water and sanitation were under the control of municipalities. In black areas, such services had been part of the political battles against the Black Local Authorities in the 1980s. As a result of this and the segregated nature of municipal tax revenues, water services to white areas were satisfactory while services to black areas – when they existed at all – were very poor. As early as 1992, during the period of the transition to political democracy, Water Sanitation Services South Africa (WSSSA), originally part of the Group Five Company, signed a long-term contract between a private company and a local authority for the provision of water and sanitation in Queenstown. The arrangement had elements of a Build–Operate–Transfer with the giant French company, Lyonnaise des Eaux. Operating under the concept of delegated management, the municipality delegated the responsibility for operating and managing a municipal service to a private company while retaining the ownership of assets, the monitoring and control of the services, and tariff control. Under this system, local people were consulted and then trained and employed to run the process, with the partnership supplying the training, technology, and injection of capital. In the first 3 years of the 25 year contract in Queenstown, services were upgraded and extended to disadvantaged communities, reportedly at a 20 percent reduction in cost. In May 1995, Group Five and Lyonanaise des Eaux announced the formation of a new company, Lyonnaise Water Southern Africa. The WSSA became a subsidiary of LWSA. By early 1995, LWSA was operating at 36 sites, including major operations in Queenstown, Stutterheim, Sundumbili, and Esikhawini (*Star*, 1995; Allen, 1995). The delegated management contracts received the nod of approval from Water Affairs Minister Kader Asmal, so long as the contracts were in the public interest and the views of organized labor taken into account. According to NALEDI's Steven Rix (1995), the unions didn't particularly like the arrangement, but they lived with it, in large part because it produced results and delivered water to people who never had it before.

South African private sector operators and also by offshore private
sector operators. (quoted in Fleming Martin Ltd., 1995: 5)

This did not mean, however, a slackening of the rhetoric of commitment to public ownership. Jordan also made it clear he considered
Telkom a national asset that must be protected from overseas competitors who will "cherrypick" its more lucrative business, leaving it unable
to meet its RDP commitments (*Financial Mail*, 1995a; also African
National Congress, 1994a: 5). Jordan also walked a tightrope on labor
matters, publicly expressing support for labor's concerns but doing little
to intercede with Telkom's internal restructuring plans. He stated that
restructuring had to be approached cautiously "so as not to exacerbate
existing social problems such as unemployment" (Wilkinson, 1995).
But the fact that he did nothing to halt restructuring must be interpreted that Telkom had his blessing. Given the many intimations from
Telkom Board Chairman Dikgang Moseneke that Telkom was looking
for a partner, the restructuring was probably done with an eye to
making the company appear more businesslike. Indeed, Moseneke confirmed to the business press in March 1995 that the appointment of
Brian Clark as Telkom's new managing director was specifically geared
toward driving the organization to evolve a proper strategy toward privatization (*Computing SA*, 1995). According to Clark (1996), Minister
Jordan always encouraged Telkom on the strategic equity partner issue.
The release that same month of the Fleming Martin analysis of Telkom's
potential as an investment must also be seen in this context. Fleming
Martin not only claimed that privatization of Telkom would enable it
to meet its targets for expanding and modernizing the network, but it
could offer investors at least 20 percent annual earnings growth for the
remainder of the decade (Fleming Martin Ltd., 1995). The book value
of Telkom's investments, including buildings, and so forth, was only
about R14.8 billion, but the parastatal's potential market value was estimated between R31 and R35 billion. Moseneke was consistently quoted
in the press as looking for a strategic equity partner (SEP) of 25 to 30
percent. If Telkom's market value was, for purposes of argument, R30
billion, a 30 percent SEP would represent a direct infusion of R9 billion.
At the time of the Fleming Martin report (1995), the South African rand
was trading at approximately 3.6 to the U.S. dollar.

Moving to address its RDP commitments, Telkom began testing the
international financial waters. Telkom Managing Director Brian Clark
was able to secure a $112.5 (U.S.) million medium-term loan facility

with a club of nine international banks – the first fund-raising on the international credit market since 1992, which was achieved without government guarantee (*Financial Mail*, 1995b). The company put out a tender in June 1995 for one million lines in various rural areas where telephone density was below 5 percent (Telkom, 1995). The million-line tender came about in part after the Swedish telecommunications company Ericsson used its political clout in government to compel an audience at Telkom. Ericsson offered to build 1.8 million lines in two years, though this proposed rollout would occur in the major cities. Telkom effectively called Ericsson's bluff and put out the tender for lines in underdeveloped areas. The one million lines was thought to be on the order of a R6 billion investment. Because it was to have no effect on Telkom's debt/equity ratio, the tender could only mean a kind of Build–Transfer–Operate arrangement as a "turnkey" project, but what exactly the tender would bring was very much a mystery. When asked if Telkom's tender undermined the Green Paper/White Paper process, Minister Jordan replied negatively. Given the immediate need for the expansion of service, he argued, it made little sense to wait for the restructuring of the sector to play itself out. The two processes could proceed simultaneously; in the end they would dovetail (Sergeant, 1995).[18]

18 In fact, the "tender" was essentially misnamed. It wasn't really a tender, rather it was a request for bids from equipment suppliers for the supply of equipment for the provision of one million lines in selected areas of the country. It was a bit of a fishing expedition to see if there were alternative mechanisms to achieve a dramatic expansion of the network. Telkom learned some important things with the bid. First, it learned that the arrangement could not easily be done without some kind of equity transfer. The notion that Telkom could gain an operating partner without this altering the company's debt/equity ratio proved to be unrealistic. Second, Telkom learned that a proposal on this scale brought much better prices than it saw previously, on the order of 30 to 40 percent lower prices. With these lessons in tow, Telkom opened up the process to a much bigger affair (Celli, 1995–96). In early November, Telkom unveiled a broad expansion plan – under the moniker "Vision 2000" – of which the one million line tender became a part. Scheduled over five years, the plan aimed at increasing the network by 75% with the addition of 2 million lines to underdeveloped areas and 1 million lines to developed areas. Another 1.2 million lines would replace obsolete lines, aiming to finalize the digitization of the network. Though Minister Jordan would not be drawn into public speculation about a strategic equity partner, he did admit that it was unlikely that government could finance the plans (Soggot, 1995a). Telkom's capital investment of about R2.4 billion per year, generated from internal funds, expanded the network at an average rate of about 190,000 lines per year over the past several years – a growth rate of less than 5 percent. The Vision 2000 rollout would require an average of 800,000 lines per year – a 20% rollout per year for four years, or 15% over five years. It is reasonable to assume from the numbers (admittedly on a simplified basis) that nearly three-quarters of the new lines would have to be financed by *new* capital. Assuming, conservatively, that Vision 2000 costs R16 billion (a figure put out by Telkom for just the equipment costs), Telkom would need another R12 billion, or R2.4 billion per year, for the plan to work.

The two policy orientations – or, rather, the search for a middle ground between the maintenance of a state monopoly oriented toward redistribution and some kind of new regime permitting a phased liberalization and the sale of equity – would also proceed simultaneously. Hence, at the same time that Minister Jordan, Brian Clark, and Dikgang Moseneke attended the 1995 International Telecommunications Union conference in Geneva, among other things presumably talking to various international telecommunications companies about possible strategic partnerships, President Mandela gave the keynote address to that conference, appealing to the ITU to assist governments in developing countries to defend state phone monopolies. "Telecommunications cannot simply be treated as one commercial sector of the economy, to be left to the forces of the free market," Mandela told the ITU conference. "Many developing countries face difficulties in raising capital for their existing operators. There is consequently pressure on governments to throw open their doors to international competition. This calls for great care, to avoid jeopardising local services unable to compete with powerful international operators" (*Financial Mail*, 1995c).

EXTERNAL PRESSURES

Beyond the immediate context of internal politics, developments outside South Africa established another set of pressures, opportunities, and constraints within which the South African telecommunications policy reform process was running its course. At the level of international trade regimes, South Africa became a signatory to World Trade Organization agreements. The 1993 WTO agreement between 130 countries defined telecommunications as a trade-related sector. Telecommunications, heretofore understood as domestic services often ensconced within a national security discourse, now were deemed tradable services. By becoming a signatory, South Africa was committed in principle to the liberalization of trade in basic telecommunications services. The formation of the Negotiating Group on Basic Telecommunications put on the negotiating table the liberalization of basic telecommunications (see World Trade Organization, 1995a,b; Nicolaides, 1995). International tariffs and accounting rates would be coming under review and would affect domestic telecommunications rates because adjustment necessarily requires a rebalancing of tariffs (see van Audenhove et al., 1999). South Africa issued a draft offer to the WTO in January 1997 (World Trade Organization, 1997).

The technological developments discussed briefly at the beginning of the chapter also weighed in on possible reform directions. Generally, new technologies, including new satellite delivery, call-back, and Internet telephony, extend possibilities for the bypass of the national network operator and make policing essentially impossible. On one specific front, AT&T floated a proposal to lay a high-capacity, 32,000-km undersea, optical fiber cable ring around Africa to carry voice and data. The Africa One proposal planned for nodal points from every coastal African country into the undersea cable through a continental consortium anchored by the Regional Africa Satellite commission (RASCOM) and national telecommunications authorities. Africa One posed a threat to Telkom's underutilized SAT-2 cable (Barber, 1995; Harris, 1995).

The presence of foreign would-be operators and international consulting companies had been clearly felt during the telecommunications Green Paper/White Paper process, but it was hard to assess how much influence they had on it. These companies, many of which made Green Paper submissions, typically championed privatization, liberalization, and competition, though most felt they should package these recommendations within several layers of gauzy statements recognizing that South Africans had, of course, to determine their own future. (AT&T's Green Paper submission, in refreshing contrast, came right out and boldly stated its recommendations.) The consulting companies and investment banks touted their roles in various parastatal restructurings and privatizations in Latin America and Eastern and Central Europe. J. P. Morgan Co., for instance, made direct contact with Willie Currie in his position as coordinator of the National Telecommunications Policy Project and delivered to him its April 1994 report on transforming the Czech telecommunications sector. The U.S. government also weighed in, both directly and indirectly. The U.S. government had posted a set of recommendations following the Green Paper and the U.S. Embassy in Pretoria made a formal response to the White Paper following the National Telecommunications Forum Plenary. These submissions reflected the U.S. policy of encouraging early privatization and competition, by making assertions about how well these worked in the United States and other countries, and so on. But behind the perfectly reasonable theoretical arguments, one could virtually smell the office of the U.S. Trade Representative and the Commerce Department doing their work as stalking horses for U.S. telecommunications companies (Hundt, Irving, Lang, and McCann, no date; United States, 1996). The constant call for liberalization, competition, and privatization – prime features of the Washington consensus – had the feel of a mantra.

In fact, indirect pressures were relatively constant throughout the South African telecommunications reform process. A first draft of a Southern Africa Transport and Communications Commission (SATCC) Protocol on Transport, Communications and Meteorology circulated through various government and sectoral circles in February 1996. The draft clearly reflected the liberalization mantra pushed through SATCC by the U.S. Agency for International Development (USAID). Member states, the draft intoned, should agree to develop national telecommunications networks for the provision of reliable, effective, efficient, and affordable telecommunications services aimed at enhancing service interconnectivity in the region and globally. This would be achieved through "the liberalisation of telecommunications, which shall include consideration of the following: (i) according service providers autonomy to fulfill the objectives of this Protocol; (ii) promoting and sustaining fair competition between telecommunications service providers where such competition is permitted" (Southern Africa Transport and Communications Commission, 1996a: 10/1). Objections to such wording and worries on the part of member countries that liberalization might compromise universal service obligations resulted in a far different document in the next draft, one which emphasized universal service above all (Southern Africa Transport and Communications Commission, 1996b). AT&T's Africa One initiative engaged in a similar process of committing African governments for the long term to the liberalization–privatization agenda as a precondition to signing on to the project.

Other U.S.-based initiatives contained similar policy prescriptions. The U.S. Agency for International Development sponsored a conference in Swaziland in April 1996 for the purpose of educating and influencing southern African countries in telecommunications reform. Another venue at which the mantra received wide play was the Information Society and Development Conference (ISAD), a high-powered gathering that brought delegations from the Group of Seven Highly Industrialized Nations (the so-called G-7) and the European Commission to South Africa in May 1996 to discuss the information society with developing nations. Among other things, ISAD featured a video-conference link with U.S. Vice-President Al Gore, who delivered a ringing reiteration of the five principles he had articulated at a telecommunications conference in Buenos Aires two years earlier: private investment, competitive service provision, flexible regulation, open access to network providers, universal access. Some South African delegates had been regaled with the mantra a week earlier by the U.S. ISAD delegation leader Larry Irving in a telephone conference call from Washington to Cape Town, under the auspices of the U.S. Information Agency.

Although one can never ignore the relationship between U.S. state agencies and the furtherance of American-based transnational corporations, U.S. policy initiatives cannot be reduced to mere "stooging" for corporations. For some of the reasons raised in the earlier discussion of the problems of state-owned enterprises in developing countries, policies of liberalization, competition, and privatization have generally resulted in the expansion of service – at least in the telecommunications sector (Wellenius and Stern, 1994; Mody, Bauer, and Straubhaar, 1995). Under certain circumstances foreign companies *can* act as agents of change within the impacted politics of developing countries. Among other things, foreign companies tend to disrupt the "quiet life" of the old parastatals. The problem was that the policy advice was packaged and delivered in an essentially neocolonialist way: I teach; you listen and do. For instance, IBM, in consultation with Parliamentary Portfolio Committee on Communications Chair Saki Macozoma, organized a day-long seminar for the committee, in May 1996, on information technology and the information society. Like the analysis of the U.S. government, it wasn't that the information conveyed by the IBM presenters on globalization and the information revolution was wrong per se; it was more a matter that the presenters adopted a particular interpretation and ran it through without equivocation or qualification, and without any real sense of the possible uniqueness of the South African situation. The punch line of all these analyses was that competition was the essential bottom line. They all partook of the kind of historical revisionism typical of neoliberalism: State intervention is counterproductive (if not bad in itself), and the free market and competition effectively harness new technologies and facilitate economic growth. But they did not acknowledge that it was state intervention in telecommunications that created the basis for competition in the advanced countries historically, or that new technologies tend to be double-edged swords in the sense that their implementation in the telecommunications sector tends to induce job loss and sometimes greater inequality of access in addition to promising general economic growth. (The job loss argument is challenged by Petrazzini, 1996.)

INTERNAL AND EXTERNAL PRESSURES JOIN
IN A BACKDOOR PLAY

The ANC alliance's post–social democratic, participatory tendency was ascendant in the telecommunications Green Paper/White Paper stakeholder process. The tension between that tendency and the ortho-dox, commandist tendency did not disappear, however. One particular event highlighted a parallel process potentially at cross purposes with the stakeholder process. New corporate ventures of international and South African companies were forming, each new venture trying to position itself as Telkom's potential strategic equity partner. The strat-egy of choice – consonant with the emerging pattern of black economic empowerment – was for hopeful international players to ally with a local South African black investment house. If and when Telkom were to take on a partner or award a large contract, so went the logic, such an action not only would have to benefit the previously disadvantaged with service, but it would have to have at least the appearance of spread-ing ownership to nonwhites (Dasnois, 1995).[19] One high-powered international telecommunications group, African Global Consortium (a multinational venture of Alcatel, the BBC, Bell Atlantic Corporation, the Commonwealth of Learning, LCC, Matra Marconi Space, Philips, and Teleglobe International) was invited to make a special presenta-tion to several Cabinet ministers shortly after the publication of the telecommunications Green Paper. African Global seemed to be posi-

19 Business's thinking was well-founded. Telkom announced the five front-runners for its million line tender in early November 1995 (though the project was cancelled 10 months later). They included three black-associated investment groups in various consortia: Kagiso Trust Invest-ments in a venture with Siemens; Trans Africa Investments (led by former Pan-African Con-gress leader Benny Alexander, renamed !Khoisan X) in a venture with AT&T; and Worldwide Africa (a consortium of black businessmen led by Wiseman Nkuhlu) believed to be allied with Marpless Communication Technologies (the consortium of Plessey and Japan's Marubeni/NEC). Also in the running were Ericsson and Alcatel (Sergeant and Dludlu, 1995). Altech/Alcatel, realizing its position was weak due to its lack of an alliance with a black invest-ment house, approached Thebe Investment Corporation, the ANC-linked investment house, with an offer the latter couldn't refuse: a 5% position in Altron, Altech's parent company, at R81.7 million, a fraction of its true worth (Vermeulen, 1995). The emerging global telecom-munications consortia also made forays into South Africa. First National Bank of South Africa signed up with Concert, the partnership of British Telecom and MCI. Telkom SA signed a memorandum of understanding to be a member of AT&T's WorldPartners. New Africa Com-munications consisted of the U.S.-based SBC Communications Inc. (formerly known as South-western Bell), Cable & Wireless, and Corporate Africa, the holding company of NAIL.

tioning itself either as Telkom's potential strategic equity partner or as a potential new entrant in competition with Telkom. Its Green Paper submission had presented a reasonable recommendation to balance the need to provide universal access with the real forces of competition. Although it recognized that Telkom must be the provider of last resort and, hence, must receive guarantees during the period that it extends its network, African Global also recommended, perhaps providing a public window on its Cabinet presentation, that "to the extent that other providers elect to participate in extending universal access to areas identified by the Government of National Unity, regulatory policy should ensure that such proposals receive prompt and serious consideration, and that there are prompt and appropriate provisions for licensing and interconnecting to Telkom's network" (African Global Consortium, 1995: 24). African Global gave a Sandton address (northern suburb of Johannesburg) but U.S. telephone and fax numbers. The Green Paper submission was written by Bell Atlantic and transmitted to the NTPP by Federal Express from the United States.

According to Telkom's Brian Clark (1996), African Global presented itself as if it would be Telkom's strategic equity partner, even though at the 1995 ITU convention in Geneva, the South African team of Minister Jordan, Telkom Board Chairman Moseneke, and Managing Director Clark indicated they were not interested in African Global's proposal. Neither Minister Jordan nor Telkom had been forewarned or consulted about African Global's presentation to Cabinet ministers. Speculation was that Deputy President Mbeki and other high-ranking ANC members were behind the invitation. African Global was subsequently invited to submit a feasibility study. Those sector players that got wind of the initial invitation became anxious as to whether the whole Green Paper process was just a public relations smoke screen for a back-channel power play (Currie, 1996b). The matter faded until the period after the publication of the White Paper and before legislation was tabled before Parliament, when African Global presented its feasibility study to various Cabinet ministers. But clearly, the telecommunications stakeholder process was taking place within broader political-economic contexts.

MOVING TOWARD THE WHITE PAPER

Following the public presentation of the Green Paper reports, Minister Jordan, in consultation with the National Telecommunications Forum executive, invited key representative stakeholders (including business, labor, black economic empowerment groups, relevant government departments, user groups, civics) to a national colloquium at the Mount Grace Hotel for an intensive three-day set of meetings to discuss how to proceed on five key policy questions. Delegates to the November 20–23 conference consisted of about 100 stakeholders, with the core of the delegates being drawn from the NTF. Addressing the opening plenary, Minister Jordan walked his familiar tightrope, stressing the need for new policy appropriate to South Africa while pointing out that it would be foolhardy to pretend South Africa could insulate itself from international developments in telecommunications. He underscored the unique political context of telecommunications policy reform in South Africa. Unlike South Korea or Singapore, Minister Jordan asserted, telecommunications reform was taking place in South Africa within a radical democratic revolution wherein there is a premium on consultation and a search for consensus. In contrast, telecommunications reform in Singapore proceeds from the authoritarian top down. Therefore any easy comparisons to other countries were suspect. The other context, the minister argued, was disillusion with postcolonial Africa. Amidst general pessimism with regard to Africa and its future, Jordan suggested, there is a great deal of hope and expectation in South Africa. As at the briefing earlier in the month in Johannesburg, he reiterated that it should be possible to arrive at mutually beneficial arrangements between Telkom and other players. He expressed satisfaction that Green Paper submissions had avoided extremes, that there seemed to be sufficient consensus on limited deregulation and limited competition and the need to protect Telkom against better funded international competitors (Jordan, 1995c).

This was Jordan's optimistic spin on the Green Paper. In fact, there was quite a range of opinion, particularly on the key questions of market structure and ownership. While most of the value-added network players, important large users, and potential competitors to Telkom stressed that full-scale liberalization and the privatization of Telkom had to occur very soon, the unions and small black business groups held out strongly for minimal change and for the continued state control and ownership of Telkom. Telkom itself proposed a fairly long period of exclusive concession and advocated that it be permitted to take on strategic equity partners.

The colloquium broke into seven working groups consisting of about eleven members each, more or less balanced in representation across the various stakeholder groups. The working groups took up questions of market structure and ownership, how the regulatory body should be constituted and what should be its functions, and whether to maintain preferences for the domestic equipment supply industry. After a long day of discussion and debate, the seven groups reported back to the plenary their belief in the inevitability of competition and their support for a market structure falling somewhere between Green Paper scenarios two and three – that is, a period of exclusivity for Telkom and a gradual but firm liberalization of telecommunications service and equipment markets. Telkom should have the primary role in universal service provision and there should be no competition with Telkom during a period of exclusivity. The telecommunications infrastructure of other parastatals should be complementary, made available to Telkom on commercial conditions. The main difference between working groups centered on the duration of Telkom's exclusivity, and here recommendations ranged from three to five years. Though there was an occasional dissenting minority view within the groups, all working groups came back to plenary supporting Telkom's taking on strategic equity partners and/or private equity participation.

The actual dynamics of arriving at this compromise position are noteworthy. For example, Working Group 3 put together the heavyweights of Telkom's Brian Clark, AT&T South Africa's Franklin Coleman, Mike van den Bergh of the value-added networks (officially representing the NTF), and Independent Broadcasting Authority Councillor Lyndall Shope-Mafole, among others. Nkosinathi Bebeza of the Posts & Telecommunications Workers Association joined the group late and made no interventions. Brian Clark dominated the discussion intellectually and politically. After an opening pro-competition gambit, van den Bergh, known as the enfant terrible of the NTF and erstwhile value-added network services' (VANS) opponent of Telkom, was effectively outmaneuvered and muted (though he may have felt hamstrung in part because he was attending the colloquium as a representative of the NTF, not as operator of FirstNet, the VANS subsidiary of First National Bank). AT&T is another story. Although in his Green Paper submission AT&T's Coleman had articulated an extremely intelligent and coherent endorsement for early competition and privatization (replete with the signature AT&T formulas for valuing interconnection charges), in the working group he behaved deferentially toward Clark and even provided the rapporteurs with the text for

Working Group 3's utterly traditional defense of Telkom's exclusivity ("universal service, particularly to unremunerative areas, is best provided under monopoly conditions with cross-subsidies"). It must be assumed that Coleman had quickly sniffed which way the wind was blowing and glided effortlessly toward the compromise position in order to safeguard his company's chances as one of Telkom's possible strategic equity partners. This was a route already traveled by New Africa Communications (NAC), the consortium composed of Cable & Wireless, SBC, and New Africa Investments Ltd. In its Green Paper submission NAC essentially supported market structure scenario two. The lesson to be drawn here is if one is wooing the dominant network provider, it is best to align one's views with those of the company. It is also best to become an equity partner under market conditions of monopoly (see Republic of South Africa, 1995g).

In the plenary session, however, the compromise came unglued. Notwithstanding the reports of the working groups, labor indicated it could not agree to the compromise recommendations. The representatives from the National Union of Metalworkers South Africa and POTWA were effectively bound to their Green Paper submission statements and could not negotiate them without further consultation from their members. Labor supported full state ownership and full monopoly for Telkom. These were "mandated" positions. This threatened to stymie further movement in the colloquium. In keeping with some of the negotiating lessons learned at CODESA, the solution was to proceed on an "exploratory" basis and to kick the disputed issues "upstairs." (On CODESA negotiation mechanics, see A. Sparks, 1995.) Taking full note of labor's positions, the plenary went ahead and arrived at a "sufficient consensus" to grant Telkom a limited period of exclusivity while phasing in a liberalization of various service segments of the telecommunications market. Telkom was encouraged to take on a strategic equity partner to enable it to roll out the network rapidly to reach the previously disadvantaged. There would be no binding contracts with local equipment suppliers, and there was a recognition that import tariffs would fall to the General Agreement on Tariffs and Trade (GATT) levels or below. All stakeholders agreed to the establishment of an independent regulator and, after a heated discussion, of a separate Universal Service Agency to keep the universal service focus paramount (Republic of South Africa, 1995h).

The fear of reform being hijacked in fact lay behind the controversy over establishing a separate Universal Service Agency to operate alongside the regulator. Expanding the telecommunications network and committing the sector toward universal service were clearly at the center of discussions all through the Green Paper/White Paper process. But how to achieve the universal service goal and safeguard good service to business gravitated quickly into technical debates among the business and policy people – who were invariably white and many of whom had associations with the old white government. As previously mentioned, the reality of political debate in the new South Africa is that, at least with regard to certain technical sectors like telecommunications, the apartheid legacy lives on. The black participants in these discussions posed the basic sectoral policy objectives with eloquence and conviction. But when the discussions took a technical turn, whether with regard to technologies or economics or existing law or international practice, those with experience in and knowledge of the sector – overwhelmingly white – took over. Under the cordial surface of the discussions lay an intense mistrust. Although everyone professed to support the universal service aim, many blacks suspected it would be abandoned by white business as the sector moved toward business-as-usual. Black representatives, led by labor, insisted on the establishment of a Universal Service Agency for fear that the future regulator would be captured by white business interests.[20] Symmetrically, business, worried about the politicization of regulation, lobbied strongly for the principle that the regulatory agency would be staffed by knowledgeable and qualified people.

The colloquium thus came to agreement in several areas except the most important ones. The disputed question of market structure was referred to an Eminent Persons Group (EPG), a group of "wise persons" to be nominated by the colloquium plenary to Minister Jordan (another negotiating mechanism learned in the Multi-Party Negotiating Council), and whose main task was to oversee that the Technical Task Team embodied the letter and spirit of the colloquium in the writing of the White Paper. The EPG now had the additional task of working on the issues on which consensus had not been reached, most importantly the question of market structure. The question of ownership of

---

20 The idea of the Universal Service Agency came from Minister Jordan himself, who offered it at the sectoral briefing in early November. The actual bearer of the proposal was Andile Ngcaba (of the Centre for the Development of Information and Telecommunications Policy) who had been favored with an occasional side-meeting with Minister Jordan during the Green Paper process. As the ANC's expert in telecommunications, Ngcaba's views always held great sway within the black delegations. This had been true within the NTF and it was true at the National Telecommunications Colloquium.

Telkom, understood as a general government policy issue with ramifications across other state assets, was referred to Minister Jordan. This was also a ploy to give labor time to caucus, meet with its rank and file, and hopefully come on board in some fashion.

In the aftermath of the colloquium the NTPP Technical Task Team was charged with writing up the elements of the consensus on the main points and presenting a first draft to the Eminent Persons Group by December 15, 1995. But the lack of consensus on the key areas of market structure and ownership made this task rather difficult. The specific question whether Telkom could take on a strategic equity partner clearly was now embroiled in the larger debate over the structure of state assets. A week after the colloquium, Willie Currie went to Lefty Monyokolo and Elias Monage, the key representatives of POTWA and NUMSA, respectively, to see whether labor would endorse a sector-specific decision on the ownership question. Currie and the union leaders held a coded discussion of options.

According to National Labour & Economic Development Institute researcher, Steven Rix, who also attended the meeting, the union leaders realized their position on the sector may not have been wholly viable, but they felt unable to move due to ideological concerns and broad labor federation deliberations on privatization (Rix, 1995). Monyokolo and Monage categorically rejected cutting a sector-specific deal. At the same time, they reiterated complaints that Telkom had never really consulted the unions on key matters, including the million line tender and the question of the strategic equity partner – or else Telkom came to a discussion with nonnegotiable items.

Thus the impasse on the Telkom ownership question was passed on to the government. In fact, POTWA sent a memorandum to the government on November 30, 1995, calling for a "National Framework Agreement" on parastatal transformation that would establish a representative (labor, parastatal management, and government) sectoral transformation task team to discuss the question. POTWA called for the representation of labor in studies to be conducted on parastatal ownership options and demanded a moratorium on unilateral restructuring. The memorandum also stated that POTWA would fight against the introduction of a strategic equity partnership (Andersson, 1996: 63). COSATU issued a parallel demand (Soggot and Dludlu, 1995). A Cabinet meeting was scheduled for December 6, 1995, to discuss how to enter into negotiations with labor on the restructuring question, with the intention of tabling a proposal before the National Economic Devel-

opment and Labour Council. Government and COSATU reached preliminary agreement to create a forum from which a proposal on state
assets would be put before NEDLAC. Pallo Jordan was hopeful
NEDLAC could come to a decision before the February date when the
telecommunications White Paper was slated to be taken to the NTF
annual plenary meeting.

The Privatization Conflict, Again

However, the December 6 Cabinet meeting appeared to undermine
any notion of a pact. The government's successfully circumspect,
though dilatory, massaging of the privatization issue *inside* the country
had evidently come up against the expectations of the international
investor community for a direct, unambiguous policy. In this contest,
the investors won out. We have seen that the ANC leadership determined that the government needed to build credibility with investors.
Speaking to the press the following day, Deputy President Mbeki pronounced Cabinet's position to support plans for strategic equity partnerships in Telkom, South African Airways, and the Airports Company.
Government would also look seriously at completely privatizing Sun
Air, Transkei Airways, and Autonet (the motor haulage arm of Spoor-
net). Other assets, notably the subdivisions of Transnet, would be
restructured to make them more efficient (Soggot, 1955b; Republic
of South Africa, 1995b).[21] The ANC's highest decision-making body,
the National Executive Committee, announced support for the
Cabinet decision, endorsing the use of income from the restructuring
to assist in the Reconstruction and Development Programme (Hadland,
1995).

Cabinet's announcement, however, seemed to come out of the blue.
Government had told a meeting of NEDLAC's executive council at the
end of November that it would meet labor to discuss privatization about
two weeks from then. Mbeki's announcement on state assets came

---

21 In fact, the ANC had announced a general policy endorsing the idea of restructuring of state
assets as early as its December 1994 convention in Bloemfontein. But the policy was finessed
through the convention in the guise of not wanting a future ANC government to have to take
on the burdens of the corrupt TBVC homeland administrations and their parastatals. At a
closed door, high-level meeting of British government and business people in October 1995,
held at the University of Sussex's Institute for Development Studies, Mbeki categorically stated
that the government would have a clear-cut policy on state assets by mid-December. He was
true to his word. Officially the First Deputy President, Mbeki seemed at this time to be moving,
in effect, toward the position of prime minister and was pulling many elements of economic
policy into the ambit of his office.

before the scheduled meeting. NEDLAC and labor were in effect bypassed – and this may have been the political point. *Business Day* columnist Greta Steyn (1996b) suggested that Mbeki may have timed the privatization announcement to make the point that government would not rubber-stamp decisions arrived at in other decision-making arenas, a position not dissimilar to one that Department of Trade and Industry Minister Trevor Manuel had staked out on Competition Policy. Whether to make the political point or to send a clear signal of government's intent to overseas investors, or both, the government's decision generated a firestorm. Labor bellowed that it had been betrayed by the ANC, arguing that Cabinet should have brought its proposal to NEDLAC and that the moratorium on restructuring had not been honored. Plans to resist privatization, including strikes, were announced by POTWA and the South African Railway and Harbour Workers Union (*Argus*, 1995). SARHWU expressed the "sense of having been stabbed in the back by our own government" (South African Railway and Harbour Workers Union, 1995). POTWA issued a scathing press release.

> POTWA detest and disapprove the approach of the cabinet recently that of allowing the State wealth be dispersed to the vicious Private Sector Wolves who have no good intention to better the lives of our workers. . . . We are therefore left with no option but to mobilise ourselves in defence against Capitalist manoeuvres that have crept in our ranks and have confused revolutionaries that the Free market will uplift the Socio-Economic conditions of our people. (Post & Telecommunications Workers Association, 1995a)

Calling government's position a "sellout," POTWA issued a memorandum to its regional offices calling upon all POTWA members to defend their jobs through sit-ins, demonstrations, strike actions, go-slows, and blockades (Post & Telecommunications Workers Association, 1995b). SARHWU and POTWA quickly made good on their threats. Transport workers slowed down domestic air, railway, and port activities on December 13; some POTWA members staged a sit-in at Telkom headquarters, demanding Brian Clark's resignation. Perhaps to strengthen its hand with government in their "national framework agreement" discussions, COSATU called for a national two-hour work stoppage the week before Christmas and a one-day strike in January (Leshilo, 1995).

Some of the dispute must be seen as uncertainty around where the authority over the parastatals rested. The unions assumed that the shareholder, that is, the state, should exercise control, and saw moves of parastatal boards of directors as preempting that control. But the government was in many ways quite happy that commercialization had taken the day-to-day operation of parastatals out of the line departments and vested them in management boards that would run the parastatals more along business lines. Commercialization of parastatals may have been instituted under the old apartheid government, but it had begun the difficult process of dragging the parastatals out of their apartheid, state bureaucratic ways – a development welcomed by the ANC. In Telkom, for example, the appointments of Brian Clark and Dikgang Moseneke were clearly designed to move the parastatal further and faster from that culture. But the fact that Telkom's top management *was* moving – sizing up potential partners (Telkom had contracted with one of the investment banks to help it choose an equity partner), moving to restructure internally by hiving off noncore divisions – even as the larger, general restructuring debate was going on in Public Enterprises, evinced a deep distrust on labor's part. As labor interpreted the situation, government said no changes would happen until there was an overall policy; yet Telkom management was moving ahead, doing what it perceived was its job – and, moreover, doing so without consulting labor. The intense mistrust lay behind labor's seeming intransigence on the state assets question. The fact that in the old days the parastatals acted badly toward black labor added another dimension of distrust, particularly since most parastatal management, with the exception of the very top, remains largely the old Afrikaner apparat (based in part on Shabalala, 1996a,b).

Emergency negotiations between labor and government produced a bilateral agreement called the "Draft National Framework Agreement" in late January 1996. The National Framework Agreement was a way of instituting a cooling out mechanism, as well as establishing an additional, bilateral negotiating arena on this contentious issue. It committed the government to a process of consultation and negotiation with labor teams in the restructuring at the enterprise level. Government stated publicly that restructuring should not occur at the expense of the workers in state enterprises. But the agreement did not rule out domestic or foreign partnerships (indeed, it stated not only that they may be necessary, but that foreign investment is beneficial), conceded nothing on the principle of privatization, and offered no

guarantee against job losses. Where restructuring has potentially negative consequences for workers, a social plan must be negotiated with the
relevant unions at the enterprise level in a manner which takes account
of the workers' interests. In short, the NFA committed the government
to working our the details on restructuring with labor's participation,
but it did not bind government to anything up-front (Republic of South
Africa, 1996c). Press reports provided no coherent sense of what was
going on, mostly they conveyed the (false) impression of a government
cave-in to labor.

The Eminent Persons Group and the Drafting
of the Telecommunications White Paper

This was the context within which the NTPP Technical Task Team
was to write up a first draft of a White Paper. The colloquium had
resolved several broad policy items, but it did not or could not determine the intricate mechanisms that would facilitate a period of exclusivity for Telkom fading into a phased liberalization. The financing and
ownership issues were handed to Minister Jordan, who had to deal with
them within the discordant NFA process. And the Eminent Persons
Group, formed to make sure the team correctly embodied the colloquium consensus, in reality turned meetings into one more negotiating forum.

On December 4, the Eminent Persons Group was announced: David
Botha (president of Electronics Industries Federation), Pinky Moholi
(Telkom Group Executive – Regulatory Affairs), Lefty Monyokolo
(POTWA president), Neel Smuts (managing director of Sentech), and
Dupree Vilikazi (chairperson of the National Black Business Caucus).
On December 6, the new postmaster general was announced: Andile
Ngcaba. But what was the position of the PMG to be in the reformed
telecommunications sector? If Telkom was state-owned but commercialized with a largely autonomous management team, if the White
Paper was effectively designed to set out the new policy guidelines, and
the future regulator would be mandated to interpret and implement the
new policy, what would be the role of the PMG? Logic would make it
the equivalent of a director-general of a department which had formal
policy-making authority, but in this instance a somewhat weak one. The
question of the authority of the PMG would prove to be a significant
subterranean issue as the telecommunications reform process moved
into its final stages.

An unexpected complication arose as members of the Technical Task Team were writing their specific sections of the White Paper. Minister Jordan informed Willie Currie that Cabinet had discussed telecommunications reform and was moving toward a position that would effectively keep the other parastatals out of telecommunications, even to the point of mandating Telkom to take over the excess telecommunications capacity of Transtel and ESKOM. An alternative strategy was to bring the parastatals' telecommunications networks under the authority of the Ministry of Posts, Telecommunications & Broadcasting. The NTPP Task Team members writing the key section on market structure had been trying to shelter Telkom in ways that would aid the company in carrying out the central tasks of expanding the network and providing universal service. At the same time the writers were anxious about the possibility that Telkom could position itself so powerfully as to inhibit competitors after the close of the period of exclusivity. In several instances internationally, reforms have increased the power of the incumbent public telecommunications operator, because restrictions on them were lifted at a time when competition was embryonic (see Noam, 1995). ESKOM and especially Transtel not only constituted the existing alternative to Telkom service, the parastatals were likely competitors to Telkom in the future. Enabling users to turn to the parastatals' alternative infrastructure meant establishing the appearance, if not the reality, of contestable markets and hence providing some protection and options to end-users, even during the period of Telkom's exclusivity (see Baumol, Panzar, and Willig, 1983).

Contestability helps immeasurably when dealing with a near-monopoly provider. South Africa's experience with radio trunking, in contrast to its experience with cellular links, was a case in point. Radio trunking is a technical means for firms to keep track of their truck fleets through the public switched telecommunications network. Three main companies applied for licenses with the Department of Posts and Telecommunications in 1993 to become network providers as this service came available. A company called Carphone asked for a regional application in Natal. Fleetcall, a joint venture of Transtel and Altech, applied for a national license. Q&D, an outfit involved in radio equipment, applied for a license in the PWV Province, but quickly ran into financial difficulties and took on Telkom as a strategic partner. That venture, renamed Q-Trunk, was 70 percent owned by Telkom. Asked to license radio trunk providers, the department had little experience in these matters, and did not think to negotiate agreements up-front for interconnection into the public switched telephone network. As it turned out, the two non-Telkom radio trunking companies had tremendous problems obtaining necessary links to the public switched telephone network – literally months of delay. Fleetcall presented the department with evidence of Telkom's stonewalling. Q-Trunk, the Telkom-held company, had no such interconnection problems.

The same problem did not arise in the area of links to the nascent cellular telephone operators, because the Department of Posts and Telecommunications had learned a lesson. It negotiated an interconnect agreement up-front and gave the cellular companies the option to self-supply if Telkom couldn't meet the demand. Not surprisingly, self-supply has not been necessary; there has been only a five-day delay on meeting the demand for cellular links (Klok, 1996). The ability of the cellular companies to build their own links to the public switched network created a condition of contestability and underlay important shifts in Telkom's behavior. As a result, in the original White Paper draft version on market structure, Telkom was given the right of first refusal in providing links to its network. But if Telkom was unwilling or unable to provide these to a user, other organizations, including the parastatals, could do so. Because of Cabinet's decision on the complementarity issue, this provision had to be amended, such that Transtel and ESKOM would lease facilities enabling Telkom to provide such links. The parastatals would be allowed to provide transmission, but not access, to telecommunications customers. Only Telkom could service end-users.[22]

---

22 This also essentially complicated any use of the ESKOM's or Transtel's excess capacity for purposes of network backup. Large telecommunications users such as ISCOR, the vertically integrated iron and steel manufacturer, transmit large amounts of electronic communication between various geographical sites and also from the sites to the divisional and group headquarters. ISCOR had been negotiating with Telkom to secure reliable Diginet backup services as alternate routes for its inter-center network. In none of the fifteen different locations where it had a legitimate need for a backup service using totally separate Telkom infrastructure was ISCOR able to satisfy this need at affordable rates within reasonable time limits. ISCOR claimed, e.g., that Telkom was unable to satisfy the steel producers' critical communications needs at its Durban harbor office. As an ISCOR executive wrote to the NTPP (van der Walt, 1996), "Iscor exports up to half our [South Africa's] steel production every year. To avoid problems with prolonged exposure of steel to the unfriendly harbour environment steel is transported to the Harbour 'just in time' for shipping. This implies high levels of business communication to the steel plants. Unfortunately Telkom has even now only one Diginet ACE in the Durban area, which implies a serious risk to the Iscor network, as it introduces a single point failure in our private network. Repeated discussions with Telkom about an alternate route based on separate infra-structure has not yet yielded an affordable solution." Satellite carriage was up to four times the cost of land-based Diginet services. ISCOR stood to lose a minimum of R36 million if the Diginet service were to

It was clear from the arcana that emerged in the writing of the market structure section that the future regulatory agency would face an enormous burden – and this in a country and situation that had no experience with independent regulation, and that had little built-in human resource capacity to deal with the responsibilities with which the regulator would soon be saddled. As the World Bank's telecommunication expert, Bjorn Wellenius (Wellenius et al., 1993), has observed, if there is a single element in the failure of telecommunication restructurings, it is the inability of the countries to establish a capable regulatory agency. This is why one of the authors of the market structure section, though possessed of old socialist leanings, wanted to inscribe more features of contestability into the telecommunications market structure.

At the same time, the pressures to build in *more* flexibility and power to the regulator were surfacing. In a meeting between the Eminent Persons Group and the Technical Task Team, Telkom's Pinky Moholi (quietly called by some "the First Lady of Telkom," because of her strong internalization of Telkom's new corporate culture) questioned the Technical Task Team's insistence on setting dates for the phasing of liberalization in the White Paper. Moholi challenged the Technical Task Team's phased timing of liberalization, arguing that Telkom needed time to fulfill its social responsibilities. The team had argued that setting fixed dates for transition was necessary to build in certainty for all players in the liberalization process. Fixed dates would enable potential entrants to plan their investments and construction. Fixed dates would put pressure on Telkom to make changes in its behavior. The colloquium had agreed with the principle. As per the consensus from the colloquium, the team designated three years until the resale by private parties of telecommunications services, and four years of Telkom exclusivity. Telkom's strategy as part of the EPG discussions with the Technical Task Team was to argue for a longer period of exclusivity and to use labor's formal opposition on the liberalization issue as a wedge. After a somewhat charged debate, Willie Currie floated an accepted compromise to leave the date for resale at three years but to increase by a year (to five years) the date at which national long-distance would be opened to competition.

be unavailable for a period of a week. Telkom was not willing to offer service level agreements, with appropriate penalties for nonperformance. So, ISCOR wanted to be able to approach any other capable party to provide backup service, and for the regulator to assess damages when failure in the Telkom service led to commercial losses to the private network operator. Ideally, ISCOR recommended having a second supplier of infrastructure on a national basis.

This debate underscored the manifest and latent functions of the EPG. The terms of reference of the EPG were to make sure that the Technical Task Team embodied the letter and spirit of the colloquium in the drafting of the White Paper. But because the details of the market structure had not been resolved at the colloquium, the EPG forum actually functioned as one more instance wherein the key stakeholder representatives could negotiate on behalf of their constituencies. Thus, Pinky Moholi held forth strongly for Telkom, challenging the Technical Task Team's understanding of the sense of the colloquium and battling to extend the period of Telkom's exclusivity. Altech's David Botha did much the same on behalf of the Electronics Industries Federation and equipment suppliers, arguing that, yes, the colloquium had agreed to be done with protectionism per se, but had not agreed to destroy the local equipment industry. That is why, Botha insisted, the White Paper had to stake out a position that tariff levels should rise to the GATT acceptable maximum of 20 percent. The colloquium may not have settled on a specific figure, Botha claimed, but it did reach consensus on the principle. Dupree Vilikazi, from the National Black Business Caucus, insisted that the White Paper draft had to reflect the consensus on black economic empowerment and must include strong language ensuring the opportunities of black small and medium enterprises. He pushed to include reference to such empowerment in nearly every chapter of the White Paper, even where such mention was essentially inappropriate. With some dissension, primarily on the question of protection of the local equipment and supply industry, the EPG essentially allowed its constituent members their hobbyhorses. The most interesting change was manifested in newly appointed Postmaster General Andile Ngcaba, who was winding up his responsibilities on the NTPP Technical Task Team. Having been outside the institutional structures for years and throwing rocks at them, now Ngcaba found himself inside the glass house and began acting accordingly. Pointing to the pressures and obligations the South African telecommunications industry was under as a signatory to the World Trade Organization and to the effect of the renegotiation of international accounting rates on domestic tariffs, he subtly suggested that the White Paper had to reflect existing trends and thus be "realistic."

The draft White Paper went to the National Telecommunications Forum plenary in February 1996. Minister Jordan had viewed this the penultimate opportunity for stakeholder input. Jordan's opening address covered familiar territory but also set out the government's thinking in a more direct manner than previously. Echoing some of the recent literature on neomodernization, he asked whether the stakeholders could generate a new conception of the public interest, in which competition could be used to expand universal service. Competition could be used as a policy tool. "Is it not time we arrived at new conceptions of the public interest and of public services?" Jordan asked. "Should we not seriously explore if and how competition can enhance the delivery of services to the people?" (quoted in Andersson, 1996: 67). He addressed the fears of the unions and the equipment suppliers and suggested that they were misplaced because of the scale of the expected expansion of telecommunications in South Africa. Jordan confirmed that government was looking at offering a minority share of Telkom, but the state would retain control.

At the plenary a lot of discussion ensued about the liberalization phasing, what complementarity meant with regard to ESKOM and Transtel, and other matters, but the changes to the White Paper draft in the end were fairly minor. Various National Telecommunications Forum parties, essentially those from business, believed the liberalization phasing to be too long and asked for the review to be undertaken earlier so that the regulator could compress the liberalization process. Labor, which had very quietly acquiesced on the principle of liberalization, saw the review as a threat to speed up liberalization, hence objected to the idea. Labor argued that the normal annual audits were sufficient. The compromise was for annual audits and a comprehensive review in year three. The Technical Task Team, given the previous sentiments of Cabinet, rejected the parastatals' argument for more flexibility on becoming telecommunications access providers. The NTF plenary ended on a familiar, cloudy note. Comments at the plenary's conclusion revealed that the fundamental suspicions on the part of many black delegates from labor and the Centre for the Development of Information and Telecommunications Policy remained strong. Notwithstanding the minister's warning that South Africa could not insulate itself from world trends in telecommunications, that is exactly what some hankered after. Ever suspicious that white business, both domestic and foreign, would burglarize the reform process, comment was made that South Africa must not be dictated to by international capital, and that "we should not be allowing participation in the NTF by those foreigners who were trying to take over our markets." It didn't help that a couple of Americans, one the economic officer from the U.S. Embassy, another the chair of the South African Cellular Service

Providers Association, had made lengthy comments from the floor in a register that brought to mind images of the arrogant "ugly American."

ELEMENTS OF THE WHITE PAPER

A third draft of the White Paper went to a Cabinet meeting on February 28, 1996, at which various ministers asked for clarification on several of the very points Minister Jordan had directed the Technical Task Team to finesse or avoid, namely, the question of a strategic equity partner (SEP) for Telkom, the question of parastatal network complementarity, and the relation between Telkom's exclusivity and the SEP. Cabinet ministers also wanted a better explanation for the reasons behind Telkom's exclusivity period and justification for its length. Minister Jordan and Postmaster General Ngcaba were in Geneva at a WTO meeting (at which the Europeans attacked the White Paper's proposed length of exclusivity for Telkom) and hence were not in Cape Town to shepherd the document. Cabinet's questions may have reflected this lack of shepherding, and some of the specific questions indicated that certain ministers (Public Enterprises Minister Stella Sigcau and Labor Minister Tito Mboweni chief among them) leaned toward positioning the parastatal networks as competitors to Telkom. Some of Cabinet's questions clearly reflected the disappointment with the White Paper that had been voiced by the business community. The SA Foundation, a roundtable of the fifty largest South African corporations, for one, heaped scorn on the White Paper's suggestion that Telkom be shielded from foreign competition for seven (*sic*: it was six) years. Its report argued that international experience showed that telecommunication sectors bloomed when exposed to competition. Touting privatization as a much needed tonic for the economy, the SA Foundation saw in it a means of boosting efficiency and helping government avoid a looming debt problem (Soggot, 1996). The general reaction of the business community to the White Paper was to applaud the policy reform process and the proposals to liberalize but strongly criticize the scope and length of Telkom's period of exclusivity (see, e.g., *Business Day*, 1996a).

The following week, armed with a Task Team explanation under the signature of the acting postmaster general, Minister Jordan was able to maneuver the White Paper through Cabinet. National Party ministers couldn't really oppose the draft, because it did in the end permit liberalization. Environment and Tourism Minister Dawie de Villiers grumbled about the length of Telkom's exclusivity, but he didn't hold up agreement. The only change Cabinet made to the draft, apart from the Ministry of Finance's insistence on the deletion of tax incentives in the chapter on human resource development, was a new clause permitting the review of liberalization and its timing by bodies other than just the Ministry for Posts, Telecommunications and Broadcasting. This addition, offered largely to satisfy Dawie de Villiers and the National Party, gave Cabinet and Parliament the authority to weigh in on liberalization.

The final version was then published in the *Government Gazette* (giving it the status of the intent of government) on March 13, 1996, and launched in a public meeting two days later in Cape Town. Draft legislation embodying the White Paper would then go to the Parliamentary Committee on Communications for a last round of discussion before a parliamentary vote. The basic elements of the White Paper were as follows:

- The state's vision is one of balancing dual requirements: to provide basic universal service to disadvantaged rural and urban communities with the delivery of high-level services capable of meeting the needs of a growing South African economy.
- Telkom is granted a limited period of exclusivity to provide most basic telecommunications services. The intention of the exclusivity period is to permit Telkom to expand the network as rapidly as possible to facilitate universal access, first, and to move toward providing universal service.[23] The period of exclusivity has the additional goal of facilitating the company's preparation for eventual competition. Telkom will not be bound to any requirement to purchase equipment from local companies, though it is encouraged to do so if prices and quality are reasonably equivalent.
- Customer premises equipment (CPE) are completely deregulated.
- Resale of communications service by other private entities is permitted in year 4.

23 One of the discussions concerned the difference between universal *access* and universal *service*. Because of the nature of black settlement, particularly in rural areas and squatter settlements, most concluded that universal service – understood as telephone service to any and all dwellings – was unrealistic in the near future. Universal access meant the ability of people to access a public telephone according to reasonable time and distance factors (see Republic of South Africa, 1995g).

- Telkom will rebalance its tariffs by year 4.
- A Universal Service Fund will collect contributions from competitive segments to cross-subsidize areas where the infrastructure must be built and to customers who cannot afford regular tariffs. The preferred method of subsidy is one of targeted subsidies to end-users.
- National long-distance will be opened to competition in year 6.
- International services and local loops will be opened to competition in year 7. Entry into these markets requires a license, and competition is understood as regulated competition.
- Telecommunications networks operated by other parastatal organizations (ESKOM, the electricity parastatal, and Transnet, the transportation parastatal) are not permitted to compete with Telkom's service offerings. They are to complement Telkom's network.
- All this is to be overseen by a strong, independent regulatory body, the South African Telecommunications Regulatory Authority (SATRA). SATRA will license all operators and providers, determine the definitions of services and boundaries, and establish performance criteria. The regulator will monitor Telkom's performance and conduct a comprehensive review in year 3. SATRA reports to Parliament through the minister of Posts, Telecommunications & Broadcasting. SATRA and the Independent Broadcasting Authority would merge in the medium term. The ministry formulates general policy for the sector and assumes the responsibility of acting as Telkom's shareholder.
- Interconnection mechanisms and charges will be a matter of contracts between private parties, with SATRA able to oversee and compel agreements and their terms where necessary.
- The self-provision of links to the network is permissible where and when Telkom cannot accommodate the request with reasonable quality in reasonable time.
- A separate Universal Service Agency (USA) will maintain the focus on the universal service imperative. It will liaise with communities, manage the Universal Service Fund, help define universal service in terms of current South African realities, and monitor technology, applications, and public expectations. The USA is appointed by the minister and answers to him or her.
- Strong efforts to expand the role of black businesses in the sector and facilitate human resource development will be undertaken.
- A human resources fund would be devoted to the training and education of employees (Republic of South Africa, 1996n).

A PROVISIONAL EVALUATION

The telecommunications reform process created a terrain of stakeholder politics that must be differentiated from party politics per se, in which building consensus among stakeholders became a key policy goal. The National Telecommunications Policy Project guided a very complex process of negotiations among virtually all of the major stakeholders resulting in a set of compromises on market structure, ownership, commitment to universal service and independent regulation, and so forth, which were embodied in a technically detailed White Paper considered a triumph by almost everyone. It represented a reasonable compromise between state control and international and domestic competitive pressures, and plotted a gradual, timed liberalization. The White Paper granted Telkom a period of exclusivity, but created mechanisms of contestability to push the parastatal to become more responsive and more efficient. The commitment to expand the network massively was designed to marry the imperatives of redistribution and development. Network expansion for universal access was also expected to mitigate the problem of potential labor retrenchments, inasmuch as such expansion would require considerable manpower, at least in the medium term.

As such, the actual policy prescriptions of the South African Telecommunications White Paper introduced no dramatically new initiatives (with the possible exception of the Universal Service Agency). The White Paper replicated in its own specifically local fashion many of the policies put in place by many other countries in both the developed and developing world: commercializing and separating operations from government; increasing private sector participation; shifting governmental responsibility from ownership and management to policy-making and regulation; containing monopolies and developing competition. It committed the sector to a massive roll-out of the network while also permitting the development of sophisticated value-added services through phased and regulated liberalization of competitive entry – first at the margins, then at the core of the infrastructure. Its universal service regulatory mechanisms were in some ways less innovative than some recent experiments (see Tyler, Letwin, and Roe, 1995). Recent debates on universal service, such as whether a subsidy system should be carried by the dominant telecommunications operator or by the social security system, made a brief appearance in the Green Paper submissions of a few international telecommunications operators and consulting firms. But they barely registered in the overall South African debate.

What was innovative in South Africa was the *process*. In marked contrast to the fenced-off, elite-driven restructurings in most countries, the South African telecommunications Green Paper/White Paper process constructed a genuine public sphere in which all relevant parties had access and the ability to participate in ongoing discussions and negotiations in substantive, rather than merely symbolic ways. Telecommunications reform in South Africa was conducted within a democratizing context and was itself a democratic process of a unique participatory and deliberative kind. To be sure, not all the participation was on an abstractly equal basis. Everybody essentially recognized that there were key players in the sector and that they had to arrive at some accommodation for policy to move forward. The key players in South Africa in the telecommunications sector in 1995 – after the end of apartheid, an ANC electoral victory of almost 63 percent, and a government of national unity – were undoubtedly Telkom, labor, and to a somewhat lesser degree, the various telecommunications business interests. The boundaries of possible reform were constrained by the global dynamic of telecommunications liberalization and South Africa's participation in the World Trade Organization negotiations on basic telecommunications. And complicating the transformation process was the legacy of apartheid: Whites, or perhaps more accurately, white business, retained a dominance over technical knowledge.

Hence, notwithstanding the broad range of responses to the Green Paper, the effective compromise looked to be some period of exclusivity for Telkom, enabling it to mobilize capital and its large workforce to roll out the telecommunications network to the historically disadvantaged and to rebalance its tariff structure gradually, within a protective envelope – and then a decisive move toward competition. This does not, however, mean the eventual policy recommendations were predetermined. The consultations and negotiations between stakeholders were real and subject to considerable substantive give and take. The process worked because it had the backing of the minister – not as a means to rubber-stamp his own preconceived ideas, but as a genuinely open forum for stakeholder discussion and compromise. In this distinctive policy-making exercise, the minister has the responsibility of initiating policy – she or he does not have the sole role in determining that policy. Indeed, if there was a criticism of Minister Jordan, it was that he had been too detached from the process, too content, it seemed, to allow the

NTPP to run its facilitating course, and too reluctant to give the Technical Task Team ministerial guidance. But neither was the policy a product of a purely corporatist consensus, as it had to pass both the minister's and the Cabinet's approval. The parliamentary process ensured via electoral representative democratic structures that the general public interest, to the extent it may have been absent from stakeholder compromise, was properly part of the reform process. The final parliamentary check presumably ensured against the possibility of a narrow corporatism.

The participatory and the electoral structures clearly interacted in some tension. The danger of stakeholder politics (and corporatist mechanisms in general) is that organized interests – particularly producer interests – dominate policy making. In corporatist processes, the state "off-loads" some of its functions to key civil society groups in a bargaining process of a usually unrepresentative, closed, and elitist kind. Consumer interests have a much more difficult time gaining relevant access to corporatist forums, and it is nearly impossible to bring in the unorganized (see Cawson, 1986). To be sure, there was no "Union of Those Without Telephones" raising hell in the telecommunications reform process. Indeed, most of the relevant consumers were "user groups" of certain kinds of business customers. This is why some observers have put forward a serious case against the forums and, by inference, the stakeholder-driven Green Paper/White Paper process. As Friedman and Reitzes argue,

> The guaranteed incorporation of civil society in the state through forums and the like runs two risks. The first is that it allows interests and organisations which have not submitted themselves to the test of public election to exert as much power as, if not more than, representatives who have. The second is that it may bypass and short-circuit the political system, in that public demands are placed not at the door of political parties and representatives in parliament, but directly at the door of state officials who are meant to be subordinate to these representatives. (Friedman and Reitzes, 1995: 9)

These are dangers, but they did not apply to the telecommunications reform process. The process was substantively open and transparent, subject to various kinds of input at various levels and periods during the course of the NTPP. Pains were taken to ensure representativeness. Individuals and organizations who could not pay meeting fees or cover the costs of accommodations were subsidized. The results were structured but hardly predetermined. This may be what marks the essential difference between the South African Green Paper/White Paper process and, for example, the American public hearing process. Though the traditional public hearing policy-making process in the American context is theoretically an open one, the mobilization of bias and the effective distribution of power means that, for the most part, most of the time, the real debate is between and among fractions of capital. There is, of course, a long literature on this, from Marxist accounts of the capitalist state to public choice accounts of how organized interests typically prevail in the public arena. In South Africa, in contrast, at least for the first few years after the first democratic election, the balance of political and economic power was in flux, and the political culture kept questions of redistribution on the front burner. The strength of that political culture must be understood to be in no small measure a reflection of the power of organized labor in South Africa (which, at a union density of 50%, is far higher than levels in most other countries undergoing a transition from authoritarian forms of government [Macun, 2000]). If the previously disenfranchised or unorganized could not always speak for themselves in political arenas, the political culture was such that the sectoral stakeholders had to address questions of redistribution or risk illegitimacy. As testament to this, nearly every Green Paper and White Paper in every sector opened with an overview to the effect that the intention of reform was to expand service delivery to the previously disenfranchised, make the sector more efficient, and enhance the sector's competitiveness in the international economy. In telecommunications the attainment of universal service, rhetorically, if not always actually, was the fundamental focus of the telecommunications White Paper, the bottom line of any possible reform.

FROM WHITE PAPER TO LEGISLATION IN THE CONTEXT OF BROADER POLITICAL EVENTS AND PRESSURES

The telecommunications policy reform process had come a long way, but was not yet complete. The White Paper had to be translated into legislative draft; a bill needed to be passed by Parliament. The writing task was made unexpectedly dicey because Department of Posts and Telecommunications lawyers were brought in to help write the legislation. Telkom managing director Brian Clark indicated this process had to be monitored extremely carefully. He clearly distrusted the motives of the department. Clark shared the sentiments of Pallo Jordan that the old Afrikaner civil service could, and if given the chance, would, sabotage progress. Like many observers, Clark (1996) attributed the success of the White Paper to the fact that it had been done outside the department. At various points in the White Paper process the old guard from the department had attempted to secure their jobs in the new dispensation. That was what lay behind several efforts to insert a provision in the White Paper permitting a "transfer" of department staff to the regulator. In the department's view, "transfer" would be automatic, a matter of the decision of the employee.

The most consequential events at this juncture in the telecommunications White Paper process occurred outside of it: a Cabinet shakeup, the finalizing of the permanent Constitution, the replacement of the Reconstruction and Development Programme with the Growth, Employment and Redistribution strategy, and the withdrawal of the National Party from the Government of National Unity (GNU). These interrelated events had both direct and indirect impact on the telecommunications reform process. Chris Liebenberg, the finance minister unaffiliated with any political party, had indicated he would step down soon after the 1997 budget had been tabled. The ANC leadership used Liebenberg's departure to effect a major Cabinet reshuffle. The new alignment of portfolios, announced by President Mandela on March 28, had Department of Trade and Industry (DTI) Chief Trevor Manuel take control of the Ministry of Finance. Alec Erwin, deputy finance minster, went over to Manuel's position as head of the DTI. The RDP ministry was shut down. RDP functions would be reassigned to line ministries by Deputy President Thabo Mbeki's office. Jay Naidoo, minister without portfolio in charge of the RDP, needed to be redeployed. Under the terms of the 1993 Interim Constitution and the power sharing agreement, the Cabinet shuffle meant the ANC had its full complement of ministries. One ANC minister had to go. Out went Pallo Jordan. In his place as minister of Posts, Telecommunications and Broadcasting came Jay Naidoo.

Speculation ran rife about Jordan's political fall. Many observers believed that a long simmering animosity between Jordan and Deputy President Mbeki had something to do with the fact that Jordan, rather than any other ANC Cabinet minister, took the fall. But rumored clashes with President Mandela himself may have been at the center of the decision. Mandela publicly said the decision was his alone, and according to the *Mail & Guardian* (Davis, 1996a), there had been no consultation with senior party officials before the decision to axe Jordan was announced. An independent Marxist intellectual, Jordan had never kowtowed to the commandist tendencies that existed within the ANC. He had been imprisoned by ANC security in Zambia in the 1980s as a consequence of this independence. Jordan had opposed proposals that the Constitution's Chapter of Rights be watered down to facilitate the police fight against crime, and earlier, at the 1994 ANC national conference in Bloemfontein, he opposed as undemocratic Mandela's bid to draw up the ANC's list of candidates. Jordan had apparently been highly critical of the way Mandela had handled the foreign policy crisis around Nigeria's execution of Ken Saro-Wiwa and other political dissidents earlier in the year (A. Johnson, 1996). His principled hands-off attitude toward the SABC and the IBA was said to have crossed both Mandela and Mbeki. Mandela was frustrated by the SABC's handling of the Afrikaans language issue. The decline of Afrikaans language programming following the South African Broadcasting Corporation relaunch angered many Afrikaners, and Mandela reportedly feared this was turning into a rallying point for the right wing and jeopardized the process of reconciliation and nation-building. Jordan also crossed Mbeki on the issue of broadcasting. Mbeki, smarting about critical press coverage of the ANC and government, proposed early in 1995 that the SABC cede a one-hour time slot for the government (see Chapter 6). Jordan, mindful of the unholy connection between government and the national broadcaster during the apartheid era, was openly disdainful of Mbeki's notion and would not alter his hands-off stance to accommodate either Mbeki or Mandela (Davis, 1996a). Whatever the ultimate reason, and despite his public silence, Jordan seemed ruffled. After arriving late for Mandela's speech to Parliament announcing the changes, Jordan sat in the back row of the gallery and appeared visibly stunned on the television screen. The transition from Jordan to Naidoo took place quickly, on April 4.[24]

24 The announced move, a few weeks later, by Cyril Ramaphosa to join the private sector after the constitutional negotiations were completed, lent credence to the complementary theory that the Cabinet shuffle had as much to do with Mbeki's grip on succession as anything else. Even though there was an informal consensus that Mbeki would succeed Mandela as leader of the ANC, the presence of the independent Ramaphosa (and Jordan) in the Cabinet may not have sat well with Mbeki or with Mandela's sense of unambiguous signals. Ramaphosa had wanted the Finance Ministry after the Constitution was finalized, but it was not offered. That two of the ANC's most intelligent and capable members were edged out of government leadership positions did not go unnoticed (Davis, 1996b; Laufer, Fine, and Forrest, 1996).

There was a potential upside to the appointment of Jay Naidoo as minister of Posts, Telecommunications and Broadcasting. Telecommunication was clearly going to be the wedge on the restructuring of state assets debate, as the White Paper was completed and legislation would soon be tabled in Parliament. Holding up everything was the unresolved question of a capital infusion for Telkom. One bit of logic was that if anyone could sell the concept of a strategic equity partner to the unions, it would be former COSATU General Secretary Jay Naidoo. Jordan, at least by this time, was not particularly liked by the unions. But in the short term, the Cabinet realignment clearly caused some loss of confidence on the part of foreign investors. The quick dissolution of the RDP without public discussion or consultation, and the silencing of a critical voice in Cabinet before his brief on telecommunications was complete combined to give investors pause. The strategic equity partner applicants became jittery (Currie, 1996c; *Financial Mail*, 1996a). Jay Naidoo's retention of Willie Currie was designed in part to restore confidence in the telecommunications reform process. It was Currie's skilled political guidance that was responsible in some substantial portion for the White Paper's success. Indeed, his role was widely recognized by the sector, and he was named the NTF's Telecommunications Person of the Year in April.

At the legislation drafting team's weekly meeting on March 29 at the NTPP office, the Department of Posts and Telecommunications lawyers seemed delighted by the news of the ministerial changes. The interpretation was that the old guard saw the change as giving them new opportunity for maneuver. And indeed, the lawyers argued for writing a draft telecommunications bill that was broad and flexible. While there is a principled case to make for such a strategy – enabling legislation is typically broad and vague, to accommodate future developments – in this instance it effectively could cede power to the department old guard given the entrance of a new minister with no experience in or knowledge of the sector.

Other personnel departures intruded during this period. Pallo Jordan was not the only significant player to drop out of the process. Earlier in the month Saki Macozoma, chair of the Parliamentary Portfolio Committee on Communications, announced he was leaving Parliament for the post of managing director of Transnet. Although the committee had played virtually no role in the telecommunications reform process thereto, Macozoma, with extensive United Democratic Front leadership experience and knowledge of communications issues, was expected to guide the legislative phase. Whoever would replace him as chair would not be as conversant with the issues. Finally, the May 16 merger of the Coloured and Indian staff associations with the far larger black Post & Telecommunications Workers Association to become the Communication Workers Union led to an unexpected result, namely, that Lefty Monyokolo (POTWA president) and Vo Tyibilika (POTWA general secretary) were not advanced to office in the new amalgamated union. Notwithstanding his public radicalism, Monyokolo at least understood the issues facing Telkom, its shortage of capital and expertise, the competition it faced. He acknowledged privately that labor recognized that some job losses were probably inevitable in restructuring. What Monyokolo consistently raised was that no one was talking about how such losses would reproduce apartheid-induced inequalities – because it was the blacks who were the sweepers, the diggers, the restaurant waiters in the Telkom workforce – many of whom would be retrenched as a result of restructuring. The departure of Monyokolo meant that there would be leadership changes at the ministerial, parliamentary, and union levels as the White Paper moved into the legislative phase.[25]

In June the government publicly unveiled its "nonnegotiable" GEAR strategy. Uncertainty on broad economic policy, including privatization, was thought to be holding back foreign investment. The common perception was that the some of the *micro*economic programs and policies assembled under the RDP label, covering small- and medium-sized enterprises, public works projects, land reform and infrastructure development, were working but too slowly to have any significant medium-term impact on growth and job creation (Gelb, 1998b). Mandela's bold pronouncement to German industrialists and financiers in late May that privatization was "the fundamental policy of the ANC" was part of the new GEAR orientation (Hartley, 1996). Several important events undergirded Mandela's timing. The permanent Constitution was passed in May. Immediately afterward, the National Party announced it would

---

25 The politics of the Communication Workers Union election contest were somewhat mysterious. It was unusual for an election in the context of a merger of union organizations to be contested. Monyokolo did not know that another slate was standing for election until quite late in the process. The eventual winner of a very close election was Tlhalefang Sekano, who told Monyokolo he had been urged to stand for election by various provincial union leaders. In an interview, Monyokolo hinted that there may have been other forces influencing the contested nature of the election. Because Monyokolo and his slate were perceived as firmly opposed to privatization, he was perceived as standing in the way of a settlement on the Telkom ownership issue. Sekano's candidacy may have been urged by certain government officials (Monyokolo, 1997).

leave the Government of National Unity and go into formal opposition. The ANC, now seeing itself *as* the government, now fully accountable for government successes and failures, likely felt it had to take the reins of power firmly. Mandela's announcement on privatization policy and the unveiling of the GEAR macroeconomic strategy were designed to take the reins of power and resolutely establish the ANC's commitment to economic orthodoxy.

GEAR featured infrastructure development and job creation through the restructuring of parastatal corporations via privatization and equity partnerships. The ANC had moved toward a position that would essentially maintain parastatal monopolies but invite private capital to participate as minority stakeholders. This, at least, was the implication of Public Enterprises Minister Stella Sigcau's presentation to Parliament in late June, in which she pledged to move toward the full and partial privatization of state assets before the end of the financial year (Republic of South Africa, 1996p).

These events and major policy shifts were occurring as the Telecommunications White Paper was being translated into draft legislation. The writing required the efforts of a small team of lawyers, whose drafts were overseen by the Eminent Persons Group and a couple of Technical Task Team members. Draft twelve was circulated to key stakeholders for a final round of input; they were to comment only on perceived contradictions between the draft and the White Paper. A meeting of the lawyers, EPG, and relevant Task Team members was held in mid-May. Telkom evinced a desire to vest more authority in the minister rather than regulator, once again calling into question the difference between policy making and regulation. In the end, the group moved a bit toward the Telkom position, requiring ministerial approval of major regulatory decisions, such as major licenses and the spectrum plan, but no further. The regulator had to retain quite a bit of authority, otherwise the line between policy making and regulation would be so hard and fast to be itself arbitrary. Transnet and ESKOM insisted the draft language be clearer on the leeway they possessed with regard to their private networks, particularly their ability to bring in international traffic (provided that such traffic is handed to Telkom at the nearest point of entry and that the traffic enhances Telkom's revenue stream). Although opposed by Telkom, changes were incorporated in the parastatals' favor. Several parties weighed in on the draft's accordance of flexibility on the minister's ability to alter the timing of the liberalization process. Telkom and those parties hoping to become its partners, notably Deutsche Telekom and its Rothschild banking advisers, argued that this violated the White Paper and that the White Paper language supported only the possibility of lengthening the period of exclusivity. As might be expected, those parties hoping to become Telkom's competitors, including ESKOM, Global One Business Solutions (formerly Sprint Communications South Africa), and Orbicom, argued the polar opposite, that is, the spirit of the White Paper supported only the possibility of shortening the period of exclusivity. In fact the White Paper, as a compromise political document, was ambiguous on the matter, and the wording was deliberately ambiguous as part of the effort to secure general agreement from the stakeholders. The oversight group left the language as it was. The Department of Posts & Telecommunications engaged in an underhanded effort to secure the old regime staff's employment. The department submitted an alternative clause 17, allowing staff now doing regulatory functions in the department to "elect" to go over to the South African Telecommunications Regulatory Authority (with full pensions and equivalent salary packages). This was the only issue in which the department's representatives to the oversight group got much involved.[26] The draft language of clause 17 stayed the same (see Republic of South Africa, 1996j,k,l).

THE PROCESS IN JEOPARDY

The Twelfth Draft of the Telecommunications Bill came back to the legislative task team marked up with suggestions from the minister. Presumably counseled by Postmaster General Ngcaba and senior department staff, Minister Naidoo called for major changes in the bill, which were reflected in the Fourteenth Draft. This included dropping any reference to a period of exclusivity for Telkom, and greatly increasing the power of the minister (which effectively included the department) vis-à-vis the regulator. All mention of the painstakingly

26 Department representatives brought a "memo" from Cabinet essentially endorsing such transfer policy. But Cabinet never discussed such a thing. This wasn't so much outright duplicity as it was an illustration of the corrupt old-boys' practices of the old regime, where departments typically wrote memos that, if it had time to consider, Cabinet "would have" written. Real animosity was evidenced in this episode between the department representatives and the black EPG members, who countered with charges that the department had been padding [white] staff during the Green Paper/White Paper process and that the new dispensation required not the protection of the old guard but, to the contrary, strong affirmative action for the previously disadvantaged. Animosity also erupted between the department and Telkom. It was clear the department staff bitterly resented the fact that Telkom (and its management) had been taken care of in the transformation of the telecommunications sector, whereas, in contrast, the department staff anticipated getting shafted.

worked out liberalization time-line was dropped in favor of the minister's prerogative on all matters of competition and liberalization. Management of the Human Resources Fund would not be the responsibility of the regulator, but would stay with the ministry. Monies collected through license fees and the like would go to the common fiscus. The department would have to approach the Finance Ministry through the normal channels to finance any of the human resource activities suggested in the White Paper. The regulator was now answerable to the *minister* rather than to Parliament. The minister's prerogative was so expanded that it was manifestly unclear what was to be the role of the regulator under the terms of the Fourteenth Draft. In effect, a version of the old governance system was being resurrected, where the ministry directed policy and effectively assumed regulatory power by vastly diminishing the proposed regulator's authority and compromising any genuine independence. Further, the new arrangement threatened to encroach on Telkom's operational authority by virtue of the government's exercise of its shareholding function (Republic of South Africa, 1996j).

The NTPP coordinator Willie Currie was distressed with the turn of events and wondered what it would take to reverse them. At a briefing on the White Paper to the Parliamentary Portfolio Committee June 11, Currie subtly alerted the members of Parliament to the differences between the draft they had received (twelve) and the most recent draft (fourteen). But the timing was inauspicious for reversal, as the Fourteenth Draft was slated to go to the Cabinet Committee June 12 and the Eminent Persons Group had not even met to discuss it. Whatever political pressure that might be applied would probably have to come through the EPG. The EPG did offer some initial resistance to what was labeled by some as a "ministerial coup." The EPG sent a memo to Minister Naidoo that the draft did not correspond to the White Paper in four key areas and, hence, refused to endorse the draft bill. Willie Currie resigned as special adviser. But Minister Naidoo spun the situation quickly, calling the EPG to a June 26 meeting and getting the five members essentially to recant their opposition. The EPG members Dupree Vilikazi and Neel Smuts attended a June 28 press conference with the minister, backing Naidoo's contention that he had not fundamentally altered the White Paper. At this press conference Naidoo claimed the ministry was still committed to liberalization and competition but did not want its hands tied by a rigid timetable (Lunsche, 1996a). Naidoo and Postmaster General Ngcaba also met with the NTF

Executive Committee to engage in damage control. As for Willie Currie, in the words of ministry spokesperson Connie Molusi (1996b), he had been acting "outside his mandate."

The changes, or in the words of the *Financial Mail*, Naidoo's "sleight-of-hand," were in direct conflict with the specific terms of consensus negotiated in the long stakeholder consultation process, and flew in the face of the culture of consultation and transparency (*Financial Mail*, 1996c). The speculation was that this turn of events represented an odd convergence of interests and personalities in the ministry. Jay Naidoo had come to the Ministry of Posts, Telecommunications and Broadcasting from heading up the RDP. Among the reasons for the failure of the RDP was that the RDP office created a new bureaucracy for the delivery of services that duplicated and, hence, invaded the turfs and complicated the functions of several other existing ministries. Coordination and cooperation were absolutely essential in delivering new or expanded services, yet very difficult to attain. But another reason for the RDP's failure was that, while in principle the RDP was bound to participatory processes and structures, in practice RDP projects often engaged in a state-oriented and state-directed kind of development that attempted but did not effectively engage people, communities, and institutions at the grassroots level. Although the RDP *document* was the product of various groups and organizations in an engaged consultative process, the actual delivery of projects and services was not often successful in drawing in the grassroots (see, e.g., Götz, 2000). Jay Naidoo had not been part of the long telecommunications reform process. And, even though he paid it lip service, Naidoo had no particular commitment to the consultations nor to the agreements reached. Naidoo had asked his top department advisers whether he would have more or less power under the Twelfth Draft of the bill as compared to existing legislation. When Koos Klok replied "less," the answer seems to have settled Naidoo on his course. According to Klok, Minister Naidoo responded, "This is unacceptable" (Klok, 1997).

Postmaster General Andile Ngcaba, on the other hand, *had* directly participated in the consultative process, had on several occasions publicly championed it, yet now seemed to be undermining it. Perhaps this was because now that he was in a position of authority and responsibility, Ngcaba was nervous about having an as yet unconstituted, untested regulatory body direct an essential infrastructure sector at this crucial and fragile moment of its transformation. But it may have been that, having finally secured a position of power and responsibility, Ngcaba was reluctant to see it diminished. Whatever the reasons or intentions behind it, the Fourteenth Draft shattered the stakeholder process and lessened the scope of the regulator's authority and removed much of its independence.[27] No doubt the restoration of the gravity of policy making and regulatory authority to the Department of Posts & Telecommunications cheered the department old guard, who had long been trying to finagle a way to retain their sinecures and power.

The changes augured by the Fourteenth Draft of the Telecommunications Bill represented a reamalgamation of power in the ministry. In the end it seemed Naidoo had returned to the old form of ad hoc ministerial control, although he dismissed that interpretation. The ministry publicly insisted that the general features of the White Paper remained intact – Telkom's exclusivity and the timed liberalization would be accomplished through licensing rather than written into statute, as contemplated by the White Paper. Again, there was precedent for this change, as many countries handled liberalization transformation through licenses and performance contracts. But nothing in principle would prevent the minister from extending Telkom's monopoly indefinitely. Without a timetable for liberalization, would-be competitors had no certainty when to commence investments. And the appearance, if not the reality, was that these changes simply scuttled the stakeholder consensus. The changes provoked a small firestorm in the business press and served to reopen the debate over competition, a debate that had been more or less settled after the publication of the White Paper. *Business Day*'s (1996b) lead editorial of June 28 conceded that lengthening the period of exclusivity might bring more cash to the government, but constituted a deeply flawed policy with regard to telecommunications development. *Financial Mail* (1996d) ran a long story in its July 5, 1996,

27 The proposed changes also posed a potential constitutional problem. Inasmuch as Minister Naidoo had earlier indicated he wanted the merger of the IBA into SATRA in the short-term, the impending non-independence of the telecommunications regulatory authority would violate the constitutional requirement for a fully independent broadcast regulatory authority. Those in the broadcast industry, including the Independent Broadcasting Authority, who had quietly harbored worries about Minister Naidoo's intentions vis-à-vis the independence of the broadcast regulator, gulped. It didn't help that Naidoo publicly legitimated the reconceived role of SATRA as a way to prevent the new regulatory body from following in the steps of the IBA (cited in *Financial Mail*, 1996c). But this was demagoguery, capitalizing on the public image of the IBA as a "gravy train" regulatory body without, however, offering any substantive analysis of its shortcomings. Naidoo brushed aside any dangers inhering in a heavier ministerial role in broadcasting by reference to the not yet passed Open Democracy Bill's (Republic of South Africa, 1998d) protection of freedom of speech (J. Naidoo, 1996).

issue blasting the ministry's abandonment of competition. Several papers ran opinion pieces critical of the policy or quoted highly disparaging remarks from Peter Archer, British Telecom's Middle East and Africa director (see, e.g., van Zyl, 1996). A new group, the National Telecommunication Co-Ordinating Group, consisting of business associations, including cellular and Internet service providers, the Information Technology Association, value-added network operators, and paging companies, protested against the ministry's handling of the Telecommunications Bill. In the words of its spokesman,

> For more than two years business organisations participated in what appeared to be a transparent and consultative process, only to have the Ministry overrule the most significant proposals without consultation. Insult was added to injury when Naidoo claimed the National Telecommunications Forum supported his action. During discussions, Naidoo undertook to address these concerns, but no evidence of this has emerged. There was no prior consultation with stakeholders regarding these changes and none of the participants of the new group supports them. . . . The removal from the Bill of the fixed dates regarding the exclusivity period of Telkom serves to potentially perpetuate its monopoly. The consumer could continue to foot the bill for an expensive and internationally noncompetitive telecoms monopoly. (Quoted in *Financial Mail*, 1996e)

There was clearly a kind of "I'm the Minister; this is government prerogative" tone to Naidoo's handling of the fallout over the changed policy. According to the *Financial Mail*, whose reports can veer toward the hyperbolic and, hence, must be taken with a grain of salt, unhappy industry representatives were upbraided by Naidoo, who opened a damage control meeting with them by saying the days of the Government of National Unity were over, "so they had better kow-tow to the ANC" (*Financial Mail*, 1996b). Less pejorative, but reasonably consonant with Naidoo's alleged comments, were ministry spokesperson Connie Molusi's remarks in a letter to the editor:

> The government is committed to a consultative process of drafting legislation, but that does not remove its sovereign right to make decisions based on the national interest. Cabinet has a right to change legislation to ensure that it conforms to the overall framework of government policy, before legislation is tabled in

268

Parliament, which is the final arbiter on all legislation. (Molusi, 1996a)

Yet, in a sense there was a kind of overdetermination to the ministry's alterations of the telecommunications White Paper. Reamalgamating power in the ministry gave the minister the ability to parlay a longer period of exclusivity for Telkom into a better price for the 25–30 percent share of the parastatal. Indeed, "sweetening" the deal for potential investors was one of the reasons behind the Fourteenth Draft changes, Naidoo intimated (Lunsche, 1996a). A high price for a share of Telkom was also in accordance with the new GEAR macroeconomic plan. Restored ministerial power also comported with the general move toward consolidating power in the now ANC-identified government and the parallel move away from the participatory structures of stakeholder forums and the like. Naidoo clearly believed that government had not had sufficient input into the White Paper process under Pallo Jordan and that stakeholder consultation promised diminishing returns at best. Jay Naidoo was more of a hands-on minister and, in the context of the ANC's policy transformation on macroeconomic strategy and its subtle political shift on the stakeholder forums, decided to put his mark on the bill as it was headed to Parliament. Indeed, Naidoo saw his actions as a corrective to the recent history of policy making in the sector. "This ministry," he declared in a barely veiled criticism of his predecessor, "has taken the lead – unlike before. Consultation was invented by the ANC and COSATU." But, Naidoo continued, "government has to move forward when consultation stops delivering" (J. Naidoo, 1997).

As the final phase of the process – the Parliamentary Committee on Communications hearings – was set to begin, Minister Naidoo led a contingent (which included labor representatives, notably Tlhalefang Sekano, new president of the Communication Workers Union, indicating some movement on that front) to foreign capitals in early July to talk with potential partners. Something happened during that trip. Naidoo announced a policy turnaround in an interview from Washington. Perhaps foreign governments already annoyed with the White Paper's stipulated length of Telkom's exclusivity expressed further disappointment with the ministry's alterations to the White Paper timetable for competition. Or, perhaps, Naidoo responded to the anxiety of potential strategic equity partners regarding the dark, potentially ad hoc, side of ministerial authority. A strong minister armed with a flexible mandate could extend the profitable reign of Telkom and its SEP, but such authority could equally easily intrude in less benevolent ways, and a skittish SEP would value certainty over a gamble that ad hoc ministerial authority would act to secure additional profits.[28] At any rate, Naidoo limited Telkom's period of exclusivity to between four and six years, but continued to insist that this not be a matter of legislation. The ministry, Naidoo explained, would determine broad policy; SATRA would issue all licenses and monitor whether Telkom was abiding by the terms of its license. Telkom's exclusivity, written into its license, would not deviate from the ball-park White Paper time periods, though the minister would take more responsibility for shortening or lengthening it as appropriate, as rollout is measured (Chalmers, 1996; Braun and Kaplan, 1996). Thus the policy seemed in some important respects to be drifting back toward the White Paper consensus.

PARLIAMENTARY HEARINGS

Behind the scenes, negotiations proceeded on the SEP bids. Although the press speculated about several large international telecommunications operators, the ministry was mum. Ministry spokesperson Connie Molusi acknowledged in late September 1996 that France Télécom, Deutsche Telekom, British Telecom, Italy's Stet, the Dutch and Swedish consortium KPN, Bell Atlantic, SBC Communications, and Telekom Malaysia were in the running. In fact, at this point, only four players, joined into two consortia, SBC-Telekom Malaysia and Deutsche Telekom with France Télécom, remained as serious candidates (*Financial Mail*, 1996f). What *was* public was the fact that labor had come on board. In mid-September, COSATU's Central Executive Committee announced its willingness to consider the involvement of private sector capital in the parastatals, so long as the state remained the majority shareholder (Congress of South African Trade Unions, 1996b). Minister Naidoo also indicated that another 10 percent of Telkom would be made available to black shareholding. The minister and Postmaster General Ngcaba were heavily involved in the assessment of the bids and wanted to settle on the SEP. But to do so required a settled policy.

28 According to Koos Klok (1997), the American telecommunications company Bell Atlantic had looked into making a bid as the strategic equity partner, but withdrew. Publicly, the reason for its decision was that the corporation had become overextended after taking over Nynex, another former Bell company. Privately, Bell Atlantic dropped out of the SEP race because it had lost faith in Minister Naidoo and Telkom.

Naidoo pushed hard for Parliament to pass the telecommunications bill before the lawmakers adjourned in November.

The Parliamentary Portfolio Committee on Communications announced public hearings on the bill in October 1996. Initially giving parties just three working days to prepare submissions, after protests the committee extended the period by a week. By this time the lines of conflict had become relatively clear. Black business and business-oriented black civic organizations and Telkom lined up to lend support for the major provisions of the draft bill and its restoration of ministerial authority. Industry and user groups, and the IBA, registered criticisms. Even as it supported the bill, Federation for African Business and Consumer Services (FABCOS), South Africa National Civic Organisation Investment Holdings, and Ilima Community Development Company (all of which submitted the same document under different covers), along with the South African Black Technical and Allied Careers Organisation, expressed disappointment that, unlike the White Paper, the telecommunications bill was not emphatic in support of black economic empowerment. They wanted concrete affirmative action guidelines written into the bill. At the same time, they praised the decision to locate the Human Resources Development offices in the director general's office and called for a third cellular license to be awarded to black shareholders (Federation for African Business and Consumer Services, 1996; Ilima Community Development Company, 1996; SANCO Investment Holdings, 1996; Mass Development Movement, 1996; South African Black Technical and Allied Careers Organisation, 1996). Telkom (1996a,b), not surprisingly, praised the bill's "new indeterminacy," that is, its reservation to ministerial discretion the determination of the period of Telkom's exclusivity and the timetable for the liberalization of the sector. Such indeterminacy, Telkom argued, permitted the government to bargain from a stronger position vis-à-vis the SEP and with the World Trade Organization in the negotiations on basic telephony. Telkom also lobbied strongly against awarding Transnet and ESKOM long-distance licenses. Indeed, asserted Telkom, the parastatals should not be permitted to prepare themselves to compete with Telkom. The parastatals should stick to business and not waste money by duplicating infrastructure. Telkom also pointed out the bill's "oversight" in not awarding the company a license to use the frequency spectrum.

The industry trade associations and business user groups formed the most prolific bloc of submissions, most of them focussing on pet sectoral complaints. The Information Technology Association (1996), for example, the trade body for suppliers of information technology equipment, systems software, and services, warned that the definition of telecommunications in the bill was too broad, and could be read to encompass computers. Similarly, the National Telecommunications Users Group (1996) complained that the bill's definition of a private network could (improperly) include all private area branch exchanges and local area networks. The South African VANS Association (1996) objected to the provision prohibiting value-added networks from carrying voice traffic during the period of Telkom's exclusivity. The South African Cellular Service Providers' Association (1996) charged that independent cellular service providers were being squeezed by the service providers owned by the cellular network operators and wanted the bill to address this abuse of market power. The Internet Service Providers Association (1996) queried why the bill made no mention of the Internet and, in a detailed submission, demonstrated how Telkom could easily favor its own Internet service provider through its direct access to Telkom exchanges. Cellular networks MTN (1996) and Vodacom (1996) complained about having to make contributions to the Universal Service Fund and the Human Resources Fund. Because they already had service and fee obligations built into their licenses by virtue of the Communication Service Obligations and Joint Economic Development Plan Commitments, the cellular network providers argued that the additional contributions represented a double taxation. They advocated a "pay or play" provision with regard to the Universal Service Fund. And NTUG (National Telematics User Group, 1996) charged that the bill contained no provisions for assessing whether the purposes of the universal and human resource funds were being fulfilled. Underneath this latter complaint was the industry's distaste that the human resource fund would become a patronage machine for Postmaster General Ngcaba.

These submissions represented a standard litany of important, yet relatively contained sectoral complaints. But the industry submissions went further than this, attacking the diminution of South African Telecommunications Regulatory Authority's independence and the seeming "unholy" alliance between Telkom and policy makers. In one of the more biting statements, the Information Technology Association (1996) expressed "little faith in the impartiality of a regulatory authority which is appointed by, and is responsible to, the Minister," who is himself "responsible for promoting the interests of Telkom." The ITA called for the total independence of SATRA. Though more discreet in its tone, Orbicom's (1996) submission made much the same points, and added that the bill should set out limitations on the discretion of the authorities to extend or shorten Telkom's period of exclusivity. In the same spirit, the South African VANS Association (1996) and South African Cellular Service Providers' Association (1996) inveighed against clause 36(5) of the bill, which stipulated that any proposed change to Telkom's license during the period of exclusivity required the company's consent. This clause presumably was to give the potential SEP security against government intervention during the period of exclusivity. The absence of a sunset clause on Telkom's license was of concern to the Telephone Attachment Association (1996), representing the major importers of telephone attachments in South Africa.

Other critics tried to bolster the independence of SATRA in more modest ways. The NTUG (1996) urged that SATRA report to the minister without interference from the Department of Posts & Telecommunications. The NTF (1996) suggested that if and when the minister disapproves a SATRA regulation, he or she should remand it back to SATRA with reasons explaining the disapproval. Then SATRA could amend its proposed regulation in light of the minister's comments. The National Telecommunications Co-Ordinating Group (1996), the newly constituted, broad umbrella industry and users group, made no specific complaints or recommendations in its written submission but upbraided Minister Naidoo and Postmaster General Ngcaba for their dismissal of the efforts of the industry stakeholders. Earlier in the parliamentary committee's deliberations, the minister had advised parliamentarians not to allow themselves to be "influenced by the smooth talk from the privileged classes." The NTCG took great exception to this characterization and to the minister's thinly veiled disparagement of industry's contributions to the stakeholder process. Indeed, Minister Naidoo's "struggle" rhetoric and the NTCG's complaints signalled that the politics of consultation had shifted. Whereas in the period of the political transition and the first couple of years of the Government of National Unity consultation and stakeholder participation constituted a means of entry by black people into the policy-making arena, by the time the National Party quit the GNU the same processes were perceived as the means by which the old order was stifling transformation.

A few government bodies and parastatals filed submissions. Transtel (Transnet, 1996) and ESKOM (1996), as expected, submitted documents designed to safeguard their special private networks. But the parastatals also tried to make sure they would not be prevented by statute from becoming future competitors to Telkom. The Independent Broadcasting Authority delivered a thoughtful submission on the question of SATRA's independence. Conceding that the bill's provisions on the appointment of councillors and the approach to telecommunications regulation generally were consistent with the practices in most democracies, the IBA nonetheless argued that a different approach was appropriate because the establishment of SATRA came at a special historical moment. The democratization of South Africa, the end of the monopoly of the state-owned telecommunications company, and the convergence of communication technologies dictated a new regulatory model, the IBA asserted, to the effect that SATRA should be wholly independent from the state and its administration. Especially given the fact that the IBA was slated to merge into SATRA in the near future and that the traditional separations between content and conduit, between broadcasting and telecommunications were likely to diminish – hence most regulatory rulings would directly or indirectly impact freedom of expression issues – SATRA should be wholly independent (Republic of South Africa, 1996i).[29]

This was the argument the ministry endeavored to rebut in its written submission. The ministry presented comparative ITU data on the powers of various national regulatory agencies and their relative degrees of "independence." The ministry's plan for SATRA, it argued, was wholly in keeping with most democratic countries. Moreover, SATRA, as envisaged in the bill, would be more independent and would possess more power than the regulatory agencies of France, Mexico, and Sweden, for instance. The ministry also took pains to show that many countries wrote exclusivity conditions into the dominant operator's license rather than into the legislation (Republic of South Africa, 1996m). A development-based argument was posed to buttress Telkom's contention that the ministry needed to have flexibility to better negotiate with the SEP and the WTO. A submission from Siyanda Women's Investments (1996) articulated the position (made also by several ANC parliamentarians) that independence was a relative term,

29 The White Paper stipulated that the Independent Broadcasting Authority would merge into SATRA after some unspecified interval. But any merger would require constitutional scrutiny. According to the Constitution, the IBA is an independent body and its councillors must be appointed by the president. The Telecommunications Bill stipulated that SATRA councillors be appointed by the minister of Posts, Telecommunications and Broadcasting and that the regulatory body answer to the minister.

and at this stage in South Africa's evolution there was a need for the government to direct the sector toward addressing the imbalances of the past. Full regulatory independence was a luxury of a few advanced industrial nations (see Republic of South Africa, 1996s; Moeti, 1997). The ministry had long set the stage for a closer hand in SATRA. It had been publicly disparaging the IBA for months as ineffective and, when IBA councillors' spending irregularities surfaced, as an agency "out of control."

The written submission of the Department of Posts & Telecommunications (Republic of South Africa, 1996b) pressed for expanded ministerial authority. Submitted after the public hearings, it registered those suggestions and objections deemed reasonable by the department's policy mavens and thus offered a shorthand for the parliamentarians, particularly the ANC caucus. The department tightened up on some definitions, acknowledged Telkom as holder of a license to provide local exchange services by way of wireless local loop and fixed wireless facilities, and replaced the word "authority," as in "regulatory authority," with the word "minister" in several places. Notably, this included giving the minister the power over interconnection and rate-setting for three years and responsibility for the award of licenses to Telkom. These additions to ministerial authority were inserted into the final draft bill under pressure from the winning SEP, the consortium of SBC Communications and Telekom Malaysia. The SEP insisted that the ministry, rather than SATRA, issue the Telkom licenses. According to Pinky Moholi (1997), this was not so much because the SEP was in bed with the ministry as due to anxiety about timing. SATRA would not be named until February 1997 at the earliest and would not be ready to take up the difficult task of licensing of Telkom until well after that. In the eyes of the SEP, the deal had to be consummated, which included a guarantee that the licenses would be granted quickly.

The department put forward a new clause giving the minister formal authority to transfer the government's equity interest in Telkom (with Cabinet approval) for purposes of economic empowerment of historically disadvantaged communities and for obtaining additional management, technology, and necessary capital for Telkom. It met the objection to clause 36(5) – the requirement that Telkom concur with any changes to its license – by opening up the initial licensing process to public debate. The department's submission also tightened up possible language in the bill that might allow for the bypass of Telkom's network. Finally, it recommended the addition of a new clause to the section on the act's objectives, to "promote the empowerment and enhancement of women" (Republic of South Africa, 1996b).

In the parliamentary committee debate, the ANC caucus steered to acceptance virtually all the changes recommended by the department (Republic of South Africa, 1996v). The Democratic Party, and to a lesser degree, the National Party, championed those complaints of the business community (and, for that matter, much of the spirit of the White Paper) that had broad policy ramifications. On the question of SATRA, the DP recommended that SATRA function without any political or other bias or interference and be wholly independent and separate from the state and its administration. To ensure against the indefinite extension of Telkom's exclusivity, the DP asked for SATRA to conduct an inquiry four years after the commencement of the act and make recommendations to Parliament on the desirability of extending or curtailing Telkom's exclusivity. Telkom's ability to vet changes to its license [clause (36.5)] should be deleted. The value-added networks should be permitted to carry voice traffic. Acknowledging the cellular networks' concerns, the DP argued that the "pay or play" principle should apply to the Universal Service Fund. And finally, the DP wanted to remove language requiring that preferences be given to applications for telecommunications licenses to persons from historically disadvantaged groups. Instead of preferences, due regard should be given to the provisions of the objectives of the act, which include encouraging ownership and control of telecommunications services by persons from historically disadvantaged groups (Democratic Party, 1996).

With the exception of some changes to SATRA, the proposed amendments were voted down by the ANC caucus. In the heat of the debate, the motives of the NP and DP were impugned and the comments by industry dismissed as vested, privileged interests. The minister in particular employed struggle rhetoric to dispatch the arguments arrayed in opposition to the bill (Republic of South Africa, 1996t).[30] But there was some compromise on the question of SATRA's independence. The word

---

30 In introducing the bill, Minister Naidoo began, "Chairperson, members of the House, I have great pleasure in moving that the Telecommunications Bill be read for the second time. For those who have suffered under apartheid, those who have had to bear the brunt of the legacy of people who sit on that side of the House will understand why this Bill is important, because the members on that side of the House have been a privileged elite which seeks, in the future, to protect its privileges. Let us understand that people who have telephones in their homes, who have telephones in their workplaces, who carry cellular phones, know nothing about the fact that it is the policies of the NP which have created the economic chaos of this country, and this Bill attempts to rectify that situation" (Republic of South Africa, 1996t).

"independent" was inserted before the word "impartial" in clause 5 ("the Authority shall be independent and impartial in the performance of its functions"), and notwithstanding objections from the ministry, the committee altered the selection procedure for SATRA councillors. In the original draft bill, the minister of Communications (Posts and Telecommunications had become simply Communications) had the power to appoint the SATRA Council. In the amended and final bill, the state president was given the power to appoint the councillors on the advice of the Parliamentary Portfolio Committee (Republic of South Africa, 1996w). The ministry proposed a clause authorizing it to appoint a task force to interview the nominees to the SATRA Council, but this was rejected (Moeti, 1997). Democratic Party MP Dene Smuts remarked that the change regarding SATRA "occurred more by accident than anything else," and was a surprise to the ANC itself (Republic of South Africa, 1996q). This was no doubt because the question of the degree of SATRA's independence opened up an institutional conflict over the power of Parliament vis-à-vis the Cabinet. Parliament already effectively appointed IBA councillors and SABC Board members. Why should the appointment of SATRA councillors be different? It was also the case that the changes may have been the price for bringing the Inkatha Freedom Party on board for the final vote (see Republic of South Africa, 1996r). With the exception of Inkatha, SATRA's small gain in independence was not enough to appease the bill's critics. The Telecommunications Act was approved by Parliament by a vote of 210 to 64 just before the end of its session in early November (Republic of South Africa, 1996y). The ANC and the Inkatha Freedom Party voted in favor. The Democratic Party voted against the bill along with the National Party and Freedom Front.

THE PROCESS CONCLUDES

The strategic equity partner was announced in March 1997. In the end only the SBC–Telekom Malaysia consortium submitted a bid. The terms of the Telkom license – decided in February – reflected the reality that the original service goals were impossible to impose on the SEP at a price the government would accept for the 30 percent stake. Although Telkom's Vision 2000 had targeted 3 million new lines and a million reconditioned lines in five years, the draft Telkom license requires a much more modest 1.8 million lines in five years. Telkom wins an extra year of exclusivity if by the fourth anniversary of its license the company has achieved a rollout of 90 percent of its cumulative five-year total line target and 80 percent of its five-year underserved line target (Republic of South Africa, 1997c). On the other side of incentives, if Telkom underachieves the projected rollout in any financial year it must pay modest penalties. For 30 percent of Telkom, the SBC–Telekom Malaysia consortium (called Thintana Communications) paid R5.45 billion ($1.26 billion, U.S.), R4.4 billion of which was retained by Telkom for infrastructure spending (Mbeki, 1997b). The government also set aside an extra 10 percent stake of Telkom for purposes of black economic empowerment. The intense push to finalize the sale of the Telkom stake, and the fact that in the end only one bidder remained, reflected the fact that South Africa may have come a bit late to the international privatization party. Brian Clark indicated that the government was anxious that world privatization had been tapped out, especially after the U.S. Telecommunications Act of 1996. Analysts speculated that the U.S. act opened up better, less risky investment opportunities in the United States and would suck up available investment capital (B. Clark, 1997).

In the big picture view, the telecommunications reform process was a largely successful political event. The parties managed to craft a pragmatic, if at times contentiously fought, balance between business desires and universal service needs, between the need to preserve a national asset and the need to open the sector to new entrepreneurs and investment. The reform committed the sector to a rapid rollout of the network while also permitting the development of sophisticated value-added services through a phased and regulated liberalization of competitive entry – first at the margins, then at the core of the infrastructure. The commitment to expand the network massively was designed to marry the post-apartheid imperatives of redistribution and development. Network expansion for universal access and eventually universal service was expected to mitigate the problem of potential labor retrenchments, inasmuch as rapid expansion would require considerable manpower. The highly charged national debate on ownership came to recognize both the benefits and the dangers of privatization. The principal benefit was the breaking of the stagnation in investment with a large infusion of capital and expertise. The dangers included the possible loss of national control over an essential national infrastructure, a new profit orientation that could focus attention and investment away from universal service and *basic* needs, and the potential repatriation of profits out of the country. The final outcome in the determination of Telkom's ownership represented another reasonable compromise: bringing in a large telecommunications operator as a minority equity partner, a percentage of equity earmarked for black economic empowerment, but the majority and controlling share of Telkom retained by the state.

In *Comrades in Business: Post-Liberation Politics in South Africa*, Adam, Slabbert, and Moodley (1997) imply that what is necessary for post-apartheid South Africa is to get blacks to accept a choiceless economic reality that largely dashes their hopes and expectations. This approach cynically conceives democracy as a mode of generating consent behind prepackaged economic policies. However, the stakeholder deliberative policy processes were rather about defining choices for a political community within economic constraints. The final outcome of the telecommunications reform process established a compromise solution between state control and unfettered market controls, between state ownership and privatization. The White Paper was a successful process both from the standpoint of participation and legitimacy, and from the standpoint of fashioning a technically coherent reasonable compromise on market structure, regulatory oversight, and the overall transformation of the sector. It was trying to ask the elements of the sector to do certain things, to wait, to agree that these policies were best for the sector and the country. The White Paper even acknowledged that it would be technically unlikely if not impossible for the regulator or minister to enforce the desired behavior. Large private networks already allegedly engage in resale without permission. New technologies, or perhaps more accurately, new deployments of existing technologies, increase the possibilities of national network bypass and make policing virtually impossible. The VANS operators can easily offer voice as well as data on their networks. Many companies, as well as private individuals, use the call-back operators for international calls, effectively bypassing Telkom's tariff structure. Satellite operators such as PanAmSat require no official national signatory, and multiple direct access to satellite services is possible. Access to satellite service outside the national signatory process allows any large organization to relay its telecommunication traffic outside the national carrier. Once a company sets up a link to a satellite without going through the national carrier, there can be no way to know or control the kind (voice or data) or amount of traffic the company sends. Because the White Paper process involved the stakeholders in genuine and substantive ways, it strove to create the conditions for its own success. The purpose of putting the market structure timetable into legislation was to lend the government's backing to the stakeholder compromise, to provide confidence as to times when the market would open up (something that is crucial for making business plans), and give Telkom both the assurance that it would not be attacked for x years, but that it must face up to competition in year z. While it may be broad international practice to enunciate liberalization timetables in licenses rather than legislation, the White Paper and Twelfth Draft of the bill did not tie policy-makers' hands. The draft language gave the minister ample opportunity to check whether the goals for the sector were being served by the timetable and general market structure provisions.

On the other hand, the denouement does point to tensions between participatory and electoral politics and underscores the tension within the ANC around its often commandist leadership style. Naidoo's handling of the end-game, particularly the apparent pushing aside of stakeholder consensus (only to readmit many of its basic provisions later, through the back door), reflected a turn away from the politics of consultation and toward the commandist style. The stakeholder forums had served as the access point for the formerly excluded black majority to enter policy deliberations during the democratic transition period. And in so doing, the forums had functioned to serve notice to the last white government that it could no longer make policy unilaterally. In the post-election period the political meaning and import of the stakeholder processes became more complicated as far as the ANC was concerned. The forums had evolved into pluralistic, nonstatutory, quasi-corporatist bodies whose authority to make policy was perceived by some as treading upon, even compromising, the government's policy-making authority. Hence the nature of the tensions between participatory and electoral structures changed after the elections, and changed still further after the National Party announced its departure from the Government of National Unity.

More than any particular change in the translation from White Paper to legislation, it was the reassertion of ministerial authority that is noteworthy. The changes to the telecommunications White Paper were consonant with the spirit and timing of the government's adoption of GEAR and reflected the move toward centralizing power in the now ANC-identified government more generally. Given the broad policy orientation of the ANC's macroeconomic plan, the reassertion of ministerial control in telecommunications gave the minister more flexibility in the search for a partner for Telkom (an ability to trade a higher sale price for greater concessions on exclusivity) and more leeway to bring labor and black economic empowerment groups into an overall settlement. Telecommunications policy had to be brought into line with the broader policy framework on the economy and the role of parastatals within it – that parastatals become a source of revenue. There is some legitimacy to the argument that, in the absence of a yet-to-be-created regulator, some authoritative body – to wit, the ministry – had to negotiate the terms of the SEP deal and the service contracts and regulatory policies associated with it. But this does not explain the zeal with which the ministry tried to establish its control over SATRA. The ANC was leery about giving new bodies of unknown political loyalties significant regulatory authority. Still, at the end of the day, it is not clear that the final outcome was appreciably different from that contemplated by the original White Paper. And the final electoral check worked in the sense that it restored some independence to SATRA.

CHAPTER 6

Free but "Responsible": The Battle over the Press and the Reform of the South African Communication Service

The final reform process in the communications sector revolved around the South African Communication Service (SACS), the state bureaucracy that performed information functions and had long served as the apartheid government's public relations mouthpiece. Like so many other institutions in the immediate post-apartheid period, SACS was targeted for transformation. Indeed, there was sentiment for eliminating the service entirely. The organization was seen by many as irredeemable, its mission regarded as an anathema in a now democratic polity. Others saw SACS as an important means to disseminate the new government's policies. But should a democratic government have an official information service? The debate over the fate of SACS after 1994 was a fight, in complicated fashion, over the vision of the post-apartheid communications system. In some respects that vision had already been decided along the way, albeit in piecemeal fashion. Broadcasting, as we have seen, would be a mixed system of three levels: a public service broadcaster formally independent of political control; a limited domain of commercial broadcasting with significant local content obligations and black shareholding; and locally controlled community radio – all overseen by a constitutionally mandated Independent Broadcasting Authority. In the telecommunications sector, the Green Paper/White Paper consultative reform process envisioned a majority state-owned Telkom, but infused by foreign shareholding capital, it would take on the task of expanding the telephone network to the previously disadvantaged as a responsibility fixed in its license. Subsequent to a five-year period of exclusivity, nearly all market segments would be opened to some degree of competition. The relative settledness of these matters opened debate over the elements of the post-apartheid media system *not* covered by broadcast or telecommunications legislation: the print press and the government information service.

With the structure of broadcasting now essentially settled and in principle independent of government and political parties, the debate about the media and public communications hung on the familiar dispute over the function of the press in a postliberation context. Should the press be "objective," that is to say, nonpartisan and adversarial, or rather a responsible "partner" in development and nation building? In the South African context, this debate was complicated by the clearly oligopolistic tendencies in the print press and in newspaper distribution, and the legacy of apartheid in racializing media ownership and control. The African National Congress's official stance on the broader question of freedom of the press, as represented in its 1988 Constitutional Guidelines, was expectedly expansive, albeit brief: the state "shall guarantee the basic rights and freedoms, such as freedom of association, expression, thought, worship, and the press" (African National Congress, 1989: 131). But the broad church that was the ANC included a strong current of support for a politically committed press or what has come to be known in the literature as the "developmental" or "nation-building" theory of the press. On this theory, a Western-style adversarial press is seen as inimical to the progressive developmental goals of (usually postcolonial or postrevolutionary) government. A press concerned about reconstruction and nation-building should augment and assist, not criticize and disparage, governmental efforts (see, among others, Siebert, Peterson, and Schramm, 1956; McQuail, 1987).

The liberation movement had long been critical of the role the establishment press had played during the apartheid years. The culture of intense partisanship and secrecy that is necessary to sustain a liberation movement under armed attack makes it difficult to support the principle of a nonpartisan, adversarial press – even after the revolutionary struggle is over. As future United Democratic Front leader Alan Boesak told a group of black journalists in 1979, "Neutrality in the struggle is a crime which the community will not forgive" (quoted in Battersby, 1981: 6). The politics of ungovernability did not foster a culture of tolerance between or within the liberation organizations. (See the accounts of black journalists regarding the intimidation and attacks on them by township activists and liberation groups during the 1980s in Mazwai et al., 1991.) It is not surprising that the subtleties of the establishment English language press's bounded, delimited opposition to the apartheid government tended to get lost in the charges of white monopoly and the accurate, if Manichaean, observation that all whites benefited from the apartheid system. The historic accommodation between the English and Afrikaner power blocs, between capitalism and apartheid, was not lost on the liberation groups. As a result, there was no clear ANC policy on the press beyond broad assurances of press freedom. Even as stalwart a supporter of press freedom as Pallo Jordan (1985: 8) hinted in the ANC journal *Sechaba* at the necessity for some kind of bold transformation of the press. "Monopoly control and ownership of the press correlate directly with the system of White domination and exploitation. The prerequisite for a truly free press to emerge in South Africa is the destruction of both the racist state and the economic interests it serves." In the post-election period, ANC officials began voicing complaints about hostile press treatment of the ANC-led Government of National Unity, and called for a "responsible" press, a press that would participate in the transformation of the country. According to John Battersby (1997), editor of the *Sunday Independent,* the attacks on the press, surfacing toward the end of 1994, were fairly unsophisticated, along the lines of, "You (the white establishment press) supported the old government. We were elected. Now you need to support *us.*" Even President Mandela attacked the press, deriding senior black newspaper journalists of doing "the dirty work of their reactionary white bosses by running down government" (*Cape Times,* 1996). In the ANC leadership's frustration with press coverage lay the seeds of SACS's possible redemption. Deputy President Thabo Mbeki was one of several who believed that SACS could be transformed and reoriented to get out the new government's message, to facilitate reconstruction and development.[1]

The complaints of the ANC about the press were not in any simple way the rantings of neophyte government officials who chafed and bristled at routine press criticism. Nor were the complaints a simple reflection of ANC statist tendencies. Like almost every other sector of the South African economy and society, press ownership

1 Normally it is a mistake to equate the ANC with the Government of National Unity, or to see no difference between government leaders speaking as party spokespeople and as officials of government. In fact, to so equate was in many respects an ideological move on the part of the ANC's opponents to tar every government policy initiative, every mistake the government made, as the ANC's responsibility. The press, too, was sometimes guilty of this elision. In the case of the government's criticism of the press, however, I find it essentially impossible to separate the ANC leadership's political or party positions from those of the government.

was, in fact, highly concentrated, and was monopolized by whites on top of that. Black reporters in the establishment white press were generally few, junior, and far between. There was virtually no independent black press, and the alternative and community papers that had flourished in the 1980s were dying quickly as foreign donors scaled back their support in the aftermath of the 1994 election. With the end of apartheid and the advent of a democratically elected government ready to serve the previously disenfranchised people of South Africa, there was clearly a huge role for government communications of a purely educational variety. Social reconstruction, economic development, and political changes would entail enormous shifts in both large policy matters and in the everyday understandings and expectations of the people on the ground. And government officials were concerned that this information and the government's intentions were not getting out to the public. In their view, much of the fault lay with the concentrated white establishment press, an institution that historically had demonstrated little interest in the black majority, and which moreover had not done much to transform its own house.

Recall that the ownership of the South African press was concentrated under the four white media groups, and, pushed a little further, under the corporate umbrellas of Anglo-American and Sanlam. Quite apart from the press's historic role in the political and cultural struggles between English and Afrikaner communities, the white-owned, white-managed newspapers had and still have identities as primarily white publications. As commercial entities funded primarily by advertising, the establishment press operated according to the logic of what should be understood as "market censorship." Put simply, newspapers must attract advertisers. Advertisers chase readers with disposable cash to purchase the advertised commodities. Newspapers will tend to orient coverage according to what they believe appeals to those coveted readers (see, among others, Jansen, 1988; Underwood, 1993; Baker, 1994). In South Africa those coveted readers are predominantly white.

High entry costs typically preclude new entry in the newspaper business in most markets in the late twentieth century. In South Africa an additional factor in the constricted newspaper sector is control over distribution. The costs of newspaper distribution in South Africa are high, in large part because South Africa is geographically a large country, but also because distribution was essentially monopolized. Historically, the Argus Group dominated English language newspaper distribution through its company, Allied Publishing Ltd. According to Anton Harber (1997), longtime editor of the alternative *Weekly Mail*, Allied Publishing operated a centralized distribution system and was itself a very flabby organization interested primarily in servicing Argus papers. Allied charged very high rates to the non-Argus papers it distributed. Distribution and point of sale took upwards of 50 percent of the cover price of the *Weekly Mail*, for example. Recall that the expense of distribution underlay the effort of the rival South African Associated Newspapers (SAAN) group to escape from the Argus distribution network. SAAN's ill-fated establishment of its own distribution system was one of the key factors in the group's financial decline.

Parallel to Allied Publishing, the Afrikaans press groups operated their own distribution companies: Naspers owns Nasionale Nuusdistribueerders (NND), and Perskor has Republican News Agencies as its distributor. Of the three, Argus's Allied Publishing is the largest and probably the most important, as it is geared to national delivery of the biggest daily newspapers such as *Star*, *Sowetan*, *Sunday Times*, and *Cape Argus*. The distribution system historically constituted an important bottleneck inhibiting new publications, and it continued to do so after the 1994 elections. Would-be publishers must make use of one of the three mentioned distribution chains (though the *Mail & Guardian* began to invest in a distribution company, Central Media Distributors, in the Western Cape). The distribution chains still take a minimum of 40 percent of cover price from independent publishers, and this price can rise as high as 80 percent for low cover-price publications in far flung areas (McGregor, 1996d). The loss of such a high proportion of cover-price revenue makes it almost impossible for any independent newspaper to reach profitability. Finally, because the existing distribution systems are geared for white, primarily urban, newspaper readers, and independent publishers are in effect "hitchhikers," it is difficult to distribute to black and rural readers due to the patterns of racial geography. These conditions go some distance toward explaining why there have been so few new daily newspaper entrants, even after the end of apartheid (KMM Investments, 1996 [submission to Comtask]).[2]

2 A note on Comtask documents. Comtask assembled and bound its documents in three classifications: Submissions, Presentations, Annexures. Only the Submissions volumes were paginated.

SACS

The South African Communication Service began as the Department of Information after the 1948 National Party victory. Combining the liaison sections of Foreign Affairs and Bantu Affairs, the department's central task was to massage the image of South Africa and to quell criticism of the apartheid state in the international media. The department was thus a service thoroughly identified with the apartheid regime and was at the center of the Muldergate scandal of the late 1970s. The scandal destroyed the old Department of Information. Its functions were reestablished in a new agency in September 1985. The responsibility for internal information was transferred to a new *Bureau* for Information, while the Department of Foreign Affairs took control over external information functions (including control of Radio RSA, the South African Broadcasting Corporation's external radio service, whose primary role was to function as the propaganda arm of the apartheid government's foreign policy). During the states of emergency of the 1980s the Bureau for Information emerged as the central broker of state information and interpreter of events, as it was one of the only entities legally permitted to report in areas of unrest. Indeed, the bureau was a mechanism for the promotion of an official news culture through which news was transmitted from government to the media. Hence the bureau was inexorably bound up with the militarization of the government and its "total strategy" of the 1980s. Among other responsibilities, the Bureau for Information was instructed to communicate with the population on behalf of other government departments about their activities and to coordinate the pronouncements coming out of various state agencies. The bureau put out regional publications such as *Light/ Khanya* and *Metropolitan Digest*, and published many newssheets on behalf of the official (and largely illegitimate) black local councils, such as *Duduzani, Diepmeadow News*, and *Bekkersdal News* (R. Muller, 1996).

The Bureau for Information was the "above ground" organization handling government communications and information during the 1980s. "Below ground," communications were an important function of the centralized security apparatus reorganized under P. W. Botha, and operated much like the old Department of Information under Mulder. The State Security Council (SSC) was served by a secretariat of around 100 functionaries seconded from various government departments. It had four branches, including a Strategic Communications branch, known as Stratkom. Stratkom established a network of agents in the mass media, and it set up a number of specialist fronts whose responsibility was to ensure that public perceptions were influenced in a manner considered appropriate by the apartheid regime and its allies. These included the establishment of Dixon Soule Associates to promote the image of Bophuthatswana, the National Students Federation to counter the liberation-identified National Union of South African Students (NUSAS), the International Freedom Foundation to demonize the ANC and promote the image of UNITA (Unaio Nacional para a Independencia Total de Angola) and Renamo (Resistencia Nacional Moçambicana) abroad (the South African–allied rebel groups in Angola and Mozambique, respectively). According to the ANC's submission to the Truth and Reconciliation Commission, the Stratkom branch of the State Security Council was charged with working out a package of strategy alternatives in response to requests from ministries, government departments, or Joint Management Committees. These plans could include tactics such as assassinations, attacks on neighboring countries, economic sabotage by spreading negative propaganda about a particular country, campaigns of character defamation and disinformation, setting up various front companies to engage in operations to influence the media and decision makers – in general, the entire gamut of what have become known as "dirty tricks" operations, and which continued to function into the 1990s (African National Congress, 1997: 11–13).

The aim and functions of the Bureau for Information were again altered in 1990. The bureau continued to provide a communication center that, in its own version of its history, "monitor[ed] domestic and foreign newsmedia 7 days a week on a 24-hour basis in order to identify communication problems and opportunities for the Government." Government, of course, until April 1994, was the National Party, at this point looking for any advantage in the political negotiations at CODESA and the Multi-Party Negotiating Council – and many suspected the Bureau for Information of continuing to work in the service of the National Party. The bureau was renamed the South African Communication Service in May 1991. SACS did make efforts to reinvent itself prior to the 1994 election, according to people who worked at the Independent Media Commission, the organization that monitored the media coverage of the election. SACS endeavored to be less a tool of the National Party and more a neutral government agency seeking to build two-way communication between government and the people (R. Muller, 1996). SACS's operational emphasis shifted to "professional service" at the request of ministries, government departments, and other government offices. It continued to provide a media-monitoring service for governmental units; made available exhibition material; acted as media liaison; supposedly gave media advice to governmental units; and gave production support.

In the period following the 1994 election, SACS tied its fortunes to the Reconstruction and Development Programme. The revamped service conceived as part of its purpose the promotion of "nation-building by empowering the population to take part in reconstruction and development" (Republic of South Africa, 1995o). SACS continued to put out several publications: the "RDP News" (a newsletter on the Reconstruction and Development Programme); "SA Now" (an overview of constitutional, economic and social development in South Africa); *South Africa Yearbook* (the official reference publication on the Republic of South Africa); "Visitors A–Z of South Africa" (tourist information); "This is SA" (booklet containing general information on South Africa); *In Touch* (a youth magazine).

THE ARNISTON CONFERENCE AND MBEKI'S CHARGE TO COMTASK

The South African press celebrated the miracle of the political negotiations and subsequent democratic election of 1994. But, as noted, the essential adversarial character of the mainstream print press quickly grated on the ANC leadership once it came to power as the preeminent partner in the Government of National Unity. No doubt the press's new-found critical zeal was nourished by the politics of the transition, inasmuch as the relaxation of government pressure gave the press far more latitude in reportage and the confidence that it would no longer be harassed. The press engaged in innumerable disquisitions on the benefits of a free and independent press, and reveled in the new ease of its freedom. But many found press criticism galling. In the ANC leadership an important segment came to believe that the government's accomplishments were not receiving adequate coverage, that the press seemed to delight in stories of black incompetence with an eagerness that betrayed a continuing racism, and that ANC figures in particular had not received fair treatment in the press. This judgment underlay Deputy President Thabo Mbeki's persistent public criticism of the white media establishment. Mbeki, the leading ANC voice in the matter, stated on several occasions that he had a "serious problem" that a major segment of political opinion was not well represented in the media (Ludski, 1996). In a 1996 speech before Parliament, Mbeki stated (Republic of South Africa, 1996o):

> Because of the particular evolution of our own society, we find the remarkable situation that . . . the political tendency represented by the liberation movement is by and large not represented in our media. The problem gets more compounded when that tendency becomes the government of the day because the lack of representation is then extended to the government. It is for this reason that the issue of media diversity becomes very important because, quite frankly, the situation cannot be considered normal where a majority political school of thought finds no way of taking its place alongside other schools of thought in the mass media.

The new South Africa must have an "equitable and balanced" media, he argued. As a testament to how much the issue concerned him, Mbeki spent a remarkable 30 minutes of a 1-hour interview with the *New York Times* attacking South African journalists as "uneducated" and "deploring a lack of support for the new Government" (Daley, 1996). Mbeki's campaign echoed an observation that President Mandela (1994a) had made to the International Press Institute Congress in 1994:

> With the exception of *The Sowetan*, the senior editorial staffs of all South Africa's daily newspapers are cast from the same racial mould. They are White, they are male, they are from a middle class background, they tend to share a very similar life experience. The same holds true for the upper echelons of the electronic media, again with a very few recent exceptions. While no one can object in principle to editors with such a profile, what is disturbing is the threat of one dimensionality this poses for the media of our country. It is clearly inequitable that in a country whose population is overwhelmingly black (85%), the principal players in the media have no knowledge of the life experience of that majority.

At bottom, as Mbeki argued on another occasion, now that apartheid was gone, an "anti-system attitude was no longer appropriate." At this point in South Africa's history, the media could best serve the country by practicing "responsible journalism" rather than adversarial criticism (Fabricius, 1996; *Star*, 1996b; de Beer, 1997).

The position was put most clearly in a January 1997 address Deputy President Mbeki (1997a) delivered to the launch of the Forum of Black Journalists, where he was trying to articulate the proper role of civil society in a transforming state.

> Indeed, the most pertinent question that can be posed at the birth of such a forum is: what role should it play in the current phase of our democratic transformation. What is certain is that your forum occupies that social space which can be found between the family unit and the state in which citizens can initiate independent action with the aim of promoting the well-being of society as a whole. It is the space commonly called civil society.... Clearly, the establishment of democratic institutions of government and state is not enough, not only in expanding democracy, but also in ensuring a more efficient service machinery to the people. Organs of civil society have got an important role to play in this regard. The answer to this question, however, must derive from a correct understanding and appreciation of the main characteristics of the current phase of democratisation and transformation. For example, given the daunting task of emancipating our people, we believe that it is inadequate to perceive of the role of the Forum of Black Journalists simply as to keep in check the power of government, or to hold the leadership accountable. Surely, that is only part of the role. We believe that it is wrong to see the chief virtue of democratic organs of civil society as an organised counterweight to the democratic state.... The point we are trying to drive home is that democratic organs of civil society, of necessity, ought to define their place and role in relation to the task of emancipating our people.... The Forum of Black Journalists has a critical role to play in this regard. It has a responsibility to continue to engage the question of what we as a country should do to promote the aspirations of the marginalised. We have the responsibility to tell the people the truth. Part of that truth is that we are set on the path towards the transformation of our country. Deviation from that path would constitute a betrayal of the interests and aspirations of all our people, both black and white.

Mandela (1997) made much the same analysis in his address to the Fiftieth ANC National Conference in December 1997. In this analysis, civil society is paid its due as a crucial institution of South African society.

But the achievement of political democracy changes the nature of civil society as an independent, critical counterweight to state power. Both the democratic state and civil society now are working toward the same end: emancipation. Organizations of civil society – particularly the press – that engage in criticism beyond some certain degree engage in a betrayal of the emancipatory project.

It must be emphasized, again, that the ANC's criticism of the establishment white press had real basis in fact. Many progressive journalists and editors, sympathetic to but not necessarily ANC, echoed the ANC's critique. Anton Harber (1997), longtime editor of the *Weekly Mail*, and Pippa Green (1997), political editor of the *Sunday Independent*, for example, believed the press *was* slow to transform with respect to covering black issues and hiring black reporters. The press *did* have problems with accuracy in its reporting and with overall quality. According to John Battersby (1997), editor of the *Sunday Independent*, ANC journalists had been shut out of the establishment press after the ANC was unbanned in 1990. Identifiably ANC would-be journalists, in Battersby's words, "were seen as terrorists" by the establishment publishers; "it was unthinkable to hire them." Even where eventually blacks are brought in to be editors of the English language newspapers, the vast majority of the second layer of leadership below them remains white. In keeping with its history, the English language press endorsed the Democratic Party in the 1994 election, a party that won less than 2 percent of the vote. Thami Mazwai, chairperson of the Black Editors' Forum and publisher of Mafube Publishers (whose magazine titles, such as *Enterprise*, are aimed at black business and political elites), described senior white journalists as having no real relations with black people outside a master–servant context. Hence they are ignorant of black life and display "Pavlovian racist tendencies" (Mazwai, 1997b).[3] Similar sentiments were echoed in *Mayibuye* (1991), the ANC's monthly magazine.

These features made the establishment white press vulnerable to attack from an otherwise curious alliance of ANC leadership and black business leaders such as Mazwai, whose Black Consciousness orientation evinced contempt for white liberalism and the institutions thought to embody white liberalism. The English language press came in for

---

3 Mazwai, a former deputy editor of the *Sowetan*, was harassed and detained as a journalist during the apartheid years. He and Jon Qwelane, who edits *Enterprise*, are among the most prominent black journalists in South Africa (see Finnegan, 1988). Both view the mainstream white press with profound scorn.

particular criticism, in large part because of the perception of hypocrisy. The ANC's submission to the Truth and Reconciliation Commission hearings on the media (African National Congress, 1997: 9) captures a bit of this sentiment.

> A key issue here is hypocrisy. While the state-run media and the newspapers owned by Afrikaner capital made no bones about their loyalty to the apartheid state, the newspapers owned by English capital trumpeted a liberal commitment to balance and objectivity – while failing to apply these principles in their own columns. They failed dismally to reflect the feelings of "ordinary" South Africans. They relied heavily on government sources of information, no matter how discredited they were, and made very little effort to obtain information from alternative sources. In their coverage of the struggle against apartheid, including the armed struggle, the English-language press relied almost exclusively on information from arms of the state. Contacts with the liberation movement were insufficient, and the paradigm remained the "white world view." This served to entrench the polarisation of apartheid, rather than exposing readers to a range of views.

Thami Mazwai (1996) was particularly outspoken in his criticism of the white press groups, calling for their "deconcentration" and for limits on foreign ownership. Although some of his comments appeared to demand divestment, his actual proposals fell short of this. Mazwai called for legislation prohibiting vertical and horizontal integration of media holdings, limits on foreign ownership, and for government to use its advertising muscle to induce newspapers to engage in serious affirmative action.

Prior to the general election the ANC had sought to ameliorate its media "problem" by looking into the possibility of launching a party newspaper, an idea that had been surfaced several times over the years. The proposal was set aside, as it had been many times before, because of the costs involved. Another gambit focused on the SABC. Several months after the 1994 election, Deputy President Mbeki floated a proposal that the government be given "special," that is to say, mandatory, access to the SABC to communicate government positions and policies. Indeed, SACS head David Venter had made submissions to the SABC Board in a bid to secure TV time for government representatives (see Sibongo and Lush, 1997: 34; also Republic of South Africa, 1996o; Zaina, 1996). But the ANC leadership was itself divided on such matters.

There was no indication that the SABC, struggling to establish itself as a bona fide public service broadcaster, looked at all kindly on the proposal. Minister of Posts, Telecommunications and Broadcasting Pallo Jordan quickly scotched the proposal for mandatory government access to the SABC, even publicly heaping derision on the very idea in a speech in Parliament. Government access to the SABC would damage the SABC's independence and image.

> There is an obvious need for effective Government communication with the public. About that there can be no question. It is, however, imperative that the boundaries between Government information services and public service broadcasters remain clear and very distinct. We are currently putting a lot of effort into producing credible and impartial public broadcasting services, which enjoy the trust and confidence of all South African citizens. I think it would be unwise to jeopardise this enterprise with ill-advised projects. Due consideration also needs to be given to the unanticipated effect of such a proposal, namely breaking down the citizens' confidence in the impartiality of our public broadcasting services. (Republic of South Africa, 1995n: cols. 2285–2286)[4]

With prospects of an ANC newspaper and mandatory time on the SABC effectively closed off, SACS, now housed in Deputy President Thabo Mbeki's office, became one of the ANC leadership's few potential tools to influence press coverage. SACS originally had been slated to be included in the Ministry of Posts, Telecommunications and Broadcasting, but Pallo Jordan refused to accept it as part of his portfolio. Indeed, Jordan earlier had nixed an ANC proposal, floated during the preelection discussions of Cabinet portfolios, for a Ministry of Information. For Jordan, a ministry of information smacked of government control of communication, and reflected the antidemocratic pedigree of those authoritarian African and Soviet bloc states that boasted such ministries. Deputy President Mbeki's office became SACS's ministerial home (Andersson, 1997; S. de Villiers, 1997).

Mbeki was quite open about the resurrection of SACS. If it were possible to redress the inequities in the media, he argued, there would probably be less need for government intervention and for a vehicle like

---

4 Jordan's forthright defense of the independence of the new SABC was reputed to be one of the factors behind his sacking in April 1996. And with Jordan out of that ministry, later in the year the government once again asked the SABC Board to consider the proposal of special access (*Star*, 1996a).

SACS (Ludski, 1996). Moving to boost the profile and capabilities of SACS, the deputy president certified the racial transformation of its staff (Republic of South Africa, 1994b) and complained that its budget was set "at an abysmally low level." He urged Parliament to support the service (Republic of South Africa, 1996o). But SACS, with its direct historic links to the apartheid government, and whose R 50-odd million annual budget and 500-plus staff produced little tangible benefit, was a department embattled. After the military and the police, SACS was among the most hated of the apartheid structures. Tainted by its long-time role as apartheid's mouthpiece, SACS had stumbled around after 1994 to find a mission for itself, alighting, as we have seen, on the role of facilitating the RDP. But the civil society groups long involved in media struggles, and some within the ANC leadership itself, were not convinced that SACS could reform, and, more fundamentally, did not believe a SACS-like department had a place in a democratic polity. SACS already was organizationally troubled. In the words of Chris Vick (1997), former head of communications for Gauteng province and media liaison officer for Gauteng Premier Tokyo Sexwale, the service was "imploding." Morale within SACS was low. Sue de Villiers, who was brought onto the Comtask inquiry as a researcher and writer, and whom most credit with putting the final report together, described SACS as filled with "demotivated, depressed people in a shipwreck of a structure" (S. de Villiers, 1997). The old guard saw the writing on the wall and large numbers had taken retirement. The new recruits tended to be people who could not get jobs elsewhere because they lacked formal qualifications.

With his media strategies more or less blocked, Deputy President Mbeki called a meeting of government communicators and media workers to the Western Cape village of Arniston in late August 1995 to investigate government communications and recommend ways to improve them. Thus in some respects the Conference on Government Communications represented the concerns of those in the ANC who advocated a thorough-going transformation of the media, including, perhaps, the breakup of the white press conglomerates. This ANC faction and their hopes to break up the white press were buttressed by the segment of black business that remained close to Black Consciousness principles. Prominent black journalists Thami Mazwai and Jon Qwelane also supported the general idea of a nation-building or "patriotic" media, in which the public good takes precedence over some abstract notion of the public's right to know. This stance took center stage in 1997, when Denel, the publicly owned armaments company, invoked apartheid legislation to suppress an article ready to run in the Independent Newspapers exposing a Middle East arms deal in which Denel was engaged. Denel did not want the name of the purchasing state divulged (*Sunday Times*, 1997). Thami Mazwai attacked Independent Newspapers and its coverage, suggesting that the press's insistence in publicizing details of the arms sales was nothing but a "secret agenda" to harm the government, now that it was black (Mazwai, 1997a; see also Jacobs, 1999).

But there was another key force behind the Arniston conference – the discontent of the new ministerial communications officers of the Government of National Unity. The press officers and spokespeople (sometimes called ministerial liaison officers or media liaison officers [MLOs]) of the new ANC Cabinet ministers had had an inordinately difficult time doing their jobs. The continuing power of the old guard in the government departments, strategically deploying the old rules still in force as per the transition agreements and the Interim Constitution, made sure the new ministerial communications officers were appointed at a very low level. This undercut the authority of the new MLOs. The old guard in the departments had their ways and clearly did not intend to give ground or cede control to the new interlopers.[5] In addition, several of the new ministerial communications officers found that they could not pursue essential public communications functions because everything had to go through SACS. Stephen Laufer, for example, who worked as Housing Minister Joe Slovo's MLO and whose task it was to organize the Masakhane campaign (designed to alter the culture of nonpayment and convince township residents to pay their rent and services charges now that there was a democratic government), found that SACS

5 In Chris Vick's (1997) view, while the old guard did engage in some direct sabotage of new initiatives, much of the sabotage was indirect, through the enforcement of old rules and red tape so typical of bloated apartheid officialdom. In Vick's experience, this affected nuts and bolts stuff: how to get things printed, how to requisition a car to take a photographer to x township, and so on. But the rule books were never brought out. The old guard used information as a power base in the face of new challenges and potential claim on their jobs. Even when there was no conscious effort at sabotage on the part of the old guard, the built-in bureaucratic culture of the public service impeded initiative. In an article for the *Saturday Star*, Vick (1996) related a telling incident. Engaged in a discussion with some of the senior and middle managers in the Transvaal Provincial Administration's Communications Department about their definition of graphic art quality, the head of the directorate's graphic art division pronounced in bald apparatchik simplicity: "Quality is about correctness. It is about obeying the rules. It is about doing things right."

controlled his money for publication and advertising. And SACS, Laufer quickly discovered, was both incompetent and grossly ill-suited for such delicate political responsibilities as Masakhane. Laufer shared his complaints with other MLOs, who indicated they had run into similar problems with SACS. Muff Andersson, MLO for Pallo Jordan, had experienced great difficulties with the Department of Posts & Telecommunications bureaucracy and with SACS on the printing and publicity campaign for the telecommunications Green Paper. The ANC-aligned MLO caucus went to Deputy President Mbeki's office, complaining about SACS and demanding that something be done (Andersson, 1997). Their complaints had important bearing on the decision to initiate a process to examine government communications.

The Arniston Conference on Government Communications thus reflected interrelated but separate political thrusts. The ANC leadership, concerned that its message was not getting out, promoted the transformation of the media, including a possible breakup of the white press conglomerates and a revitalizing of SACS as a revamped government information agency. Although the caucus of new MLOs acknowledged the problem about the government's message, it implicitly argued that the source of the problem was government itself. Arniston thus was as much an opening for MLOs to reinvent government communications as it was a venue for the deputy president and his allies to attack the white press and promote the developmental model of the media.

The Arniston Conference on Government Communications brought together members of the press, government communicators, relevant government departments (including SACS), media unions, and civil society media groups – in short, another community of stakeholders – to discuss the problems of communications in the new South Africa. The conference was in effect a stakeholders' forum. After many papers were given and perspectives shared, participants proposed that a Communications Task Group, "Comtask," investigate government communications. Comtask was established in the spirit of the Green Paper reform processes that had encompassed so many other South African institutions. The conference mandated Deputy President Mbeki to appoint a ten-member board of inquiry, following a public nomination process. Nominees to Comtask were forwarded to Mbeki's office, and he appointed a committee broadly representative of the stakeholder community and knowledgeable about communications issues.[6] Comtask's brief was to examine the structure and function of government communications, to look at training and affirmative action in the field, and to recommend policy choices. In addition to that broad charge, Mbeki included in Comtask's brief the review of the "ownership and control of South African media and to interpret how these affect government communication" (Republic of South Africa, 1996x: 10).

THE COMTASK INQUIRY

The Communications Task Group engaged in its own particular version of the stakeholder consultation – deliberative democracy politics characteristic of the post-1994 policy-making environment. Funded by the Commonwealth Secretariat, the Friedrich Ebert Stifftung Foundation, and the United Nations Development Programme, the Comtask team was constituted as a representative nonstate body, whose brief, parallel to that of the Green Paper task teams, was to consult with the general public and affected parties, engage in research and internal debate, and then put forward recommendations regarding government communications. The Comtask team met with institutions, professional bodies, and all levels of government in a series of 37 public meetings. Written submissions were taken from 150 parties following advertisements in newspapers and radio in 9 languages inviting individuals and institutions to comment on the issues. Comtask also heard 61 direct presentations. The group surveyed ministries, departments, and provincial governments on their communication practices, requirements, expectations, and criticisms. Comtask team members visited provinces to meet with provincial government, experts, and community groups. They spoke about the issues on community radio. They

6 The Comtask team of ten had varied experience in the media, information, and news production, as well as varied experience in civil society activist organizations. They included Mandla Langa (an accomplished writer who had once run the ANC's London office, and a member of the SABC Board) as chair, Stephen Mncube (an information specialist at the Development Bank of South Africa), Val Pauquet (national communications coordinator of the National Peace Accord), Willem de Klerk (former editor of *Rapport* and brother of F. W. de Klerk), David Dison (media lawyer and codrafter of the IBA Act), Raymond Louw (former editor of the *Rand Daily Mail* and head of the Freedom of Expression Institute), Sebiletso Mokone-Matabane (IBA cochair), Mathatha Tsedu (political editor of the *Sowetan*), Tshepo Rantho (president of the National Community Media Forum), and Steve Godfrey (from the Commonwealth secretariat). Sue de Villiers was brought in to do background research, and ended up editing and writing a good portion of the final report.

attended a two-day presentation by SACS. The team also conducted research on the communication systems of 19 countries, including 10 developing countries. Various experts were commissioned to provide studies for the inquiry. The Media Monitoring Project (1996), which had produced a respected study of media coverage in and around the 1994 election, undertook a content analysis of the media's coverage of government. Robin McGregor (1996a,b,c), the noted analyst of South African business ownership, was commissioned to describe current ownership and patterns of control of the South African media. An information analyst for the Development Bank of Southern Africa, Jeremy Berlyn, put together a questionnaire and statistical study of government departments' communications practices, needs, and problems (Comtask, 1996a). Toward the end of the investigation, in October 1996, Comtask convened a national public colloquium to present its findings.

At the time Comtask got under way, the widespread feeling in government circles was that the central issue at stake in the debate on communication in the new South Africa was the concentration of ownership of the press. It was the concentrated and racially based nature of press ownership that explained why the press was anti-ANC and why the government's message was not getting out to the public. That sense of the problem was shared by several Comtask members. Accordingly, at Comtask's second meeting the members engaged in a hotly contested debate whether or not the group should begin its work with the press ownership issue. In Willem de Klerk's (1997) recollection, by the end of that meeting the focus had shifted. Comtask members decided to step back from the ownership question and to address, rather, the broader issue of government communications. *Why* was the message of government failing to reach the people, especially people in rural areas and the functionally illiterate? When the issue was considered in this light, the ownership concentration and editorial distortions of the print press took on less significance. The print press may set the scope and tone of the news agenda, but the workings of the print press were and remain for the most part barely material to the communication and information needs, practices, and gaps of very large segments of the population (Rantho, 1997). Radio, in this light, was obviously far more important than was the print press. The early argument about Comtask's central focus was, according to Raymond Louw (1997), the only contentious debate within the group. The submissions and testimony delivered to Comtask came in so unconflicted and in so transparent a fashion that the analysis of the South African communications situation became abundantly evident to the group. The analysis and the concrete recommendations for change were adopted in a consensual and almost self-obvious manner.

The submissions in themselves constitute a fascinating exercise in communication. Many letters from individuals are seemingly far off the point of the Comtask inquiry, registering complaints about local problems of varying kinds: continued oppression, a racist landlord, a desperate need for money or work and request to Comtask for assistance. But while not all that useful to the formulation of policy options, these individual submissions in fact construct a revealing window onto some of the problems of South Africans and their new government – some of which do, indeed, highlight deficiencies of government communication. Many submissions complain about the lack of reply from government offices, how hard it is to get accurate and timely information, poor RDP delivery, how local government was thwarting civil society participation (see Comtask, 1996d).

Thus what the Comtask inquiry found was not really news to anyone with a passing acquaintance with government communications and what was actually happening on the ground in the previously disenfranchised communities. The inquiry found a set of government communications functions, structures, and personnel that were largely uncoordinated and of very broad range in competence and effectiveness. The information released to the public by ministers was often not in sync with communiqués issued by their own departments; there was little or no strategic planning or coordination at any level of government – between ministries and departments, between ministries, between ministries and SACS, or even between ministries and the president's and deputy president's offices (Media Liaison Officers Forum, 1996). If such coordination was the responsibility of SACS, the service was not getting the job done. According to the survey data, SACS lacked credibility in the eyes of most government communicators and its services were not all that useful to governmental units trying to get information out. The completed questionnaires from government communications officers in ministries, departments, and provinces indicated that the vast majority consulted SACS "only from time to time" (Comtask, 1996a). Government department liaison officers judged SACS's services as "patchy" and "unsatisfactory" (Comtask, 1996b). Provincial media officers complained that the SACS regional structures were generally not integrated into the work of provincial government communicators, and that at times SACS duplicated work done by regional communicators to the detriment of both (Provincial Government Communications Forum, 1996). For example, a SACS video project on the RDP was not coordinated with the government departments responsible for RDP delivery. And, in the end, a completed video never appeared (Vick, 1997).

The overall assessment was that the inherited government communication structures in the ministries, departments, and SACS were not suited to a new democratic dispensation that prizes accountability, openness, and public participation. Compounding the problem of its deplorable history, SACS was structurally too far removed from the policy formulation and decision-making processes (Laufer, 1996b). Its history, holdover staff, and structural remove led many to conclude the service was hopeless and irreclaimable. The fact that SACS still existed angered many provincial communications officers, inasmuch as SACS had ample facilities and resources and the provinces had very few. SACS, moreover, displayed the typical apartheid government departmental centralism and featherbedding. It did everything by itself and at great expense, operating in-house video and photographic studios, printing presses, television and radio monitoring (S. de Villiers, 1997). Despite these resources, SACS communicated rather poorly, in large part because it was at bottom a security/intelligence institution, not a communications institution.

THE QUESTION OF MEDIA BIAS

Comtask also received a report on the character and extent of press coverage of government from the Media Monitoring Project (1996). Somewhat contrary to the ANC leadership's charge that "the major segment of political opinion was not well represented in the media" and that the media were "running down" government, the MMP found that coverage of Parliament and the Constitutional Assembly and related negotiation sessions had been rather extensive. Furthermore, the MMP judged that media coverage of the government had been by and large neutral or positive. Of the news stories that the MMP surveyed during monitoring across various media outlets, 30 percent reflected a positive view of government, 49 percent were neutral, and 21 percent could be regarded as negative. SABC and the *Sowetan* were the most positive; the national weekly newspapers (*Sunday Times, Mail & Guardian, Rapport, City Press,* and *New Nation*) had a much more critical view of government. The English language radio service, SAFM, also tended to air more critical reports (Media Monitoring Project, 1996). If news was not being covered or important information not being presented (SACS contended that 80% of information generated within the parliamentary complex and/or disseminated by ministries never reached the public via the media), a good part of the problem lay in government communication practices, according to the MMP.

The absence of coordination of communication strategies and lack of clarity as to responsibility between ministerial and departmental levels, and between these levels and SACS, were major structural impediments to the dissemination of information. Augmenting the structural problems were serious deficiencies at the staff and operational levels. Government media liaison personnel were not properly empowered, and neither were they particularly competent, in the MMP's appraisal. Most MLOs were drawn from political party sources and had little or no specialist training. They tended to understand neither the professional conventions of journalism nor what reporters need from officials in order to write a viable news story. The single most important feature affecting the flow of newsworthy information from government, in the judgment of the MMP (1996: 27), is "the degree of openness and interactivity in the relationships between government media liaison personnel, on the one hand, and media practitioners, on the other. Access to good quality, verifiable information – preferably directly from the source to ensure accuracy and to facilitate clarification and follow-up – is the most crucial resource in news production." But such access was extremely variable across departments and ministries at all levels of government. Government was also faulted for failing to format and package information – and to prime its release with appropriate background and follow-up briefings – in ways that would be easily usable to the media. The submission of the MLOs reiterated the findings of the MMP and then some, pointing to the severe underrecognition of MLO responsibilities by Public Service Commission job definitions and the corresponding paucity of resources devoted to government communications apart from SACS (Media Liaison Officers Forum, 1996).

The news media did not go uncriticized in this evaluation. MMP accepted that the journalistic profession in South Africa was generally understaffed and undertrained – an assessment strongly echoed by Allister Sparks (1996a), executive director of the Institute for the Advancement of Journalism at the University of the Witwatersrand and former *Rand Daily Mail* editor. In fact, staffing problems in government were mirrored by similar problems in the press. Because few reporters had more than three or four years of work experience, argued Sparks, there was an unacceptably high rate of misjudgment and error. Inexperienced reporters practice a kind of "stenographic journalism," rewriting government press releases as news stories, but stories bereft of context, history, or explanatory background. Inexperienced journalists interacting with poorly trained government media liaison officers create a vicious cycle. Poor reporting causes antagonism on the part of government officials, which results in insubstantial and uninformative briefings, which in turn results in even poorer reporting. Government media officers, now suspect in their competence by their ministerial and departmental bosses because of poor news stories, tend to get left out of the information flow. Media officers begin to see their jobs as one of keeping the press away. The fact that a major source of news about government was the South African Press Agency (SAPA) contributed to the shoddy quality of reporting. SAPA typically featured lots of brief, descriptive items, but which were absent of much analysis. A structural bias in the press in favor of political correspondents over beat reporters meant that stories on the day-to-day functioning of government typically received less prominence. A particular problem was that the news media tended to conflate parties and government. But the overall tenor of the Media Monitoring Project's (1996: 51–56, 60) evaluation was that the communication problem rested primarily with government.

Still, a central problem did clearly come out of the submissions to the Comtask inquiry. Communication was inadequate, especially in rural areas and particularly among people who were either illiterate or functionally illiterate (reputed to be a majority of the population). According to a figure offered by Deputy President Mbeki, the penetration of the print media was estimated at only 5 percent of the population (cited in Independent Newspapers, 1996: 332). SACS, among others, focused on this problem in its presentation to Comtask. The SACS submission highlighted the new government's struggles against the legacy of apartheid and its lack of capacity "to disseminate objective information on all government activities to *all* our people, thus empowering them to participate in and influence the course of government." In SACS's rather statist view, the remedy requires "a national communication/information institution with a clear statutory mandate and policy," and "an adequate budget to enable the institution to function optimally" (South African Communication Service, 1996: 2, 3). Solomon ("Solly") Kotane, former Radio Freedom official and the newly appointed director-general of SACS, floated a proposal for a government news agency, an overture that elicited broad criticism in the press.[7] But that was the extent of the SACS submission, and the service clearly did not address the other problem characteristic of existing government communications – that, RDP-inspired rhetoric notwithstanding, communication tended to be understood as a one-way affair from government to the communities. It is perhaps ironically paradigmatic that SACS provided Comtask with a detailed description of its establishment and breakdown of its operations, but Comtask declined to include the SACS submission, even as an appended document. The Comtask Final Report indicated that the SACS information "is bulky and was found to be impossible to analyse in the state presented" (Republic of South Africa, 1996x: 19). In other words, the official government communications service could not communicate its own case in a coherent form.

Thus, to the extent that SACS was supposed to carry the ball for the ANC leadership's "media-as-partner-in-nation-building" stance, it did not do a very credible job articulating the position. What SACS did do, in the view of many of the Comtask members, was engage in attempts at sabotage of the Comtask process. At the Arniston conference, SACS officials spent a lot of time publicly justifying themselves and their mission; they clearly did not want to be subject to an inquiry and made noises about boycotting the Comtask process altogether (de Klerk, 1997; S. de Villiers, 1997). With Comtask up and running, SACS engaged in small-scale obstruction. It put roadblocks before Comtask's ability to use money. Indeed, someone from SACS set in motion an investigation by the auditor-general into the legality of Comtask's budget, a move widely interpreted as a stratagem to divert attention from Comtask's recommendations (Laufer, 1996a). Comtask was required to use SACS staff as its secretariat for the inquiry, but the particular individuals seconded from SACS came with no secretarial skills. Comtask members in fact suspected that the SACS secretaries were reporting the minutes of meetings back to SACS officials. Comtask asked SACS for all kinds of information, cost breakdowns, and the like, but could not get them. And SACS tried to block Comtask's hiring of Sue de Villiers as a researcher and writer. In this regard SACS behaved much like the Department of Posts & Telecommunications did vis-à-vis the National Tele-

7 Kotane (1997) claimed to have been misrepresented, that he was not proposing the establishment of a government news agency, only that the establishment of a state news agency should be an option under consideration.

communications Policy Project. The difference was that, unlike the Department of Posts & Telecommunications, which still represented the old guard, the top leadership of SACS *had* been transformed, taken over largely by a cadre of former Radio Freedom comrades loyal to the deputy president. Indeed, the appointment by Deputy President Mbeki of Solly Kotane as director-general of SACS *after* Comtask had been established led some to question whether the fix was in with regard to Comtask and what the government would do about SACS. Kotane placed ads in newspapers announcing searches for senior positions in SACS, even though Comtask was debating its future. And inasmuch as Kotane had been talking about the possibility of a state news agency, many wondered if this was Mbeki's overture. For these reasons, many in the press were highly dubious about the Comtask inquiry (R. Louw, 1997). Perhaps one should not be surprised that by 1996 both the apartheid old guard and the ANC leadership cadre in control of SACS possessed parallel statist tendencies. Still, such consonance was jarring.

Throughout the Comtask inquiry, the establishment press alternated between a strong wariness of Comtask and its brief and a celebration of the changes in the press that had taken place since 1994, changes that, in its eyes, demonstrated the success both of political transformation and the workings of the market. Independent Newspapers (1996), the new holding company of the old Argus Group (to be discussed later in this chapter), delivered a self-congratulatory submission to Comtask hailing its corporate vision and calling attention to its new titles and its transformation efforts. The clear subtext of the submission was that these achievements had come to pass as part of market forces, the commitment of management to internal change, and the financial strength provided to Independent Newspapers from its overseas shareholding – pointedly, that is, without any government policy or compulsion. Independent, as the only press group with significant overseas shareholding, was particularly sensitive to the possibility of controls being placed on ownership. Likewise, the submission of the Print Media Association of Southern Africa (1996: 508), representing four bodies of press associations, claimed that the print media were adjusting quickly and successfully to changes in the marketplace and to changes in the political environment. Again, the subtext was that the market was, in fact, working. "Today," the PMA claimed, "there are no less than 27 independent daily and weekly metro newspapers, 117 regional newspapers, and more than 500 published titles which are members of the PMA.

Diversity is continuing on a voluntary and viable basis." Implicitly supporting some combination of the libertarian and social responsibility theories of the press, the PMA also darkly advised that in a free society the press "should be reader driven, not government driven." The entry from Nasionale Pers (van Deventer, 1996: 169) was much the same. Recounting its corporate history as one of independence and pluck, Naspers touted its role in the reform within Afrikaner nationalism and called attention to its more recent commitment to black empowerment. Getting to the heart of the matter, Naspers, on the one hand, challenged the term "monopoly" as applied to the press and, on the other, argued that "diversity" needs were being met voluntarily through partnerships and cooperation. Diversity must be left to market forces. "Diversity cannot be achieved by waving [the] magic wand [of government intervention]. . . . The electronic and the printed media are so sensitive to the market situation that they will naturally reflect the changing market pattern."

Between, on the one hand, the failure of SACS to make a credible case for the developmental or nation-building model of media and, on the other, the self-serving social responsibility presentations of the print press, came submissions from the civil society media policy organizations and independent media practitioner groups. These groups included the National Community Media Forum, South African Students Press Union, the National Community Radio Forum, Community Print Sector of South Africa, and the Open Window Network, which continued to represent the post–social democratic tendency within the ANC alliance (and which ironically had suffered with the coming of electoral democracy because their foreign funders began withdrawing support in favor of direct support of the new government). As had been the case in the debates over broadcasting, the civil society media groups were able to offer an incisive critique of government communications because their analysis was embedded in a coherent, political-economic theoretical framework. Although these groups did not dispute the concentration of press ownership and essential irrelevance of the existing press to the majority of the previously disadvantaged, they balked at any prospect of a centralized government communication service. Rather, they argued, government should foster and encourage an expansion of ownership and titles in what is an obviously difficult and constrained marketplace. Contrary to the claims of the establishment publishers, the unfettered market clearly did *not* work. Indeed, the decline of the alternative press had precipitated a decrease in the numbers and kinds of titles. The entry barriers to, and the commercial pressures on, the newspaper business in South Africa, mirroring trends in other countries, produce a strong impetus toward concentration (Berger, 1996; also Bagdikian, 1997; Smith, 1991; Kaniss, 1991). Notwithstanding these pressures, any possible divestiture program must be considered very carefully. A palpable subtext to the civil society media groups was that, while there was little love lost between them and the establishment press, government response to the perceived problem of inadequate communications (and sub-subtext, the perception of poor press treatment of government) should neither be one that compels divestiture willy-nilly nor establishes a formal government media presence. A "Ministry of Information" or centralized information service has no place under a democratic government as a matter of political principle. As a pragmatic matter, the civil society groups argued forcefully that centralized government communications were a waste of resources, because, as a long line of academic research has shown, few pay attention to this kind of communication except under the peculiar conditions that support propaganda (see, e.g., Lazarsfeld and Merton, 1948; Katz and Lazarsfeld, 1955). This old communications research finding was reiterated by people Comtask team members interviewed while on their international visits (see Comtask, 1996c).

In this respect, the post-apartheid press policy debate was not the Manichaean choice between libertarian/social responsibility versus developmental/nation-building models discernible in the pronouncements of the establishment press, on the one hand, and some government representatives, on the other. An alternative model was put forward, a proposal for a mixed system that was not an unreflective, simple compromise between the libertarian and development exemplars, but rather a theoretically justified third way. An essentially private, but mixed media system of commercial, public, subsidized semicommercial, and nonprofit print and broadcast entities was articulated by civil society media groupings such as the Independent Media Diversity Trust (1996), National Community Media Forum (1996), the Learn and Teach Publications Trust (1996), and Berger (1996). These groups proffered proposals borrowed from European countries to establish press and broadcast trusts empowered to subsidize print and broadcast ventures outside the existing media conglomerates and outside a strict reliance on advertising as the funding source. The idea behind the trust proposal was not only to foster press pluralism, it also underlay an assumption that community media could best serve as the interactive, participatory conduit between people on the ground in communities and government efforts at reconstruction and development. Such efforts would best implement the democratic vision of the ANC's original RDP document that "democracy is not confined to periodic elections," that the "people affected must participate in decision-making" (National Community Radio Forum, 1996). In other words, the civil society media organizations articulated a theory of government communications premised on the central idea of the active and interactive *citizen*.

Somewhat complementary though less overtly political submissions advocated a government role in expanding the infrastructure to establish an "information society." These submissions tended to avoid political judgments, either about SACS or the wisdom of state intervention in the print press. But their proposals were essentially in keeping with the post–social democratic agenda of civil society media groups. These included proposals for the expansion of telecommunications, the creation of community telecenters and libraries, and the uploading of government information on the Internet (Wild, 1996; African National Congress, 1996b; Mackie, 1996; National Information Technology Forum, 1996). Such proposals contemplated providing citizens not with information delivered from on high, but rather with informational tools with which they could empower themselves.

Chief among the virtues of the political culture of the new South Africa was the recognition of the importance of public discourse and the need to establish the conditions that foster and extend it. This was one legacy of the early transition period demand for a politics of "consultation and transparency." As one would expect from a polity making a transition from authoritarianism to democracy, most of the attention focused on the government side – the decisions of government in a democracy should be made publicly, through free and open discussion. Hence an important piece of legislation was the Open Democracy Bill (Republic of South Africa, 1998d), a bill, still under discussion at this writing, that would guarantee the transparency of government operations and provide a constitutional right of access to information held by the state. But there was also recognition, especially on the part of the civil society groups, that the goals of citizenship, including the formation of a common identity and sense of purpose within the heterogeneity that characterizes South Africa, could be fostered only if people participated in public life and learned the virtues of public reasonableness. This was especially true given the reverberations of the legacy of the liberation movement's tactic in the struggle against apartheid, the "culture of ungovernability," and the continuing ethnic violence particularly in KwaZulu-Natal province. Campaigns such as Masakhane were not simply to get people to pay their rent and service fees, but to inculcate the spirit that all now had a stake in society and must act as responsible members of the new social compact. Similarly, the introduction of new educational curricula was not just undertaken to provide school texts free of apartheid ideology but also embodied efforts to teach the virtues of public reasonableness. The stakeholder policy forums themselves constituted sites for the exercise of politics and public reasonableness. The Truth and Reconciliation Commission represented an extraordinary effort of the society to come to terms with the violent and divisive past with an eye on the future. Such a grand social reckoning and hoped-for cleansing could only occur if done on a grand scale through the media – hence government assistance in expanding media coverage and communication access was crucial. The fostering of democratic citizenship required the state's help in establishing material points of access into public discourse, such as telecenters, more libraries, better schools, and support for community media within a broadly accessible mixed media system. Communication rights and capabilities and citizenship thus were understood by the civil society media groups as inexorably linked. Here, again, as in the broadcasting policy debate, South Africa found itself at odds with the postmodern declaration of the death of the grand narrative of citizenship. The debate over government communication and the future of SACS was a deliberation not simply over the proper forms of governmental communications per se, but an effort to define the basic entitlement of citizenship in the new South Africa – how to secure the complex right to participate fully in social life with dignity and without fear, and to help formulate the forms that social life might take in the future.[8]

---

8 The scholarly debate on citizenship has grown immensely in recent years. For an introduction see Kymlicka and Norman (1994). The communicative basis of citizenship has been taken up by scholars such as Graham Murdock and is captured in an early essay on the structure of television. "Full and effective citizenship," Murdock (1990: 78) writes, "requires access to the range of information, insights, arguments, and explanations that enable people to make sense of the changes affecting their lives, and to evaluate the range of actions open to them both as individuals and as members of a political community. Without these resources, they are excluded from effective participation. They become the victims not the subjects of change, unable to pursue their rights and press for their extension. Precisely because of its cultural centrality the television system has become a key site on which the struggle to secure and develop resources for citizenship takes place."

OWNERSHIP REDUX

The ownership issue and the desire to break up the white press conglomerates may have been the secret kernel of Mbeki's brief to Comtask.
But in most respects the die had already been cast. The terms of the
negotiations between the government and the ANC, and enshrined
in the Interim Constitution, had left property arrangements intact
(Republic of South Africa, 1993a: sect. 28). This meant that in the most
significant respect the press was probably protected from nationalization or forced divestment. The political negotiations at CODESA and
Kempton Park implicitly worked off an assumption that there was no
justification for regulation of the press other than self-regulation. Thus,
realistically, dissolution of the white press conglomerates was probably
an idle hope. In Raymond Louw's view, the ANC antipress faction was
likely hoping instead for a strengthened SACS and the establishment of
a press commission (R. Louw, 1997).

Nonetheless, the attacks on the press groups probably did have some
impact at the ideological level. The deputy president's early attacks
on the press, backed up on occasion by President Mandela and by prominent black businessmen like Thami Mazwai, surely had the consequence
of helping convince the white owners that they must engage in some kind
of transformation, if not for fear of government-imposed divestment
then for fear of their business opportunities being obstructed in the new
South Africa. The Independent Broadcasting Authority's cross-media
rules essentially forced the press conglomerates to become minority-
share partners of mixed ownership consortia if they wanted to be serious
contenders in the future rush for private broadcasting licenses (Dison,
1997b). The IBA guidelines constituted just one aspect of what was
widely believed would become standard operating procedure for the new
government: Government contracts for goods and services would favor
black-owned businesses, or white businesses in joint ventures with black
ones, or historically white businesses that had "transformed" themselves
by bringing in significant numbers of black directors. Thus the incentives were there for the owners of the press to transform the industry on
their own. They seem to have reached the conclusion, in the words of
Thami Mazwai, that "to be multiracial is [now] in the logic of business"
(cited in K. Tomaselli, 1997: 17).

Thus in some respects the newspaper submissions to Comtask were
on target – the South African press *was* changing. But those changes
were only nominally a function of market forces. Ownership changes

and internal transformation were more the *political* fallout of the transition to a post-apartheid dispensation. In anticipation of domestic political transformation, Anglo-American and its Johannesburg Consolidated Investments (JCI) unit initiated moves to unbundle some of their holdings after February 1990. This unbundling would include the newspaper groups. The first move was the Argus's sale in 1993 of 52 percent of the *Sowetan*, now South Africa's largest daily newspaper, to Corporate Africa, the black-owned consortium headed by Dr. Nhato Motlana. Corporate Africa is the umbrella for New African Investments Ltd. (NAIL), the leading black-owned investment company.[9] The sale made Motlana the chairman of the *Sowetan's* board of directors. The *Sowetan* subsequently acquired the financially ailing *New Nation* (though NAIL closed that publication in May 1997).

The following year Anglo-American moved to unbundle its JCI conglomerate further. Its first divestment was the Argus Group, the investment furthest from its core mining and manufacturing business. According to Robin McGregor (1996b: 9), Anglo-American had been peddling its press interests for some time and had attracted several potential buyers, including, once rumored, the ANC. But it was not until the irreversible abandonment of apartheid that a deal was done. In early 1994, in advance of the election, Anglo-American listed Argus Newspapers Ltd. on the Johannesburg Stock Exchange and sold 31 percent of the shares under its control to the Irish-based Independent Newspapers PLC (a division of the H. J. Heinz Company). Included in the sale were the *Cape Times*, which Argus had bought from Times Media Ltd. in April 1994, along with TML's interests in Natal Newspapers (principally the *Natal Mercury*) and the Cape Joint Operating Agreement, and its 45 percent share in *Pretoria News*. Both JCI and Heinz head Tony O'Reilly sought an endorsement from the ANC of Independent Newspapers' acquisition of the Argus Group. In its submission to Comtask, Independent Newspapers indicated that it had received the backing of Nelson Mandela (Independent Newspapers, 1996: 339). Mandela's

---

9 Motlana was the head of the Soweto Committee of Ten, precursor to the Soweto Civic Association, established in the wake of the 1976 uprising. He was considered by many the unofficial "mayor" of Soweto. Corporate Africa Ltd. is controlled by Motlana, Jonty Sandler, Cyril Ramaphosa, and Dikgang Moseneke, each of whom has a 25% stake in the holding company. These stakes give each an effective 3.6% share of New African Investments Ltd., the operating company with positions in companies such as Metropolitan Life, African Bank, MTN, as well as the *Sowetan* newspaper. In McGregor's (1996b) appraisal, the 3.6% share of NAIL means that any three Corporate Africa principals could control NAIL with only an effective 10.8% ownership. Corporate Africa has since been restructured (see Chapter 7).

backing was contingent upon agreement to expand black participation at shareholder and director levels and end inequalities in employment conditions (Matisonn, 1998). According to Moeletsi Mbeki (1995), who, with Pallo Jordan negotiated with O'Reilly on behalf of the ANC, the endorsement was given, but Independent Newspapers did not live up to the quid pro quo. Subsequent negotiations to create black share-holding and black advancement were broken off by the Independent Newspapers – even though it had indicated in its Comtask submission its intention to place up to 20 percent ownership in black hands. Independent Newspapers increased its stake in the Argus Group to 58 percent in 1995. With 60 percent held by Independent Newspapers PLC of Ireland, Independent Newspapers is the only South African press group with significant overseas shareholding. Independent Newspapers inaugurated "Business Report," a business section included in its dailies, revamped the *Cape Times* and *Natal Mercury*, and launched a new title, the *Sunday Independent.*

The next phase of restructuring is a bit more complicated. Recall that by the 1980s the Times Media Ltd. group was owned principally by Argus and Anglo-American's JCI. As part of the unbundling of JCI, Anglo announced late in 1995 that two of JCI's three units would be sold. One of those was Johnnic, Johnnies Industrial Corporation, a $2 billion diversified company with controlling interest in Times Media Ltd. (through its media holding company, Omni Media Ltd.). Anglo-American sold Johnnic to a consortium of black investing groups called the National Empowerment Consortium (NEC). Originally a loose association of smaller businessmen and COSATU-affiliated union retirement funds (the largest of which were the National Union of Mineworkers and S.A. Railway and Harbour Workers Union), NEC was joined by the major black business groups, the first of which was Worldwide Africa Investment Holdings, another significant player in black empowerment led by Wiseman Nkuhlu (chairman of the Development Bank of South Africa, the government-originated development agency). New African Investments Limited originally bid against the NEC but it was brought into the NEC consortium after ANC General Secretary Cyril Ramaphosa joined NAIL in April 1996. The Johnnic deal was clinched in August 1996 (see Table 7).[10] Ramaphosa, now a 25

10 The NEC initially bought 20% of Johnnic for R1.5 billion at a 7% discount, with an option to increase its stake to 35%, which it did at a 5% discount. The cost of the full 35% was R2.9 billion. Voting rights for the entire 35% were agreed to with immediate effect. Anglo-American retained 6.4% of its original 47.4% of Johnnic (McGregor, 1996a; *Enterprise*, 1997a).

Table 7. *Original Shareholding of National Empowerment Consortium*

Shareholder	Percentage
Labor[a]	
National Union of Mineworkers	12.94
S.A. Railway and Harbour Workers Union	10.15
S.A. Commercial, Catering & Allied Workers Union	4.81
Food & Allied Workers Union	3.85
Mineworkers Investment Corporation	3.69
Metal & Electrical Workers Union of S.A.	2.43
S.A. Clothing & Textile Workers Union	1.70
SACTWU Investment Group	1.48
Ikhwezi	1.48
Building Construction & Allied Workers Union	0.93
Construction & Allied Workers Union	0.92
BCAWU/CAWU/MEWUSA Investment Company	0.55
CACCWU Investment Company	0.37
PPWAWU Investment Company	0.37
Business	
Worldwide Africa Investment Holdings	9.82
Metropolitan Life (owned by NAIL)[b]	9.82
Siphumelele Investments	9.82
National Empowerment Corporation	8.71
Nozola Investments	6.05
Tswelopele Investments	4.62
Vuya Investments	0.80
New World Foundation	0.36

[a] The National Empowerment Consortium consists of equal parts of labor and business components.

[b] Metropolitan Life played a role in helping some of the smaller groups – Siphumelele, Nozola, and Tswelopele – to acquire their stakes.

percent shareholder in Corporate Africa, chairman of Johnnic, and deputy executive chairman of NAIL, was named chairman of Times Media Ltd. in April 1997.

The historic parallel to the unbundling of JCI, widely commented upon in South Africa, was Anglo-American's discounted sale of General Mining to the Afrikaner firm Federale Mynbou (the mining subsidiary of the Sanlam-controlled Federale Volksbeleggings) in 1964. That sale thrust Afrikaner-controlled business into the big time, bringing Afrikaner ownership through the 7 percent level of market capitalization on the Johannesburg Stock Exchange (JSE). The sale was executed to help shore up a moderating tendency in Afrikaner nationalism and to curry favor with the National Party regarding general economic policy and the more concrete allocation of government contracts and leases (O'Meara, 1996: 120).[11] The Johnnic sale, which pushed black business to approximately 9 percent market capitalization of the JSE, could be seen as having similar impetus. But, like the General Mining story, the JCI story is also somewhat more complicated. Anglo-American did not unbundle JCI purely out of politically far-sighted motives. According to Robin McGregor (1997), Anglo-American sold Johnnic at a premium.

Interestingly, apart from Anglo-American's unbundling of JCI, it is largely Afrikaans institutions that undergird many of the black empowerment ventures. Afrikaners, understanding the use of the state to boost ethnic capital, have partially underwritten or have gone into joint ventures with black empowerment groups. Sanlam, for example, held at least 17 percent of NAIL as of 1997.[12] Perhaps more to the point is that Afrikaans companies worry that the ANC will use the state as Afrikaners did and, hence, are laboring to attract black shareholding so that Afrikaans institutions will not be frozen out of the post-apartheid economy. And in fact, the awarding of state contracts is now pretty much dependent upon the bidding companies being black-owned or in partnership with black entrepreneurs. A government procurement policy announced in July 1997 would have government paying a premium of up to 12 percent for goods and services bought from businesses owned by or involving the historically disadvantaged. The parastatals now have empowerment goals both within and without the organizations. Telkom, for example, set a R54 million goal to purchase from emerging black suppliers, a goal it exceeded in 1996–97 (*Business Day*, 1997e). Transnet waived normal tendering procedures in awarding a multimillion-rand scrap metal contract to Xisaka, a company in which the South African Railway and Harbour Workers Union has a

---

11 J. D. F. Jones (1995: 130–134) partly goes along with this assessment, though he contends that the story is much more complicated and that Anglo-American's motives were not quite so disinterested and politically motivated. Jones argues that Anglo-American's sale to Federale Volksbeleggings of General Mining carried with it a key quid pro quo, to limit any inroads by the Afrikaners into the diamond sector.

12 The reason for the numerical imprecision is that South African corporate ownership is highly pyramided, and often particular investors will use names – typically called "nominee" companies, that do not reveal the ultimate identity of the owner. For example, in this case, a 5.1% shareholder of NAIL is Eighty One Main Street Nominees, Ltd., which McGregor identifies as Nedcor (*McGregor's Who Owns Whom in South Africa*, 1997: 498, 1127).

stake (*Business Day*, 1996c). The Independent Broadcasting Authority's criteria for license applications for the sell-off of the six SABC radio stations constituted an early indication of the approach to black empowerment (Republic of South Africa, 1996f). This approach encourages joint ventures between existing white-owned businesses and emerging black ones (Sikhakhane, 1997; see also Gevisser, 1997).

In a typical joint venture, an "empowerment group" trades its historical disadvantage characteristics and legitimacy for equity. Because equity has to be funded, the empowerment group attracts loans from either its consortium partners or from financial institutions. But the lenders may not ordinarily use their loans as an instrument of control of the empowerment partner or else the requirement that ownership and control by historically disadvantaged South Africans be encouraged would thus be defeated. In order to avoid diluting the empowerment stake, loans cannot be secured against the shares of empowerment partners other than as a last resort (Janisch and Kotlowitz, 1998: 20). In the media area, the list of black–Afrikaner joint ventures is surprisingly extensive and underscores the transformation of that sector in particular. For example, Nasionale Pers signed a R110 million joint venture deal to set up City Press Media with a black business consortium. The deal earmarks 51 percent of the black-targeted Sunday *City Press* (a mass Sunday paper aimed at an urban black readership, with a circulation of 115,000) for black investment goups, two of them being Ukhozi Media and the Dynamo Group, the latter a Durban-based company headed by Oscar Dhlomo, former secretary general of the Inkatha Freedom Party (*Business Day*, 1997a). In October 1996 Naspers and Thebe Investments announced a joint venture to publish and distribute school textbooks and to operate private- and distance-education interests through their respective Boekhandel and Vuna Industrial Holdings subsidiaries. Naspers would finance Thebe's 30 percent stake. Most significant, Perskor, the smaller of the Afrikaans publishing groups, sold a stake to the Kagiso Trust, the former liberation-oriented non-governmental organization. The Kagiso Trust, the Rembrandt Group, and the Dagbreek Trust now form a voting pool that is the major shareholder in the Perskor Group at 33.33 percent. According to McGregor, it was Rembrandt's influence that was instrumental in setting up this structure – the Afrikaans conglomerate prevailed upon Naspers to abstain from voting when it was clear Naspers was not prepared to support the plan. Rembrandt's support would appear to give the Kagiso voting bloc effective control of Perskor. Kagiso is now the effective publisher of the still editorially conservative *Citizen*. Speculation was that Perskor's deal with Kagiso was designed in large part to "shed its *verkrampte* image and regain some of the government's book printing contracts," which it had dominated during the apartheid era (Efrat, 1996). What this means is that between the JCI unbundling and the sale of a stake of Perskor to Kagiso, the two smaller white press conglomerates – Times Media Ltd. and Perskor – have passed to nominal black control. And this has impact beyond newspapers. Perskor's holdings in M-Net and MIH (formerly called Multichoice, the holding company for M-Net) effectively pass to Kagiso, as do TML's holdings in MIH to the National Empowerment Consortium. Naspers sold part of its holdings in M-Net to the Phutuma Trust.

Moreover, the 1994 election had begun to effect at least the semblance of editorial transformation. Naspers, for example, appeared to have altered its historical relation to the National Party, having made monetary donations to the Democratic Party and declaring that the publishing group, in the word of managing director Ton Vosloo, had learned that being too close to a political party was no longer "expedient" (Golding-Duffy, 1996). These changes were not confined to the Afrikaans language press. Independent Newspapers intimated it planned to launch new titles, preferably with black partners, aimed at markets currently not penetrated by existing newspapers. Independent Newspapers, like Naspers, spent much ink in its Comtask submission touting its affirmative action and training programs, its commitment to the new democratic order, and to internal transformation. Many of these changes were unfolding as Comtask was carrying out its brief. And though the impact of these ownership changes at the level of actual newspaper product and editorial orientation was not clear, they signaled the racial transformation of ownership in media and served to undercut the call for the breakup of the press groups.

THE COMTASK FINAL REPORT AND ITS RECEPTION

The Comtask Final Report conceptualized the delicate issues of government communication and the ownership and control of media largely in the terms articulated by the post–social democratic civil society media groups. "South African democracy inherited a concentrated media," the report stated. "Concentration of ownership and control is a matter of concern for all governments. In the case of the media, there is an additional concern: lack of diversity allows for control of information and opinion. Media diversity is thus vital to democracy" (Republic of South Africa, 1996x: 15, 17). Government's central role, the report argued, should be to assist the development of a plurality of voices and encourage media diversity. Several actions would serve this aim. The bottleneck in newspaper distribution should be alleviated with an elegant regulatory solution, that is, imposing common carrier status on the currently anticompetitive and restrictive distribution networks. Affirmative action strategies, more transparent criteria for selecting and awarding contracts in order to promote empowerment, and the support of the public broadcaster and community media were identified as essential elements in fostering media diversity. To overcome the economic disincentives to market entry in small, noncommercial media outlets, government should institute a Media Development Agency to operate a subsidy system for community and independent newspapers in certain instances. And government must address the funding crisis of the SABC, particularly as radio appeared to be the best way to reach rural populations and the functionally illiterate. Finally, government must do the kinds of things only government can do: facilitate the expansion of the telecommunications infrastructure, improve libraries, assist in the creation of telecenters, and endeavor to make government information widely and easily accessible.

Absent from these recommendations was support of government as a direct communicator. Relying on its survey of international practices Comtask (1996c) suggested that didactic messages or government "slots" are not particularly effective communication tools and, although the latter do exist in some democracies, they tend to be limited. Instead, the report focused on removing the many bottlenecks in the structure and operational practices of government communications. This meant, along with familiar recommendations for more training, affirmative action, and resources devoted to a more professionalized government communication function, the elimination of SACS. SACS was seen as too politically compromised and too anachronistic an organization to continue in a democratic South Africa. In its place Comtask recommended a new framework for government communications, at the center of which would be a Government Communication and Information System (GCIS) coordinated centrally from the office of the president or from Cabinet. A Cabinet Committee on the Information Economy was proposed to ensure top level consideration and interministerial coordination of all relevant aspects in this sector. The GCIS would develop an infrastructure to ensure coordination between national departments (horizontally), between the three tiers of government (vertically), and between other government bodies and parastatals (laterally). All remaining laws that restrict media freedom should be scrapped.

In sum, Comtask conceptualized the communications tasks of government as providing information quickly, transparently, and with accountability to the people and the press, and enacting policies to spur the growth of communications structures so as to enable people to function as active citizens in a democratic polity. Communication in a democracy was understood, metaphorically, as dialogue; the role of the citizen was conceived as far greater than simply as a voter in periodic elections (Republic of South Africa, 1996x: 33). Comtask thus recommended a new, differently conceived government communications agency, very much distinct from the SACS model and its ministry of information pedigree. The proposed GCIS was envisioned as a small central agency that delivers, accesses, and outsources essential communication services and serves as a government–media–community liaison (Republic of South Africa, 1996x: 56–66). Finally, Comtask finessed the issue of the concentration of press ownership. Acknowledging the dangers of concentration, the report asserted that the issue could not be considered in isolation of the general question of industrial concentration and thus should be referred to the Competition Board and be dealt with under the broad policy framework of competition policy and emerging antitrust law.

Rhodes University Professor of Journalism Guy Berger (1996) had worried about the politics of the reception of the Comtask report. As he noted in his Comtask submission, the final report would be taken up in the context of a preexisting government position that the SACS budget was too low, of government's desire for time on the SABC, and of criticism of the white character of the press.[13] Berger fretted publicly

13 Berger's concerns were not idle ones. As Comtask compiled its recommendations and moved toward writing its report, skirmishes continued within the press and between the press and government. Anticipating the ownership and hence significant "transformation" changes, the Times Media Ltd. editorial staff initiated an "editorial charter" that would guarantee their independence, a move many charged as racist. At the same time, senior members of the Black Editors Forum (co-founders of the new South African National Editors Forum, SANEF) called for the establishment newspapers to place themselves before the scrutiny of the Truth and Reconciliation Commission (TRC). The TRC took up hearings on media as part of its investigation of human rights violations, to examine the question of press collusion with the old government (de Beer, 1997: 36). And in November, President Mandela unloaded his broadside that senior black newspaper journalists were doing "the dirty work of their reactionary white bosses by running down government" (*Cape Times*, 1996). Mandela took up the cudgel again

that the Comtask report could be used to legitimize a final strategy that would amalgamate Comtask and government proposals but contradict the Comtask philosophy. Indeed, this scenario seemed to be playing itself out in the immediate aftermath of the public delivery and discussion of the Comtask Final Report in the town of Caledon. The press, which had been rather cynical about the Comtask inquiry, was pleasantly surprised by the final report's analysis and recommendations. Deputy President Mbeki's office in contrast showed annoyance toward the report. Essop Pahad, Mbeki's deputy minister and key adviser, was disappointed with the recommendations. Thami Ntenteni, the deputy president's communications chief, lectured Comtask Chair Mandla Langa at Caledon (Dison, 1997a). SACS head Solly Kotane walked out of the Caledon meeting just before the question of SACS's continued existence was discussed. Mbeki himself did not attend Caledon nor did he meet with Comtask in advance of its final report. According to Willem de Klerk, Mbeki initially was displeased, but came around after consulting with Comtask Chair Mandla Langa, and accepted the report's broad outline (de Klerk, 1997). Mbeki took the report to Cabinet in early 1997 but apparently soft-pedaled the recommendations. Cabinet accordingly endorsed the broad thrust of the report but declined to support the elimination of SACS. Cabinet empowered Mbeki to appoint an "implementation committee" to refine the report and to study the implications of effecting Comtask's recommendations.

The decision by government to sidestep the Comtask recommendations on SACS unleashed a firestorm of criticism in the press (see, e.g., *Business Day*, 1997c). Asking why was the deputy president's office so anxious to keep SACS going in the face of so much evidence that the service was an anachronism, the *Mail & Guardian* (1997) editorialized:

> The answer seems self-evident: he and his advisers are nursing the fantasy of centralised control of information pertaining to the workings of the government. In other words, they would like to say what the public is allowed to know – a common enough dream

during his state visit to Zimbabwe in May 1997. He asserted that the South African media are run by conservative whites who do not share black aspirations and cannot accept majority rule. Black journalists are used by the reactionary white press barons to shield their masters from charges of racism, Mandela asserted. His remarks indicated that his earlier attack on the press was not a fluke. Finally, July 1997 was the Denel episode, in which the publicly owned armaments company invoked apartheid legislation to suppress an article ready to run in the Independent Newspapers exposing Denel's sale of weapons to Saudi Arabia (*Sunday Times*, 1997).

among the politically powerful, but one which runs completely contrary to the ethos of our Constitution.

Notwithstanding the political fears over the Implementation Committee, the validity of the Comtask findings was hard to dispute. The committee's audit of the personnel, assets, and performance capacity of SACS found a bloated, ineffectual service, many of whose tasks could be farmed out to the private sector (Laufer, 1997). By May, when Essop Pahad, chair of the Implementation Committee, testified before the Parliamentary Communications Committee, he stated that SACS's current budget would be its last and that a dedicated government information body would be set up in its place (Dlamini, 1997). It was essential, Pahad averred, that any new government communications service treat all political parties equally (*Citizen*, 1997). The Implementation Committee's recommendations for a GCIS Secretariat, operating as a think-tank for government communications, located in the office of the deputy president, linking directly to Cabinet through a Cabinet Committee on the Information Economy, for all intents and purposes recapitulated Comtask's blueprint and were accepted by Cabinet on October 8, 1997. "The GCIS will develop ways to ensure that there is delivery of information to the people of South Africa and that a two way system is set up to facilitate a dialogue between government and the broadest possible public." Existing SACS staff would have to apply for positions in the new structure (Republic of South Africa, 1997d).

CONCLUSION: THE CITIZENSHIP MODEL OF GOVERNMENT COMMUNICATIONS

Like the telecommunications and the broadcast reform processes, Comtask was a participatory, consultative exercise in political and institutional reform in which a largely post–social democratic, mixed system vision of communication held ultimate sway. The replacement of SACS by a GCIS represented the replacement of the ministry of information, top–down government-knows-best model of communication by a model that conceptualized the relations between the government and the governed as, in principle, interactive, dialogic, and participatory. The rejection of the call to break up the white press groups in favor of a set of more narrowly tailored government policies to assist community and noncommercial media represented an embrace of the principle of freedom of the press, on the one hand, and the recognition that

normal market forces in the media sector necessitated positive government intervention, on the other. It didn't hurt that the mainstream press
had begun to transform the racially exclusive nature of its ownership
during the period Comtask conducted its inquiry.

There was, of course, nothing inevitable in the triumph of this vision.
The usual complicated interweaved set of forces and circumstances
must be understood. Notwithstanding clear patterns of ownership
concentration in the press, the supporters of the developmental/
nation-building model of media probably could not have prevailed in
the desire to break up the white press groups. The press was probably
protected by the political transition agreements on the retention of
property rights.[14] And the political fallout – both domestic and international – from such an effort likely would have been counterproductive, regardless. Backers of the developmental model had to put their
eggs in the SACS basket. The problem was that, at bottom, SACS was
an intelligence organization that had not successfully made the transition to become a bona fide communications organization. Essentially
put in the position of defending itself and promoting a version of
the developmental/nation-building model of media, SACS did neither
competently.

Comtask, as a manifestation of the South African pattern of consultative policy reform processes rooted in civil society activism, was effectively governed by principles of deliberation and transparency. Though
there may have been a desire on the part of the government to use
Comtask's legitimacy as a consultative forum to ram through its policy
program, Comtask could not be easily "wired" or hijacked from within
or from without. Under the conditions of South African political
culture since 1990, the appointment of members to Comtask had to
manifest a strong measure of stakeholder representivity for the inquiry
to be legitimate. Comtask was accountable not just to government but,
more directly, to the stakeholders who attended the Arniston conference. Likewise, the public presentations, submissions, and expert
reports had to be taken seriously, or the final report would lack legitimacy. The data that came into Comtask clearly indicated that a large

14 My hesitation on a definitive statement about the newspaper groups' property rights stems
from the fact that the government was engaging in a process to determine competition policy.
Antitrust was to be a part of competition policy, and presumably newspaper group concentration could be found to violate its antitrust provisions. But the competition policy was itself
mired in controversy and was stymied at the time of the Comtask inquiry (B. Cameron, 1996;
Steyn, 1996a).

part of the government's communication problem was the organization of government communication itself. And here the post–social democratic civil society organizations, buttressed by the complaints of the media liaison officers (many of whom were veterans of these organizations), were able to articulate the most coherent analysis of the situation. Coherent analysis aside, the power of the post–social democratic civil society groups' proposals stemmed from the fact that the subject of their vision – the active citizen – was most congruent with the participatory politics vision at the heart of the Reconstruction and Development Programme. And this remained a vision of great force. The government's ultimate acceptance of the Comtask recommendations may also have been a matter of timing. Carl Niehaus, Ambassador to the Netherlands and an ANC parliamentarian and official ANC spokesperson prior to that posting, conceded that the government had entered a period – beginning around the time of the closing of the RDP – where, in his words, "consultation was poor." The government's unconsultative temperament could be seen in the closing, without public debate, of the RDP and its replacement by GEAR, the changes to the telecommunications White Paper, the decision to solve the political tensions in the Free State by stripping provincial Premier Terror Lekota of his position. According to Niehaus (1997), there had been no general strategy to move off the consultation route, but the ANC National Executive Committee came to recognize these incidents as mistakes and resolved to improve the consultative process. Acceptance of the Comtask recommendations may well have been a manifestation of government's return to consultation.

This is also not to argue that the battle over vision is settled. The pressure from the ANC leadership and elements of black business for a nation-building or patriotic press continues unabated. In late 1998 the Black Lawyers Association and the Association of Black Accountants of South Africa, whose members constitute the growing black elite and have moved into leading public and private sector positions, lodged a complaint with the Human Rights Commission to institute an inquiry into racism in the media. The call for an investigation highlighted the divide over the vision of the press that seemed at a quick glance to shake out racially: The idea found support from within government and its black allies in the media, and it was denounced by the white press (Haffajee, 1998a).

CHAPTER 7

Conclusion: Black Economic Empowerment and Transformation

Surprisingly, a good deal of continuity can be found between the apartheid government's concrete proposals to reform the communications sector during the final years of white rule and those pursued after the ANC alliance gained access to and dominance within the policy-making arena. Several of the main recommendations of the Viljoen Task Group report on broadcasting were effectively replicated in the Independent Broadcasting Authority Act and the IBA's Triple Inquiry Report. Likewise, the 1992 study of the telecommunications sector conducted by Coopers & Lybrand for the old Department of Posts and Telecommunications looks rather like an early blueprint of the Telecommunications Act of 1996. No doubt this is in part due to the structure of (dare it be said in such old-fashioned terms) the objective conditions and forces shaping events in the communications sector and to the limited number of reasonable reform options. Largely irrespective of their apartheid pedigree, bloated and debt-ridden state-owned and -operated South African monopoly enterprises in both broadcasting and telecommunications faced market and technological conditions that had begun to erode their monopoly control. Would-be competitors, both domestic and international, were poised at the ready to take advantage of this erosion. This predicament has affected virtually all broadcast and telecommunications monopolies worldwide in recent years. Some accommodation of the erosion of monopoly and the reality of competition was virtually inevitable. The fact that new institutional strategies such as liberalization and privatization were being adopted by states worldwide, and constituted the baseline assumptions of multilateral institutions such as the World Bank and World Trade Organization, posed additional pressures, incentives, and rationales for particular kinds of reform.

At a quick glance, then, South Africa's reform of its communications institutions brought the sector well in line with international trends. Yet these reasons for policy continuity disguise more historically specific explanations and mask important differences in the politics of the policy outcomes. And in this respect they conceal the particular success of South African institutional reform and the distinctive features of South Africa's accommodation of racial and class conflicts in its transition to democracy.

The National Party's broad reform impetus of the 1980s can be attributed to the economic crisis of apartheid and a transformation in Afrikaner class composition. Though apartheid "worked" for decades, all indications were that the continued application of apartheid policies threatened the viability of the economy. The South African political economy was a racialized version of autarkic state capitalism: The state operated as the instrument of national development by shielding the economy from the world market and by using internally generated surplus built around an apartheid labor market to carry out the primary tasks of industrialization. An extensive complex of state-owned enterprises, known as the parastatals, provided infrastructure-related services (and more) and served as an important source of employment for whites, particularly Afrikaners. The country's main export, gold and diamonds, rested on the exploitation of unskilled black labor, and fueled its economy for decades. But by the 1970s the general, import substitution industrialization model – in South Africa and elsewhere – came to be increasingly dysfunctional. Gross domestic product and productivity had fallen, and South African corporations were less competitive in an increasingly liberalized world economy. The parastatals showed some of the classic symptoms of poor management, low productivity, and increasing debt. Economic activity had in general moved from a primacy on extractive industry toward manufacturing, but apartheid-imposed Bantu education left a labor force ill-equipped for the skills, literacy, and workplace agility required for manufacturing. Apartheid passbook and residence laws made the development of a stable workforce difficult, as did the absence of effective labor unions. The black insurrection and the government's campaign of violence against it in the years following the 1976 Soweto uprising led to a loss of confidence in South Africa on the part of foreign investors and governments. This constricted access to foreign capital, creating a squeeze with serious economic consequences for the apartheid state. At the same time, the historic effort of Afrikaner uplift having largely succeeded, Afrikaner interests (especially those of the middle class, who had arrived in part because of the state's policies of job reservation and support of Afrikaanse capital) could now be protected by the seemingly natural and impersonal workings of the market rather than by direct state power. The Botha government's reform moves of the early 1980s were part of a dual effort to overhaul and reformulate the traditional class and ethnic composition of the National Party and, at the same time, to liberalize the racial state but retain effective white control of the institutions of power. The reform of the parastatals was a component of a broad undertaking to scale back state interventionism and steer those enterprises toward market controls and private, obviously inordinately white, ownership.

But the effort to liberalize apartheid while maintaining white dominance was contested by a mobilized civil society of organized political resistance. The United Democratic Front brought under its umbrella of nonracial democratic socialism a myriad of organizations against the apartheid state and its reforms. Allied to the ANC in spirit, if not in direct organizational ties, the township civic organizations and the labor movement played the key roles in the opposition to the state's reform agenda. The dialectic of mass political resistance and state repression dashed reform apartheid and brought the equivalent of martial law to South Africa. The palpable sense of dangerous political stalemate in the aftermath of the violent struggles of the 1980s gave skilled leaders in strong political organizations the impetus to move toward a negotiated political settlement – the elite-pacting process discussed by theorists of democratic transitions. By the time general political events advanced toward the likelihood of some kind of transition to democracy, the particular politics of the reform of the parastatals became inexorably intertwined with the struggle to define the shape of the post-apartheid state and economy. The apartheid government's reform efforts were pursued under the old political structure of white supremacy and in the old top–down style of National Party politics. Although they may have been propelled by objective economic problems, the government-sponsored reforms in communications and other sectors appeared to be a clever, dastardly political scheme for transferring state assets to the private sector. Privatization would ensure that the control of those apparatuses remained in white hands and could not be used by a potential black-majority government for redistribution or patronage. The white employees would be protected by such a reform effort, as well.

After February 1990, South African politics entered into a period of uncertainty in which the political parties, the state apparatuses, and civil society organizations engaged in a kind of Gramscian "war of position" within an overall political negotiating process whose outcome was wildly indeterminate. The National Party still in effect operated the state and attempted to pursue the tasks of day-to-day governing, but the state itself was now up for negotiation. The tripartite alliance challenged the government's legitimacy to engage in that day-to-day governance, and particularly repudiated its policy maneuvers as unacceptable because of their unilateral nature. In the matter of parastatal reform, the ANC's threat to renationalize staved off the government's privatization gambit. Brandishing political culture almost as a political weapon during the 1990–94 transition period, the anti-apartheid alliance trumpeted the culture of transparency and consultation that had vitalized the UDF's internal political insurrection to establish alternative policy-debating arenas outside of government. These stakeholder forums brought black South Africans into policy making for the first time. The forums functioned both to institutionalize the ANC alliance's efforts to thwart the government's policy options in a great many areas of economic and social life and to instill the principles of participatory democracy in all aspects of political life. The forums represented the direct antithesis to apartheid authoritarianism, embodying a post-1990 manifestation of the UDF/labor/civic movement program of multiracial participatory democracy. The latter was a bit of a mixed bag for the ANC, whose exiles and prisoners returned to take up most of the leadership positions in the newly legalized organization, and who believed the UDF and the civics, perceived as ANC proxies, should now move aside, even disband. The forums were clearly of great political benefit to the ANC in the early 1990s when the congress was making the arduous transition from an exiled liberation movement to a political party and needed every edge in sparring with a clearly better prepared National Party/South African government. But participatory democracy and the culture of transparency and consultation were almost as out of step with the political inclinations of the ANC exiles, who tended toward statism and a leaders-know-best style, as they were with the apartheid government. The civil society activist groups that energized the stakeholder forums, though intimately allied with the ANC and often a source of expertise for it, in many instances also served as a brake on the discretion and some of the proclivities of the ANC leadership.

These dynamics were first seen in the reform of broadcasting, the first major state-owned enterprise and state-dominated sector to undergo structural transformation. At a concrete level, the content of apartheid authoritarianism and racism was directly visible in broadcasting, and this made the South African Broadcasting Corporation an early candidate for transformation. The future of South African broadcasting was a major focus of anti-apartheid civil society groups, in part because the South African Broadcasting Corporation was such a hated institution, but also because of the homologous relationships among a free, open, and accessible mass media, the culture of consultation and transparency, and the practice of participatory democracy. Civil society–based campaigns mobilized public debate on broadcasting through various conferences, seminars, and protest actions after February 1990, and succeeded in driving the debate toward the acceptance of the idea of a transformed SABC as a nonpartisan, independent public broadcaster. The activism of civil society media organizations propelled broadcasting policy directly into the Convention for a Democratic South Africa negotiations in the wake of the government's announced intention to table a bill before Parliament that embodied the Viljoen Task Group's recommendations. Fearing unilateral government action to "marketize" broadcasting in the guise of reforming the SABC, and watching the apartheid government surreptitiously commence the privatization of broadcasting through quiet license grants to favored white constituencies, the civil society media groups pushed the ANC leadership to demand that broadcasting be taken up by CODESA. Because both the National Party and the ANC saw the question of the control of broadcasting as crucial in the election to come and in the political dispensation to follow, both parties assented. In the ensuing compromise at CODESA, both the National Party and the ANC agreed to an impartial public broadcaster overseen by an independent regulatory authority as the most viable, if a second best, policy option. Here, as in the constitutional negotiations generally, bargaining worked because there were a small number of strong political parties – essentially two – at the center of negotiations. The ANC was anxious about continued NP control of broadcasting before the 1994 election; the NP feared the possibility of ANC control of broadcasting after the election. Thus it was essential to both parties that the SABC be reconstituted as an independent, nonpartisan, if still state-owned, broadcaster. The model of an independent nonpartisan broadcaster comported with the basic principles of the small, occasionally influential Democratic Party, but the DP was unimportant to the actual politics of compromise.

The drafting of the Independent Broadcasting Authority Act was then in effect handed over to the "experts" attached to the major political parties. The CODESA negotiators had many more questions to settle, including the terms of the upcoming election, whether there would be an interim constitution, how to deal with the widespread civil violence, and other matters of immediate import. This gave a remarkable leeway to some of the principals in the ANC-aligned civil society media groups in the writing of the draft broadcast legislation. They wrote draft legislation establishing the public broadcaster as the anchor of a mixed system of public, commercial, and community broadcasting. Public service obligations were to be shared by all broadcasters, with substantial local content requirements and tough cross-media limitations to ensure the diversity of ownership and voices. The draft legislation and subsequent law, the Independent Broadcasting Authority Act, stipulated that applicants for new commercial broadcast licenses demonstrate substantial evidence of the inclusion of the historically disadvantaged in the ownership and operation of those enterprises. The future domain of commercial broadcasting could not be exclusively white.

I have called these principles post–social democratic, in that they endeavored to create a mixed public–private broadcast system with a substantial nonstate and noncommodified presence built into the system's structure. Both state broadcasting and commercial broadcasting, for all their differences, were understood by the civil society media groups to render citizens passive and uninformed. Even traditional public service broadcasting often displayed a tendency toward cultural and big-city hegemony, a tendency that would be inappropriate for a new South Africa. The model of broadcasting embodied in the IBA Act sought to avoid the worst aspects of both market and state controls in broadcasting, while pragmatically placing market forces and public forms in a hoped-for creative tension. The triumph of the model rested in no small measure on the fortuitous fact of a deadlocked negotiated struggle between the ANC and the National Party, representing, in caricature, state versus market, and thus creating a space for the effective intervention of civil society media groups and their post–social democratic vision. Again, this is not to oversimplify or caricature the ANC's position on broadcasting and media policy. Like the tripartite alliance itself, there were many tendencies. The official ANC Media Charter (African National Congress, 1992a: 67–71) clearly was consonant with the general aims of the civil society media groups (though the charter was a general manifesto and not a concrete policy blueprint). Moreover, the civil society media groups did not stand apart from the ANC but were constituents internal to the alliance. But there *was* also an important faction in the ANC supportive of the idea of state broadcasting, notwithstanding the Media Charter.

The post–social democratic model could not be complete, however. It could not encompass the broadcast sector as a whole because the transition agreements on the retention of property rights rendered the white pay television corporation, M-Net, untouchable. The property rights agreements had broken the deadlock between the government and the ANC and enabled the democratic transition to move forward (see Republic of South Africa, 1993a: sects. 28, 245). But those same transition agreements also meant that a significant portion of the public budget would go toward paying for years to come the pensions of white, apartheid-era bureaucrats – including those of the old-guard SABC staff – and thus starving the budget for funds dedicated to rectifying the damage of apartheid.

With the general structure set, the political battles in broadcast policy shifted somewhat after the 1994 election from one that pitted the ANC against the National Party to a struggle within the ANC alliance over the size of the SABC station portfolio – a complicated question not reducible to the conflict between statist versus post–social democratic visions but, nonetheless, with clear elements thereof. Many supported a large SABC because of the need to deliver broadcast programming to all South Africans and in the now eleven official languages. But others supported a large SABC because they still at bottom conceived the public broadcaster as, essentially, a state broadcaster. And now that the leadership of the SABC was in principle in the hands of trusted ANC comrades, the purview of the public broadcaster should remain expansive. At the very least, many proponents of the large SABC portfolio flirted with the "developmental" or "nation-building" theory of the media, in which the media are to augment and assist, not criticize and disparage, governmental efforts at reconstruction and nation-building. The SABC was conceived as a cardinal ally in the nation-building project. The SABC itself lobbied heavily for a large portfolio but envisioned the broadcast system, particularly in television, as essentially market driven. Anticipating – correctly – that little money would come from government, the corporation planned for two of its television channels to become commercial, and with their proceeds would cross-subsidize the third, the public service channel. In contrast, those who argued for a smaller SABC portfolio, including the Independent Broadcasting Authority and several of the civil society media groups, fought for a leaner SABC better able to concentrate on its public service mission and for more opportunities for new broadcast innovators, particularly at the regional or provincial level. Commercial broadcasting, delimited and regulated, could galvanize the medium and prod the SABC to raise the quality and pluck of its program offerings. Regional broadcasting could decenter programming away from its over-whelmingly Johannesburg–Pretoria–Cape Town orientation. But public service obligations and local content requirements would be imposed on *all* broadcasters so as to establish an overall public service broadcast *system*, rather than to ghettoize public broadcasting as the sole responsibility of the SABC.

Party politics did not disappear from the debate over the size of SABC's portfolio, and their dynamics played a major factor in the debate's resolution. Because the National Party had consistently striven to diminish the power of the SABC after 1994 (which included a constant and malignant public denigration of the new SABC as the ANC's mouthpiece) and to create more space for private broadcasters, the ANC's natural political response was to protect the public broadcaster and bolster its portfolio. The civil society media groups had almost nothing in common with the National Party's market-based broadcast policy vision, but they found themselves on the same side of the SABC portfolio fight. This would prove to be a factor in the distancing of the ANC leadership from the civil society media organizations. With the ANC leading the way, Parliament rejected the Independent Broadcasting Authority's Triple Inquiry recommendation that the SABC portfolio be trimmed from three television channels to two. Parliament restored some of the radio stations to the portfolio as well. A large SABC was seen as necessary to do its part in the tasks of reconstruction and nation-building. Here, however, the dismal budget situation inherited from the last white government doomed even the positive feature of this vision. With housing, education, and health care desperately in need of public monies, and with a sizeable portion of the budget precommitted to honoring state pensions, the government declined to allocate funds to an institution that *had* a proven source of funding. Advertising for decades had constituted the primary source of SABC's funding, and under the new ANC-led Government of National Unity it would continue to do so. But the reliance on advertising to fund SABC's three television channels and numerous radio stations could only pit the SABC's public service mission against its desperate need for revenue, thus reinforcing the commercializing dynamic in broadcasting found worldwide. Paradoxically, the ANC's statist tendency served to reinforce the power of the market in South African broadcasting.

In telecommunications a slightly different set of forces came to bear on the process of reform, though the overall political dynamic closely resembled that of broadcasting. Like broadcasting, telecommunications were targeted for liberalization and privatization by the last white government. The government's hope to enact the recommendations of the de Villiers Report and privatize South Africa's telecommunications parastatal was defeated by labor opposition and the ANC's threat to renationalize. But the government did manage to pass a more limited reform bill in 1991, whose provisions generally comported with the worldwide trend in telecommunications policy. Posts were separated from telecommunications and the ministry would no longer operate the telecommunications parastatal. Parliament created a new telecommunications company, Telkom, that, though state-owned, was expected to behave like a normal, private corporation. But the legislation did not, and, given the overall politics of the transition period, could not, create a comprehensive policy for the sector. The upshot was that the environment within which Telkom was to operate was left undefined. The failure of a stakeholder forum to coalesce in telecommunications until 1994 meant there was no arena in which the major players could engage in debate and negotiate new policy during the transition years. As a consequence, telecommunications policy served as a flashpoint between the ANC alliance and the government between 1990 and the 1994 election. Amidst great controversy, the government managed to license two cellular telephone providers in 1993. But to gain the ANC alliance's acquiescence, one of the licensees had to include a substantial percentage of black shareholding. The cellular deal initiated an important pattern in black economic empowerment and the deracialization of the economy, where state tenders and contracts are used to foster private black capital. Another consequence of the cellular story was that the rapid introduction and success of cellular telephony provided real-world evidence – especially to ANC leaders – that competition could be beneficial.

Following the 1994 election and the formation of a stakeholder forum in telecommunications, Pallo Jordan, the new (ANC) minister of Posts, Telecommunications and Broadcasting, initiated a Green Paper/White Paper policy process. Jordan's initiative institutionalized and gave government blessing to the broad consultative policy-making processes that had been the hallmark of the UDF and were reinscribed in the stakeholder forums. The National Telecommunications Policy Project (NTPP) clearly represented some version of a corporatist mechanism, but it departed from classic corporatism (if there is such a thing) in that participation was general and open, not restricted to large, powerful institutional stakeholders. Classical corporatism brings together business, labor, and government in a closed negotiating forum. In this instance, called "concertation" to distinguish it from corporatism (see Baskin, 2000), other players, interests, and civil society groups were also directly part of the discussions and negotiations. Another distinguishing feature was that for much of the process government played a rather circumspect role. Government was there, in the personage of Minister Jordan, initiating the process, selecting (with the consultation of others) the persons to facilitate it, and providing very general policy guidelines. The broad policy guidelines essentially followed the election results and the compromises of the political transition: Commit the sector fundamentally toward the provision of telecommunications service to the previously disadvantaged while providing the kinds of sophisticated services to business that are essential to economic growth and job creation. But for the most part government was not directly active in the telecommunications reform process, in part because Minister Jordan did not trust his own bureaucracy (another instance where the transition agreements protecting the apartheid civil service had consequences), in part because he was committed to deliberative democracy. Jordan evidently believed a better policy result would come from the structured interaction of public and open negotiations among stakeholders.

In this regard the telecommunications reform process followed the Reconstruction and Development Programme, the tripartite alliance's post-apartheid political-economic policy framework, in both spirit and in deed. The RDP document, pressed upon a somewhat reluctant ANC by its COSATU and South African Communist Party alliance partners, the civics, and other civil society organizations, called for the direct inclusion of civil society in policy making, and it conceived the new democratic state as a social power that would facilitate, at the minimum, Keynesian-based economic development directed toward the previously disadvantaged. Accordingly, the National Telecommunications Policy Project consisted of an open, consultative set of discussions and negotiations conducted largely within the realm of civil society, and wherein the principle of universal service stood at the core. In the struggle to reform South African telecommunications, a homology could be identified between the goal to equalize access to information and communication embodied in the commitment to universal service and the understanding of democracy as, in part, expanding the number of active participants in the process of public deliberation and expanding the social basis of communication generally. The expansion of communication was manifested both in the ends (the goal of universal service) and in the means (citizen participation in policy determination). Like the broadcasting struggle, the post–social democratic effort to reform telecommunications displayed a Deweyan pragmatism, where democracy was both a goal and a means.

The first phase of the stakeholder reform process in telecommunications resulted in a set of politically and technically viable compromises embodied in the White Paper on Telecommunications Policy, in which Telkom was given a limited period of exclusivity to meet extensive network expansion obligations. The White Paper plotted a sectoral liberalization in which various service markets would be gradually opened to competition at explicit time intervals over a period of six years. A strong independent regulatory body, the South African Telecommunications Regulatory Authority, or SATRA, was to oversee the sector generally, license new entrants, administer the liberalization timetable, and settle the inevitable disputes that would result from bold policy reform. As in broadcasting, new business entrants in telecommunications would be expected to include the previously disadvantaged in ownership and operation as a condition of licensing. The telecommunications White Paper thus envisioned another mixed system in which state and market forces were balanced against each other in a hoped-for creative tension to expand service, and in which a timed liberalization would abet black entrepreneurship. Telkom, the large and dominant state-owned telecommunications provider, was reaffirmed as the sector's main actor, but conditions for contestability and accountability were established at several junctures and explicit provisions for competition were written into the policy document. Traditional cross-subsidy mechanisms for universal service were built into the new regime, but, recognizing that the era of monopoly provision was soon to be over, the White Paper targeted subsidies toward end-users rather than to Telkom. The liberalization timetable was to be fixed in legislation so as to build certainty into transformation and elicit "buy-in" from the sector's players. SATRA's independence was to guard against improper ministerial interference. The establishment of the Universal Service Agency represented an additional institutional check to keep SATRA's attention focused on the universal service goal. Of course, universal service meant the obligatory expansion of telecommunications service to blacks and to historically black geographic areas.

It was the stakeholders who essentially hammered out the telecommunications White Paper, but they did so within a tightly prestructured political framework established by the electoral victory of the ANC and the policy environment fabricated by the RDP. This was why even the white business interests had to embrace universal service as the fundamental orientation of the reform effort. The central sticking point was whether Telkom should remain entirely state-owned or whether some portion of its equity could be sold to an international telecommunications operator. This issue highlighted tensions within the tripartite alliance, as labor had proclaimed a no privatization stance and insisted upon separate discussions with government regarding the disposition of state assets as a general policy. Yet without some large infusion of capital and new management skills, Telkom would not be able to succeed in the fundamental mission to expand telecommunications service to blacks. Government reentered the politics of telecommunications reform in a direct fashion when Cabinet considered the White Paper. Here, like the space created by the stalemated negotiations between the ANC and National Party in the broadcast arena earlier, the divided nature of the Government of National Unity Cabinet actually eased the acceptance of the telecommunications White Paper. The ANC could support the White Paper because it retained the state-owned Telkom as the key player in a sector reoriented toward the delivery of universal service; the NP could support the White Paper because it plotted the opening of the sector to competition. Indeed, the fact that the NP strongly backed competition made it politically difficult for those market-oriented ANC Cabinet ministers to side with the NP against the central thrust of the White Paper. The fact that the White Paper came to Cabinet under the general imprimatur of the RDP meant that its civil society–stakeholder consultation pedigree had to command respect from the ANC, even from those who quietly wished for more extensive privatization and a quicker path to competition. And that was important, as was soon to be underscored when telecommunications reform entered into a second phase.

Soon after the publication of the telecommunications White Paper, general political dynamics shifted. In short succession, the government closed the RDP ministry; Pallo Jordan was removed as minister of Posts, Telecommunications and Broadcasting and replaced by Jay Naidoo. Parliament passed the final version of the Constitution, and the NP announced its withdrawal from the Government of National Unity. Economic performance had been generally disappointing, and in 1996 the rand fell in value. The ANC replaced the RDP with the more orthodox Growth, Employment and Redistribution (GEAR) macroeconomic policy, and the ANC turned away from the politics of consultation. The turn away from consultation manifested itself in the telecommunications arena with the reassertion of ministerial authority. The minister substantially altered the language of the draft legislation on telecommunications policy. The bill Minister Naidoo brought to Parliament removed the White Paper's liberalization timetable in favor of ministerial discretion, and diminished the functions and independence of SATRA. The new draft elevated the role of the ministry in the substantive regulation of the sector. Just as the White Paper had been written under the political imprimatur of the RDP, the telecommunications *bill* was written under the political imprimatur of the GEAR. The GEAR comprised a largely orthodox macroeconomic policy of deficit reduction and fiscal and monetary discipline. With GEAR, strict attention would be paid to the budgetary implications of government-delivered services. Parastatals should not lose money; indeed, they could be a new source of revenue through privatization. GEAR was predicated on the assumption, following the "Washington consensus" on economic policy, that if the government demonstrated its credibility to such discipline, private investment, particularly direct foreign investment, would materialize. To pull

GEAR off, the ANC leadership, again following the Washington consensus script, insulated the politics of GEAR's adoption from participatory democratic structures.

The changes to the telecommunications White Paper were consonant with the spirit and timing of the government's adoption of GEAR and reflected the move toward centralizing power in the now ANC-identified government. The telecommunications bill's reassertion of ministerial control gave Minister Naidoo more flexibility in the search for a partner for Telkom (an ability to trade a higher sale price for greater concessions on exclusivity) and more leeway to bring labor and black economic empowerment groups into an overall settlement. This had its desired effect. With the muted acquiescence of COSATU, the government was able to sell a 30 percent stake of Telkom to an international telecommunications consortium of SBC Communications and Telekom Malaysia. Government held out another 10 percent of Telkom for black economic empowerment. Of the U.S. $1.2 billion the consortium paid for the 30 percent stake, U.S. $1 billion was to stay in the telecommunications sector.

The contest over the independence of SATRA assumed outsized importance because it represented a fight over the power of the state in the new South Africa. Those backing the reduction of SATRA's independence asked rhetorically from what was SATRA to be independent: From the first democratically elected government? From the society's commitment to development and reconstruction? At this stage in South Africa's evolution, so went the argument, there was a need for the government to direct the telecommunications sector toward addressing "the imbalances of the past." The position had some salience, particularly given the long fear that SATRA might be captured by the old white business interests. But the alignment of the ministry and black economic empowerment groups in the effort to weaken SATRA pointed to something more, to wit, the general ANC political strategy represented by GEAR: increase the power of the state and use the state for development by way of establishing patronage for a politically loyal black bourgeoisie through selected privatizations, tenders, and contracts.

In the end, this gambit in telecommunications was turned back to some degree. The final legislation reinscribed many of the elements of the White Paper, including the restoration of some independence to SATRA. There were several reasons for this development. One was the technical acuity of the overall White Paper liberalization plan, a chunk of which returned in the language of Telkom's new license. The question of SATRA's independence fed into some institutional tension within the ANC alliance over the power of Parliament vis-à-vis the Cabinet. Giving the state president the power to appoint SATRA councillors on the advice of the Parliamentary Portfolio Committee simply mirrored existing practice in the appointment of IBA councillors and SABC board members. Maintaining the practice would preserve parliamentary authority vis-à-vis the minister of Posts, Telecommunications and Broadcasting and permit Parliament to keep a hand in telecommunications policy. Finally, restoring some independence to SATRA was part of coalition party politics. With the Democratic Party and National Party in acrimonious opposition, the partial restoration of SATRA's independence may have been the price for bringing the Inkatha Freedom Party on board with the ANC for the final vote. Whatever the combination of reasons, the appearance, if not the reality, of a stronger, more independent SATRA served to resuscitate the post–social democratic vision that was attached to the telecommunications White Paper.

The power of the state and the character of state-directed development were again at issue in the debate over the fate of SACS, the old South African Communication Service. Because the agreements on a nonpartisan broadcasting system effectively put that medium off limits (notwithstanding Deputy President Mbeki's standing claim for government time on the SABC), statist elements within the ANC leadership alighted on a two-front strategy of assailing the print press and striving to reinvigorate SACS. The ANC leadership, smarting from press criticism, attacked the established white press groups in the name of a nation-building theory of the media. Now that South Africa had a democratically elected government dedicated to deracialization and reconstruction, so went the argument, the press should be a partner in the nation-building effort. The media should be free, but responsible. Instead, the press, in the eyes of many in the ANC leadership, engaged in destructive criticism and race-baiting, and did little to disseminate the government's message to the vast majority of South Africans. The press reflected its white owners and its white readers. In Deputy President Mbeki's words, "[The] majority political school of thought finds no way of taking its place alongside other schools of thought in the mass media."

The ANC leadership's problems with the press superficially coincided with the problems that new government media liaison officers (MLOs) had experienced in disseminating ministerial and departmental information in the new democratic dispensation. Latching on to the political climate of stakeholder consultation, Deputy President Mbeki convened a gathering of communicators to discuss the problem of government communications at the town of Arniston in 1995. This was the origin of the Communications Task Group, or Comtask, the stakeholder-driven policy process in the area of government communications. The ANC leadership's intentions for Comtask included the rejuvenation of SACS and the establishment of a process to explore the possible divestiture of the concentrated white press groups. But Comtask didn't just take on the appearance of a stakeholder consultative process, it *was* one. Comtask was accountable to the government, but also to the communication sector stakeholders assembled at Arniston and to the South African public beyond them. Comtask took up the concerns of the media liaison officers, many of whom were political veterans from the United Democratic Front and anti-apartheid civil society media organizations. The MLOs had complained that SACS was useless to their needs and responsibilities; indeed the state communications service was still, at bottom, an intelligence service inimical to democratic communication. Three narratives coursed through the Comtask consultative process: a statist discourse that vilified the concentrated white press and that extolled the idea of a state information agency as an instrument for development; a free market discourse emanating from the establishment press touting a libertarian press philosophy and warning of the dangers of state intervention; and a post–social democratic discourse from the civil society media organizations that proposed a mixed media system of commercial, public, subsidized semicommercial, and nonprofit print and broadcast entities. The civil society groups argued that the state *did* have a role to play in a democratic media and that unfettered market controls were inadequate to that task. But government media was not the answer; neither was breaking up the press groups, notwithstanding their concentrated white ownership. Rather, government should expand the information and communications infrastructure and create institutional and funding mechanisms to facilitate community and nonprofit media. In other words, government should help foster a diversity of voices by nurturing and sustaining a tier of nonstate, noncommodified media. The civil society media groups articulated a vision of government communications premised not on a predetermined notion of the common good, but on the central idea of active and interactive citizens linked in a common public concern to forge a new democracy.

This was the vision that informed the Comtask final report (Republic of South Africa, 1996x). Comtask rejected the concept of a top–down government communications agency. Its report recommended the elimination of SACS and creating in its stead a slim government communications service whose purpose was to facilitate coordination among government agencies and act as a liaison between government and community. Acknowledging press concentration as a genuine worry, Comtask referred the issue to South Africa's Competition Board but insinuated that a concentrated press was not the root of the government's communication problem. Public awareness, communication, and democratic debate, Comtask suggested, would be much better served by the government acting to expand the communications and information infrastructure and by fostering community and non-commercial media – in other words, by broadening the infrastructure of the public sphere. With some hemming and hawing, the Comtask recommendations were implemented by the government and the GCIS, the Government Communication and Information System, was established.

Broadcasting and telecommunications were among the first sectors to transform as part of South Africa's transition to democracy. Is this just coincidence or is there something about communications that is central to democratic transition in the contemporary period? Scholars of the transition to democracy in Eastern Europe have noted that the oppositional civil societies emerged at a stage of development in which the means of cultural production and transmission were highly socialized. This meant that from fairly early on, the oppositional social movements were forced to try to come to terms with the mass media. In the case of Poland, at least, the democratization of the mass media was one of the key issues for the civil society opposition movement, Solidarity (C. Sparks, 1994; Jakubowicz, 1990). This was no less true for the anti-apartheid civil society opposition in South Africa. In societies that are media saturated, and where communication systems have become central to other basic processes of society, the mass media and telecommunications become a focus for structural reform. South Africa's was a transition to democracy distinguished by the mobilization of civil society, and in which the relationship between communication and democratic citizenship were joined at the hip in both theory and practice. The struggle to transform South African communications was a fight for access to information that enables citizens to pursue their rights effectively; a fight for access to the broadest possible range of information, interpretation, and debate on areas that involve political choices, and to use communications facilities in order to register criticism, mobilize opposition, and propose alternative courses of action; a fight for the ability of especially black South Africans to recognize themselves and their aspirations in the range of representations offered within the central communications sectors and be able to contribute to developing their representations; and a fight of especially black South Africans to participate in the ownership and control of the means of communication (see Murdock and Golding, 1989). The general success of this struggle was due to the ability of civil society groups aligned with the ANC to articulate a coherent vision of democratic communication and their surprising capacity in implementing the vision – which essentially meant winning political struggles within the ANC alliance itself. This favorable outcome was possible because of the fluid, open politics characteristic of transition periods and the particular character of the political conflict between the ANC and the National Party, which also provided openings for participatory democracy.

FROM TRANSITION TO CONSOLIDATION:
THE DECLINE OF PARTICIPATORY DEMOCRACY

The stakeholder reform processes in the communications sector established structures that in many respects embodied the post–social democratic vision of the anti-apartheid civil society groups. Although I have highlighted the importance of civil society in this exercise in policy reform, it was not a matter of civil society activism per se. Successful civil society struggle depends on a state open to such interventions. Participatory politics works when the state is hospitable to such politics. In the 1990–94 period the South African state was open because it was in fundamental transition and was being contested on all fronts. In the 1994–96 period the state was open because of the way that the RDP embodied the general, if sometimes politically conflicted, aims of the tripartite alliance, in particular the privileging of the stakeholder forums and other forms of participatory democracy. In other words, effective civil society participation in policy determination needs both a strong state and viable, hospitable points of political entry (see Evans, 1997). This book has told that story in some detail. But the story cannot and does not end there. The structures and institutions created during the period of the transition to democracy in South Africa become part of the conflicts and politics of the *consolidation* of that democracy, a process and period generally more structured, more bureaucratic, more prone to clientelism, and less open especially to participatory democracy. If SATRA, the IBA, and the GCIS embody, to some degree, the participatory politics and post–social democratic vision of the transition period, they are now institutional players (subject to their own internal tendencies toward bureaucratization) within ongoing contests between statist tendencies, market forces, and post–social democratic inclinations, all of which take place in the context of the overall political-economic milieu established by GEAR, and behind GEAR, the government's assessment of South Africa's position in the global economy. The struggle among these tendencies gets played out through the politics of the ANC alliance.[1] There is clearly a considerable degree of animosity within the ANC leadership toward the new political agencies – like the IBA and to a lesser degree SATRA – that possess some independence from government. And notwithstanding the Comtask report, the ANC leadership's attacks on the white press and its efforts to instill the vision of a nation-building media continue unabated.

The most clearcut example of the animosity toward the independent agencies was the continuing tumult over broadcast policy and the concerted efforts on the part of the Ministry and Department of Communications to diminish the authority of the IBA. The department initiated a Green Paper/White Paper process to establish policy on broadcasting in 1997 (Republic of South Africa, 1997b, 1998b). Ostensibly required because the Independent Broadcasting Authority Act had not established a coherent policy for the sector as a whole, the broader political justification of the new policy process, in the words of Sam Moeti (1997), chairperson of the Parliamentary Portfolio Committee on Communications, was that the "Kempton Park agreements [which included the IBA] were illegitimate because the people who

---

1 Hein Marais' (1998: 247) observation that the ANC is both the subject and object of hegemonic struggle is apropos. The ANC is both the historic incarnation of black liberation and, for the foreseeable future, the dominant party in government. Hence the ANC is subject both to the long-standing ideological tensions and political expectations that historically characterize the organization as a liberation movement, and it is subject to the exigencies and constraints of being the governing party in a middle-income, mixed economy in a global economic system.

negotiated them were not elected." Broadcast policy likewise, asserted Joe Mjwara (1997), special adviser to the Ministry of Communications, "must now be determined within the democratic political framework." Coherence was to be built in broadcasting by bringing policy making back into the Department of Communications, a government apparatus directly tied through the vote to the democratic will of the people. This would require, among other things, reducing the authority of the IBA, a body tied to the pre-election, "undemocratic," transition compromises.

The department's manner of accomplishing this aim was to conduct a stakeholder consultative process that many participants viewed as a charade, the appearance of a democratic process whose results were entirely foreordained. Many of the key people and groups in the broadcast arena were named to a stakeholders' committee, but the process was pre-scripted and discussions highly constrained. Certain key questions, such as the merger of the IBA into SATRA, were off the table and nonnegotiable. International experts who were brought in to assist a Technical Team were declared off limits to the stakeholders committee, and the documents written by the internationals were not made available to the committee. Stakeholder committee suggestions or objections were routinely ignored, according to participants (Sekha, 1997; Duncan, 1998; R. Muller, 1998). If the Comtask stratagem represented a failed effort on the part of government to drive policy through a manipulated consultative forum in 1996, by the time of the Broadcast Green Paper the Department of Communications senior officials had learned how to run a sham consultative process.

The deadline for public comment on the broadcast Green Paper had barely expired in February 1998 when Minister Naidoo presented draft legislation to Parliament on the future of the SABC and the authority of the IBA. The timing lent some credence to the charge that the broadcast policy Green Paper/White Paper consultative process was window dressing for a broad, predetermined policy maneuver. The bill called for the corporatization of the SABC, the sale of some of its channels, and the reduction of the IBA's authority. The central aim of the bill was to transform the SABC into a public company with the state as sole shareholder, and the minister of communications, in effect, the custodian of the shares. In the new structure, the public service and commercial operations of the SABC would be separated. The commercial arm, to consist of one television and four radio stations (along with some other operations), may be used to cross-subsidize the public service arm, but the money would have to be redirected to the fiscus first before a decision is taken by the minister as to the extent of state funding. Eventually, the commercial arm may be privatized (Republic of South Africa, 1998a).

As several of the civil society media organizations suggested, the bill was less a play for government control over the content of the SABC programming (though that could happen indirectly inasmuch as the minister would exercise considerable discretion over SABC funding), as it represented a new broadcast policy in line with GEAR imperatives. It had become clear that government would not fund the public service broadcaster. Indeed, recall that the proceeds from the sale of the SABC radio stations went to the central fiscus, not back to the SABC. The SABC, like all other parastatals, was required not only to be self-financing but was now expected to become export-oriented as well. Minister Naidoo hoped to see the commercial arm of the SABC operating in neighboring African markets. SABC head Zwelakhe Sisulu declared the SABC a "gold mine" (Spira, 1997). In the most sanguine interpretation, the broadcast bill was an attempt to rescue some features of the SABC's RDP-linked goals (universal access to broadcast signals, programming in the eleven official languages, educational programs, local content) by tying them to GEAR goals (broadcasting as a commercial growth and export-oriented sector). But there was no assurance that the commercial dynamic would not become its own imperative. To the contrary, the GEAR climate encourages expanded commercialism, including the privatization of the SABC commercial channels. Yet any privatization of the SABC's commercial wing would eliminate the public service broadcaster's cross-subsidy source. A continually cash-starved public service broadcaster, reliant on a combination of advertising as well as the ad hoc munificence of the minister, is hardly in a position to act as a bold, independent broadcaster. Subject to both commercial and political pressures (even if indirect in the latter), the SABC will find it difficult to program to the South African audience in the mode distinctive to public service broadcasters, to wit, addressing the audience as citizens rather than as consumers or as political subjects (Freedom of Expression Institute, 1998; Media Monitoring Project, 1998; Berger, 1998; Duncan, 1998).

The ANC leadership, committed to fiscal discipline and efficient parastatals, could not see that broadcasting was in fact distinct from other infrastructure parastatals. Broadcasting provides content, not just service; it is a central conduit for cultural representation and political discussion and hence it is an institution at the heart of a democratic public sphere. Commercializing and privatizing parts of the sector without supporting the public service broadcaster will inevitably lead to a shell of public broadcasting – somewhat like that of the United States. And to achieve this GEAR-linked transformation of broadcast policy, the government must centralize power and curb the independence of the IBA, reducing the IBA's authority to that of a mere licensing body. Once again in broadcasting, the ANC's statist tendency served to reinforce the power of the market. And it should be noted that the South African broadcast market is politically idiosyncratic, largely in keeping with one of the key trends in black economic empowerment. The diminished SABC has outsourced some of its programming to favored ANC-linked business organizations. The lucrative contract for SABC breakfast television, as well as several other programs, went to Urban Brew, an affiliate of New African Investments Limited (NAIL), and headed by newly departed SABC chief, now NAIL principal, Zwelakhe Sisulu (Haffajee, 1998b).

FINAL REFLECTIONS: TRANSFORMATION, STATE, SOCIETY, AND THE MEANING OF BLACK ECONOMIC EMPOWERMENT

Much has changed in South Africa since 1990. At the most obvious level, a country for decades characterized by a brutal, racially exclusivist authoritarianism now has free elections, one person–one vote, a constitution that guarantees civil liberties and equal protection before the law. Racial and gender discrimination are constitutionally forbidden. South African labor laws are the envy of trade unions in even the developed countries. That's on the political side. The socioeconomic side displays a much more mixed picture. GDP has risen slightly but unemployment is very high, by some estimates approaching 40 percent (Economist Intelligence Unit, 1999: 21). The legacy of Bantu education continues to circumscribe the life-chances of a large portion of the black population. Crime is a major social problem, instilling a destructive level of fear and despair throughout the society and negatively affecting investment decisions. On the other hand, infant mortality has dropped and life expectancy has risen. The delivery of basic services has increased significantly since 1994 (see Table 8).

Table 8. *Expansion of Basic Services in South Africa, 1994–1998/99*

Households with:	1994 (%)	1998–99 (%)
Electricity	31	63
Water	30	44
Telephones	25	35
Television reception[a]	70	85

[a] Based on total population, not households.
Sources: Government Communication & Information System; Statistics South Africa; cited in Murphy, 1999: 16.

One of the most noticeable developments is the rise of a small, but rapidly growing black middle class. This black middle class has grown as a consequence of various schemes that encourage black economic empowerment. Its emergence constitutes a window on the nature, strengths, and limits of South Africa's transformation.

Empowerment has tended to take the form of the ascent of black-owned investment companies that have acquired stakes in existing, historically white, South African corporations. A good deal of the impetus for such empowerment derives, directly and indirectly, from the continued significant presence of the state in the economy. By the time the Government of National Unity came to power in 1994, state tenders and contracts were no longer being awarded as a matter of course to favored Afrikaanse companies. The unwritten rule, soon to be formalized, was that companies bidding for state contracts had to demonstrate, at the minimum, significant participation by the previously disadvantaged black majority. Recall that the issuance of tenders for the cellular telephone licenses in 1993 required bidders to show evidence of substantial black investment. Indeed, even before this, white companies saw that they would need to bring in black partners and to engage in internal "transformation" – the hiring and promotion of blacks to management positions – as a condition of doing business in the new South Africa. Much of this transformation was tokenism, to be sure, but some was genuine. In part because broadcasting and telecommunications reformed relatively early, and in part because of high state-related demand in information and telecommunications, many of the initial black empowerment deals occurred in the communications sector. The significant ownership changes in the print press, and the new business consortia forged to bid for private broadcast licenses, highlight these early empowerment deals. According to Business Map, the consultancy that tracks black economic empowerment, identifiable black empowerment deals in the information and telecommunications industries amounted to R4.5 billion for the period 1996–98 (Block, 1999). The rush of joint ventures between black investment houses and white companies in communications and other sectors has been remarkable, pushing the black share of market capitalization of the Johannesburg Stock Exchange, according to one estimate, to 10.3 percent in 1998 (*F&T Weekly*, 1998: 33).

At issue is the meaning of this development. What is changed by the fact that, for example, two of the four historically white press conglomerates, Times Media Ltd. and Perskor, are now nominally controlled by black-owned firms? Is the ANC following the classic script of modernization theory and the history of Afrikaner nationalism, that is, consolidating an emergent democracy by establishing, largely through state policy, a (black) middle class with a strong stake in the system? Is black economic empowerment simply capitalism with a black face; indeed, is it part of the unfolding of economic orthodoxy with the attached political benefit of creating a clientelistic black middle class that is loyal to the ANC? While this *is* a trend, there is no "simply" about it. Black economic empowerment is a many faceted, contradictory phenomenon that must be assessed in the context of an analysis of what kind of transformation is possible and desirable in light of three largely interrelated issues: the nature of the compromises that underlay South Africa's transition to democracy, the opportunities and constraints established by economic globalization, and what, concretely, constitutes the emancipatory project in a post-socialist world.

The transition to democracy in South Africa rested on compromises that safeguarded past capitalist accumulation. The retention of property rights meant that, while the transition entailed a political revolution, the social revolution would be truncated. Not only would class continue to be the basis of socioeconomic dominance, but historically determined class position would continue to predominate as well. As Mahmood Mamdani (1997) points out, radical economic redistribution was characteristic of several post–World War II success stories, such as Germany, Japan, South Korea, Taiwan. Economic growth and domestic stability in these countries rested to a large extent on this redistribution. The political and economic establishments in each case accepted radical redress because of the fear that if they did not they might meet a fate worse than redress: communism. This did not apply in the case of South Africa. The South African paradox is that while the elimination of the fear of communism in part allowed the National Party to negotiate a political transition with the ANC, the elimination of the fear also meant the arrest of a more progressive social transformation. The property rights and protection of civil service compromises not only meant the instantiation of historic class domination, they meant the ANC's acceptance of responsibility for a public budget that was already overextended and a good portion of which was promised for the state pension funds (which largely benefitted white civil servants). And, though it is a question whether it was really necessary, the compromises also meant the ANC's agreement on the near-total independence of the Reserve Bank, whose sole constitutionally mandated task to protect the value of the rand could only further constrain the tripartite alliance's economic policy prerogatives when it came to power.

The new South Africa has been joyously welcomed back into the community of nations. But this is a new community of nations, characterized by an increasingly global capitalist economy, by the end, for the time being, of an anticapitalist alternative, and hence dominated by multilateral organizations that compel the reassessment of domestic policies by a set of international market standards. The new South Africa has been forced to adapt to this reality. The autonomy of the liberal democratic state has always been constrained by the overriding need to maintain business confidence. This is the basic lesson of much political sociology. The state depends on business to invest, to produce goods and services, provide jobs, and create the tax base upon which the state funds its activities. A major function of the state in a capitalist social formation is to see to it that businessmen perform their tasks. The globalization of the economy ratchets up the state's burden. Globalization is the worldwide integration of key markets, especially the international finance system, and the transformation of multinational enterprise into global enterprise. Perhaps the easiest way to conceptualize globalization is the recognition of the new hegemony of trade in world affairs. As international linkages are increasingly institutionalized or guided by organizations designed around liberal trade and investment principles, they instigate an exogenous evaluation of the role and form of national states, and the types of policies they pursue with respect to internal economic policies and strategies of development. South Africa, a newly democratic middle-income state intent on spurring capital investment, guarding against the flight of skill and capital, and protecting the value of its currency, ignores international models at its peril. The ANC has adapted to these pressures and constraints by showing its commitment to previous economic reforms and by adopting a mostly orthodox macroeconomic policy of deficit reduction, relaxation of exchange controls, and reduction of tariffs.

In light of the new South African state's relative economic weakness, black economic empowerment becomes a transformation strategy. So what kind of transformation does it entail? One route into this discussion is to examine concretely who owns and controls Johnnic, the black holding company of Times Media Ltd. and other corporations (see Table 7 in Chapter 6). Recall that the National Empowerment Consortium (NEC) is made up of business and labor components. NAIL and Worldwide Africa Investment Holdings are, for the most part, black investment houses whose aim is to make money for a very small number of rising, big-time black capitalists. The principals of NAIL in particular are either close to or are important members of the ANC. NAIL and Worldwide Africa each has a direct stake of just under 10 percent in a business component that itself makes up 50 percent of the National Empowerment Consortium. But the business component of the NEC is somewhat more than just this. Beyond NAIL and Worldwide Africa, another 10 percent is owned by Siphumelele Investments, a cooperative made up of 79 Western Cape organizations purportedly representing 150,000 people – each group, including fruit sellers and fishermen, women real estate agents on the Cape Flats, the Food and Allied Workers Union, among others, put up R20,000 to join. Nozola Investments is a vehicle for the empowerment of African women. Tswelopele Investments is a smaller black investment company whose principals are old political activists. And as part of the deal with Anglo-American, Johnnic offered a share scheme (called *Ikageng*, Tswana for "develop yourself") making available 9.1 million shares (6% of share capital, on top of the NEC's 35%), at reduced rates, to disadvantaged black South Africans. The offering was nearly seven times oversubscribed with 32,000 people applying for shares, raising about R190 million. Innovative financing arrangements made it possible for the disadvantaged to participate in Ikageng, by giving people the ability to buy shares at R66 in three years' time against payment of a nonrefundable deposit of R6. The business component of Johnnic is thus made up of straight-out big black capitalists, community group cooperatives, African businesswomen, and very small shareholders from the disadvantaged black majority (*Enterprise*, 1997a). The other 50 percent of NEC's share of Johnnic is held by the trade unions through the pension and provident funds and the union investment companies, with the largest single stake held by the National Union of Mineworkers at just under 13 percent.

But is ownership the same as control? At the present moment, there is little evidence that black ownership makes much difference with regard to patterns of corporate behavior, job creation, or workplace relations. Most of the NEC members are highly geared, and require a dividend return from Johnnic in the range of 12 to 14 percent simply to retain control of their investments. Thus there is intense interest in the performance of Johnnic, particularly dividend payments, which means the new owners are unlikely to make large changes that might risk reducing the profit stream (Singh, 1997; *Enterprise*, 1997b). Perhaps saying much the same thing, one business writer argued that many of Johnnic's holdings, though well situated in some of South Africa's key industrial companies, are "passive." They do not allow much room for active managerial involvement, "which is fine if the intention is merely to sit on solid investments but not so clever if the desire is to participate meaningfully in management" (Gleason, 1997: 15–16). It may not make very much difference, in the short run at least, that a Cyril Ramaphosa is the head of Johnnic, or for that matter, the chairman of Times Media Ltd. Those investments must be profitable; the companies must engage in actions that best secure profitability in their particular markets. (Still, it is noteworthy that the only new titles in the South African press scene have been introduced by TML. In a joint venture with NAIL, TML launched the *Sunday World* in March 1999, a new title aimed at a wealthy top-end black readership. TML also inaugurated the country's first daily sports paper, *Sportsday*.)

Thus a widespread criticism is that, so far, black economic empowerment has not meant the creation of "organic" black capital, that is, businesses organized by blacks from the ground up, which produce entrepreneurial skills and new job opportunities in the process of producing commodities or services. Rather, empowerment has consisted largely of get-rich-quick schemes for a small elite. Government policies to empower small, medium, and micro-enterprises (SMMEs), considered the key to organic black capital and job creation, have been desultory at best (Adam, Slabbert, and Moodley, 1997; Cronin, 1998; Brown, 1998). At the same time, the *corporate* version of black economic empowerment – the version that engenders black investment houses taking stakes in existing (white) companies which then can bid on state contracts and privatization tenders – seems to bind the small newly empowered black elite to the new status quo. So, for example, one now finds major black businessmen deploying and defending the use of pyramid structures of ownership – precisely those structures that ANC-linked economists historically condemned because they close off the South African economy from competition and easy entry (Singh, 1997; D. Lewis, 1995).[2] The commitment of the new black bourgeoisie to the status quo paradoxically accomplishes what the *verligte* Nationalists had in mind in the 1980s – an uneasy, but workable coalition among property holders and rising economic actors – but with a center–left ANC the political beneficiary rather than a center–right National Party.[3]

But this is not all there is to black economic empowerment. One has to consider the steady, significant growth of basic services as a form, however modest, of black economic empowerment (see Table 8). The expansion of basic services provides the previously black disadvantaged with a kind of property – in Amartya Sen's (1999) term, "capabilities," that forms the basis for the augmentation of life-chances. Still modest in practical consequences, this enabling property is in keeping with the longstanding claim that increased access to basic services not only enhances people's quality of life but facilitates economic activity (see Ghosh, 1984; United States, 1991; Howe and le Roux, 1992; Saunders,

---

2 Of course, one reason for the defense of pyramid structures in the black economic empowerment arena was to permit the control of the companies by blacks, rather than by the white sources of the initial capital. NAIL was a case in point. But NAIL's pyramid structure got the holding company into trouble in mid-1999. An attempt by directors to award themselves a R136 million share option bonus sparked a revolt by the group's institutional shareholders and prompted a demand for reorganization. The reorganization creates more accountability to shareholders, but means the company no longer will be controlled by blacks (Block and Soggot, 1999; McNeil, Jr., 1999).

3 This is the basis of the political comparison between the ANC-led South Africa to the PRI-led Mexico. The Party of the Institutional Revolution (PRI), which ruled Mexico for several decades, was able to do so by trading on its revolutionary credentials at the ballot box and by controlling the state, bureaucracy, and patronage in so tight a manner that there was virtually no civil society independent of the state. Groups, organizations, and civic life were in a real sense defined by their relation to the PRI and the PRI's distribution of funds and patronage.

Warford, and Wellenius, 1994). A good part of the success in expanding basic services must be attributed to the post–social democratic
nature of the parastatal policy initiatives. The expansion of basic
services is something that pure state ownership and state operation of
parastatal organizations probably could not have accomplished as easily,
because of a shortage of capital for investment and because of ingrained
patterns of monopoly-related incentive problems.[4] What matters, in
the matter of the parastatals, is not ownership per se, but rather the
creation of institutional structures that can facilitate and realize
the fundamental goal of expanding basic services to the disadvantaged.
The partial privatization of Telkom facilitated that expansion in the area
of telecommunications service; the partial commercialization of South
African broadcasting brought new formats, content, and audiences.
Thus in some respects, in sectors like communications, the corporate
version of black economic empowerment, in conjunction with the
careful, limited privatization and liberalization parastatal policy since
1994, fostered a "capabilities" version of black economic empowerment.
Privatization had an additional unanticipated consequence in the area
of race. The stake in Telkom was purchased by the consortium of SBC
Communications and Telekom Malaysia. SBC brought in a high-level
management team of several score people to Telkom, a large percentage of whom were African-American. Telkom, for so long a white
organization at the management level, was instantly transformed by
the presence of black managers with expertise and clout.

There is still another side to black economic empowerment: labor.
All the unions but one, and even the South African Communist Party,
have set up investment companies. The various union funds promise
significant capital for joint private ventures and for the purchase of
stakes in state-owned enterprises if and when they come available.[5] The
Mineworkers Investment Company (MIC), for example, commencing
with a modest R3 million in seed money from the union, now has assets
(in addition to Johnnic) in companies listed on the Johannesburg Stock

---

4 Electricity is an exception to this statement, largely because of the peculiar history of ESKOM
and its built-up excess electricity-generating capacity (see Horwitz, 1994a).
5 According to one report, actuarial estimations suggest that, on average, as much as 60% of the
domestic finance for locally listed firms could come from institutional investors, mainly retirement funds. The Katz Commission estimated the assets of the retirement industry in 1996 at
about R500 billion. At the absolute minimum, the Congress of South African Trade Unions
funds account for 10 percent of "self-administered funds," the largest category of fund type.
Transnet, Telkom, and the Post Office operate separate categories of retirement funds, some of
which are also COSATU-linked (R. Naidoo, 1997: 3, 6).

Exchange, including Mathomo (mining-related clothing), Hosken Consolidated Investments (financial services, telecommunications, broadcasting, and information technology), and Rebhold (food and liquor distribution, industrial catering, and freight). These investments have begun to bring economic returns (Simon, 1997).

The union investment companies evolved in part as a form of self-protection when the government moved toward economic orthodoxy and privatization. Highly politicized and organizationally powerful, a constituent in the tripartite alliance, the COSATU unions espouse socialism and denounce privatization. Yet, as the Post & Telecommunications Workers Association's former general secretary confided about his union, though the communications workers union fought hard against privatization and vigorously opposed Telkom on outsourcing, in the meantime it set up investment companies capable of bidding on potentially outsourced units (Monyokolo, 1997). But the motivation behind the union investment companies was not just defensive. As John Copelyn, former general secretary of the South African Clothing and Textile Workers Union (SACTWU) and, with Marcel Golding of the mineworkers, an originator of the union investment company idea, argued in the *South African Labour Bulletin*:

> Progressive worker leaders in the trade union movement need to focus not only on the traditional areas of trade union activity, which centre around organising industrial combinations of workers, but also on building new and different institutions which can help working class people with solutions to problems they have in capitalist societies and which are essentially outside that competence. (Copelyn, 1997: 76)

Such institutions include those that develop the consumer power of workers, such as credit cards, and create opportunities for workers outside the workplace, such as housing, creches (day-care centers), and retirement homes provided by union-owned businesses. The SACTWU and Mineworkers investment companies have returned capital back to their unions in the form of bursaries (educational scholarships and loans) for workers' children. SACTWU's bursary fund swelled to R8 million in 1997 as a result of the holdings of SACTWU Investments. The Mineworkers Investment Company also has funded the Mineworkers' Development Agency, which trains retrenched mineworkers for other occupations. Hosken Consolidated Investments

(HCI), the holding company of the National Union of Mineworkers and SACTWU trusts, bought a large stake in a bank, which now provides mortgages to union members at three to four points lower than commercial lenders. Union trust funds bought the assets of a bankrupt clothing company in Durban and started up a union-owned company, Zenzeleni Clothing (Zulu for "we help ourselves"), putting 150 retrenched clothing workers back to work (Golding, 1997; Haffajee, 1997; Copelyn, 1998). COSATU's investment company, in the words of its director, Tumelo Motsisi, aims to invest in the "commanding heights" of the South African economy, using its investment stake to make sure that the economy performs in the interests of COSATU's members (Koch, 1997).

No one disputes these benefits. The debate within the labor movement is whether union investments are simply a form of "labor capitalism," in which the unions act as capitalists and find themselves mired in the contradiction of having to adopt hard-nosed, antiworker tactics in order to survive (see R. Naidoo, 1997; Dexter, 1997; McKinley, 1997). As one union leader remarked, in a quote that made the rounds, "You can't invest in a capitalist economy in a comradely manner" (quoted in R. Naidoo, 1997: 2).[6] The question for labor posed by former union leader, now (ANC) Member of Parliament, Phillip Dexter (1997: 71–72) "whether or not their [union] investment activities contribute to developing a separate, distinct capital outside of the control and influence of monopoly capital, which is engaged in a conscious programme of transforming the economy," can in fact be posed to black economic empowerment and post-apartheid transformation in general. This is the South African version of the classic dilemma confronting a socialist movement. As Adam Przeworski has noted,

Any movement that seeks to transform historical conditions operates under these very conditions. The movement for socialism developed within capitalist societies and faced definite choices that arise from this particular organization of society. These choices have been threefold: (1) whether to seek the advancement of

6 The precise nature of the association between a union, its investments, and its investment company has been muddled, and this has added a tension to the debate within the labor movement. Workers have had little control over their union investment companies, which are often run by businessmen or union officials. There have been instances where union rank-and-file have taken to the streets against government plans for the privatization of a state-owned enterprise, only to find their own investment company one of the primary bidders.

socialism within the existing institutions of the capitalist society or outside of them; (2) whether to seek the agent of socialist transformation exclusively in the working class or to rely on multi- or even non-class support; and (3) whether to seek reforms, partial improvements, or to dedicate all efforts and energies to the complete abolition of capitalism. (Przeworski, 1985: 3)

The difficulty of the dilemma also now inheres in the problem of conceptualizing transformation in an era when the models of the state and of property utilized to criticize capitalist relations hail, especially after the fall of the Soviet Union, from a theory that many believe has been discredited. One way out of this difficulty is to reconsider the relationship between property and the socialist project. This is the method of "market socialist" theorists, such as John Roemer and Pranab Bardhan (1993), and may be a basis of the argument for the union investment companies advanced by John Copelyn and Marcel Golding, among others. In *A Future for Socialism*, Roemer (1994: 11–23) argues that socialists have made a fetish of public ownership. Public ownership has been viewed as the *sine qua non* of socialism. But this is built on a false inference, he claims. Socialists should want those property rights that will bring about a society that best promotes equality of opportunity for everyone. What is it, at bottom, that socialists want, Roemer asks? Running a theory of socialism through egalitarian theories of justice, he argues that socialists want equality of opportunity for (1) self-realization and welfare, (2) political influence, and (3) social status. The choice of property rights over firms and other resources is an entirely instrumental matter and should be evaluated according to the likelihood they will induce the three equalities. State ownership, particularly of the Soviet design, has proven incapable of securing socialist goals. At the economic level, centrally planned economies failed primarily because of the principal–agent problem (where one actor must engage another – or others – to perform a task) and the "soft budget constraint," where firm managers entered into bargaining relationships with politicians to obtain loans and tax exemptions to firms that, from the viewpoint of economic efficiency, should not have received them. At the political level, the hierarchical structure of the planned economy is paralleled by a similar hierarchical structure of society as a whole, resulting in political domination. Political authoritarianism need not necessarily follow from command economies, but there seems to be an

easy movement in that direction. Complex societies require markets –
only markets appear capable of providing the decentralized information necessary for firms or other large economic agents to act efficiently (see, among others, Nove, 1983). The problem, of course, is that
unregulated markets necessarily distribute profits in the extremely
unequal way characteristic of capitalism. And in liberal democracies,
economic power quickly translates into entrenched political power
as well.

The difficulty is designing a system that takes advantage of markets
but prevents the accumulation of economic and political power in a
small class. Social democracy characteristically met this challenge with
statist solutions that, over time, tended to generate bureaucratic exter-
nalities and fiscal overextension (and also tended to generate nonplu-
ralistic cultural formations – we saw this in, e.g., the complaint about
traditional public service broadcasting). Social democracy's exhaustion
at century's end derives from the diminishing returns of its solutions in
an increasingly globalized economy and from the objection to the often
statist, paternalist, and culturally centralist politics that accompanied its
policies. Hence the efforts to conceive a "third way" (see, for instance,
Giddens, 1994).

Social revolution traditionally has been understood at the level of
class transformation and the redistribution of property. But perhaps
this is too narrow, or at least too time-constricted, a reading of social
revolution. As Chantal Mouffe (1993: 103) has suggested, the post-
socialist project is the expansion of democracy to a wide range of social
relations. Relations of domination have to be challenged to enable the
liberal principle of equal rights of self-development to be realized. The
peculiarity of South Africa, of course, was that class domination historically mapped onto domination by race. The latter is now prohibited
by law. It is surely revolutionary that in the South African transition,
race and class are in principle now delinked. Black economic empowerment and union investments represent the realization that to end
racial domination under the present circumstances, economic power
must be exercised not just through the state, but through participation
in ownership, through the market.

Social transformation was always a central part of the South African
emancipatory project, from the Freedom Charter to the RDP to GEAR.
How social transformation happens is another matter. Under the
current conditions, social transformation takes the form of black
economic empowerment within a capitalist framework. As I hope the

preceding pages make clear, black economic empowerment is a complicated and contradictory phenomenon, ranging from a big business-based black-white joint-venture version to a union investment version. All the contending elements of post-apartheid politics are also found in the black economic empowerment phenomenon. The danger is that the version of black economic empowerment in which black corporate clientelism is joined to ANC statism crowds out the post–social democratic version of transformation and empowerment.

Appendix

Table A. *State-Owned Enterprises and Their Classifications*

Category 1 Clear public interest[a]	Category 2 Some public interest[b]	Category 3 No public interest[c]	
		Profitable	*Unprofitable*
ESKOM	Denel		
Telkom	Petronet		
Spoornet	Atomic Energy Board		
SA Post Office	Armscor		
SABC	Mossgas		
Portnet	SAA	Sun Air	Transkei Air
SARCC	Strategic Fuel Fund	Autonet	Aventura
Airports Company	Association Soekor	SAFCOL	Parcel Express
Air Traffic Navigational Services (ATNS)		Alexkor	Abacor

[a] Explicit role in the provision of basic needs, essential infrastructure, or services.
[b] No precise role in providing essential services; historically in public sector for national security or strategic reasons.
[c] No visible role in Reconstruction and Development Programme.
Source: Republic of South Africa (1995j: 13). Some of the parastatals changed positions in the period between the second draft and this document. Notably, SAA moved from category 1 to category 2; Portnet, the Airports Company, and Air Traffic Navigational Services moved from category 2 to category 1.

Table B. *Value of Parastatals (in 1995 rand)*

Parastatal	Total Assets	Total Liabilities	Turnover	Profit	No. of Employees
Category 1 – public policy value					
ESKOM	49,761,000	39,162,000	12,891,000	2,601,000	39,173
Telkom	16,464,387	11,387,603	8,365,412	1,206,032	60,000
SABC	1,285,883	467,673	1,393,297	108,461	4,397
Spoornet	21,583,000	5,204,472	7,624,000	618,261	65,452
S.A. Post Office	2,576,417	2,316,398	1,457,472	22,704	24,183
Portnet	4,138,000	2,652,894	2,539,000	687,684	11,005
SARCC	4,788,155	1,370,797	474,228	(1,051,030)	10,815
Airports Co.	846,566	87,575	150,811	33,823	1,531
Air Traffic & Navigation Services Co.	211,556	13,463	89,817	12,706	467
Category 2 – public policy/strategic value					
Armscor	681,700	342,000	311,400	5,000	1,016
Atomic Energy Board	515,686	746,319	745,401	15,406	2,623
Denel	4,078,500	1,337,900	3,014,500	324,900	11,523
Mossgas	11,219,840	10,504,026	1,188,276	516,703	1,290
Petronet	1,432,417	911,504	446,000	141,685	653
SAA	4,355,000	2,377,622	3,999,000	217,000	10,367
SFF Assn.	3,689,233	731,264	2,641,536	1,030,027	320
Soekor	199,268	1,356,210	5,657	(52,996)	310
Category 3 – no public policy value					
PROFITABLE					
Alexcor	257,970	41,862	228,005	46,409	1,661
Autonet	234,000	142,849	399,000	3,664	1,883
Safcol	691,541	201,307	448,921	56,798	5,433
Sun Air	86,252	26,597	46,253	(4,047)	257
UNPROFITABLE					
Abakor	314,344	95,060	338,769	(15,429)	2,600
Aventura	100,731	54,516	109,586	(6,772)	1,585
Parcel Express	593,000	981,543	557,000	(297,000)	8,757
Transkei Airways	6,743	7,838	9,244	(6,420)	45
Transnet – other	6,085,966	3,091,116	359,631	194,487	47,810
TOTAL	138,343,722	76,612,408	49,632,585	6,409,275	315,156

Source: Ministry for Public Enterprises, cited in Lunsche (1996b).

References

Abedian, Iraj, and Barry Standish. 1985. "An Economic Inquiry into the Poor White Saga." Southern Africa Labour and Development Research Unit Working Papers, No. 64. Cape Town: SALDRU.

Adam, Heribert, and Hermann Giliomee. 1979. *The Rise and Crisis of Afrikaner Power.* Cape Town: David Philip.

Adam, Heribert, and Kogila Moodley. 1993. *The Opening of the Apartheid Mind: Options for the New South Africa.* Berkeley: University of California Press; also published as *The Negotiated Revolution: Society and Politics in Post-Apartheid South Africa.* Johannesburg: Jonathan Ball.

Adam, Heribert, Frederik van Zyl Slabbert, and Kogila Moodley. 1997. *Comrades in Business: Post-Liberation Politics in South Africa.* Cape Town: Tafelberg.

Adelzadeh, Asghar. 1996. "From the RDP to GEAR: The Gradual Embracing of Neo-liberalism in Economic Policy." *Transformation* 31: 66–95.

Adler, Glenn, and Eddie Webster. 1995. "Challenging Transition Theory: The Labor Movement, Radical Reform, and Transition to Democracy in South Africa." *Politics & Society* 23: 75–106.

African Communist, The. 1995. Vol. 141 (2d quarter).

African Global Consortium. 1995. Submission to Green Paper on Telecommunications Policy. Johannesburg: NTPP.

African National Congress. 1987. "Apartheid South Africa: Colonialism of a Special Type." <anc.org.za/ancdocs/history/special.html>

—— 1989. "Constitutional Guidelines of the African National Congress." In *South African Journal on Human Rights* 5: 129–132.

—— 1991. "Resolutions Adopted at the DIP National Media Seminar." Johannesburg: author, November 23–24.

—— 1992a. *ANC Policy Guidelines for a Democratic South Africa.* (Adopted at National Conference.) Johannesburg: author, May 28–31.

—— 1992b. "ANC Position on Telecommunications Sector Strategy Study Report for the Department of Posts and Telecommunications." Press release. August.

—— 1992c. Department of Information and Publicity. "Negotiations: A Strategic Perspective" (as adopted by the National Working Committee). Johannesburg: author, November 18.

—— 1994a. "The ANC Policy for Equity and Efficiency in the Telecommunications Sector." Draft Discussion Paper. February.

1994b. *The Reconstruction and Development Programme: A Policy Framework.* Johannesburg: Umanyano Publications.

1996a. Statement to the Truth and Reconciliation Commission. <www.anc.org.za/ ancdocs/misc/trctoc.html>

1996b. Technology Unit. Submission to Comtask. *Annexure 19.* Johannesburg: Comtask.

1996c. "The State and Social Transformation: An ANC Discussion Document." <www.anc.org.za/ancindex.html>

1997. "The Role of the Media under Apartheid." Submission to the Truth and Reconciliation Commission. <www.anc.org.za/ancdocs/misc/mediasub.html>

Alchian, Armen. 1965. "Some Economics of Property Rights." *Il Politico* 30: 816–829.

Alexander, Neville. 1989. *Language Policy and National Unity in South Africa/Azania.* Cape Town: Buchu Books.

Allen, Anita. 1995. "Getting Water to the People." *Star,* May 11.

Anderson, Benedict. 1991. *Imagined Communities: Reflections on the Origin and Spread of Nationalism.* 2d edition. London: Verso Press.

Andersson, Muff. 1996. "The Consultative National Telecommunications Process: South Africa." Unpublished manuscript (third draft). Johannesburg: author, April 22.

1997. Media Liaison Officer, Ministry of Posts, Telecommunications and Broadcasting. Interview by author. Johannesburg, October 25.

Argus. 1995. "Assets Sale Row." December 8.

Armstrong, Amanda. 1987. " 'Hear No Evil, See No Evil, Speak No Evil': Media Restrictions and the State of Emergency." In Glenn Moss and Ingrid Obery, eds., *South African Review 4.* Johannesburg: Ravan Press, pp. 199–214.

Ash, Timothy Garton. 1990. *We The People.* Cambridge, U.K.: Granta Books.

1997. "True Confessions." *The New York Review of Books.* July 17, pp. 33–38.

Averch, Harvey, and Leland L. Johnson. 1962. "Behavior of the Firm under Regulatory Constraint." *American Economics Review* 52: 1052–1069.

Bagdikian, Ben. 1997. *The Media Monopoly.* 5th ed. Boston: Beacon Press.

Baker, C. Edwin. 1994. *Advertising and a Democratic Press.* Princeton: Princeton University Press.

Barber, Simon. 1995. "SA Aloof as Move to Wire Africa Gets Under Way." *Business Day,* May 23.

Baskin, Jeremy. 1991. *Striking Back: A History of Cosatu.* Johannesburg: Ravan Press.

2000. "Labour in South Africa's Transition to Democracy: Concertation in a Third World Setting." In Glenn Adler and Eddie Webster, eds., *Trade Unions and Democratization in South Africa, 1985–1997.* London: Macmillan; New York: St. Martin's Press, pp. 42–56.

Battersby, John. 1981. "When We Look at the World, Do We All See It the Same Way?" *Journalist.* March.

1990. "ANC Tempers Hard-Line Rhetoric on Economic Policy." *The Christian Science Monitor,* May 10.

1997. Editor, *Sunday Independent.* Interview by author. Johannesburg, October 22.

Baumol, W. J., J. C. Panzar, and R. D. Willig. 1983. *Contestable Markets and the Theory of Industry Structure.* New York: Harcourt Brace Jovanovich.

Berger, Guy. 1996. Remarks to Comtask on Ownership of the Press. *Annexure 14*. Johannesburg: Comtask.

———. 1998. "Broadcasting Through a Glass Darkly." *Sunday Independent*, October 18.

Berlin, Isaiah. 1980. *Against the Current: Essays in the History of Ideas*. New York: Viking Press.

Bester, Alan. 1995a. National Telecommunications Manager, ESKOM. Interview by author. Johannesburg, December 4.

———. 1995b. "Telecommunications in Eskom." Johannesburg: ESKOM, December 13.

Bethlehem, Lael. 1995. "Employment in South African Parastatals – A Preliminary Investigation." Johannesburg: NALEDI, November.

Bets, Ben. 1992. Senior General Manager, Telkom. Interview by author. Pretoria, June 8.

Bierbaum, Neil. 1995. "M-Net Vows to Keep its Share of Ad Spend." *Mail & Guardian*, November 17–23.

Biko, Steve. 1978. *I Write What I Like*. Aelred Stubbs, ed. San Francisco: Harper.

Block, Donna. 1999. "IT's Africa's Calling." *Mail & Guardian*. April 30. <www.sn.apc.org/wmail/issues/993004>

Block, Donna, and Mungo Soggot. 1999. "Hammer to Fall on Top NAIL Executives." *Mail & Guardian*, April 30. <www.sn.apc.org/wmail/issues/990430>

Blumler, Jay G. 1989. *The Role of Public Policy in the New Television Marketplace*. Washington, D.C.: Benton Foundation.

———. ed. 1992. *Television and the Public Interest: Vulnerable Values in West European Broadcasting*. London: Sage Publications in association with the Broadcasting Standards Council.

Blumler, Jay G., and T. J. Nossiter, eds. 1991. *Broadcasting Finance in Transition: A Comparative Handbook*. New York: Oxford University Press.

BMI-TechKnowledge. 1997. *Communication Technologies Handbook 1997*. Johannesburg: author.

Bohman, James. 1996. *Public Deliberation: Pluralism, Complexity, and Democracy*. Cambridge, MA: MIT Press.

Boraine, Alex, Janet Levy, and Ronel Scheffer, eds. 1994. *Dealing with the Past: Truth and Reconciliation in South Africa*. Cape Town: IDASA.

Botha, David. 1996. Group Technical Executive, Altech. Personal communication. February 6.

Brand, S. S. 1988. "Privatization: An Economist's View." *South African Journal of Economics* 56: 235–250.

Braun, Robin, and David Kaplan. 1996. Members of NTPP Technical Task Team and Oversight Committee, respectively. Personal correspondence with author. September 4 and 5.

Brown, Andy. 1998. Senior researcher, Business Map. Interview by author. Johannesburg, November 27.

Buchanan, James, and Gordon Tullock. 1962. *The Calculus of Consent: Logical Foundations of Constitutional Democracy*. Ann Arbor: University of Michigan Press.

Business Day. 1993a. "Compromise Deal on Cellular Phones." September 30.

———. 1993b. "Government 'Will Not Back Down' on Phone Licenses." September 13.

———. 1996a. "Holding the Line." February 6.

1996b. "Phone Monopoly." June 28.

1996c. "Transnet Contract Aimed to Promote Black Empowerment – Director." October 29.

1997a. "Black Consortium Is to Own 51% of City Press." May 28.

1997b. "Cellphone Industry." May 28.

1997c. "Distorting Mirror." February 24.

1997d. "SA Warned on Poor Urban Underclass." September 16.

1997e. "Telkom Uses R67M For Empowerment." July 11.

Cameron, Bruce. 1995. "Cabinet Guide to Privatisation Held Back." *Cape Times*, June 29.

1996. "Manuel Scraps Competition Law Proposals." *Cape Times*, March 20.

Cameron, Robert. 1996. "The Reconstruction and Development Programme." *Journal of Theoretical Politics* 8: 283–294.

Cape Times. 1996. "Press Freedom Not Under Threat." November 22.

Carver, Richard. 1995. "South Africa." In Article 19 and Index on Censorship, *Who Rules the Airwaves? Broadcasting in Africa.* London: author, pp. 76–98.

Castells, Manuel. 1996. *The Rise of the Network Society.* Oxford: Blackwell.

Cawson, Alan. 1986. *Corporatism and Political Theory.* London: Blackwell.

Celli, Gabriele. 1992. General Manager for Corporate Strategy, Telkom. Interview by author. Pretoria, June 8.

1995–96. Personal communications with author. December, 1995 to February, 1996.

Chalmers, Robyn. 1996. "Exclusivity Period for Telkom Limited." *Business Day*, July 10.

Chimutengwende, Chenhamo C. 1978. *South Africa: The Press and the Politics of Liberation.* London: Barbican Books.

Citizen. 1993. "Government, ANC Impasse on Cellular Phone Controversy." September 15.

1997. "SACS Not Propaganda Service: Pahad." May 16.

Clark, Brian. 1996. Chief Executive and Managing Director, Telkom. Interview by author. Cape Town, March 28.

1997. Personal communication with author. March 24.

Clark, Nancy L. 1994. *Manufacturing Apartheid: State Corporations in South Africa.* New Haven: Yale University Press.

Clarke, Jack. 1991. Chairman of the Board of Directors, Telkom. Personal communication with Libby Brydolf. Sun City, Bophuthatswana, November 3.

Clifford, A. Jerome. 1965. *The Independence of the Federal Reserve System.* Philadelphia: University of Pennsylvania Press.

Collinge, Jo-Anne. 1986. "The United Democratic Front." *South African Review II.* Johannesburg: Ravan Press, pp. 248–266.

Collins, Richard. 1993. "Public Versus the Market Ten Years On: Reflections on Critical Theory and the Debate on Broadcasting Policy in the UK." *Screen* 34: 243–259.

Commission of the European Communities. 1984. *Television without Frontiers: Green Paper on the Establishment of the Common Market for Broadcasting, Especially by Satellite and Cable.* Brussels: author.

Computing SA. 1995. "Spotlight Falls on Telkom's Ownership." December 4.

Comtask. 1996a. Analysis of the Questionnaires Sent to Ministries, Departments and Provinces. *Annexure 7.* Johannesburg: Comtask.

1996b. Report of Meeting with Departmental Liaison Forum. *Annexure 9.* Johannesburg: Comtask.

1996c. Reports of International Visits. *Annexure 4.* Johannesburg: Comtask.

1996d. Submissions to the Task Group on Government Communications. Vols. 1–6. Johannesburg: Comtask.

Congress of South African Trade Unions. 1996a. "A Draft Programme for the Alliance Presented to the EXCO." COSATU discussion paper. Johannesburg: COSATU, November 22.

1996b. Press Statement on Decisions of the Central Executive Committee. Johannesburg: COSATU, September 14.

Cooper, Carole, and Linda Ensor. 1981. *PEBCO: A Black Mass Movement.* Johannesburg: S.A. Institute of Race Relations.

Coopers & Lybrand, 1992. *Telecommunications Sector Strategy Study for the Department of Posts and Telecommunications.* Pretoria: Government Printer.

Copelyn, John. 1997. "Seizing the Moment: Union Investment Companies." *South African Labour Bulletin* 21: 74–78.

1998. Chief Executive Officer, Hosken Consolidated Investments. Interview by author. Johannesburg, December 2.

Cornelius, Wayne A. 1996. *Mexican Politics in Transition: The Breakdown of a One-Party-Dominant Regime.* La Jolla, CA: Center For US-Mexican Studies, University of California, San Diego.

Cowhey, Peter, and Jonathan Aronson. 1988. *When Countries Talk: International Trade in Telecommunications Services.* Cambridge, MA: Ballinger.

Crawhall, N. T. 1993. *Negotiations and Language Policy Options in South Africa: The National Language Project Report to the National Education Policy Investigation Sub-committee on Articulating Language Policy.* Salt River, South Africa: National Langauge Project.

Cronin, Jeremy. 1998. Deputy General Secretary, South African Communist Party. Interview by author. Johannesburg, November 25.

Crwys-Williams, Jennifer. 1994. *Penguin Dictionary of South African Quotations.* London: Penguin Books.

Curran, James, and Jean Seaton. 1985. *Power Without Responsibility: The Press and Broadcasting in Britain.* London: Methuen.

Currie, Willie. 1991. "The Control of Broadcasting: Transition Period." In *Jabulani! Freedom of the Airwaves: Towards Democratic Broadcasting in South Africa.* Conference Report. Amsterdam: African-European Institute, pp. 9–13.

1993. "The People Shall Broadcast! The Battle For the Airwaves." In P. Eric Louw, ed., *South African Media Policy: Debates of the 1990s.* Bellville, S.A.: Anthropos, pp. 41–63.

1995a. Secretary-General, Film and Allied Workers Organisation; Coordinator, National Telecommunications Policy Project. Interview by author. Johannesburg, November 21.

1995b. Interview by author. Johannesburg, November 28.

1996a. Interview by author. Johannesburg, March 8.

1996b. Interview by author. Johannesburg, May 16.

1996c. Personal communication with author. April 4.

Dahl, Robert. 1971. *Polyarchy*. New Haven: Yale University Press.

Daley, Suzanne. 1996. "Mandela's Successor Skillful but Lacks a Common Touch." *New York Times*, July 23.

Dasnois, Alide. 1995. "Telkom Not Keen on Strong Foreign Stake." *The Argus*, September 14.

Davies, Rob, Dan O'Meara, and Sipho Dlamini. 1984. *The Struggle for South Africa: A Reference Guide to Movements, Organizations and Institutions*. Two vols. London: Zed Books.

Davis, Gaye. 1996a. "Crossing Madiba Cost Jordan His Job." *Mail & Guardian*, April 4–11.

1996b. "How Cyril Was Edged Out by Thabo." *Mail & Guardian*, April 19–25.

de Beer, Arnold. 1997. "The South African Media as Conflict Generator or Facilitator in the Post-Apartheid Democratization Process." Paper to International Communications Association Meeting. Montreal, May 24.

de Klerk, Willem. 1997. Member of Comtask. Interview by author. Johannesburg, October 27.

Deloitte & Touche. 1995. "Report on the Free to Air Broadcast Industry." In Independent Broadcasting Authority, *Appendices to Triple Inquiry Report*. Johannesburg: IBA.

Democratic Party. 1996. "Democratic Party Amendments: Telecommunications Bill." Cape Town: author.

Demsetz, Harold. 1967. "Toward a Theory of Property Rights." *American Economics Review* 57: 347–359.

de Villiers, Dawid. 1983. "The State of the Press." *Leadership SA* 2: 38–48.

de Villiers, Sue. 1997. Writer, Comtask Final Report. Interview by author. Cape Town, October 29.

Dewey, John. 1954. *The Public and Its Problems*. Denver: Swallow Press.

Dexter, Phillip. 1997. "Union Investment: Towards a Political Strategy." *South African Labour Bulletin* 21: 71–73.

Di Palma, Giuseppe. 1990. *To Craft Democracies: An Essay on Democratic Transitions*. Berkeley: University of California Press.

Dison, David. 1996. Co-author of Independent Broadcasting Authority Act; member of Comtask. Interview by author. Johannesburg, February 6.

1997a. Interview by author. Johannesburg, October 24.

1997b. Personal communication with author. December 14.

Dlamini, Jacob. 1997. "Govt to Replace Communications Service." *Business Day*, May 13.

Drake, William J. 1994. "Asymmetric Deregulation and the Transformation of the International Telecommunications Regime." In Eli M. Noam and Gerard Pogerel, eds., *Asymmetric Deregulation: The Dynamics of Telecommunications Policies in Europe and the United States*. Norwood, NJ: Ablex, pp. 137–203.

Duch, Raymond M. 1991. *Privatizing the Economy: Telecommunications Policy in Comparative Perspective*. Ann Arbor: University of Michigan Press.

Duffy, Andy. 1995. "Telkom Unions Threaten to Take Industrial Action." *Cape Times*, July 25.

Duncan, Jane. 1998. Publications and Education Coordinator, Freedom of Expression Institute. Interview by author. Johannesburg, November 23.

Dyson, Kenneth, and Peter Humphreys, eds. 1990. *The Political Economy of Communications: International and European Dimensions.* London: Routledge.

Economist Intelligence Unit. 1992. *South Africa: Country Profile, 1991–92.* London: author.

1994. *Country Report: South Africa* (3rd quarter). London: author.

1997. *Country Profile 1996–97.* London: author.

1998. *Country Profile: South Africa 1997–98.* London: author.

1999. *Country Report: South Africa* (1st quarter). London: author.

Edmunds, Marion. 1997. "Concerns Grow Over 'Africanist Cabal.'" *Mail & Guardian,* May 23–29.

Efrat, Z. 1996. "New Ownership Scramble." *Natal Witness,* November 27.

Eidelberg, P. G. 2000. "The Tripartite Alliance on the Eve of a New Millennium: COSATU, the ANC and the SACP." In Glenn Adler and Eddie Webster, eds., *Trade Unions and Democratization in South Africa, 1985–1997.* London: Macmillan; New York: St. Martin's Press, pp. 129–158.

Electronics Industries Federation. 1995. Submission to Green Paper on Telecommunications Policy. Johannesburg: NTPP.

Emdon, Clive. 1993. "Postscript – Appointing a New SABC Board." In P. Eric Louw, ed., *South African Media Policy: Debates of the 1990s.* Bellville, S.A.: Anthropos, pp. 64–78.

1996. "South Africa." In Vicki MacLeod, ed., *Media Ownership and Control in the Age of Convergence.* London: International Institute of Communication, pp. 191–213.

Enloe, Cynthia. 1980. *Military and Ethnicity: Foundations of State Power.* London: Transaction Books.

Enterprise. 1997a. "Black Grassroots Empowerment, at Last." November.

1997b. "Ikageng Benefits 2 Million." November.

ESKOM. 1996. Submission to the Portfolio Committee on Communications on the Telecommunications Bill. October 15.

Evans, Peter, ed. 1997. *State-Society Synergy: Government and Social Capital in Development.* Research Series No. 94. Berkeley: International and Area Studies.

F&T Weekly. 1998. "Black Economic Empowerment." Supplement, July 24.

Fabricius, Peter. 1996. "SA Journalists Lack Training, Says Mbeki." *Star,* July 25.

Fanaroff, Bernie. 1993a. National Secretary of Organising Department, National Union of Metalworkers South Africa. Interview by author. Johannesburg, August 31.

1993b. "The Role of Telecommunications in Economic Growth: Projects for Southern Africa." Paper to the Telecommunications Regulatory Symposium, sponsored by the Centre for the Development of Information and Telecommunications Policy (CDITP). Johannesburg, July 28–30.

Federation for African Business and Consumer Services (FABCOS). 1996. Submission to the Portfolio Committee on Communications on the Telecommunication Bill. October 15.

Film and Television Federation. 1994. Submission on Local Television Content and Independent Production. IBA Triple Inquiry.

Finance Week. 1993. "Dial for Fair Play." January 21–27.

1994. "Mandela on the Record: What the SA Business Community Can Expect of and from the ANC." March 31.

Financial Mail. 1986. "Posts and Telecommunications." Survey Supplement. October 3.

1990. "Privatisation: No Stomach for the Fight." April 13.

1992. "Holding the Airwaves Hostage." June 12.

1993a. "Networking Pays Off." June 25.

1993b. "Squeezing the Cellular-Phone Industry." April 16.

1995a. "Green Light for National Debate." October 6.

1995b. "Ringing the Changes." September 8.

1995c. "Strategic Partner in the Wings?" November 10.

1996a. "Blows to Privatisation." April 19. <http://www.fm.co.za>

1996b. "Jay's Game of Cloak and Daggers." July 5.

1996c. "Naidoo's Sleight-of-Hand." June 21.

1996d. "Protecting a Monopoly Compounds the Problem." July 5.

1996e. "Soaking the Customers." September 6.

1996f. "Telkom Bids: Sound as a Bell," November 8.

Finnegan, William. 1988. *Dateline Soweto: Travels with Black South African Reporters.* New York: Harper & Row.

Fleming Martin, Ltd. 1995. "Telkom Investment Report." Johannesburg: author.

Forrest, Drew. 1997. "Ministers in 'Racial Rift' over Top Job." *Business Day,* October 27.

Foster, C. C. 1992. *Privatization, Public Ownership and the Regulation of Natural Monopoly.* Oxford: Blackwell.

Frankel, Philip. 1980. "Race and Counter-Revolution: South Africa's Total Strategy." *Journal of Commonwealth and Comparative Politics* 18: 272–292.

Frankel, Philip, Noam Pines, and Mark Swilling, eds. 1988. *State, Resistance and Change in South Africa.* London: Croom Helm.

Frankel, S. Herbert. 1938. *Capital Investment in Africa: Its Course and Effects.* London: Oxford University Press.

Frederikse, Julie. 1990. *The Unbreakable Thread: Non-Racialism in South Africa.* London: Zed Books.

Fredrickson, George M. 1995. *Black Liberation: A Comparative History of Black Ideologies in the United States and South Africa.* New York: Oxford University Press.

1997. *The Comparative Imagination: On the History of Racism, Nationalism, and Social Movements.* Berkeley: University of California Press.

Free, Fair and Open. 1992. "Submission to Codesa, Working Group 1" (dated February 5, 1992). In P. Eric Louw, ed., *South African Media Policy: Debates of the 1990s.* Bellville, S.A.: Anthropos, pp. 316–328.

Freedom of Expression Institute. 1998. "Response to Broadcasting Bill, 1998." Johannesburg: author.

Freund, Bill, and Vishnu Padayachee. 1998. "Post-Apartheid South Africa: The Key Patterns Emerge." *Economic and Political Weekly,* May 16, pp. 1173–1180.

Friedman, Steven. 1987. *Building Tomorrow Today: African Workers in Trade Unions, 1970–1984.* Johannesburg: Ravan Press.

Friedman, Steven, ed. 1993. *The Long Journey: South Africa's Quest for a Negotiated Settlement.* Johannesburg: Ravan Press.

Friedman, Steven, and Maxine Reitzes. 1995. "Democratic Selections? Civil Society and Development in South Africa's New Democracy." Development Paper 75. Halfway House, South Africa: Development Bank of Southern Africa.

Gagiano, J. I. K. 1986. "Meanwhile Back on the 'Boereplaas'." *Politikon* 13: 3–21.

Gans, Herbert. 1979. *Deciding What's News.* New York: Pantheon.

Garnham, Nicholas. 1986. "The Media and the Public Sphere." In Peter Golding et al., eds., *Communicating Politics.* Leicester: Leicester University Press, pp. 37–55.

Gelb, Stephen. 1991. "South Africa's Economic Crisis: An Overview." In Stephen Gelb, ed., *South Africa's Economic Crisis.* Cape Town: David Philip, pp. 1–31.

1998a. Senior Economist, Development Bank of Southern Africa. Interview by author. Midrand, December 2.

1998b. "The Politics of Macroeconomic Reform in South Africa." Paper presented to the conference on Democracy and the Political Economy of Reform. Cape Town, January 16–18.

General Agreement on Trade and Tariffs. 1994. *Final Act Embodying the Results of the Uruguay Round of Multilateral Trade Negotiations: Legal Instruments Embodying the Results of the Uruguay Round of Multilateral Trade Negotiations.* 33 I.L.M. 1140. April 15.

Gevisser, Mark. 1994. "Tension at SABC over 'Weak' TV Proposal." *Weekly Mail & Guardian,* October 21–27.

1997. "Ending Economic Apartheid." *The Nation,* September 29.

Ghosh, P. K., ed. 1984. *Energy Policy and Third World Development.* Westport, CT: Greenwood Press.

Giddens, Anthony. 1994. *Beyond Left and Right: The Future of Radical Politics.* Stanford: Stanford University Press.

Giliomee, Hermann. 1979a. "Afrikaner Politics: How the System Works." In Heribert Adam and Hermann Giliomee, *Ethnic Power Mobilized: Can South Africa Change?* New Haven: Yale University Press, pp. 196–257.

1979b. "The Afrikaner Economic Advance." In Heribert Adam and Hermann Giliomee. *Ethnic Power Mobilized: Can South Africa Change?* New Haven: Yale University Press, pp. 145–176.

1982. *The Parting of the Ways: South African Politics, 1976–82.* Cape Town: David Philip.

1992. "Intra-Afrikaner Conflicts in the Transition from Apartheid." *African Affairs* 91: 339–364.

Giliomee, Hermann, and Johannes Rantete. 1992. "Transition to Democracy Through Transaction? Bilateral Negotiations Between the ANC and the NP in South Africa." *African Affairs* 91: 515–542.

Giliomee, Hermann, and Lawrence Schlemmer. 1989. *From Apartheid to Nation-Building.* Cape Town: Oxford University Press.

Giliomee, Hermann, and Lawrence Schlemmer, eds. 1994. *The Bold Experiment: South Africa's New Democracy.* Halfway House: Southern Book Publishers.

Gillwald, Alison. 1996. Manager of Policy Development, Independent Broadcasting Authority. Interview by author. Johannesburg, March 6.

Ginsburg, David. 1996. "The Democratisation of South Africa: Transition Theory Tested." *Transformation* 29: 74–102.

Ginsburg, David, Eddie Webster, et al. 1995. *Taking Democracy Seriously: Worker Expectations and Parliamentary Democracy in South Africa.* Durban: Indicator Press.

Gitlin, Todd. 1983. *Inside Prime Time.* New York: Pantheon.

Glaser, Daryl. 1997. "South Africa and the Limits of Civil Society." *Journal of Southern African Studies* 23: 5–25.

Gleason, David. 1997. "Joining the March Abroad." *Finance Week,* July 10–16.

Golding, Marcel. 1997. "Pioneers or Sell-Outs? Exploring New Lands." *South African Labour Bulletin* 21. June, pp. 85–90.

Golding-Duffy, Jacquie. 1996. "Papers Lose Faith in NP." *Mail & Guardian,* May 24–30. 1997. "Argus 'Mea Culpa' Row." *Mail & Guardian,* March 7–13.

Götz, Graeme A. 2000. "Shoot Anything That Flies, Claim Anything That Falls: Labour and the Changing Definition of the Reconstruction and Development Programme." In Glenn Adler and Eddie Webster, eds., *Trade Unions and Democratization in South Africa, 1985–1997.* London: Macmillan; New York: St. Martin's Press, pp. 159–189.

Gramsci, Antonio. 1971. *Selections from the Prison Notebooks of Antonio Gramsci.* Quinton Hoare and Geoffrey Nowell Smith, eds. New York: International Publishers.

Green, Pippa. 1997. Political Editor, *Sunday Independent.* Interview by author. Johannesburg, October 22.

Greenberg, Stanley B. 1980. *Race and State in Capitalist Development: Comparative Perspectives.* New Haven: Yale University Press.

1987. "Ideological Struggles within the South African State." In Shula Marks and Stanley Trapido, eds., *The Politics of Race, Class and Nationalism in Twentieth-Century South Africa.* London: Longman, pp. 389–417.

Grest, Jeremy, and Heather Hughes. 1984. "State Strategy and Popular Response at the Local Level." *South African Review II.* Johannesburg: Ravan Press, pp. 45–62.

Group of Thirteen. 1994a. "The Group of Thirteen Organisations Oral Representations and Expert Evidence to the IBA Triple Inquiry." Johannesburg: author.

1994b. "The Joint Submission to the Independent Broadcasting Authority's Inquiry into the Protection and Viability of Public Broadcasting Services in a Democratic South Africa." Submission to IBA Triple Inquiry. Johannesburg: author.

Gumede, William. 1997. "SANCO, Struggling to Find a Role, Should Change from Being ANC Lapdog to a Watchdog." *Star,* May 10.

Habermas, Jürgen. 1996. *Between Facts and Norms: Contributions to a Discourse Theory of Law and Democracy.* William Rehg, trans. Cambridge, MA: MIT Press.

Hadland, Adrian. 1995. "Privatisation Initiative Backed by ANC Body." *Sunday Independent,* December 10.

Haffajee, Ferial. 1992. "Stamp of Approval for Post Office Changes." *Weekly Mail,* January 10–16.

1997. "Union Investment Pays Off." *Mail & Guardian,* May 23–29.

1998a. "Pityana's Probe Anathema to Media." *Mail & Guardian,* November 20–26.

1998b. "Replicating the Rot." *Mail & Guardian,* August 28–September.

Haggard, Stephan, and Robert R. Kaufman. 1995. *The Political Economy of Democratic Transitions*. Princeton: Princeton University Press.

Haggard, Stephan, and Robert R. Kaufman, eds. 1992. *The Politics of Economic Adjustment: International Constraints, Distributive Conflicts, and the State*. Princeton: Princeton University Press.

Hainebach, Geoff. 1993. Joint Managing Director, Siemens Ltd. Interview by author. Johannesburg, September 6.

Hall, Stuart. 1980. "Encoding/Decoding." In Stuart Hall et al., eds., *Culture, Media, Language: Working Papers in Cultural Studies, 1972–79*. London: Hutchinson, pp. 129–138.

Hamilton, Carolyn, ed. 1995. *The Mfecane Aftermath: Reconstructive Debates in Southern African History*. Johannesburg and Pietermaritzburg: University of Witwatersrand and University of Natal Presses.

Harber, Anton. 1997. Editor, *Mail & Guardian*. Interview by author. Johannesburg, October 21.

Harris, Lance. 1995. "The Year in Review: Change Growth and Innovation in 1995." *Computing SA*, December 4.

Hartley, Ray. 1996. "Who's in Charge, Anyway?" *Sunday Times*, June 2.

Hartyani, Karl. 1992. Senior Executive, Telephone Manufacturers of South Africa. Interview by author. Johannesburg, July 23.

Hachten, William A., and C. Anthony Giffard. 1984. *The Press and Apartheid: Repression and Propaganda in South Africa*. Madison: University of Wisconsin Press.

Hayek, Friedrich von. 1935. "The Nature and History of the Problem." In F. A. Hayek, ed., *Collectivist Economic Planning*. London: Routledge & Kegan Paul, pp. 1–40.

1940. "Socialist Calculation: The Competitive 'Solution.'" *Economica* 7: 125–149.

1960. *The Constitution of Liberty*. London: Routledge.

Hayman, Graham, and Ruth Tomaselli. 1989. "Ideology and Technology in the Growth of South African Broadcasting, 1924–1971." In Ruth Tomaselli, Keyan Tomaselli, and Johan Muller, eds., *Currents of Power: State Broadcasting in South Africa*. Bellville, S.A.: Anthropos, pp. 28–83.

Heard, Anthony Hazlitt. 1992. "The Struggle for Free Expression in South Africa." In Larry Diamond, ed., *The Democratic Revolution: Struggles for Freedom and Pluralism in the Developing World*. New York: Freedom House, pp. 167–180.

Hepple, Alex. 1960. *Censorship and Press Control in South Africa*. Johannesburg: self-published.

1974. *Press Under Apartheid*. London: International Defence and Aid Fund.

Herbst, Jeffrey. 1994. "South Africa: Economic Crises and Distributional Imperative." In Stephen John Stedman, ed., *South Africa: The Political Economy of Transformation*. Boulder, CO: Lynne Rienner, pp. 29–46.

1997–98. "Prospects for Elite-Driven Democracy in South Africa." *Political Science Quarterly* 112: 595–615.

Herman, Edward S., and Robert W. McChesney. 1997. *The Global Media: The New Missionaries of Corporate Capitalism*. London: Cassell.

Hills, Jill. 1993. "Back to the Future: Britain's 19th Century Telecommunications Policy." *Telecommunications Policy* 17: 186–199.

Hobsbawm, Eric, and Terence Ranger, eds. 1983. *The Invention of Tradition*. Cambridge, U.K.: Cambridge University Press.

Hofmeyr, Isabel. 1987. "Building a Nation from Words: Afrikaans Language, Literature and Ethnic Identity, 1902–1924." In Shula Marks and Stanley Trapido, eds., *The Politics of Race, Class and Nationalism in Twentieth Century South Africa*. London: Longman, pp. 95–123.

Horowitz, Donald. 1991. *A Democratic South Africa?: Constitutional Engineering in a Divided Society*. Berkeley: University of California Press.

Horrigan, John. 1998. Review of Milton Mueller, "Universal Service: Competition, Interconnection, and Monopoly in the Making of the American Telephone System." *Journal of Policy Analysis and Management* 17: 564–568.

Horwitz, Robert B. 1989. *The Irony of Regulatory Reform: The Deregulation of American Telecommunications*. New York: Oxford University Press.

———. 1991. "The First Amendment Meets Some New Technologies: Broadcasting, Common Carriers, and Free Speech in the 1990s." *Theory and Society* 20: 21–72.

———. 1994a. "Apartheid, Its Demise and Electricity: The Development of the Institutional and Regulatory Structure of the South African Electricity Industry." Energy for Development Research Centre Working Papers, No. 14c. Cape Town: EDRC.

———. 1994b. "Judicial Review of Regulatory Decisions: The Changing Criteria." *Political Science Quarterly* 109: 133–169.

Howe, G., and Pieter le Roux, eds. 1992. *Transforming the Economy: Policy Options for South Africa*. Bellville: Indicator Project South Africa and Institute for Social Development.

Hoynes, William. 1994. *Public Television for Sale: Media, the Market, and the Public Sphere*. Boulder: Westview Press.

Hundt, Reed, Larry Irving, Jeffrey M. Lang, and Vonya B. McCann. No date. "Comments on Green Paper." Submission to Green Paper on Telecommunications Policy. Johannesburg: NTPP.

Huntington, Samuel P. 1991. *The Third Wave: Democratization in the Late Twentieth Century*. Norman: University of Oklahoma Press.

Hutt, W. H. 1964. *The Economics of the Colour Bar: A Study of the Economic Origins and Consequences of Racial Segregation in South Africa*. London: Institute of Economic Affairs.

Ibrahim, Anwar. 1996. *The Asian Renaissance*. Singapore: Times Books International.

Ilima Community Development Company. 1996. Submission to Parliamentary Portfolio Committee on Communications on the Telecommunications Bill. October 15.

Independent Media Diversity Trust. 1996. Submission to Comtask. *Presentations*. Vol. I. Johannesburg: Comtask.

Independent Newspapers. 1996. Submission to Comtask. *Submissions*. Vol. 4. Johannesburg: Comtask.

Information Technology Association. 1996. Submission to the Portfolio Committee on Communications on the Telecommunications Bill. October 15.

Innes, Duncan. 1984. *Anglo-American and the Rise of Modern South Africa*. London: Heinemann Educational Books.

International Telecommunications Union. 1992. *Yearbook of Common Carrier Telecommunication Statistics*. 19th ed. Geneva: ITU.

1994. *African Telecommunication Indicators, 1994.* Geneva: ITU.

Internet Service Providers Association. 1996. Submission to the Portfolio Committee on Communications on the Telecommunications Bill. October 21.

Jabulani! Freedom of the Airwaves: Towards Democratic Broadcasting in South Africa. 1991. Conference Report. Amsterdam: African-European Institute.

Jackson, Gordon S. 1993. *Breaking Story: The South African Press.* Boulder: Westview Press.

Jacobs, Sean. 1999. "Tensions of a Free Press: South Africa after Apartheid." Research Paper R-22. Cambridge, MA: The Joan Shorenstein Center of Press, Politics, and Public Policy, Harvard University.

Jakubowicz, Karol. 1990. "Solidarity and Media Reform in Poland." *European Journal of Communication* 5: 333–353.

Janisch, Hudson N., and Danny M. Kotlowitz. 1998. "African Renaissance, Market Romance." Paper to Symposium of Columbia University Institute of Tele-Information. New York, June 12.

Jansen, Sue Curry. 1988. *Censorship: The Knot That Binds Power and Knowledge.* New York: Oxford University Press.

Joffe, Avril, David Kaplan, Raphael Kaplinsky, and David Lewis, eds. 1995. *Improving Manufacturing Performance in South Africa: The Report of the Industrial Strategy Project.* Cape Town: University of Cape Town Press.

Johnson, Anthony. 1996. "Power Shifts in Cabinet." *Cape Times,* April 3.

Johnson, Shaun. 1991. "An Historical Overview of the Black Press." In Keyan Tomaselli and P. Eric Louw, eds., *The Alternative Press in South Africa.* Bellville, S.A.: Anthropos, pp. 13–32.

Jones, J. D. F. 1995. *Through Fortress and Rock: The Story of Gencor, 1895–1995.* Johannesburg: Jonathan Ball.

Jordan, Z. Pallo. 1985. "Monopoly Capitalism, Racism and Mass Media in South Africa." *Sechaba.* May, pp. 2–9.

1992. "Strategic Debate in the ANC: A Response to Joe Slovo." *The African Communist* 131: 7–15.

1995a. Minister of Posts, Telecommunications and Broadcasting. Interview by author. Magaliesburg, S.A., November 23.

1995b. "Minister Z. Pallo Jordan's Remarks to the Portfolio Committee on Communications on the IBA Report on the Future of Public Broadcasting Services." August 29.

1995c. Opening Remarks at National Colloquium on Telecommunications Policy. Magaliesburg, S.A., November 21.

1997. "The National Question in Post 1994 South Africa" (Discussion paper in preparation for the ANC's 50th National conference). <www.anc.org.za/ancdocs/discussion/natquestion.html>

Jung, Courtney, and Ian Shapiro. 1995. "South Africa's Negotiated Transition: Democracy, Opposition, and the New Constitutional Order." *Politics and Society* 23: 269–308.

Kahler, Miles. 1986. *The Politics of International Debt.* Ithaca: Cornell University Press.

1992. "External Influence, Conditionality, and the Politics of Adjustment." In Stephan Haggard and Robert R. Kaufman, eds., *The Politics of Economic Adjustment:*

International Constraints, Distributive Conflicts, and the State. Princeton: Princeton University Press, pp. 89–136.

Kahn, Alfred E. 1988. *The Economics of Regulation: Principles and Institutions.* Vol. II. Cambridge, MA: MIT Press.

Kahn, Ellison. 1959. "Public Corporations in South Africa: A Survey." *South African Journal of Economics* 27: 279–292.

Kaniss, Phyllis. 1991. *Making Local News.* Chicago: University of Chicago Press.

Kaplan, David. 1990. *The Crossed Line: South African Telecommunications Industry in Transition.* Johannesburg: Witwatersrand University Press.

  1992. "The Development of Telecommunications in South Africa: The Equipment Supply Industry." *Critical Arts* 6: 96–107.

  1999. "Out of South Africa: South Africa's Telecommunications Equipment Industry." In Eli M. Noam, ed., *Telecommunications in Africa.* New York: Oxford University Press, pp. 193–204.

Katz, Elihu, and Paul F. Lazarsfeld. 1955. *Personal Influence: The Part Played by People in the Flow of Mass Communications.* Glencoe, Il.: Free Press.

Keane, John. 1991. *The Media and Democracy.* Cambridge, U.K.: Polity Press.

Kevin Harris Productions. 1996. "Twenty Years of the SABC." Broadcast on NNTV, February 2.

Klok, J. C. 1996. Senior Manager of Communication Policy, Department of Posts & Telecommunications. Personal communication with author. April 3.

  1997. Interview by author. Johannesburg, October 27.

KMM Investments. 1996. Submission to Comtask. *Annexure 18.* Johannesburg: Comtask.

Knott-Craig, Alan, and Alwyn Hanekom. 1990. *Report on the Deregulation of Telematics in South Africa.* Pretoria: SAPT.

Koch, Eddie. 1997. "From Shop Floor to Trading Floor." *Mail & Guardian,* May 16–22.

Kornai, Janos. 1992. *The Socialist System: The Political Economy of Communism.* Princeton: Princeton University Press.

Kotane, Solomon. 1997. Director-General, South African Communication Service. Interview by author. Pretoria, October 23.

Krueger, Anne O. 1993. *Political Economy of Policy Reform in Developing Countries.* Cambridge, MA: MIT Press.

Kymlicka, Will, and Wayne Norman. 1994. "Return of the Citizen: A Survey of Recent Work." *Ethics* 104: 352–381.

Lachenicht, M. K. 1991. "ISDN and Centrex for South Africa." In *Proceedings of the Fifth National Conference on Telecommunications in South Africa.* Pretoria: Telkom, November 4–6.

LaPalombara, Joseph. 1963. *Interest Groups in Italian Politics.* Princeton: Princeton University Press.

  1974. *Politics Within Nations.* Englewood Cliffs, NJ: Prentice-Hall.

Laufer, Stephen. 1996a. "Private Complaint Led to Special Probe." *Business Day,* September 30.

  1996b. Submission to Comtask. *Presentations.* Vol. I. Johannesburg: Comtask.

  1997. "Communications Revamp Speeds Up." *Business Day,* March 10.

Laufer, Stephen, Alan Fine, and Drew Forrest. 1996. "Ramaphosa's Move Ends the ANC's Age of Innocence." *Business Day,* April 19.

Lazarsfeld, Paul F., and Robert K. Merton. 1948. "Mass Communication, Popular Taste and Organized Social Action." In Lyman Bryson, ed., *The Communication of Ideas.* New York: Harper, pp. 95–118.

Le Duc, Don R. 1987. *Beyond Broadcasting: Patterns in Policy and Law.* New York: Longman.

Learn and Teach Publications Trust. 1996. Submssion to Comtask. *Submissions.* Vol. 6. Johannesburg: Comtask, pp. 511–524.

Legassick, Martin. 1998. "Myth and Reality in the Struggle Against Apartheid." *Journal of Southern African Studies* 24: 443–458.

Lerner, Daniel. 1958. *The Passing of Traditional Society: Modernizing the Middle East.* Glencoe, IL: Free Press.

Leshilo, Thabo. 1995. "COSATU Intensifies Anti-Privatisation Call." *Cape Times,* December 15.

Levi, Margaret. 1988. *Of Rule and Revenue.* Berkeley: University of California Press.

Lewis, David. 1995. "Markets, Ownership and Manufacturing Performance." In Avril Joffe, David Kaplan, Raphael Kaplinsky, and David Lewis, eds., *Improving Manufacturing Performance in South Africa: The Report of the Industrial Strategy Project.* Cape Town: UCT Press, pp. 133–185.

Lewis, Jr., Stephen R. 1990. *The Economics of Apartheid.* New York: Council on Foreign Relations Press.

Lijphart, Arend. 1977. *Democracy in Plural Societies: A Comparative Exploration.* New Haven, CT: Yale University Press.

1985. *Power-Sharing in South Africa.* Berkeley: Institute of International Studies.

Linz, Juan J., and Alfred Stepan. 1996. *Problems of Democratic Transition and Consolidation: Southern Europe, South America, and Post-Communist Europe.* Baltimore: Johns Hopkins University Press.

Lipset, Seymour Martin. 1960. *Political Man: The Social Bases of Politics.* New York: Doubleday.

Lodge, Tom. 1983. *Black Politics in South Africa Since 1945.* London: Longman.

1992. "The African National Congress in the 1990s." In Glenn Moss and Ingrid Obery, eds., *South African Review 6: From "Red Friday" to Codesa.* Johannesburg: Ravan Press, pp. 44–78.

1996. "South Africa: A Post-apartheid Society." In Adrian Leftwich, ed., *Democracy and Development: Theory and Practice.* Cambridge, U.K.: Polity Press, pp. 188–208.

Lodge, Tom, Bill Nasson, Steven Mufson, Khehla Shubane, and Nokwanda Sithole. 1991. *All, Here, and Now: Black Politics in South Africa in the 1980s.* Cape Town: David Philip.

Louw, P. Eric. 1989. "Rejoinder to 'Opposing Apartheid': Building a South African Democracy Through a Popular Alliance Which Includes Leninists." *Theoria* 73: 49–62.

1993. "The Growth of Monopoly Control of the South Africa Press." In P. Eric Louw, ed., *South African Media Policy: Debates of the 1990s.* Bellville, S.A.: Anthropos, pp. 159–180.

1994. "Shifting Patterns of Political Discourse in the New South Africa." *Critical Studies in Mass Communication* 11: 22–53.

Louw, Raymond. 1997. Editor, *Rand Daily Mail*; Member of Comtask. Interview by author. Johannesburg, October 21.

Ludski, Henry. 1996. "'Skewed Political Coverage Needs Balancing Out.'" *Cape Times*, June 21.

Lunsche, Sven. 1996a. "New Twist in Telkom's Saga." *Sunday Times*, June 30.

1996b. "Privatisation Bogeyman Over-Inflated." *Sunday Times*, February 25.

MacDonald, Michael. 1996. "Power Politics in the New South Africa." *Journal of Southern African Studies* 22: 221–233.

Mackie, Sandy. 1996. Submission to Comtask. *Presentations*. Vol. II. Johannesburg: Comtask.

Macro Economic Research Group. 1993. *Making Democracy Work*. Bellville, S.A.: Centre for Development Studies and Oxford University Press.

MacShane, Denis, Martin Plaut, and David Ward. 1984. *Power! Black Workers, Their Unions and the Struggle for Freedom in South Africa*. Nottingham, U.K.: Spokesman.

Macun, Ian. 2000. "Growth, Structure and Power in the South African Union Movement." In Glenn Adler and Eddie Webster, eds., *Trade Unions and Democratization in South Africa, 1985–1997*. London: Macmillan; New York: St. Martin's Press, pp. 57–74.

Magnusson, Ake. 1976. "The Voice of South Africa." Research Report No. 35. Uppsala: Scandinavian Institute of African Studies.

Mail & Guardian. 1997. "Forget the Fantasy, Thabo." February 28.

Makgetla, Neva Seidman. 1995a. "The New Privatisation Debate." Johannesburg: NALEDI.

1995b. "The New Privatisation Debate." *South African Labour Bulletin* 19: 65–73.

Makhanya, Mondli. 1993. "Playing Broken Telephones." *The Weekly Mail & Guardian*, September 17–23.

Mamdani, Mahmood. 1996. *Citizen and Subject: Contemporary Africa and the Legacy of Late Colonialism*. Princeton: Princeton University Press.

1997. "Now Who Will Bell the Fat Black Cat?" *Mail & Guardian*, October 17–23.

Mandela, Nelson. 1990. Address to South African Business Executives. Johannesburg, May 23. <www.anc.org.za/ancdocs/speeches/1990/sp900523.html>

1991. "Statement to President P. W. Botha." In Sheridan Johns and R. Hunt Davis, eds., *Mandela, Tambo and the African National Congress*. New York: Oxford University Press, pp. 216–225.

1994a. Address to the International Press Institute Congress. Cape Town, February 14. <www.anc.org.za/ancdocs/history/mandela/1994/sp940214.html>

1994b. *Long Walk to Freedom*. Boston: Little, Brown.

1997. "Report by the President of the ANC, Nelson Mandela, to the 50th National Conference of the African National Congress." Mafikeng, S.A., December 16. <www.anc.org.za/ancdocs/history/conf/conference50/presaddress.html>

Mann, Michael. 1988. "The Giant Stirs: South African Business in the Age of Reform." In Philip Frankel et al., eds., *State, Resistance and Change in South Africa*. London: Croom Helm, pp. 52–86.

Manoim, Irwin. 1996. *You Have Been Warned: The First Ten Years of the Mail & Guardian*. London: Viking.

Marais, Hein. 1998. *South Africa, Limits to Change: The Political Economy of Transition*. London: Zed Books; Cape Town: University of Cape Town Press.

Marcus, Gilbert. 1984. "Blacks Treated More Severely." *Index on Censorship* 13: 14–21.

Maré, Gerhard. 1993. *Ethnicity and Politics in South Africa*. London: Zed Books.

Maree, Johann. 1985. "The Emergence, Struggles and Achievements of Black Trade Unions in South Africa from 1973 to 1984." *Labour, Capital and Society* 18: 278–303.

Markovitz, Michael. 1992. Presentation at POTWA Communications Workshop. Johannesburg, July 10.

——— 1996. Co-author, Independent Broadcasting Authority Act. Interview by author. Johannesburg. March 8.

Marlowe, John. 1976. *Milner: Apostle of Empire*. London: Hamilton.

Marx, Anthony W. 1992. *Lessons of Struggle: South African Internal Opposition, 1960–1990*. New York: Oxford University Press.

Mass Development Movement. 1996. Submission to the Portfolio Committee on Communications on the Telecommunications Bill. October 15.

Matisonn, John. 1996. Councillor, Independent Broadcasting Authority. Interview by author. Johannesburg, January 23.

——— 1998. "Making a 'Mixed' Media Work." *Mail & Guardian*, November 27–December 3.

Mayibuye. 1991. "A War of Perceptions." June, pp. 40–41.

Mazwai, Thami. 1996. Address to Conference on Government Communications. Arniston, S.A., no date.

——— 1997a. "Public's Right to Know Hides Racist Hypocrisy." *Business Day*, August 1.

——— 1997b. Publisher of *Enterprise*. Interview by author. Johannesburg, October 24.

Mazwai, Thami, et al. 1991. *Mau-Mauing the Media: New Censorship for the New South Africa*. Johannesburg: SAIRR.

Mbeki, Govan. 1996. *Sunset at Midday: Latshon 'ilang 'emini!* Braamfontein: Nolwazi Educational Publishers.

Mbeki, Moeletsi. 1995. "ANC Did Not Aid and Abet O'Reilly." *Mail & Guardian*, December 8–14.

Mbeki, T. M. 1994. "Statement by the acting President." Cape Town: Deputy President's Office, October 29.

——— 1997a. Address by Deputy President TM Mbeki at the Launch of the Forum of Black Journalists. January 24. <www.anc.org.za/ancdocs/history/mbeki/1997/sp970124.html>

——— 1997b. Speech to Tel.Com 97 Conference. Gallagher Estates, Midrand, S.A., March 25.

——— 1998a. "The African Renaissance Statement." Speech to SABC. August 13. <www.anc.org.za/ancdocs/history/mbeki/1998/tm0813.html>

——— 1998b. "The African Renaissance, South Africa and the World." Speech at the United Nations University. April 9. <www.anc.org.za/ancdocs/history/mbeki/1998/sp980409.html>

McCarthy, Jeff, and Mark Swilling. 1984. "Transport and Political Resistance: Bus Boycotts of 1983." *South African Review II*. Johannesburg: Ravan Press, pp. 26–44.

McGregor, Robin. 1996a. "Addendum to 'Control of the Media' Report." Submission to Comtask. Johannesburg: Comtask. May 13.

——— 1996b. "Control of the Media." Submission to Comtask. *Annexure 3*. Johannesburg: Comtask.

1996c. Supplemental letter on media ownership to Comtask. Johannesburg: Comtask, July.

1996d. "The Distribution of Publications." Submission to Comtask. Johannesburg: Comtask, June 28.

1997. Publisher, *Who Owns Whom in South Africa.* Interview by author. Johannesburg, October 21.

McGregor's Who Owns Whom in South Africa: Listed and Unlisted Companies. Various years. Aukland Park, S.A.: McGregor Publishing.

McKinley, Dale T. 1997. "Rethinking Union Investment Strategy." South African Communist Party, unpublished paper.

McNeil, Jr., Donald G. 1999. "South Africa Blacks Lose Control of Black Empowerment Company." *New York Times,* August 6.

McQuail, Dennis. 1987. *Mass Communication Theory: An Introduction.* London: Sage.

Media Liaison Officers Forum. 1996. Submission to Comtask. *Annexure 8.* Johannesburg: Comtask.

Media Monitoring Project. 1996. "Communicating Government: Government Coverage in the Media, 1 April 1996–23 June 1996." Submission to Comtask. *Annexure 2.* Johannesburg: Comtask.

1998. "Update." Johannesburg, February 16.

Merrett, Christopher. 1994. *A Culture of Censorship: Secrecy and Intellectual Repression in South Africa.* Cape Town: David Philip.

Merton, Robert K. 1967. *On Theoretical Sociology: Five Essays, Old and New.* New York: Free Press.

Mjwara, Joe. 1997. Special Adviser, Ministry of Communications. Interview by author. Pretoria, October 27.

Mody, Bella, Johannes M. Bauer, and Joseph D. Straubhaar, eds. 1995. *Telecommunication Politics: Ownership and Control of the Information Highway in Developing Countries.* Mahwah, NJ: Lawrence Erlbaum.

Moeti, Sam. 1997. Chairperson, Parliamentary Portfolio Committee on Communications. Interview by author. Cape Town, October 29.

Moholi, Nombulelo. 1996. Telkom Group Executive, Regulatory Affairs. Personal communication with author. June 12.

1997. Interview by author. Midrand, S.A., March 25.

Mokaba, Peter. 1997. "On Leadership" (Discussion paper in preparation for the ANC's 50th National conference). August 18.

Molusi, Connie. 1996a. Letter to the editor. *Mail & Guardian,* July 12–18.

1996b. Letter to the editor. *Sunday Times,* July 7.

Monyokolo, Ramateu. 1996. President, Post & Telecommunications Workers Association. Presentation at POTWA Workshop. Johannesburg, March 7.

1997. Interview by author. Johannesburg, October 24.

Mouffe, Chantal. 1992. "Democratic Citizenship and Political Community." In Chantal Mouffe, ed., *Dimensions of Radical Democracy: Pluralism, Citizenship, Community.* London: Verso, pp. 225–239.

1993. *The Return of the Political.* London: Verso.

MTN. 1996. Submission to the Portfolio Committee on Communications on the Telecommunication Bill. October 16.

Mueller, Jr., Milton L. 1997. *Universal Service: Competition, Interconnection, and Monopoly in the Making of the American Telephone System.* Cambridge, MA: MIT Press and Washington, DC: AEI Press.

Mufson, Steve. 1990. *Fighting Years: Black Resistance and the Struggle for a New South Africa.* Boston: Beacon Press.

Muller, Johan. 1987. "Press Houses at War: A Brief History of Nasionale Pers and Perskor." In Keyan Tomaselli, Ruth Tomaselli, and Johan Muller, eds., *The Press in South Africa.* Bellville, S.A.: Anthropos, pp. 118–140.

Muller, Ruth. 1996. Submission to Comtask. *Submissions.* Vol. 3. Johannesburg: Comtask, pp. 255–263.

1998. South African Union of Journalists representative to Green Paper on Broadcasting Policy Stakeholders Committee. Interview by author. Johannesburg, November 24.

Murdock, Graham. 1990. "Television and Citizenship: In Defence of Public Broadcasting." In Alan Tomlinson, ed., *Consumption, Identity, and Style: Marketing, Meanings, and the Packaging of Pleasure.* London: Routledge, pp. 77–101.

Murdock, Graham, and Peter Golding. 1989. "Information Poverty and Political Inequity: Citizenship in the Age of Privatized Communications." *Journal of Communication* 3: 180–195.

Murphy, Dean E. 1999. "Unfinished Revolution: South Africa after Apartheid." *Los Angeles Times.* May 26.

Naidoo, Jay. 1996. Address to Telecommunications and Broadcasting: Reaching the People Conference. University of Pretoria Law School, May 30–31.

1997. Minister of Posts, Telecommunications & Broadcasting. Interview by author. Gallagher Estates, Midrand, S.A.: March 24.

Naidoo, Prakash. 1997. "How the SABC's Efforts to Fulfil Its New Role Drove It into the Red." *Sunday Independent,* March 30.

Naidoo, Ravi. 1997. "Unions and Investments: Preliminary Assessment and Framework Development." Johannesburg: National Labour & Economic Development Institute, June.

National Community Media Forum. 1996. Submission to Comtask. *Annexure 12.* Johannesburg: Comtask.

National Community Radio Forum. 1996. Submission to Comtask. *Submissions.* Vol. 6. Johannesburg: Comtask, pp. 525.

National Information Technology Forum. 1996. Submission to Comtask. *Presentations.* Vol. V. Johannesburg: Comtask.

National Party. 1992. "Position Paper on the Regulation of the Electronic Media." Presented to Codesa Working Group 1, March 2. In P. Eric Louw, ed., 1993. *South African Media Policy: Debates of the 1990s.* Bellville, S.A.: Athropos, pp. 341–345.

National Telecommunications Co-Ordinating Group. 1996. Submission to the Portfolio Committee on Communications on the Telecommunication Bill. October 23.

National Telecommunications Forum. 1994. Proceedings of First Plenary Meeting. Johannesburg: author.

National Telecommunications Users Group. 1996. Submission to the Portfolio Committee on Communications on the Telecommunication Bill. October 21.

National Telematics User Group (NTUG). 1991. "Response to Report on the Deregulation of Telematics in South Africa." Wierda Park, S.A.: author, July 19.

Nattrass, Jill. 1988. *The South African Economy: Its Growth and Change.* Cape Town: Oxford University Press.

Nelson, Joan, ed. 1990. *Economic Crisis and Policy Choice: The Politics of Adjustment in the Third World.* Princeton: Princeton University Press.

Ngcaba, Andile. 1993a. Department of Information Systems, ANC; Director-General, Department of Communications. Interview by author. Johannesburg, September 1.

— 1993b. "Hah! Government Caught in the Act." *The Weekly Mail & Guardian,* September 17–23.

Nicolaides, Kalypso. 1995. "International Trade in Information-Based Services: The Uruguay Round and Beyond." In William J. Drake, ed., *The New Information Infrastructure: Strategies for US Policy.* New York: Twentieth Century Fund Press, pp. 269–302.

Niddrie, David. 1996. Activist in civil society media organizations; Group Manager, South African Broadcasting Corporation Strategic Planning Unit. Interview by author. Johannesburg. March 8.

Niehaus, Carl. 1997. ANC Department of Information and Publicity; Ambassador to the Netherlands. Interview by author. The Hague, October 17.

Niskanen, Jr., William. 1971. *Bureaucracy and Representative Government.* Chicago: Aldine, Atherton.

Nix, Jennifer. 1997. "Actions Against Journalists in South Africa Between 1960–1994." Johannesburg: Freedom of Expression Institute. <www.fxi.org.za/detentio.txt>

Nkwinti, Gugile. 1991. "The Front Debate." *Mayibuye.* February, pp. 30–40.

Noam, Eli M. 1991. *Television in Europe.* New York: Oxford University Press.

— 1994. "The Three Stages of Network Evolution." In Eli Noam, Seisuke Komatsuzaki, and Douglas A. Conn, eds., *Telecommunications in the Pacific Basin: An Evolutionary Approach.* New York: Oxford University Press, pp. 17–31.

— 1995. "Beyond Telecommunications Liberalization: Past Performance, Present Hype, and Future Direction." In William J. Drake, ed., *The New Information Infrastructure: Strategies For US Policy.* New York: Twentieth Century Fund Press, pp. 31–54.

Nove, Alec. 1983. *The Economics of Feasible Socialism.* London: George Allen & Unwin.

Nzimande, Blade, and Jeremy Cronin. 1997. "We Need Transformation Not a Balancing Act: Looking Critically at the ANC Discussion Document." *The African Communist* 146 (1st quarter). <www.sacp.org.za/ac/ac146.html>

Nzimande, Blade, and Mpume Sikhosana. 1991. "Civics Are Part of the National Democratic Revolution." *Mayibuye.* June, pp. 37–39.

— 1992. "Civil Society and Democracy." *The African Communist* 128 (1st quarter), pp. 37–51.

O'Donnell, Guillermo, and Philippe C. Schmitter. 1986. *Transitions from Authoritarian Rule: Tentative Conclusions About Uncertain Democracies.* Baltimore: Johns Hopkins University Press.

O'Meara, Dan. 1983. *Volkskapitalisme: Class, Capital and Ideology in the Development of Afrikaner Nationalism, 1934–1948.* Johannesburg: Ravan Press.

Forty Lost Years: The Apartheid State and the Politics of the National Party, 1948–1994. Randburg, S.A.: Ravan Press.

OECD. 1991. *Universal Service and Rate Restructuring in Telecommunications.* Paris: author.

Offe, Claus. 1996. *Modernity and the State: East, West.* Cambridge, MA: MIT Press.

Olivier, Nic. 1994. "The Head of Government and the Party." In Robert Schrire, ed., *Malan to De Klerk: Leadership in the Apartheid State.* New York: St. Martin's Press, pp. 80–101.

Oosthuizen, Ters. 1993. Postmaster General, Republic of South Africa. Interview by author. Pretoria, September 3.

Orbicom. 1996. Submission to the Portfolio Committee on Communications on the Telecommunication Bill. October 15.

Organisations Which Form Part of the Independent Broadcasting and Film Industry. No date. "Joint Submission to Codesa Working Groups 1 and 3." In P. Eric Louw, ed., 1993. *South African Media Policy: Debates of the 1990s.* Bellville, S.A.: Anthropos, pp. 294–305.

Orlick, Peter B. 1970. "South Africa: How Long Without TV?" *Journal of Broadcasting* 14: 245–258.

——— 1974. "Southern Africa." In Sydney W. Head, ed., *Broadcasting in Africa.* Philadelphia: Temple University Press, pp. 140–154.

Owen, Ken. 1997. "Media Bosses Who Played the Apartheid Game." *Mail & Guardian,* July 18–24.

Pahad, Essop. 1993. "The Media Are Too Important to Be Left to the Professionals to Plan." In P. Eric Louw, ed., *South African Media Policy: Debates of the 1990s.* Bellville, S.A.: Anthropos, pp. 123–127.

Patel, Ebrahim, ed., 1993. *Engine of Development? South Africa's National Economic Forum.* Johannesburg: Juta Press.

Pérez-Díaz, Víctor M. 1993. *The Return of Civil Society: The Emergence of Democratic Spain.* Cambridge, MA: Harvard University Press.

Petrazzini, Ben A. 1995. *The Political Economy of Telecommunications Reform in Developing Countries: Privatization and Liberalization in Comparative Perspective.* Westport, CT: Praeger.

——— 1996. *Global Telecom Talks: A Trillion Dollar Deal.* Washington DC: Institute for Global Economics.

Phelan, John M. 1987. *Apartheid Media: Disinformation and Dissent in South Africa.* Westport, CT: Lawrence Hill.

Pogrund, Benjamin. 1998. "A Cool, Clear Voice Is Still." *Mail & Guardian,* November 20–26.

Pollak, Richard. 1981. *Up Against Apartheid: The Role and the Plight of the Press in South Africa.* Carbondale: Southern Illinois University Press.

Pool, Ithiel de Sola. 1983. *Technologies of Freedom.* Cambridge, MA: Harvard University Press.

Posel, Deborah. 1991. *The Making of Apartheid, 1948–1961: Conflict and Compromise.* New York: Oxford University Press.

Post & Telecommunications Workers Association (POTWA). 1992. Communications Workshop. Johannesburg, July 10.

379

1995a. "Memorandum to POTWA Regions on Privatisation of the State Assets." December 11.

1995b. Press Statement. December 11.

Potter, Elaine. 1975. *The Press as Opposition: The Political Role of South African Newspapers.* Totowa, NJ: Rowman and Littlefield.

Powell, Ivor. 1996. "Naidoo Steps in on Radio Licensing." *Sunday Times,* May 12.

Preiss, W. 1991. "The Tariff Policy of Telkom SA." In *Proceedings of the Fifth National Conference on Telecommunications in South Africa.* Pretoria: Telkom, November 4–6.

Pretorius, Johan. 1992. "The Role of the Electronic and State Media During the Transitional Period." Paper to Free, Fair and Open: South African Media in the Transition to Democracy Conference. Cape Town, January 31.

Pretorius, Louwrens. 1996. "Relations Between State, Capital and Labour in South Africa: Towards Corporatism?" *Journal of Theoretical Politics* 8: 255–281.

Pretorius, Pierre. 1993. Special Adviser to Postmaster General. Interview by author. Johannesburg, September 6.

Price, Monroe Edwin. 1995. *Television, the Public Sphere, and National Identity.* New York: Oxford University Press.

Price, Robert M. 1991. *The Apartheid State in Crisis: Political Transformation in South Africa, 1975–1990.* New York: Oxford University Press.

1994. "South Africa: The Political Economy of Growth and Democracy." In Stephen John Stedman, ed., *South Africa: The Political Economy of Transformation.* Boulder, CO: Lynne Rienner, pp. 181–198.

Print Media Association of Southern Africa. 1996. Submission to Comtask. *Submissions.* Vol. 6. Johannesburg: Comtask, pp. 505–510.

Provincial Government Communications Forum. 1996. Submission to Comtask. *Annexure 10.* Johannesburg: Comtask.

Przeworski, Adam. 1985. *Capitalism and Social Democracy.* Cambridge, U.K.: Cambridge University Press.

1991. *Democracy and the Market: Political and Economic Reforms in Eastern Europe and Latin America.* Cambridge, U.K.: Cambridge University Press.

Putnam, Robert, with Robert Leonardi, and Raffaella Y. Nanetti. 1993. *Making Democracy Work: Civic Traditions in Modern Italy.* Princeton: Princeton University Press.

Rantho, Tshepo. 1997. Member of Comtask. Interview by author. Johannesburg, October 24.

Raubenheimer, Llewellyn. 1991. "From Newsroom to the Community: Struggle in Black Journalism." In Keyan Tomaselli and P. Eric Louw, eds., *The Alternative Press in South Africa.* Bellville, S.A.: Anthropos, pp. 93–132.

Reconstruction and Development Council. 1994. "Protection and Viability of the Public Broadcaster." Submission to IBA Triple Inquiry. Johannesburg: author.

"Record of Understanding." 1992. Meeting Between the State President of the Republic of South Africa and the President of the African National Congress. Held at the World Trade Centre, September 26. <www.anc.org.za/ancdocs/history/transition/record.html>

Rees, Mervyn, and Chris Day. 1980. *Muldergate: The Story of the Info Scandal.* Johannesburg: Macmillan.

Republic of South Africa. 1961. Commission of Enquiry into the Press. *Report of the Commission of Enquiry into the Press.* Pretoria: Government Printer.

———. 1971. Commission of Inquiry Into Matters Relating to Television. *Report of the Commission of Inquiry Into Matters Relating to Television.* Pretoria: Government Printer.

———. 1976. *Broadcasting Act* (No. 73 of 1976). Cape Town: Government Printer.

———. 1978. Commission of Inquiry into the Monetary System and Monetary Policy in South Africa. *Interim Report of the Commission of Inquiry into the Monetary System and Monetary Policy in South Africa: Exchange Rates in South Africa* (de Kock Commission Report). Pretoria: Government Printer.

———. 1979a. Commision of Inquiry into Legislation Affecting the Utilisation of Manpower. *Report of the Commision of Inquiry into Legislation Affecting the Utilisation of Manpower* (Riekert Commission Report). Pretoria: Government Printer.

———. 1979b. Departments of Labour and of Mines. Commission of Inquiry into Labour Legislation. *Report of the Commission of Inquiry into Labour Legislation.* Part 1 (Wiehahn Commission Report). Pretoria: Government Printer.

———. 1979c. Office of the Economic Adviser to the Prime Minister. *Ninth Economic Development Programme for the Republic of South Africa, 1978–87: A Strategy for Growth.* Vol. 1. Pretoria: Government Printer.

———. 1980. Commission of Inquiry into the Riots at Soweto and Elsewhere. *Report of the Commission of Inquiry into the Riots at Soweto and Elsewhere, From the 16th of June 1976 to the 28th of February 1977* (Cillié Commission Report). Pretoria: Government Printer.

———. 1984a. Commission of Inquiry into the Supply of Electricity in the Republic of South Africa. *Report of the Commission of Inquiry into the Supply of Electricity in the Republic of South Africa.* Pretoria: Government Printer.

———. 1984b. Parliament. House of Assembly Debates. Speech of Finance Minister B. J. du Plessis. Cape Town: Government Printer, March 28.

———. 1985a. Parliament. House of Assembly Debates. *Appropriation Bill.* Second reading. Cape Town: Government Printer, April 9.

———. 1985b. Parliament. House of Assembly Debates. Speech of Minister of Trade and Industry D. J. de Villiers. Cape Town: Government Printer.

———. 1985c. *White Paper on Industrial Development Strategy in the Republic of South Africa.* Pretoria: Government Printer.

———. 1986a. *Condensed Report of the Study by Dr. W. J. de Villiers Regarding the Strategic Planning, Management Practices and Systems of the South African Transport Services.* Pretoria: Government Printer.

———. 1986b. Economic Advisory Council of the State President. *Proposed Long-Term Economic Strategy.* Pretoria: Government Printer.

———. 1987. *White Paper on Privatisation and Deregulation in the Republic of South Africa.* Pretoria: Government Printer.

———. 1988. Parliament. Debates of Parliament. State President's Opening Address. Cape Town: Government Printer, February 5.

———. 1989. *Summarized Report on the Study by Dr. W. J. de Villiers Concerning the Strategy, Policy, Control Structure and Organisation of Posts and Telecommunications.* Pretoria: Government Printer.

1990. Parliament. Address by State President F. W. de Klerk, DMS, at the Opening of the Second Session of the Ninth Parliament of the Republic of South Africa. Pretoria: Government Printer, February 2.

1991a. Parliament. Debates of Parliament. *Post Office Amendment Bill.* Cape Town: Government Printer, March 15.

1991b. Parliament. Debates of Parliament. *Post Office Appropriation Bill.* Cape Town: Government Printer, February 28 and March 1.

1991c. *Post Office Amendment Act* (Act No. 85 of 1991). Pretoria: Government Printer.

1991d. Task Group on Broadcasting in South and Southern Africa. *Report of the Task Group on Broadcasting in South and Southern Africa* (Viljoen Commission Report). 1991. Pretoria: Government Printer.

1992. Department of Posts & Telecommunications. "Estimates of Revenue and Expenditure for Year Ending March 31, 1992." Pretoria: Department of Posts & Telecommunications.

1993a. *Constitution of the Republic of South Africa* (Act No. 200 of 1993). Cape Town: Government Printer.

1993b. *Independent Broadcasting Authority Act* (Act No. 153 of 1993). Cape Town: Government Printer.

1993c. Transitional Executive Council. "Statement of Economic Policies." Cited in *Business Day,* 1994. March 24.

1994a. *Amendment of the Independent Broadcasting Authority Act, 1993* (No. 55 of 1994). Cape Town: Government Printer.

1994b. Parliament. Debates of Parliament. Opening Speech by Deputy President Thabo Mbeki. SACS Budget Vote No. 19. Cape Town: Government Printer, September 23.

1994c. *White Paper on Reconstruction and Development.* Cape Town: Government Printer.

1995a. *Amendment of the Independent Broadcasting Authority Act, 1993* (No. 36 of 1995). Cape Town: Government Printer.

1995b. Government of National Unity. "Press Statement – Restructuring of State Assets." December 11.

1995c. Independent Broadcasting Authority. *Appendices to Triple Inquiry Report.* Johannesburg: IBA.

1995d. Independent Broadcasting Authority. *Report on the Protection and Viability of Public Broadcasting Services; Cross Media Control of Broadcasting Services; Local Television Content and South African Music* (Triple Inquiry Report). Johannesburg: IBA.

1995e. Ministry of Posts, Telecommunications and Broadcasting. *A Green Paper for Public Discussion: Telecommunications Policy.* Pretoria: Government Printer.

1995f. Ministry of Posts, Telecommunications and Broadcasting. *Interim Narrative Report on the Responses to the Green Paper on Telecommunications Policy.* Johannesburg: NTPP, November 7.

1995g. Ministry of Posts, Telecommunications and Broadcasting. National Telecommunications Policy Project. Telecommunications Green Paper Submissions. Volumes 1–12. Johannesburg: NTPP.

1995h. Ministry of Posts, Telecommunications and Broadcasting. *Report on the Proceedings of the National Colloquium on Telecommunications Policy.* Muff Andersson, compiler. Johannesburg: NTPP.

1995i. Ministry of Posts, Telecommunications and Broadcasting. *Statistical Analysis of Responses to the Green Paper on Telecommunications Policy 1995 – Interim Report.* Bacchialoni, A. and A. Wills, eds., Johannesburg: BMI, November 7.

1995j. Ministry of Public Enterprises. "Discussion Document by the Government of National Unity on the Consultative and Implementation Framework for the Restructuring of the State Assets." Pretoria: Ministry of Public Enterprises, July 25.

1995k. Ministry of Public Enterprises. "Official Launch of Guidelines for Restructuring of State Enterprises." Press release. August 30.

1995l. Ministry of Public Enterprises. *Proceedings of the Bosberaad Held by the Portfolio Committee on Public Enterprises and the Office for Public Enterprises.* Pretoria: Ministry of Public Enterprises, November 13–15.

1995m. Ministry of Public Enterprises. "Restructuring of State Owned Enterprises." Second Draft. Pretoria: Ministry of Public Enterprises, June 13.

1995n. Parliament. Debates of the National Assembly. Debate on Vote No. 13 (Finance). Cape Town: Government Printer, June 8.

1995o. South African Communication Service. "Vision, Mission and Objectives." Pretoria: SACS.

1996a. *Constitution of the Republic of South Africa* (Act 108 of 1996). Cape Town: Government Printer.

1996b. Department of Posts & Telecommunications. Submission to the Portfolio Committee on Communications on the Telecommunication Bill. October 28.

1996c. Government of National Unity. "Draft National Framework Agreement (NFA)." <www.polity.org.za/govdocs/misc/framework/html>

1996d. *Growth, Employment and Redistribution: A Macroeconomic Strategy.* Pretoria: Government Printer.

1996e. Independent Broadcasting Authority. *Discussion Paper on Private Broadcasting Services.* Johannesburg: IBA.

1996f. Independent Broadcasting Authority. *Position Paper on Private Sound Broadcasting Services.* Johannesburg: IBA. <http://wn.apc.org/iba/pvstoc.htm>.

1996g. Independent Broadcasting Authority. *Reasons for the Decision in Relation to the Application for Private Sound Broadcasting Licence for Radio Jacaranda/RMFM by: Newshelf 71 (Proprietary) Limited and Naledi Media Investments.* Johannesburg: IBA.

1996h. Independent Broadcasting Authority. *Report on Private Sound Broadcasting.* Johannesburg: IBA.

1996i. Independent Broadcasting Authority. Submission to the Parliamentary Portfolio Committee on Communications on the Telecommunication Bill. October 22.

1996j. Ministry of Posts, Telecommunications & Broadcasting. "Fourteenth Draft of Telecommunications Bill." Johannesburg: Ministry, June 7.

1996k. Ministry of Posts, Telecommunications & Broadcasting. Submissions to the 12th Draft of Draft Legislation on Telecommunications Policy. Johannesburg: Ministry.

1996l. Ministry of Posts, Telecommunications & Broadcasting. "Twelfth Draft of Telecommunications Bill." Johannesburg: Ministry, May 3.

1996m. Ministry of Posts, Telecommunications and Broadcasting. "Telecommunications Regulatory Regime: An International Comparison of Legislation." Pretoria: Ministry, October 16.

1996n. Ministry of Posts, Telecommunications and Broadcasting. *The White Paper on Telecommunications Policy.* Pretoria: Government Printer, March 13.

1996o. Parliament. Debates of Parliament. National Assembly. Speech by Mr. T. M. Mbeki, Deputy President, S.A. Communication Service Budget Vote No. 31. Cape Town: Government Printer, June 10.

1996p. Parliament. Debates of Parliament. National Assembly. Speech by Ms. S. N. Sigcau, Minister for Public Enterprises, on the Occasion of the Budget Vote on Public Enterprises in the National Assembly. Cape Town: Government Printer, June 21.

1996q. Parliament. Debates of Parliament. National Assembly. *Telecommunications Bill* (Second Reading debate). Remarks of Ms. N. Smuts (unrevised copy: tape 231, disk 189), October 30.

1996r. Parliament. Debates of Parliament. National Assembly. *Telecommunications Bill.* (Second Reading debate). Remarks of Ms. S. C. Vos (unrevised copy: tape 226, disk 184), October 30.

1996s. Parliament. Debates of Parliament. National Assembly. *Telecommunications Bill.* (Second Reading debate). Remarks of N. N. Kekana (unrevised copy: tape 233, disk 191), October 30.

1996t. Parliament. Debates of Parliament. National Assembly. *Telecommunications Bill.* (Second Reading debate). Remarks of the Minister for Posts, Telecommunications & Broadcasting (unrevised copy: tape 220, disk 178; tape 240, disk 198), October 30.

1996u. Parliament. Portfolio Committee on Communications. National Assembly. Amendments to Independent Broadcasting Authority Triple Inquiry Report. Cape Town: Committee.

1996v. Parliament. Portfolio Committee on Communications. National Assembly. Amendments to Telecommunications Bill (B 85A-96). Cape Town: Committee.

1996w. Portfolio Committee on Communications – National Assembly. *Telecommunications Bill* (as amended by the Portfolio Committee on Communications – National Assembly). B 85B-96. Pretoria: Government Printer.

1996x. Task Group on Government Communications. Report of the Task Group on Government Communications to Deputy President Thabo Mbeki. *Communications 2000: A Vision for Government Communications in South Africa: Final Report.* Johannesburg: Comtask.

1996y. *Telecommunications Act* (Act No. 103 of 1996). Cape Town: Government Printer.

1997a. Independent Broadcasting Authority. *Reasons for the Decisions of the Independent Broadcasting Authority in Respect of Applications to Provide Private Sound Broadcasting Services in Johannesburg on 95.9 MHZ, 99.2 MHZ and 102.7 MHZ.* Johannesburg: IBA.

1997b. Ministry of Posts, Telecommunications and Broadcasting. *A Green Paper for Public Discussion of Broadcasting Policy.* Pretoria: Government Printer.

1997c. Ministry of Posts, Telecommunications and Broadcasting. *Licence Issued to Telkom*. Pretoria: Government Printer.

1997d. Office of the Deputy President. "Press Statement on Cabinet Acceptance of Recommendations of Committee Appointed to Implement the Comtask Report." October 15.

1998a. *Broadcasting Bill* (94–98). <www.polity.org.za/govdocs/bills/1998/broadcasting.pdf>

1998b. Department of Communications. *White Paper on Broadcasting Policy*. Pretoria: Government Printer.

1998c. Independent Broadcasting Authority. *Reasons for Decision Regarding Private Free-to-Air Terrestrial Television Broadcasting License*. Johannesburg: IBA.

1998d. *Open Democracy Bill* (67–98). Cape Town: Government Printer.

1998e. Truth and Reconciliation Commission. *Truth and Reconciliation Commission of South Africa Report*. Cape Town: Truth and Reconciliation Commission.

Reynolds, Andrew, ed., 1994. *Election '94 South Africa: The Campaigns, Results and Future Prospects*. New York: St. Martin's Press.

Rich, Paul B. 1996. "Apartheid, the State and the Reconstruction of the Political System." In Paul B. Rich, ed., *Reaction and Renewal in South Africa*. Houndmills, U.K.: Macmillan, pp. 47–72.

Riding, Alan. 1984. *Distant Neighbors: A Portrait of the Mexicans*. New York: Vintage Books.

Ritchken, Edwin. 1989. "Trade Unions and Community Organisations: Toward a Working Alliance?" *Transformation* 10: 40–53.

Rix, Steven. 1995. Adviser, National Labour & Economic Development Institute. Telephone interview by author. December 1.

Rodrik, Dani. 1996. "Understanding Economic Policy Reform." *Journal of Economic Literature* 34: 9–41.

Roemer, John E. 1994. *A Future for Socialism*. Cambridge, MA: Harvard University Press.

Roemer, John E., and Pranab Bardhan, eds., 1993. *Market Socialism: The Current Debate*. New York: Oxford University Press.

Rose-Ackerman, Susan. 1992. *Rethinking the Progressive Agenda: The Reform of the American Regulatory State*. New York: Free Press.

Rosenthal, Eric. 1974. *You Have Been Listening . . . The Early History of Radio in South Africa*. Cape Town: Purnell.

Rumney, Reg. 1994. "We'll Keep Our Jewels." *The Weekly Mail & Guardian*, November 18–24.

Ryan, Alan. 1995. *John Dewey and the High Tide of American Liberalism*. New York: Norton.

SABC. 1994a. "Delivering Value" (I). Submission to IBA Triple Inquiry. Johannesburg: IBA, June.

1994b. "Delivering Value, part 2." Submission to IBA Triple Inquiry. Johannesburg: IBA, December.

1995a. "Developing Delivering Value: Particulars and Financial Implications of the SABC Radio and Television Portfolios." Supplementary Submission by the SABC to the IBA. Johannesburg: IBA, May 30.

1995b. Presentation to the Parliamentary Select Committee on the IBA Triple Inquiry. Pretoria, November 8.

1995c. "The IBA Report on the Viability and Protection of Public Broadcasting Services." Submission to the Portfolio Committee of the National Assembly on Communications. October 20.

1995d. "The SABC as a PBS in the RDP" (Part of "Delivering Value III"). Submission to IBA Triple Inquiry. Johannesburg: IBA.

Annual Report. Various years. Johannesburg: author.

SACS Gauteng Provincial Office. 1996. Submission to Comtask. *Submissions.* Vol. 5. Johannesburg: Comtask, pp. 352–502.

Salgado, Ingrid. 1995. "SABC Submits Radio Options." *Business Day*, June 1.

1996. "Govt Cautioned on Radio Stations' Sale." *Business Day*, June 3.

SANCO Investment Holdings. 1996. Submission to Parliamentary Portfolio Committee on Communications on the Telecommunications Bill. October 15.

Saul, John, and Stephen Gelb. 1981. *The Crisis in South Africa: Class Defence and Class Revolution.* New York: Monthly Review Press.

Saunders, Robert J., Jeremy J. Warford, and Bjorn Wellenius. 1994. *Telecommunications and Economic Development.* Baltimore: Johns Hopkins University Press.

Savage, Michael. 1986. "The Cost of Apartheid." Cape Town: University of Cape Town.

Scholtz, Cobus. 1996. Presentation to Telecommunications and Broadcasting: Reaching the People Conference. University of Pretoria Law School, May 30.

Schrire, Robert. 1991. *Adapt or Die: The End of White Politics in South Africa.* New York: Ford Foundation and Foreign Policy Association.

Schulze, Alf. 1993. Executive Manager, Transtel. Interview by author. Johannesburg, September 6.

Schulze, Peter. 1992. General Manager of Group Strategic Planning, Siemens Ltd. Interview by author. Johannesburg, July 24.

Seegers, Annette. 1994. "The Head of Government and the Executive." In Robert Schrire, ed., *Malan to De Klerk: Leadership in the Apartheid State.* New York: St. Martin's Press, pp. 37–79.

Seekings, Jeremy. 1988. "Political Mobilisation in the Black Townships of the Transvaal." In Philip Frankel et al., eds., *State, Resistance and Change in South Africa.* London: Croom Helm, pp. 197–228.

1992. "Civic Organisations in South African Townships." In Glenn Moss and Ingrid Obery, eds., *South African Review 6: From 'Red Friday' to Codesa.* Johannesburg: Ravan Press, pp. 216–238.

1993. *Heroes or Villains? Youth Politics in the 1980s.* Johannesburg: Ravan Press.

Segal, Simon. 1994. "The R135-bn RDP Shock." *The Weekly Mail & Guardian*, June 3–9.

Seidman, Gay W. 1994. *Manufacturing Militance: Workers' Movements in Brazil and South Africa, 1970–1985.* Berkeley: University of California Press.

Sekha, Felleng. 1997. Chairperson, Independent Broadcasting Authority Council. Interview by author. Johannesburg, October 22.

Sen, Amartya. 1999. *Development as Freedom.* New York: Knopf.

Sergeant, Melanie. 1993. "Are Cellular Phones Just Another Party Line?" *Business Day*, September 2.

1995. "Stiff Telecommunications Deadline Set." *Business Day*, July 10.

Sergeant, Melanie, and John Dludlu. 1995. "Five Front-Runners for R6 Billion Telkom Contract." *Business Day*, November 3.

Shabalala, Sipho. 1996a. Deputy Director-General, Office for Public Enterprises. Interview by author. Cape Town, February 28.

1996b. "The Restructuring of State Enterprises: A Political Economy Perspective." Paper to NALEDI Mini-Conference on the Restructuring of State Enterprises. Midrand, S.A., February 20.

Shubane, Khehla. 1991. "Politics in Soweto." In Tom Lodge, et al., *All, Here, and Now: Black Politics in South Africa in the 1980s.* Cape Town: David Philip, pp. 261–272.

Shubane, Khehla, and Pumla Madiba. 1992. *The Struggle Continues? Civic Associations in the Transition.* Johannesburg: Centre for Policy Studies.

Shubane, Khehla, and Mark Shaw. 1993. *Tomorrow's Foundations?: Forums as the Second Level of a Negotiated Transition in South Africa.* Johannesburg: Centre for Policy Studies.

Sibongo, Daniel, and D. Lush, eds. 1997. *So This Is Democracy? State of the Media in Southern Africa 1996.* Windhoek, Namibia: The Media Institute of Southern Africa.

Siebert, Frederick S., Theodore Peterson, and Wilbur Schramm. 1956. *Four Theories of the Press: Authoritarian, Libertarian, Social Responsibility and Soviet Communist Concepts of What the Press Should Be and Do.* Urbana: University of Illinois Press.

Siemering, William. 1996. Personal correspondence with author. March 25.

Siemering, William, Jean Fairbairn, and Noma Rangana. 1998. *Community Radio Stations in South Africa: Six Case Studies.* Cape Town: Open Society Foundation for South Africa.

Sikhakhane, Jabulani. 1997. "Empowerment Enters New Phase." *Cape Times*, July 2.

Silke, Daniel, and Robert Schrire. 1994. "The Mass Media and the South African Election." In Andrew Reynolds, ed., *Election '94: South Africa.* Cape Town: David Philip, pp. 121–143.

Simon, Bernard. 1997. "NUM Investment Arm Earns Its Pinstripes." *Business Day*, October 23.

Singh, Shareen. 1997. "Black Business Is Learning Harsh Lessons." *Business Day*, April 23.

Siyanda Women's Investments. 1996. Submission to the Parliamentary Portfolio Committee on Communications on the Telecommunication Bill. October 15.

Slovo, Joe. 1990. *Has Socialism Failed?* London: Inkululeko Publications.

1992. "Negotiations: What Room For Compromise?" *The African Communist* 130: 36–40.

Smit, Dennis. 1993. Managing Director, BMI TechKnowledge. Interview by author. Johannesburg, September 1.

Smith, Anthony. 1991. *The Age of Behemoths: The Globalization of Mass Media Firms.* New York: Priority Press Publications.

Smuts, Neel. 1996. Member, SABC Managment Board; Member, Eminent Persons Group for NTPP. Interview by author. Midrand, S.A., March 6.

Soggot, Mungo. 1995a. "Equity Partner Urged for Telkom." *Business Day*, November 6.

1995b. "Govt Seeks a Partner in SA Airways." *Business Day*, December 8.

1996. "Privatisation Will Help Govt Dodge Looming Debt Trap." *Business Day*, March 1.

Soggot, Mungo, and John Dludlu. 1995. "Labour Calls for State Assets Pact." *Business Day*, December 4.

South African Black Technical and Allied Careers Organisation (Sabtaco). 1996. Submission to the Portfolio Committee on Communications on the Telecommunication Bill. October 21.

South African Cellular Service Providers' Association. 1996. Submission to the Parliamentary Portfolio Committee on Communications on the Telecommunication Bill. October 14.

South African Communication Service. 1996. Submission to Comtask. *Annexure 11*. Johannesburg: Comtask.

South African Communist Party. 1997. "Time to Shift the Terrain of Debate." *The African Communist* 146: (1st quarter). <www.sacp.org.za/ac/ac146.html>.

South African Communists Speak: Documents from the History of the South African Communist Party, 1915–1980. 1981. London: Inkululeko Publishers.

South African Institute of Race Relations. Various years. *Race Relations Survey*. Johannesburg: author.

South African Labour Bulletin. 1995. Vol. 19, March.

1996. Vol. 20, April.

South African Posts and Telecommunications (SAPT). *Annual Report*. Various years. Pretoria: SAPT.

South African Railway and Harbour Workers Union (SARHWU). 1995. "On the Cabinet Statement on Restructuring of State Assets." Press statement. December 8.

South African Reserve Bank. Various years. *Quarterly Bulletin*. Pretoria: Government Printer.

South African VANS Association. 1996. Submission to the Parliamentary Portfolio Committee on Communications on the Telecommunication Bill. October 15.

Southern Africa Transport and Communications Commission – Technical Unit. 1996a. "Protocol on Transport, Communications, and Meteorology." Maputo, Mozambique: author, February 5.

1996b. "Second Draft Making Document, Transport, Communications and Meteorology – Protocol Development." Maputo, Mozambique: author, March 25.

Sparks, Allister. 1995. *Tomorrow Is Another Country: The Inside Story of South Africa's Road to Change*. New York: Hill and Wang.

1996a. Institute for the Advancement of Journalism. Submission to Comtask. *Annexure 15*. Johannesburg: Comtask.

1996b. "TML Attitude Smacks of Racism," *Cape Times*, August 21.

Sparks, Colin. 1994. "Civil Society and Information Society as Guarantors of Progress." In Slavko Splichal, Andrew Calabrese, and Colin Sparks, eds., *Information Society and Civil Society: Contemporary Perspectives on the Changing World Order*. West Lafayette, IN: Purdue University Press, pp. 21–49.

Spira, John. 1997. "Bullish SABC Predicts Its First Profit Ever." *Sunday Independent*, August 31.

Splichal, Slavko. 1994. *Media Beyond Socialism: Theory and Practice in East–Central Europe.* Boulder, CO: Westview Press.

Stallings, Barbara. 1992. "International Influence on Economic Policy: Debt, Stabilization, and Structural Reform." In Stephan Haggard and Robert R. Kaufman, eds., *The Politics of Economic Adjustment: International Constraints, Distributive Conflicts and the State.* Princeton: Princeton University Press, pp. 41–88.

Standish, Barry. 1987. "Some Statistics on Public Sector Employment in South Africa, 1920–1980." Southern Africa Labour and Development Research Unit Working Papers. No. 69. Cape Town: SALDRU.

Star. 1995. " 'Private Sector Has the Answer.' " March 21.

1996a. "Call to Give Government Its Own Voice on News." June 3.

1996b. "Free Press in All Our Interests." December 2.

Starr, Paul. 1988. "The Meaning of Privatization." *Yale Law & Policy Review* 6: 6–41.

Steyn, Greta. 1996a. "Competition Bill Dropped After Criticism." *Business Day*, April 29.

1996b. "Passage of Time Robs 'Golden Triangle' of Some of Its Lustre." *Business Day*, January 18.

Stone, Alan. 1989. *Wrong Number: The Breakup of AT&T.* New York: Basic Books.

Sunday Times. 1996. "An Attempt to Repeat History." July 10.

1997. "Denel's Gift to Democracy – A Gagging Order." July 27.

Swilling, Mark. 1988a. "Introduction: The Politics of Stalemate." In Philip Frankel et al., eds., *State, Resistance and Change in South Africa.* London: Croom Helm, pp. 1–18.

1988b. "The United Democratic Front and Township Revolt." In William Cobbett and Robin Cohen, eds., *Popular Struggles in South Africa.* London: James Currey, pp. 90–113.

Switzer, Les. 1997a. "Bantu World and the Origins of a Captive African Commercial Press." In Les Switzer, ed., *South Africa's Alternative Press: Voices of Protest and Resistance, 1880–1960.* Cambridge, U.K.: Cambridge University Press, pp. 189–212.

1997b. "Introduction: South Africa's Alternative Press in Perspective." In Les Switzer, ed., *South Africa's Alternative Press: Voices of Protest and Resistance, 1880–1960.* Cambridge, U.K.: Cambridge University Press, pp. 1–53.

Switzer, Les, and Donna Switzer. 1979. *The Black Press in South Africa and Lesotho.* Boston: G.K. Hall.

Taylor, W. J. 1990. "Privatisation – Issues to Consider." *Proceedings of the Fourth South African National Telematics Conference.* Durban. May.

1992. Deputy Postmaster General, Republic of South Africa. Interview by author. Irene, S.A., July 7.

1997. Personal correspondence with author. September 11.

Teer-Tomaselli, Ruth. 1993. "Militancy and Pragmatism: The Genesis of the ANC's Media Policy." In P. Eric Louw, ed., *South African Media Policy: Debates of the 1990s.* Bellville, S.A.: Anthropos, pp. 227–240.

1995. "Moving Toward Democracy: The South African Broadcasting Corporation and the 1994 Election." *Media, Culture and Society* 17: 577–602.

Telephone Attachment Association. 1996. Submission to the Parliamentary Portfolio Committee on Communications on the Telecommunication Bill. October 16.

Telkom. 1991. *Proceedings of the Fifth National Conference on Telecommunications in South Africa.* Pretoria: author.

1993. *The First Annual Report, 1991-10-01 to 1993-10-31.* Pretoria: author.

1995. "Important Conditions and Undertakings by Vendors in Respect of Proposal No. DP1408." Pretoria: author, June 2.

1996a. Submission to the Parliamentary Portfolio Committee on Communications on the Telecommunication Bill. October 14.

1996b. Submission to the Parliamentary Portfolio Committee on Communications on the Telecommunication Bill. Second Submission. October 22.

Annual Report. Various years. Pretoria: author.

Temin, Peter, with Louis Galambos. 1987. *The Fall of the Bell System: A Study in Prices and Politics.* Cambridge: Cambridge University Press.

Thomas, Wolfgang. 1995. "Privatisation: Big Bang Shrinks to a Whimper." *Democracy in Action* 9. October 15, pp. 5–10.

Tomaselli, Keyan. 1997. "Media Ownership and Democratization: The Political Economy of South African Media." Paper presented at College of Journalism and Communications. University of Florida, Gainesville, March 1–4.

Tomaselli, Keyan, and P. Eric Louw, eds., 1991a. "The South African Progressive Press Under Emergency. 1986–1989." In Keyan Tomaselli and P. Eric Louw, eds., *The Alternative Press in South Africa.* Bellville, S.A.: Anthropos, pp. 175–190.

1991b. *The Alternative Press in South Africa.* Bellville, S.A.: Antropos.

Tomaselli, Keyan, and Ruth Tomaselli. 1989. "Between Policy and Practice in the SABC, 1970–1981." In Ruth Tomaselli, Keyan Tomaselli, and Johan Muller, eds., *Currents of Power: State Broadcasting in South Africa.* Bellville: Anthropos, pp. 84–152.

Tomaselli, Ruth, and Keyan Tomaselli. 1987. "The Political Economy of the South African Press." In Keyan Tomaselli, Ruth Tomaselli, and Johan Muller, eds., *The Press in South Africa.* Bellville, S.A.: Anthropos, pp. 39–117.

Transnet. 1996. Submision to the Parliamentary Portfolio Committee on Communications on the Telecommunication Bill. October 15.

Transtel. 1995. *Operations Overview.* Johannesburg: author.

Trapido, Stanley. 1963. "Political Institutions and Afrikaner Social Structures in the Republic of South Africa." *American Political Science Review* 57: 75–87.

Truu, M. L. 1988. "Economics of Privatization." *South African Journal of Economics* 56: 251–269.

Tyibilika, Vo. 1996. Presentation at POTWA Workshop. Johannesburg, March 7.

Tyler, Michael, William Letwin, and Christopher Roe. 1995. "Universal Service and Innovation in Telecommunication Services." *Telecommunications Policy* 19: 3–20.

Underwood, Doug. 1993. *When MBAs Rule the Newsroom: How Marketers and Managers Are Reshaping Today's Media.* New York: Columbia University Press.

Union of South Africa. 1934. *Report on Broadcasting Policy and Development* (Reith Report). Pretoria: Government Printer.

1936. *Broadcasting Act* (No. 22 of 1936). Pretoria: Government Printer.

1948. Commission of Enquiry into Broadcasting Services. *Report of the Commission of Enquiry into Broadcasting Services* (Schoch Commission Report). Cape Town: Cape Times Ltd.

1958. *Post Office Act* (No. 44 of 1958). Pretoria: Government Printer.

1960. *Broadcasting Amendment Act* (No. 49 of 1960). Pretoria: Government Printer.

United States. 1939. Federal Communications Commission. *Investigation of the Telephone Industry in the United States.* Washington, DC: Government Printing Office.

1968. National Advisory Commission on Civil Disorders. *Report of the National Advisory Commission on Civil Disorders* (Kerner Commission Report). Tom Wicker, introduction. New York: Dutton.

1991. Department of Commerce. National Telecommunications and Information Administration. *The NTIA Infrastructure Report: Telecommunications in the Age of Information.* Washington, DC: NTIA.

1996. Embassy of the United States of America. "USG Comments on South African Draft Telecomms White Paper." Pretoria: U.S. Embassy, February 12.

Uys, Stanley. 1985. "A Silenced Voice." *Index on Censorship* 14: 7–8.

Vail, Leroy, ed. 1991. *The Creation of Tribalism in Southern Africa.* Berkeley: University of California Press.

van Audenhove, Leo, Jean-Claude Burgelman, Gert Nulens, and Bart Cammaerts. 1991. "Information Society Policy in the Developing World: A Critical Assessment." *Third World Quarterly* 20: 387–404.

van der Walt, J. C. L. 1996. Group General Manager for Business Information, ISCOR. 1996. Letter to National Telecommunications Policy Project, February 9.

van Deventer, J. H. 1996. Nasionale Pers Beperk. Submission to Comtask. *Submissions.* Vol. 2. Johannesburg: Comtask, pp. 160–177.

van Rensburg, Eugene. 1992. Adviser of the Policy Unit, Ministry for Economic Co-ordination and Public Enterprise. Interview by author. Pretoria, June 11.

van Rooyen, Jeff. 1995. Special Adviser, Ministry for Public Enterprises. Interview by author. Pretoria, November 8.

van Zyl, Gerrie. 1996. "Monopoly-Minded Jay Has Better Options." *Business Day,* July 8.

VANGUARD Initiative Steering Committee. 1992. "The South African VANGUARD Initiative." Johannesburg: author.

Vermeulen, Amanda. 1995. "Thebe Buys Into Technology Group." *Business Day,* November 8.

Vick, Chris. 1996. "Lighting a Fire Under the Public Service." *Saturday Star,* July 6. 1997. Media Liaison Officer for Gauteng Premier. Interview by author. Johannesburg, October 22.

Vickers, John, and George Yarrow. 1988. *Privatization: An Economic Analysis.* Cambridge, MA: MIT Press.

Vodacom. 1996. Submission to the Parliamentary Portfolio Committee on Communications on the Telecommunication Bill. October 15.

Wassenaar, A. D. 1977. *Assault on Private Enterprise: The Freeway to Communism.* Cape Town: Tafelberg.

Waterbury, John. 1992. "The Heart of the Matter? Public Enterprise and the Adjustment Process." In Stephan Haggard and Robert R. Kaufman, eds., *The Politics of*

Economic Adjustment: International Constraints, Distributive Conflicts, and the State. Princeton: Princeton University Press, pp. 182–217.

Waterman, Peter. 1991. "Social-Movement Unionism: A New Model for a New World." Working Paper Series No. 110. Institute of Social Studies: The Hague.

Webb, Lindo Carvel. 1993. Group Executive, Information Technology and Systems, Transnet Ltd. Interview by author. Johannesburg, September 6.

Webster, Eddie. 1984. "New Force on the Shop Floor." *South African Review II.* Johannesburg: Ravan Press, pp. 79–89.

——— 1988. "The Rise of Social Movement Unionism: The Two Faces of the Black Trade Union Movement." In Philip Frankel, Noam Pines, and Mark Swilling, eds., *State, Resistance and Change in South Africa.* London: Croom Helm, pp. 146–173.

Wellenius, Bjorn, et al. 1993. "Telecommunications: World Bank Experience and Strategy." World Bank Discussion Papers. Washington, D.C.: World Bank.

Wellenius, Bjorn, and Peter A. Stern, eds. 1994. *Implementing Reforms in the Telecommunications Sector: Lessons From Experience.* Washington, D.C.: World Bank.

Wellisz, Stanislaw H. 1963. "Regulation of Natural Gas Pipeline Companies: An Economic Analysis." *Journal of Political Economy* 71: 30–43.

Wessels, Ewald. 1995. "The Fifth Column in the Economy." *Financial Mail,* December 1.

——— 1996a. Member of the Executive of the Cape Chamber of Commerce and Industry. Personal correspondence with author. August 31.

——— 1996b. "Protectionism the Culprit Behind High Manufacturing Costs." *Business Day,* May 8.

White, Matthew. 1991. Publisher, *IPS.* Personal communication with author. Sun City, Bophuthatswana, November 5.

Wild, Kate. 1996. Submission to Comtask. *Annexure 16.* Johannesburg: Comtask.

Wilensky, Harold L. Forthcoming. *Rich Democracies: Political Economy, Public Policy, and Performance.* Berkeley: University of California Press.

Wilkins, Ivor, and Hans Strydom. 1978. *The Super-Afrikaners: Inside the Afrikaner Broederbond.* Johannesburg: Jonathan Ball.

Wilkinson, Bronwyn. 1995. "Telecommunications Reforms Must Not Affect Jobs, Minister Warns." *Star,* October 21.

Williamson, John. 1994. "In Search of a Manual for Technopols." In John Williamson, ed., *The Political Economy of Policy Reform.* Washington, D.C.: Institute for International Economics, pp. 11–28.

Williamson, John, and Stephan Haggard. 1994. "The Political Conditions for Economic Reform." In John Williamson, ed., *The Political Economy of Policy Reform.* Washington, D.C.: Institute for International Economics, pp. 525–596.

World Bank. 1995. World Bank Policy Research Report. *Bureaucrats in Business: The Economics and Politics of Government Ownership.* New York: Oxford University Press.

——— 1999. *World Development Report.* New York: Oxford University Press.

World Trade Organization. 1995a. Negotiating Group on Basic Telecommunications. "Communication from the United States: Pro-Competitive Regulatory and Other

Measures for Effective Market Access in Basic Telecommunications Services." S/NGBT/W/5. Geneva: WTO, February 9.

1995b. *Trading Into the Future*. Geneva: WTO.

1997. Group on Basic Telecommunications. "South Africa: Draft Offer on Basic Telecommunications." Geneva: WTO, January 29.

Zaina, Jacqueline. 1996. "Communications Task Group to Weigh Media Options." *Business Day*, January 16.

Index